Peacekeeping i

MW01716873

This book provides a comprehensive analysis of peacekeeping in Africa.

Recent events in the Democratic Republic of Congo and Mali remind us that violence remains endemic and continues to hamper the institutional, social and economic development of the African continent. Over the years, an increasing number of actors have become involved in the effort to bring peace to Africa. The United Nations has been joined by regional organizations, most prominently the African Union and the European Union, and by sub-regional organizations such as the Economic Community of West African States. Meanwhile, traditional and emerging powers have taken an increased interest in Africa and, as a consequence, in peacekeeping.

This book provides a comprehensive analysis of the trends and challenges of international peacekeeping in Africa, with a focus on the recent expansion of actors and missions. Drawing upon contributions from a range of key thinkers in the field, *Peacekeeping in Africa* concentrates on the most significant and emerging actors, the various types of missions, and the main operational theaters, thus assessing the evolution of the African security architecture and how it impacts on peace operations.

This book will be of much interest to students of peacekeeping and peace operations, African politics, war and conflict studies, security studies and international relations.

Thierry Tardy is a Senior Analyst at the European Union Institute for Security Studies. He is the editor of *European Security in a Global Context* (2009) and *Peace Operations after 11 September 2001* (2004).

Marco Wyss is a Senior Lecturer in Politics and Contemporary History at the University of Chichester, UK. He is the author of *Arms Transfers, Neutrality and Britain's Role in the Cold War* (2013) and *Un Suisse au Service de la SS* (2010).

This book makes a major contribution to understanding the genesis and evolution of the African peace and security architecture and the multi-dimensional peace support operations environment. This is a highly readable and informative book that will be useful for practitioners, policymakers and academics alike and anyone seeking deeper and more nuanced knowledge of the operational environment within which the African Union's evolving peace and security structures will be responding. The critical suggestions by the authors concerning how to improve responses are most welcome. There is no doubt that this is an essential must-read for those interested in and concerned about Africa's responses to its security challenges.

Kwesi Aning, *Kofi Annan International Peacekeeping Training Centre, Ghana*

Peacekeeping in Africa provides a long-needed comprehensive analysis. Its chapters by leading and emerging experts map recent trends and draw out important lessons. Must read for policy makers, academics and activists interested in African peace and security.

Alex Vines, *Chatham House, London, UK*

CSS Studies in Security and International Relations
Series Editor: Andreas Wenger
Center for Security Studies, Swiss Federal Institute of Technology (ETH), Zurich

The *CSS Studies in Security and International Relations* examine historical and contemporary aspects of security and conflict. The series provides a forum for new research based upon an expanded conception of security and will include monographs by the Center's research staff and associated academic partners.

War Plans and Alliances in the Cold War
Threat perceptions in the east and west
Edited by Vojtech Mastny, Sven Holtsmark and Andreas Wenger

Transforming NATO in the Cold War
Challenges beyond deterrence in the 1960s
Edited by Andreas Wenger, Christian Nuenlist and Anna Locher

US Foreign Policy and the War on Drugs
Displacing the cocaine and heroin industry
Cornelius Friesendorf

Cyber-Security and Threat Politics
US efforts to secure the information age
Myriam Dunn Cavelty

Securing 'the Homeland'
Critical infrastructure, risk and (in)security
Edited by Myriam Dunn Cavelty and Kristian Søby Kristensen

Origins of the European Security System
The Helsinki Process revisited
Edited by Andreas Wenger, Vojtech Mastny and Christian Nuenlist

Russian Energy Power and Foreign Relations
Edited by Jeronim Perovic, Robert W. Orttung and Andreas Wenger

European–American Relations and the Middle East
From Suez to Iraq
Edited by Daniel Möckli

EU Foreign Policymaking and the Middle East Conflict
The Europeanization of National Foreign Policy
Patrick Müller

The Politics of Nuclear Non-Proliferation
A pragmatist framework for analysis
Ursula Jasper

Regional Organisations and Security
Conceptions and practices
Edited by Stephen Aris and Andreas Wenger

Peacekeeping in Africa
The evolving security architecture
Edited by Thierry Tardy and Marco Wyss

Peacekeeping in Africa

The evolving security architecture

Edited by Thierry Tardy and Marco Wyss

Routledge
Taylor & Francis Group
LONDON AND NEW YORK

First published 2014
by Routledge
2 Park Square, Milton Park, Abingdon, Oxfordshire OX14 4RN

and by Routledge
711 Third Avenue, New York, NY 10017

First issued in paperback 2015

Routledge is an imprint of the Taylor & Francis Group, an informa business

British Library Cataloguing in Publication Data
A catalogue record for this book is available from the British Library

Library of Congress Cataloging in Publication Data
Peacekeeping in Africa : the evolving security architecture / [edited by] Marco Wyss, Thierry Tardy.
pages cm. – (CSS Studies in security and International relations)
Includes bibliographical references and index.
1. Peacekeeping forces–Africa. 2. Peace-building–Africa. 3. Conflict management–Africa. 4. Security, International–Africa. 5. National security–Africa. 6. Africa–Politics and government–21st century. I. Wyss, Marco. II. Tardy, Thierry.
JZ6377.A35P45 2014
355.3'57096–dc23 2013031696

ISBN 13: 978-1-138-94024-6 (pbk)
ISBN 13: 978-0-415-71572-0 (hbk)

Typeset in Baskerville
by Wearset Ltd, Boldon, Tyne and Wear

Contents

Contributors

David Ambrosetti is a Senior Research Fellow at the French Centre national de la recherche scientifique (CNRS). He holds a PhD in political science (Institut d'études politiques de Bordeaux, 2005). His work explores the international social sector in charge of the regulation of violence in sub-Saharan Africa, through a political sociology of peace and security organizations, their agents and their practical norms. His book *Normes et rivalités diplomatiques à l'ONU* (Peter Lang 2009) and several academic articles (appearing in *Etudes internationales, Cultures & Conflits, Security Dialogue, Global Society, Politique africaine, African Security*) have dealt with the social sanction of violence among diplomats in the United Nations Security Council during the armed conflicts in Rwanda, Sierra Leone and Sudan. His current research focuses on African experts in peacekeeping and security sector reform with a focus on Burundi.

Romain Esmenjaud holds a PhD from the Graduate Institute of International and Development Studies, Geneva. In 2012 he completed his thesis on the Africanisation and African ownership of peace operations. His research deals with the politics of African interventions and aims to unearth the power relations and the ideological foundations shaping African peace operations. He has published several academic articles on peace and security issues in Africa, including "Who Owns African Ownership? The Africanisation of Security and its Limits", co-authored with Benedikt Franke and published in the *South African Journal of International Affairs* (2008).

Meike Froitzheim is a PhD candidate in Peace and Development Research at the School of Global Studies, University of Gothenburg, Sweden. Her research focuses on the implementation of international peace operations in sub-Saharan Africa with a specific focus on the Great Lakes Region and the Democratic Republic of Congo. Her wider research interests include examining the EU's role as a global actor, specifically regarding the intersection of security and development policies. She has recently published on these topics in *African Security* (under the name Meike Lurweg) and *Africa Spectrum*.

Megan Gleason-Roberts is a Program Officer with the Southeast Asia Program at the International Foundation for Electoral Systems. Prior to this she was with the Global Peace Operations Program at the Center on International Cooperation (CIC) at New York University. Her research interests include peace operations, political settlements, emerging power engagement on development and security issues, and post-conflict peacebuilding and statebuilding. She holds a Master of Science in International Relations from New York University's Center for Global Affairs, and Bachelor's degrees in Finance and Political Science from Rutgers University.

Alischa Kugel is a Senior Program Officer at the Center on International Cooperation (CIC) at New York University, where she conducts research on various issues related to global peace operations. In 2013, Alischa, together with Megan Gleason-Roberts, was co-editor and lead researcher for the *Annual Review of Global Peace Operations*, which for the first time combines analysis and data on military and non-military peace operations in one volume, providing a new and expanded overview of multilateral contributions to peacekeeping, conflict prevention and post-conflict peacebuilding. Alischa holds a Master of Science in International Affairs with a focus on socioeconomic development from the New School University in New York.

David Lanz is a PhD candidate at the University of Basel (Switzerland) and is about to complete his thesis, *Saving Strangers in Darfur: International Norms Lost in Translation.* He has experience with the UN Mission in Sudan and currently works in the Conflict Prevention Centre of the Organization for Security and Co-operation in Europe. He has published on different aspects of the Darfur conflict and on international conflict management, in journals including *African Affairs*, *Journal of Modern African Studies*, *International Negotiation*, and *Global Responsibility to Protect.*

Zachariah Mampilly is an Associate Professor of Political Science and Chair of the Africana Studies Program at Vassar College in New York. He was a Fulbright Visiting Faculty member at the University of Dar es Salaam, Tanzania, in 2012–2013. He is the author of *Rebel Rulers: Insurgent Governance and Civilian Life during War*, published by Cornell University Press in 2011. He is currently working on a monograph on popular protests in Africa with Adam Branch. In addition, he was the co-editor of the two-volume *Peacemaking: From Practice to Theory*, published in 2011, and is currently co-editing a volume on rebel governance.

Esther Marijnen is a PhD candidate at the Institute for European Studies at the Vrije Universiteit Brussel. She holds an MA in Conflict Studies and Human Rights from Utrecht University. In her PhD research project Esther analyses the approach the EU pursues towards the Democratic Republic of Congo and how this interacts with conflict transformation processes in the Great Lakes region from a bottom-up perspective. Her work thus sits at the intersection of African, European and conflict studies. Her other research interests include conflict transformation, peacebuilding, Rwandan politics and European Foreign and Security Policy.

Alexander Mattelaer is the Assistant Director of the Institute for European Studies at the Vrije Universiteit Brussel. His research interests include European defence policies, civil-military relations and operation planning. He teaches conflict studies at Vesalius College and guest-lectures at the European Security and Defence College. He obtained his PhD in Political Science from the Vrije Universiteit Brussel. and Master's degrees from the University of Bath and the University of Leuven. He also graduated in the Higher Studies Security and Defence of the Belgian Royal High Institute for Defence and the Joint Operations module of the Belgian Advanced Staff College (123rd Div.). His book *The Politico-Military Dynamics of European Crisis Response Operations: Planning, Friction, Strategy* was published by Palgrave Macmillan (2013).

Karen A. Mingst is Lockwood Chair in the Patterson School of Diplomacy and International Commerce and Professor of Political Science at the University of Kentucky. She is a specialist on international organizations and Africa, and has held two Fulbright fellowships in the region. Dr. Mingst is co-author with M.P. Karns of *International Organizations: The Politics and Processes of Global Governance* (2nd edn, 2009), and *The United Nations in the 21st Century* (4th edn, 2011); and co-editor of *The United States and Multilateral Institutions: Patterns of Changing Instrumentality and Influence* (2004). She is also the author of *Politics and the African Development Bank* (1990), as well as of *Essentials of International Relations* (6th edn, 2013), which has been translated into Spanish, Chinese, Portuguese, Albanian, and Polish.

Jide Martyns Okeke recently joined the Peace Support Operation Division of the African Union Commission, Ethiopia. He also serves as a non-stipendiary research fellow at the Department of International Relations, University of the Witwatersrand, in Johannesburg, South Africa. Previously, he worked as a Senior Researcher on the African Peace and Security Architecture at the Institute for Security Studies, Addis Ababa office. He holds a PhD in Politics and International Studies from the University of Leeds, UK, and has published widely on the Responsibility to Protect and on peace and security issues in Africa.

Giulia Piccolino gained her PhD from the University of Florence in 2012. Her thesis explored the interplay between nationalism and international intervention in Côte d'Ivoire. She also participated as associate researcher at the University of Milan in an EU-funded project on the consequences of democratic reforms. She is currently a post-doctoral fellow at the Centre for the Study of Governance Innovation, Department of Political

Sciences, Univeristy of Pretoria. She is contributing to the international project REGIOCONF, which focuses on the effects of the promotion of regional integration on regional conflicts. She is interested in African politics, civil conflicts and peacekeeping and peacebuilding. Her publications have appeared in *African Affairs, Conflict, Security & Development*, and *European Foreign Affairs Review*, as well as in other journals. In addition to her academic experience, she has worked as an election observer for the Carter Center and the Organization for Security and Cooperation in Europe, and as an electoral advisor for the United Nations Operation in Côte d'Ivoire.

Thierry Tardy is a Senior Analyst at the European Union Institute for Security Studies. Previously he was a Senior Fellow at the Geneva Centre for Security Policy. He has researched and published extensively on military and civilian crisis management with a particular focus on the United Nations and the European Union, inter-institutional cooperation in security governance, security regionalism, and the EU Common Security and Defence Policy. He is currently co-editing the *Oxford Handbook on United Nations Peacekeeping Operations* (Oxford University Press, with J. Koops, N. MacQueen and P.D. Williams). He is a member of the editorial board of *International Peacekeeping*. He has taught at the Graduate Institute of International and Development Studies (IHEID) in Geneva, as well as at the Institut d'Etudes Politiques and the War College in Paris.

Ian Taylor is Professor in International Relations and African Politics at the University of St. Andrews and also Chair Professor in the School of International Studies, Renmin University, China – the highest rank a non-Chinese academic can hold at a Chinese university. He is also Professor Extraordinary in Political Science at the University of Stellenbosch, South Africa, an Honorary Professor at the Institute of African Studies, China, and a Visiting Scholar at Mbarara University of Science and Technology, Uganda. Focusing largely on sub-Saharan Africa, he has authored seven academic books and edited another eight, and has published over 60 peer-reviewed scholarly articles and more than 60 chapters in edited books. He has conducted research in and/or visited 38 African countries, plus Réunion island.

Lori-Anne Théroux-Bénoni is a Senior Researcher with the Institute for Security Studies in Dakar, where she covers West Africa. She is currently working on a variety of human security issues in West Africa and the Sahel. She previously worked as a Researcher on Peace and Security issues with the Network on Peace Operations at the University of Montreal. In that context, she developed various projects relating to UN and AU peace operations in New York and Addis Ababa. She holds a PhD in Anthropology from the University of Toronto in Canada (2009). Her thesis focused on media, conflict and democratisation in Côte d'Ivoire, where she conducted regular field research between 2003 and 2011.

Judith Vorrath is an Associate in the International Security Division of the German Institute for International and Security Affairs (SWP). She is working on different aspects of peace and security in sub-Saharan Africa, among others on the African peace and security architecture. She is responsible for a research project on organized crime in West Africa and the implications for development cooperation. She has been a post-doc fellow at SWP, at the US Institute of Peace in Washington DC and the European Union Institute for Security Studies in Paris. She holds a Doctor of Science from the Swiss Federal Institute of Technology (ETH), Zurich. From 2005 to 2010, she pursued studies at the Center for Security Studies, Zurich, and as a member of a national research center (NCCR Democracy). Prior to this, she worked as a Research and Programme Coordinator at the Development and Peace Foundation (SEF) in Bonn.

Marco Wyss is a Senior Lecturer in Politics and Contemporary History at the University of Chichester. Previously he worked as a Senior Researcher at the Center for Security Studies at the Swiss Federal Institute of Technology (ETH), Zurich. His current research focuses on Britain's and France's post-colonial security roles and peacekeeping in Africa. Marco gained his PhD from the Universities of Nottingham and Neuchâtel, and holds Master's degrees from the Graduate Institute of International and Development Studies Geneva and the University of Neuchâtel. Currently he serves as Secretary General of the Bibliographical Committee of the International Commission of Military History and the Scientific Editor of the *International Bibliography of Military History* (Brill). He is the author of *Arms Transfers, Neutrality and Britain's Role in the Cold War* (Brill 2013) and *Un Suisse au Service de la SS* (Alphil–Presses universitaires suisses 2010).

Acknowledgment

Earlier versions of the chapters of this volume were presented at an academic conference held at the Center for Security Studies (CSS) of the Swiss Federal Institute of Technology (ETH), Zurich, in November 2012. The editors are grateful to the CSS and its director, Professor Andreas Wenger, for their generous support for the conference.

Abbreviations

ACIRC	African Capability for the Immediate Response to Crisis
ADF	Allied Democratic Forces
AFDL	Alliance of Democratic Forces for the Liberation of Congo
AFISMA	African-led International Support Mission to Mali
AMIB	AU Mission in Burundi
AMIS	AU Mission in Sudan
AMISOM	AU Mission in Somalia
APSA	African Peace and Security Architecture
AQIM	Al-Qaeda in the Islamic Maghreb
ASF	African Standby Force
ASWJ	Ahlu Sunna Wal Jama'a
AU	African Union
AUPSC	AU Peace and Security Council
BRICS	Brazil, Russia, India, China and South Africa
CAR	Central African Republic
CEMAC	Economic and Monetary Community of Central Africa
CEN-SAD	Community of Sahel-Saharan States
CFSP	Common Foreign and Security Policy [EU]
CNDP	National Congress for the Defence of the People
CPC	Chinese Communist Party
CPLP	Community of Portuguese Language Countries
CPX	Command Post Exercise [ASF]
CSDP	Common Security and Defence Policy [EU]
DDR	disarmament, demobilization and reintegration
DDRRR	disarmament, demobilization, repatriation, resettlement and reintegration
DFID	Department for International Development [UK]
DITF	Darfur Integrated Task Force
DRC	Democratic Republic of Congo
ECOMIB	ECOWAS Mission in Guinea-Bissau
ECOMOG	ECOWAS Monitoring Group
ECOWARN	ECOWAS Early Warning and Response Network
ECOWAS	Economic Community of West African States

EU	European Union
EUPOL	EU Police Mission
EUSEC	EU Security Sector Reform Mission
EUSR	EU Special Representative
EUTM	EU Training Mission
FDLR	Democratic Forces for the Liberation of Rwanda
FN	*Forces Nouvelles*
FPI	*Front Populaire Ivoirien*
FRCI	*Forces Républicaines de Côte d'Ivoire*
HRE	High Representative for Elections
IBSA	India, Brazil and South Africa
ICC	International Criminal Court
ICG	International Crisis Group
IDP	internally displaced person
IEC	Independent Electoral Commission
IGAD	Intergovernmental Authority on Development
IGO	intergovernmental organization
ISSSS	International Security and Stabilization Support Strategy
IWG	International Working Group
KDF	Kenyan Defence Forces
LRA	Lord's Resistance Army
M23	March 23 movement [Democratic Republic of Congo]
MICEMA	ECOWAS Mission in Mali
MINUSMA	UN Multidimensional Integrated Stabilization Mission in Mali
MISSANG	Angolan Military Mission in Guinea-Bissau
MLC	Movement for the Liberation of the Congo
MNLA	Mouvement National de Libération de l'Azawad
MONUC	UN Mission in the DRC
MONUSCO	UN Organization Stabilization Mission in the DRC
MUJWA	Movement for Unity and Jihad in West Africa
NARC	North African Regional Community
NATO	North Atlantic Treaty Organization
NCP	National Congress Party
NGO	non-governmental organization
OAU	Organization of African Unity
ONUB	UN Mission in Burundi
OPA	Ouagadougou Political Agreement
PoC	protection of civilians
PRC	People's Republic of China
PSC	Peace and Security Council [AU]
PSO	peace support operation
RCI-LRA	Regional Cooperation Initiative for the Elimination of the LRA
RDC	rapid deployment capability

RDC-Goma	Rally for Congolese Democracy
REC	Regional Economic Community
RM	Regional Mechanism
RPF	Rwandan Patriotic Front
RtoP	Responsibility to Protect
SADC	Southern African Development Community
SADCC	Southern African Development Coordination Conference
SRSG	Special Representative of the Secretary-General [UN]
SSR	security sector reform
STAREC	Stabilization and Reconstruction Plan for War-Affected Areas
TCC	troop-contributing country
TFG	Transitional Federal Government
TNG	Transitional National Government
UIC	Union of the Islamic Courts
UK	United Kingdom
UN	United Nations
UNAMID	AU-UN Hybrid Mission in Darfur
UNAMSIL	UN Mission in Sierra Leone
UNDPKO	UN Department of Peacekeeping Operations
UNIOGBIS	UN Integrated Peacebuilding Office in Guinea-Bissau
UNMIL	UN Mission in Liberia
UNMIS	UN Mission in Sudan
UNOCA	UN Regional Office for Central Africa
UNOCI	UN Operation in Côte d'Ivoire
UNOM	UN Office in Mali
UNOSOM	UN Operation in Somalia
UNOWA	UN Office for West Africa
UNPOS	UN Political Office for Somalia
UNSC	UN Security Council
UNSOA	UN Support Office for AMISOM
UNSOM	UN Assistance Mission in Somalia
US	United States
USAID	US Agency for International Development
WACI	West Africa Coast Initiative

Introduction

Africa – the peacekeeping laboratory

Thierry Tardy and Marco Wyss

On 19 February 2013, United Nations (UN) Under-Secretary-General Hervé Ladsous commented on the adoption of Security Council resolutions 2071 (2012) and 2085 (2012) on the situation in Mali by stating that "a multi-pronged approach to help facilitate the resolution of the crisis ha[d] been pursued by the United Nations, in close partnership with the Malian authorities, ECOWAS, and the African Union, as well as other key stakeholders".[1] These remarks on the potential deployment of a UN mission to Mali are illustrative both of the evolution of the African security architecture over the last decade and of current peacekeeping challenges in Africa. A UN multidimensional operation in Mali is to take place not only in partnership with the "Malian authorities", but also with the Economic Community of West African States (ECOWAS), the African Union (AU), and "other key stakeholders". Among the latter are states of the region, the European Union (EU), which has established a training mission for the Malian armed forces, and UN humanitarian and development agencies, as well as the International Criminal Court.

On the threshold of the new millennium, when the last comprehensive volumes on peacekeeping in Africa were published,[2] the AU had not yet succeeded the Organization of African Unity (OAU), while ECOWAS was struggling to assert its role at the sub-regional level. The trend towards regionalisation of peacekeeping in Africa was already making itself felt at the time. Yet the active participation of regional and sub-regional organisations, whether African or European, was far from being a given. Throughout the 1990s, despite the tragedies of Somalia and Rwanda, the UN had remained by far the most prominent peacekeeping actor on the African continent. The second half of the 1990s had witnessed a relative withdrawal of the great powers from Africa – even France had opted for a less interventionist and more indirect African policy.

Against this background, over the last decade, Africa's rise to new strategic prominence has led old and new great powers, notably the United States and China, to (re-)discover the African continent and become increasingly involved in African security affairs and, in China's case, peacekeeping – leading to what some have called the "new scramble for Africa".[3]

Even the French, who had never been entirely absent, have also made a forceful return – as their recent Ivorian and Malian interventions demonstrate.

Simultaneously, the UN, which multiplied its peacekeeping operations in Africa over the last decade in the wake of the so-called Brahimi Report of 2000,[4] is no longer "holding out" almost on its own. As noted in the case of Mali, the UN increasingly operates in cooperation with regional and sub-regional organisations, such as the AU, the EU and ECOWAS, as well as individual countries.[5]

The UN and other peacekeeping actors, however, remain confronted with substantial challenges, which affect their partnerships and individual peacekeeping activities. The UN itself is overstretched, with large-scale and complex operations that, from Darfur to the Democratic Republic of Congo (DRC), have pushed the organisation to the limits of its political and operational capacity. Despite the much praised "Africanisation" of peacekeeping, the AU and the Regional Economic Communities (RECs) are in dire need of military, civilian and financial capabilities, and are largely dependent on external, mostly Western, support. After an initial enthusiasm for putting its Common Security and Defence Policy (CSDP) into practice, notably on the African continent, the EU has kept a relatively low profile, and to an extent has shifted towards an indirect commitment to African security governance. Furthermore, against the background of Africa's colonial past, renewed great power rivalry and regional competition, sovereignty remains a key characteristic of statehood, and the involvement of outside actors – be they African or not – thus appears often contested.

This book presents and assesses the evolution of the African security architecture and examines how its main trends and challenges impact on African peacekeeping. Thereby it focuses on the most significant and emerging actors, the various types of peacekeeping missions, and the main operation theatres. In view of the proliferation of peace operations on the African continent, there has been much scholarly writing on the issue. Yet this literature focuses predominantly on the UN.[6] The recent expansion of actors and missions and the parallel development of norms have made Africa a laboratory of peacekeeping, with all the challenges that come with the notion of experimentation. Such evolutions need to be constantly analysed. This is what this book aims to do by providing a comprehensive assessment of peacekeeping in Africa.

The epicentre of peacekeeping

In recent years, in light of continuous economic growth and ongoing democratisation processes, an increasing number of experts have foreseen a brighter future for Africa.[7] The continent remains, however, haunted by violence. Intrastate and regional crises and conflicts continue to hamper the political, economic, and social development of many African countries and societies, even though according to statistics, violence has significantly diminished since the 1990s.

External actors have not stood by idly, and a myriad of ways to bring peace to the African continent have been tried. "The proliferation of peace operations was", according to Paul D. Williams, "arguably the most visible international response to Africa's wars".[8] Indeed, from the end of the Cold War, the number of peace operations in Africa strikingly increased – more than on any other continent. As a result, Africa developed into an "experimental laboratory", in which many of today's peacekeeping norms and practices came into existence. The UN has been responsible for the great majority of these operations, and thus remains the most important crisis management actor in Africa.

In the 1990s, though, setbacks in Somalia and Rwanda led to disillusionment, and as a consequence UN missions decreased between 1994 and 1998. It was only after a long introspection phase of several years, and prominent operations in Kosovo and East Timor (1999), that UN peacekeeping returned on the African scene and was reformed in line with the Brahimi Report (2000). In the meantime, over the last 20 years the UN has been joined by regional and sub-regional organisations, as well as individual states.[9] With this process, Africa has to an extent shifted from being a mere venue for peace operations to becoming a real stakeholder – through its regional and sub-regional bodies.[10] Meanwhile, organisations such as the EU began to build up their own crisis management capacities. It was the beginning of a new phase, in which Africa has become the epicentre of peacekeeping.[11]

From a UN perspective, Africa remains at the centre of its peacekeeping activities. Operations there have absorbed 70 percent of all UN peacekeepers since the turn of the millennium, and come at a cost of more than US$30 billion over the same period. This expansion began in 1999 with the authorisation of two new missions, the UN Mission in Sierra Leone (UNAMSIL) and the UN Mission in the DRC (MONUC). Although these operations were confronted with major difficulties and put severe strain on the organisation, the demand for UN troops increased and the expansion continued unabated. In addition to the enlargement of the operations in Sierra Leone and the DRC, new extensive missions were established, notably in Liberia, Côte d'Ivoire, Sudan and, most recently, Mali.[12] At the end of 2012, the UN was running seven out of its 15 peacekeeping operations in Africa.[13] As of April 2013, of roughly 111,000 UN peacekeepers worldwide, almost 85,000 were based on the African continent, and out of a peacekeeping budget of US$7.33 billion, more than US$5 billion are spent on operations in Africa.[14] Most of these operations are multidimensional, and in addition to "traditional" peacekeeping tasks – such as monitoring a ceasefire or a peace agreement – they include the protection of civilians (PoC), disarmament, demobilisation and reintegration (DDR), security sector reform (SSR), humanitarian tasks, and the promotion of human rights, rule of law, economic recovery, etc.[15]

Africans are not, however, mere peacekeeping objects, or "peacekept".[16] In the early 1990s, major Western powers and various African governments began to call for "African solutions to African problems". While the African side insisted on the principle of non-interference, the United States (US), the United Kingdom (UK), and France saw "African solutions" partly as a means to reduce their own commitments in Africa. Simultaneously, both Western and African proponents argued that Chapter VIII of the UN Charter required African organisations to take on a leading role in the resolution of conflicts in their own neighbourhood. In 1994, the genocide in Rwanda and the passivity of international actors – be they African or not – reinforced the necessity of establishing new African security governance mechanisms. In this context, African states began to build a new continental security architecture with improved peacekeeping instruments. The OAU was disbanded and in its place the AU was launched in 2002. In contrast to its predecessor organisation, the AU's Constitutive Act (Article 4h) allows for military intervention on humanitarian grounds, i.e. in the case of war crimes, genocide and crimes against humanity. Moreover, the AU established a political-military structure for conflict management, through the Peace and Security Council (PSC), dedicated units within the AU Commission, and in particular the African Standby Force (ASF).[17]

Although the ASF has yet to become operational, the AU launched its first peace operation, the AU Mission in Burundi (AMIB), in 2003.[18] This was followed by six more missions, deployed to the Comoros, Sudan, Somalia and Mali.[19] Since 2007, the AU has taken the lead in the Horn of Africa with the AU Mission in Somalia (AMISOM), and in 2008 it began to operate alongside the UN through the AU-UN Hybrid Operation in Darfur (UNAMID). With approximately 17,700 and 24,500 peacekeepers respectively (as of June 2013),[20] these are the largest AU missions so far, and have extensive mandates, reaching from election monitoring to peace enforcement.[21]

In its peacekeeping activities, the AU relies on its member states and the sub-regional organisations or RECs, which have also carried out their own peace operations. The most prominent examples are ECOWAS and, to a lesser degree, the Southern African Development Community (SADC). ECOWAS was founded in 1975 on Nigeria's initiative, mainly to promote market integration. However, in light of the Liberian civil war, ECOWAS deployed a peace operation in 1990 (lasting until 1999), namely the ECOWAS Monitoring Group (ECOMOG). This was followed by missions in Sierra Leone (1997–2000), Guinea-Bissau (1998–1999), Côte d'Ivoire (2003–2004) and, again, Liberia (2003–2004).[22] While Nigeria is the driving force in ECOWAS, the other regional power, South Africa, dominates SADC. Paradoxically, the latter organisation emerged in 1992 from the Southern African Development Coordination Conference (SADCC), which had been founded in 1980 to reduce the sub-region's economic dependence on Apartheid South Africa. At the turn of the millennium, SADC conducted two legally disputed peace enforcement operations in Lesotho (1998–1999) and the DRC (1998–2002).[23] Besides these "REC-heavyweights", since the turn of the millennium, the Community of Sahel-Saharan States (CEN-SAD), the Economic and Monetary Community of Central Africa (CEMAC), and the Intergovernmental Authority on Development (IGAD) have also become active in peacekeeping with one operation each.[24]

Almost simultaneously with the African organisations, the EU also became a security actor in Africa. During the Cold War, European foreign policy was dominated by the former colonial powers and focused mainly on Africa's economic and social development. With the proliferation of conflicts and reawakened European Common Foreign and Security Policy (CFSP) aspirations in the early 1990s, the EU became concerned about the security challenges in Africa.[25]

Yet it was only in the new millennium that the EU put words into deeds. In 2003, the EU deployed – at the UN's request – Operation Artemis to the DRC, which was its first peace operation in Africa.[26] This was followed by another operation in the DRC in 2006 (EUFOR RD Congo), and in 2008 the EU deployed troops to Chad and the Central African Republic (EUFOR Chad/CAR).[27] These ground operations were followed by the anti-piracy maritime operation established in 2008 in the Gulf of Aden, and then training missions in Somalia (2010) and Mali (2013). In parallel, the EU has run a series of civilian missions, in the DRC, Niger, Guinea-Bissau, the Horn of Africa, and most recently Libya.

By 2013 the EU was running eight operations in Africa, of which none are particularly substantial and only three are of a military character.[28] The operations focus mainly on capacity-building, SSR and fighting piracy. Consequently, the EU has not only reacted to specific crises with punctual peace operations, as was the case in the DRC and Chad; since the adoption of the EU Strategy for Africa in 2005, and the Strategic Partnership with the AU in 2007, it has also become increasingly active in inter-institutional cooperation and long-term capacity-building.[29]

Notwithstanding their role in the EU's African policy and Common Security and Defence Policy (CSDP), former colonial powers France and, to a lesser extent, Britain also act individually in the African peacekeeping landscape.[30] Despite a reduced military footprint in Africa, France retains the capacity and will to intervene militarily in its traditional sphere of influence, if possible under a UN mandate or in partnership with African and UN troops. It also plays a central role at the UN Security Council, where it has taken the lead on many African peacekeeping issues. France's political and operational activism has been demonstrated by its recent interventions in Côte d'Ivoire and Mali.[31]

The contributions of both the UK and the US to African peacekeeping are negligible, at least with respect to their military capacities.[32] After the US withdrawal from Somalia back in 1993, and with the exception of the British intervention in Sierra Leone in 2000, both the Americans and the British have pursued an indirect peacekeeping agenda in Africa through their respective capacity-building programmes, as well as through the funding of UN and AU operations.[33] Both countries remain, however, active at the UN Security Council on African matters, to the extent that together with France, the three Western permanent members of the Council (P3) dominate the African peace and security agenda.

In contrast to its Western Security Council peers, China does not pursue a peacekeeping agenda in Africa outside of the existing institutional frameworks, but participates actively in UN peace operations. Despite its staunch adherence to the principles of sovereignty and non-interference, Beijing has become more supportive of UN peacekeeping. Over the last decade, China has increasingly deployed uniformed personnel to UN operations, mainly in Africa, and, as a consequence, has become the largest troop-contributing country (TCC) among the five permanent Security Council members. Although Chinese units have mainly been confined to support and logistics, China's UN peacekeeping commitment, as well as its financial support to the AU operations in Somalia and Sudan and the AU more generally, are illustrative of and a consequence of its expanding role and interests in Africa and the wider world.[34] The other Asian heavyweight, India, has also become, albeit less significantly, "an important economic and political player in Africa".[35] However, in contrast to China, India is no newcomer to UN peacekeeping and has been one of the first contributors to UN operations in Africa since the very first mission in the Congo in 1960. In 2013, India is the third largest TCC to UN peace operations, and contributes key enablers, such as helicopters.[36]

While "older" peacekeepers such as India and the UN have reinforced their peacekeeping commitments in Africa, new ones such as China and the AU have arrived. The number of actors having an impact on peacekeeping has thus significantly increased. This has influenced peace operations at the conceptual and normative levels, as well as on the ground – where actors cooperate or compete – and has led to ever more complex, ambitious and often intrusive missions. One consequence has been some forms of hybridisation of peacekeeping, by which operations bring together two or more international actors that operate simultaneously or sequentially and the activities of which imply a certain degree of inter-institutional cooperation.

While such proliferation of peacekeepers might look good "on paper", in light of often complex conflicts and difficult operational theatres, peacekeeping in Africa has been confronted with a host of challenges, and in some countries or regions peace remains a distant ideal. For a start, all peacekeeping actors struggle with the effectiveness of their own policies, i.e. their ability to positively influence the environment in which they operate. In most cases, the deployment of multidimensional operations creates expectations of an improved situation that prove to be extremely difficult to meet. This is particularly the case for PoC, which has become a prominent mandated task of all African missions. In Darfur or the DRC, while PoC is one of the priorities of the UN, the nature of the terrain and the determination of some of the spoilers confronting the format and military readiness of the UN contingents make civilian protection a political and operational challenge. Furthermore, all peacekeeping actors suffer from a legitimacy deficit that tends to develop or increase with the duration of their presence and that is dependent upon the nature of the host state's initial consent as well as the degree of intrusiveness of the mission. Third, the global financial and economic crisis has constrained conflict management actors and in particular the African ones. As illustrated in Somalia and Mali, the difficulty of funding African missions has reinforced a Southern dependency towards the North that the emerging powers have not yet palliated. Finally, the hybridisation of peace operations has made inter-institutional cooperation even more necessary, yet such cooperation is hampered by a series of political and technical obstacles that ultimately undermine the overall coherence of peacekeeping missions.

Book structure

The constellation of peacekeeping actors can be – inasmuch as they are "individual" actors – both an advantage and a challenge to peace operations in Africa, and thus to the security of the continent. Therefore, and as mentioned earlier, this book examines the architecture of peacekeeping in Africa and its impact on peace operations by focusing first on international and regional organisations and then on state actors, and finally on their policies and impact on the ground.

The UN is and will remain for the foreseeable future the most important peacekeeping actor on the African continent. However, the demand for ever larger and more complex missions over the last decade has overstretched the organisation in manpower as well as administratively and financially.[37] This was followed by operational, political and financial pressure from member states – not least because of the global financial crisis – to reduce ongoing peacekeeping commitments. While this did not provoke a withdrawal from Africa, UN peacekeeping has entered a consolidation phase, and remains under pressure from powerful member states.[38]

Against this background and starting from a UN perspective, Megan Gleason-Roberts and Alischa Kugel identify in the first chapter a contraction of multilateral peacekeeping in Africa, which is related not only to strains on international support, but also to the evolution of the nature of conflicts. Yet rather than striking a negative chord, they argue that peacekeeping in Africa is currently in a transition period, which sees – despite the enduring pre-eminence of multidimensional operations – the emergence of alternative models of UN peacekeeping, namely civilian-led political missions, regional deployments, and over-the-horizon security guarantees. The key to success for these alternative models is, however, strengthened partnerships between peacekeeping actors.

In line with the "regionalisation" or "Africanisation" of peacekeeping, international observers harbour great hopes for partnerships with African organisations, especially the AU. Yet often the "partners" pursue different goals in accordance with their contrasting security outlook; consequently, the much praised "Africanisation" is confronted with many obstacles from within and outside the continent – ranging "from the selective support and hidden agendas of the international community to the reluctance and ulterior motives of the African states themselves".[39] The ultimate goal of "African ownership" is thus being increasingly questioned. In the second chapter, Jide Martyns Okeke tackles the issue of "Africanisation", and questions – on the basis of the AU interventions in Burundi, Sudan (Darfur) and Somalia – whether there is an evolving model of African-led peace support operations (PSOs). He recognises that since its establishment the AU has undergone a substantial normative and institutional transformation, namely with the establishment of a legal basis and instruments for crisis management. However, he comes to the conclusion that instead of a model, African-led PSOs rather illustrate an ad hoc process, in which they remain heavily dependent on external support. Furthermore, because of the unwillingness of many African states to take over more political, material and financial responsibility, the dependence on external actors is likely to endure and even increase.

After the UN, the EU is probably the most important external institution on which African crisis management depends. Besides offering support to other institutions, the EU has also acted as a peacekeeper in its own right. However, after the series of military operations of the last decade, and with the exception of the anti-piracy operation in the Horn of Africa, the EU focus in Africa has been concentrated on SSR and other capacity-building activities. Furthermore, the EU's means remain relatively modest and the EU's African presence continues to be dominated by national policies of a few states, especially France. In the third chapter, Alexander Mattelaer and Esther Marijnen examine the trend from direct to indirect engagement in EU peacekeeping in Africa. In their assessment, the indirect European approach is explained by a strategy of "affordable influence", which results from an intertwining of political and financial constraints. In other words, the EU tries to remain a major player in African security at modest cost through a combination of training programmes, capacity-building and financial assistance.

The EU has developed specific instruments to financially support African peace operations. But European and other external financial assistance comes with political strings attached, and thus raises the issue of African ownership. David Ambrosetti and Romain Esmenjaud emphasise in the fourth and last chapter of Part I that African ownership requires Africans funding their own operations. Nevertheless, external donors' increasing reluctance to systematically pay for African missions has not led African states to re-assert their ownership on their operations. They lack not only the material and financial means, but also the necessary political will, especially as their motivations to participate in peace operations are often more financial or self-centred than driven by a sense of African empowerment.

Meanwhile, in parallel to Africa's increasing geostrategic importance, the circle of potential donor countries has widened, new security actors have arrived, and old powers have reclaimed their pre-eminent role. The second part of this book turns to those major emerging powers that play a significant role in peacekeeping on the African continent: China and India. It also examines the case of France as the only former colonial power that intervenes regularly, and lately increasingly with its own operations on African soil under the guise of multilateralism.

China is critical of the West's liberal peace project, to which it continues to oppose the principle of sovereignty. China's increasing peacekeeping commitment in Africa is thus seen by many Africans as a welcome counterbalance to the Western influence in African security affairs. The growth of Beijing's peacekeeping role seems, however, to have been accompanied by a subtle shift in China's position on state sovereignty. In the first chapter of Part II, Chapter 5, Ian Taylor investigates the reasons for China's growing peacekeeping commitment in Africa against the background of its increasingly influential position in sub-Saharan Africa. In doing so, he analyses the evolution of Beijing's peacekeeping role, and the challenges it faces therein. Although China's aspirations to be seen and to act as a responsible power have led to substantial contributions to UN operations, the Chinese leadership still considers the consent of the host government to be a condition *sine qua non* for the deployment of and participation in a peace operation. Thus China's position towards UN peacekeeping has been "normalised" rather than "revolutionised".

In contrast to China, India's participation in UN peacekeeping is not only of less recent vintage but also more substantial, in terms of both quantity and quality. Nevertheless, in parallel to the Chinese "discovery" of peacekeeping, the Indians have redoubled their commitment to UN operations over the last decade, and thereby rendered their troops and military hardware essential to peacekeeping on the African continent. However, as Zachariah Mampilly observes in Chapter 6, little is known about the performance of Indian peacekeepers on the ground. Drawing on the experience of Indian peacekeepers in the DRC, Mampilly examines India's peacekeeping role in Africa, and reveals a tension between the work of Indian troops on the ground, and New Delhi's international agenda. The

Indian government has discovered its peacekeeping troops as a foreign policy tool, often at the expense of operational performance. This in turn could undermine India's ambitions to use its peacekeepers as a means to strengthen its ties with Africa, and receive African support to improve its status and position within the UN. The growing roles and aspirations of China and India in peace operations can also be felt in normative debates on peacekeeping, and it is thus questionable whether the West will remain "in a position to impose its vision on emerging powers".[40] Moreover, the Indian and, especially, the Chinese "incursions" into the African continent have provoked concerns in some Western capitals about loss of influence.

Despite its declared policy of multilateralism and support for "African solutions", France has not refrained from national interventions in Africa. Even though in the Ivorian case the French acted at various points alongside the UN, the AU, ECOWAS and individual regional and sub-regional powers, they were arguably disproportionately influential. Against this background, Marco Wyss questions (Chapter 7) France's peacekeeping policy through its role in the Ivorian crisis (2002–2011) and its aftermath. He argues that French military action resulted from a combination of self-interest and African inaction. Furthermore, while French peacekeeping as well as peace enforcement provided essential support to UN troops and most likely helped prevent more bloodshed, it arguably also undermined UN impartiality.

France has also played a prominent role in Mali; the multidimensional peacekeeping efforts in this country provide the second case study of Part III. Although in January 2013 the French entered the fight for Mali with their counteroffensive dubbed Operation Serval, and were only later joined by African troops, the initial response to the armed groups in Northern Mali was supposed to be African, first sub-regional and then regional. In Chapter 9, Lori-Anne Théroux-Bénoni examines the evolving response of the international community to the Malian crisis. She looks at the inner workings of the multilateral security architecture in ECOWAS, the AU and the UN, especially at the shift from the planned ECOWAS mission (MICEMA) to the AU-sponsored African-led International Support Mission to Mali (AFISMA) and, ultimately, the UN Multidimensional Integrated Stabilization Mission in Mali (MINUSMA). The African responses to the crisis in Mali were not only overtaken by events and French "reactivity", they also illustrated the weaknesses of Africa's crisis management capabilities, as well as of the functioning and suitability of the African Peace and Security Architecture (APSA), which have finally rendered a UN mission necessary.

What in Mali had been planned as an African peace enforcement operation, and became a French-led counterinsurgency campaign, eventually turned into a UN operation. The UN has thus become responsible for yet another mission that could reach proportions similar to those of MONUSCO in the DRC, UNAMID in Darfur, or even the AU-led AMISOM in Somalia. The UN and AU operations in the DRC and Somalia respectively are examined in Chapter 8. Through the concept of regional conflict transformation, Judith Vorrath analyses how MONUSCO and AMISOM have responded to and dealt with parallel regional interventions by neighbouring countries that have tried to "keep a foot in the door". Thereby she questions whether the AU as a regional organisation is in a different position from that of the UN, when it is faced with regional interference. Seemingly, the responses by both MONUSCO and AMISOM depended, as so often, on the mission's setup and composition, as well as on the local, regional and international context at the time.

The importance of both local and regional dimensions to peacekeeping, as well as to peacebuilding, are evident in Chapter 10, which is again – but this time specifically – concerned with the seemingly intractable conflict in the DRC. Meike Froitzheim focuses on the implementation of the International Security and Stabilization Support Strategy (ISSSS), which aims to integrate peacebuilding, statebuilding, and development. The chapter focuses not only on MONUSCO itself, but also on the other UN agencies involved in the DRC, as well as international and local non-governmental organisations (NGOs). If one focuses on the outcomes, rather than the outputs, it is apparent that the stabilisation strategy has so far been a failure. Not only has the international community failed to grasp the regional dimension and resurgence of the conflict, but the Congolese government has also not been particularly cooperative, which raises once again the question of the merits and limitations of national ownership.

The final two chapters are also, to varying degrees, concerned with the position and attitude of host states. In Chapter 11 David Lanz, through the case of Darfur, questions how peacekeeping interacts with the contentious concept or emerging norm of the Responsibility to Protect (RtoP), which runs contrary to the Westphalian conception of sovereignty. He argues that while the RtoP discourse surrounding the Darfur crisis made UNAMID and its mandate for the protection of civilians possible, it has also soured the relations with the Sudanese government, which considered the peacekeepers a threat.[41] Moreover, UNAMID has been discredited as the RtoP language raised unrealistic hopes among the civil population in Darfur, which have been disappointed.

The RtoP concept and mandates for the protection of civilians are often viewed with suspicion by host states, and this – among other factors – has led some of them to withdraw or weaken their consent to ongoing UN missions.[42] Against this background, in the final chapter (12), Giulia Piccolino tackles the issue of consent through the case of the UN Operation in Côte d'Ivoire. She examines the continued relevance and significance of the consent principle in UN peacekeeping, and its role in the relationship between peacekeepers and the host government. Although the norm of consent remains essential, it may clash with other UN-supported norms and principles such as the use of force. As a result, peacekeepers get caught between conflicting imperatives and have to "manage consent", as the Ivorian case has illustrated.

New and emerging peacekeeping norms challenge or are resisted by "old norms", which survive and evolve. These evolution and tension at the normative level are directly related to the emergence of new peacekeeping actors, the changing role of traditional ones, and the parallel adaptation of missions' mandates. Over the last two decades, Africa has provided a laboratory for these evolutions. It is the aim of this volume to reflect upon these changes by providing a comprehensive overview of the complexities of African peacekeeping, with the hope that it will add value to the work of academics, but also to that of policymakers and practitioners.

Notes

1 "Remarks of Hervé Ladsous, Under-Secretary-General for Peacekeeping Operations, to the Special Committee on Peacekeeping Operations", United Nations Department of Peacekeeping Operations (UNDPKO), 19 February 2013, available at www.un.org/en/peacekeeping/articles/hl_speech_C34_19_February%20_with_french.pdf, accessed 28 March 2013.
2 See for example O. Furley and R. May (eds), *Peacekeeping in Africa*, Aldershot: Ashgate, 1998; E.G. Berman and K.E. Sams (eds), *Peacekeeping in Africa: Capabilities and Culpabilities*, Geneva and Pretoria: United Nations Institute for Disarmament Research (UNIDIR) and Institute for Security Studies (ISS), 2000; R.I. Rotberg (ed.), *Peacekeeping and Peace Enforcement in Africa*, Cambridge MA: World Peace Foundation, 2000.
3 C. Pádraig, *The New Scramble for Africa*, Cambridge: Polity Press, 2011; R. Southall and H. Melber, *A New Scramble for Africa? Imperialism, Investment and Development*, Scottsville: University of KwaZulu-Natal Press, 2009.
4 "Report of the Panel on United Nations Peace Operations", United Nations (UN), A/55/305–S/2000/809, 21 August 2000, available at www.un.org/peace/reports/peace_operations/, accessed 28 March 2013.
5 M. Brosig, "The Multi-actor Game of Peacekeeping in Africa", *International Peacekeeping* 17, 2010, pp. 327–342.
6 See for example N. MacQueen, *United Nations Peacekeeping in Africa since 1960*, London: Longman, 2002; A. Adebajo, *UN Peacekeeping in Africa: From the Suez Crisis to the Sudan Conflicts*, Boulder CO: Lynne Rienner, 2011.
7 M. Edward, "Africa Unleashed", *Foreign Affairs* 90, 2011, pp. 155–160.
8 P.D. Williams, *War and Conflict in Africa*, Cambridge: Polity Press, 2011, p. 184.
9 *Ibid.*
10 D. Morin, "Introduction: L'Afrique: théâtre et acteur des opérations de paix", in D. Morin and L.-A. Théroux-Bénoni (eds), *Guide du maintien de la paix 2011: L'Afrique et les opérations de paix*, Outremont: Athéna Editions, 2011, p. 11.
11 Adebajo, *UN Peacekeeping in Africa*, pp. 9–20; A.J. Bellamy and P.D. Williams, *Understanding Peacekeeping*, Cambridge: Polity Press, 2010, pp. 71–152.
12 Williams, *War and Conflict in Africa*, pp. 185–192.
13 UN Mission for the Referendum in Western Sahara; UN Mission in Liberia; UN Operation in Côte d'Ivoire; AU-UN Hybrid Operation in Darfur; UN Organization Stabilization Mission in the DRC; UNISFA – UN Interim Security Force for Abyei; UN Mission in the Republic of South Sudan.
14 "United Nations Peacekeeping Operations Fact Sheet", UNDPKO, 28 February

2013, available at www.un.org/en/peacekeeping/documents/bnote0213.pdf, accessed 3 April 2013.

15 "Current Peacekeeping Operations", UNDPKO, available at www.un.org/en/peacekeeping/operations/current.shtml, accessed 3 April 2013.

16 C. Clapham, "Being Peacekept", O. Furley and R. May (eds), *Peacekeeping in Africa*, Aldershot: Ashgate, 1998, pp. 303–319.

17 P.D. Williams, "Keeping the Peace in Africa: Why 'African Solutions' are Not Enough", *Ethics and International Affairs* 22, 2008, pp. 309–314.

18 E. Svensson, *The African Mission in Burundi: Lessons Learned from the African Union's First Peace Operation*, Stockholm: FOI, Swedish Defence Research Agency, Division of Defence Analysis, 2008.

19 MIOC – AU Military Observer Mission in the Comoros (2004); AMIS – AU Mission in Sudan (2004–7); AUSTF – AU Special Task Force Burundi (2006–9); AMISEC – AU Mission for Support to the Elections in the Comoros (2006); MAES – AU Electoral and Security Assistance Mission to the Comoros (2007–8); Operation Democracy in Comoros (2008).

20 "Frequently Asked Questions", AMISOM, http://amisom-au.org/about/frequently-asked-questions/, accessed 11 June 2013; "UNAMID", UNDPKO, available at www.un.org/en/peacekeeping/missions/unamid/facts.shtml, accessed 11 June 2013.

21 P.D. Williams, *The African Union's Conflict Management Capabilities*, Working Paper, New York: Council on Foreign Relations, 2011.

22 ECOMOG 2 – Sierra Leone; ECOMOG 3 – Guinea Bissau; ECOMICI – ECOWAS Mission in Côte d'Ivoire; ECOMIL – ECOWAS Mission in Liberia. C.I. Obi, "Economic Community of West African States on the Ground: Comparing Peacekeeping in Liberia, Sierra Leone, Guinea Bissau and Côte d'Ivoire", *African Security* 2, 2009, pp. 119–135.

23 Operation Boleas – Lesotho; Operation Sovereign Legitimacy – DRC. M. Schoeman and M. Muller, "Southern African Development Community as Regional Peacekeeper: Myth or Reality?", *African Security* 2, 2009, pp. 175–192.

24 CEN-SAD Operation – Central African Republic (2001–2002); FOMUC – *Force multinationale en Centrafrique* (later MICOPAX – *Mission de consolidation de la paix en Centrafrique*) (2002–); IGAD Verification Monitoring Team – Sudan (2003–5). M. Malan, "Africa: Building Institutions on the Run", in D.C.F. Daniel, P. Taft and S. Wiharta (eds), *Peace Operations: Trends, Progress and Prospects*, Washington DC: Georgetown University Press, 2008, pp. 90–91; A. Meyer, "Regional Conflict Management in Central Africa: From FOMUC to MICOPAX", *African Security* 2, 2009, pp. 158–174; T. Murithi, "Intergovernmental Authority on Development on the Ground: Comparing Interventions in Sudan and Somalia", *African Security* 2, 2009, pp. 136–157.

25 G. Rye Olsen, "The EU and Military Conflict Management in Africa: For the Good of Africa or Europe?", *International Peacekeeping* 17, 2009, p. 245.

26 See S. Ulriksen, C. Gourlay and C. Mace, "Operation Artemis: The Shape of Things to Come?", *International Peacekeeping* 11, 2004, pp. 508–525.

27 C. Morsut, "Effective Multilateralism? EU–UN Cooperation in the DRC, 2003–2006", *International Peacekeeping* 16, 2009, pp. 264–265; H. Dijkstra, "The Military Operation of the EU in Chad and the Central African Republic: Good Policy, Bad Politics", *International Peacekeeping* 17, 2010, pp. 395–407.

28 EU Training Mission in Somalia; European Naval Force in Somalia (Atalanta); EU Training Mission in Mali. "EU Operations", February 2013, EU External Action, available at http://consilium.europa.eu/eeas/security-defence/eu-operations?lang=en, accessed 3 April 2013.

29 A. Vines, "Rhetoric from Brussels and Reality on the Ground: The EU and Security in Africa", *International Affairs* 86, 2010, p. 1091.

30 T. Chafer and G. Cumming, "Beyond Fashoda: Anglo-French Security Cooperation in Africa since Saint-Malo", *International Affairs* 86, 2010, pp. 1129–1147.
31 M. Wyss, "The Gendarme Stays in Africa: France's Military Role in Côte d'Ivoire", *African Conflict & Peacebuilding Review* 3, 2013, pp. 81–111.
32 T. Tardy, "France"; P.D. Williams, "The United Kingdom"; A.C. Smith, "United States of America", in A.J. Bellamy and P.D. Williams (eds), *Providing Peacekeepers: The Politics, Challenges, and Future of United Nations Peacekeeping Contributions*, Oxford: Oxford University Press, 2013, pp. 115–138, 93–114, 71–92.
33 B. Gebrewold, "The Cynicism of 'African Solutions for African Problems'", *African Security* 3, 2010, pp. 87–89; A.S. Bah and K. Aning, "US Peace Operations Policy in Africa: From ACRI to AFRICOM", *International Peacekeeping* 15, 2008, pp. 118–132.
34 G. Bates and C.-H. Huang, "The People's Republic of China", in Bellamy and Williams, *Providing Peacekeepers*, pp. 139–157.
35 Carmody, *The New Scramble for Africa*, p. 95.
36 D. Banerjee, "India", in Bellamy and Williams, *Providing Peacekeepers*, pp. 225–244.
37 D.S. Tull, *Die Peacekeeping-Krise der Vereinten Nationen*, SWP-Studie, Berlin: Stiftung Wissenschaft und Politik, January 2010.
38 J. Sherman and M. Gleason, "Strategic Summary 2011", in Center on International Cooperation (CIC), *Annual Review of Global Peace Operations 2012*, Boulder CO: Lynne Rienner, 2012, pp. 3–10.
39 B. Franke and S. Gänzle, "How 'African' Is the African Peace and Security Architecture? Conceptual and Practical Constraints of Regional Security Cooperation in Africa", *African Security* 5, 2012, p. 95.
40 M. Berdal, "The United Nations, Peacekeeping and Power Politics: Is the West Still in a Position to Impose its Vision on Emerging Powers?", *Normative Changes in Peacekeeping Operations*, Zurich and Geneva: Center for Security Studies (CSS) at ETH Zurich and Geneva Centre for Security Policy (GCSP), April 2013.
41 See also T. Tardy, "Protecting Civilians in Africa: The Risks of Issue-Linkage between RtoP and Peacekeeping", *Journal of International Peacekeeping* 17, 2013, pp. 201–221.
42 See also D.M. Tull, "When They Overstay Their Welcome: UN Peacekeepers in Africa", *Journal of International Peacekeeping* 17, 2013, pp. 179–200.

Part I

Institutions

1 Changing dimensions of international peacekeeping in Africa

Megan Gleason-Roberts and Alischa Kugel

Introduction

International peacekeeping deployments to Africa have reached a pivotal time. Thus far, the predominant form of international peace operations in Africa has been the UN peacekeeping operations. The number of UN peacekeepers in the region constitutes almost half of all UN deployments. Africa also hosts three out of the UN's four largest operations, namely the UN missions in Darfur (25,960 personnel), the DRC (23,470 personnel) and Côte d'Ivoire (12,395 personnel).[1] Yet multilateral peacekeeping in Africa is entering a period of change and contraction driven by a number of factors related to the evolution of both the nature of conflict, and international support to conflict-affected or post-conflict states. In addition, a number of transitions in peace operations, including those in Somalia, Sudan and South Sudan, and West Africa, exemplify how changes in conflict trends, the climate of fiscal austerity and the development of newly-defined crisis management tools have manifested themselves in the field.

This chapter will first explore trends in international peacekeeping deployments to Africa with a particular focus on those that are currently undergoing a period of transition. It then aims to demonstrate how alternative models of peacekeeping – including civilian-led political missions, regional deployments, and over-the-horizon security guarantees – are increasingly important tools for crisis response both in parallel with traditional peacekeeping operations and as deployment alternatives. Finally, the chapter will examine the increasingly dynamic partnerships between actors, both at headquarters and at the field level.

Overall, while the risks in these changing strategies are manifold, and often driven by rapidly unfolding situations rather than a strategic vision, developments over the past two years have also demonstrated the important role that peace operations continue to play in supporting post-conflict and post-crisis states as well as the continued national demand for this type of support.

Changing dimensions in conflict and crisis management

This section will examine changes in international conflict and crisis management along three paradigms, namely the changing manifestations of conflict, increasing fiscal austerity and budgetary pressures in countries financing peace operations, and a renewed focus on political processes.

Changes in the manifestation of conflict

As the 2011 World Development Report *Conflict, Security and Development* notes, the global drivers and manifestations of conflict are changing. The world has witnessed a decline in the number of civil wars and the number of deaths attributable to civil conflict over the past 25 years. In Africa, while a number of conflicts continue, meaningful progress has been registered in sustainably resolving conflicts in a number of countries including Angola and Mozambique. Considerable but still fragile peace consolidation has also been achieved in recent years in Liberia and Sierra Leone.

Yet underlying these positive trends, there are a number of countries throughout the world that are experiencing repeated cycles of violence, exacerbated by poor governance.[2] Ninety percent of all civil wars in the last decade occurred in countries that had had a previous civil war in the last 30 years. Often called failed or fragile states, these countries struggle to recover from multiple and in many cases simultaneous political and security crises. Fifteen of the top 20 countries on the Fund for Peace's 2012 Failed State Index are located in Africa.[3]

In Somalia, until recently, simultaneous security and political crises stressed the capacity of national and international actors on the ground and reduced the prospect for meaningful progress towards stabilization. Hopeful signs in 2012, including the end of the transitional period and the security gains achieved in connection with the AU Mission in Somalia (AMISOM), emphasize that there cannot be a purely military solution for the crisis in Somalia and that instead, security, governance and socio-economic spheres must be addressed simultaneously.[4] The strategic review of the UN's engagement in Somalia, conducted between September and December 2012, served to emphasize the need for continued complementary efforts by international actors across different sectors.[5]

In addition, countries are coming under increasing pressure from transnational threats including organized crime, trafficking and extremism. These three threats all particularly impact stabilization efforts in West Africa.[6] Organized crime and drug trafficking have been recognized as threats for several years, but the region is now facing a security crisis in northern Mali that highlights the risk that violent extremism poses to even more stable countries in West Africa.[7]

The impacts of increasing fiscal austerity in countries financing African peace operations

The budgets for peace operations managed to survive the first three years of the global financial crisis relatively unscathed. However, more recently states have come under increasing pressure to reduce their contributions to multilateral peace operations. In the UN, after long debates between member states, the peacekeeping budget was reduced by nearly eight percent between 2011 and 2012, while during the same period the budget requirements for civilian-led political missions were reduced by six percent. A similar trend is seen in the EU, now increasingly hesitant to deploy new large missions, and where the future of the African Peace Facility is uncertain due to budgetary pressures.[8]

These exigencies have led to disputes about how to implement cost savings, with deep divides seen among member states that provide much of the financial contributions for UN peacekeeping. In 2011, uncharacteristically public debates were seen between Western European states and the US over which missions to scale down, including those in Sudan and Liberia.[9]

In Sudan, the July 2012 reconfiguration and reduction in size of the AU-UN Hybrid Mission in Darfur (UNAMID) were driven in large part by member states' belief that during a time of financial austerity the mission should be able to achieve its mandated tasks with a smaller force level and enhanced operational efficiency.[10] However, the force reduction took place amidst a renewed increase in fighting between the government and rebel forces, and this stalled the political process.

Budgetary constraints also played a large role in the drawdown of the UN Mission in Liberia (UNMIL), which began in mid-2012 despite the UN Secretary-General's acknowledgement in April 2012 that "none of the country's security institutions is operationally independent" or "able to maintain stability without the support of UNMIL".[11] In neighboring Côte d'Ivoire, plans for a reduction in the military forces of the UN and French peacekeeping operations after the re-establishment of constitutional order have been put on hold due to the precarious security situation, including along the border with Liberia where there has been an increase in attacks by armed groups.[12]

While civilian-led political missions are now being praised by member states and the UN for their efficiency and relatively low cost,[13] member states are also carefully limiting the funding budgets for these types of missions. In 2011 the Secretary-General proposed to extend additional peacekeeping funding mechanisms to political missions.[14] These efforts failed to garner sufficient support among member states, largely because the five permanent members of the Security Council feared they would have to pay a higher percentage of these costs, as they do for the peacekeeping budget.[15]

These pressures also extend to Western support for African-led operations, though the approval in February 2012 of an expanded support package, including an authorized troop increase for the AU Mission in Somalia, temporarily overcame this trend, bolstered in part by the EU's willingness to provide increased funding for the mission through the African Peace Facility.[16] The future viability of this funding source is now in question as the EU struggles to make reductions in its overall budget.[17]

A renewed focus on political processes

In addition to changes in the conflicts confronting peace operations, there is also a greater recognition of when peacekeeping is effective and when it is unlikely to have a meaningful impact. Numerous studies have shown the important contribution that peacekeeping can make in reducing the likelihood of a resumption of conflict. Indeed, peacekeeping missions have been found to reduce the risk of another relapse into conflict by between 55 and 85 percent, all other things being equal.[18] However, the presence of multiple decades-long peacekeeping deployments demonstrates that they are not a cure-all. In some instances the continued deployment of a peacekeeping operation, in the case of some missions in Africa for a decade or more,[19] represents a vivid reminder of a failure to adequately address underlying causes of conflict. Research has shown that peacekeeping operations are most effective when deployed into environments where conflict has ended, but that when deployed in situations where war is still ongoing, they have little or no impact.[20] This has meaningful implications for how and when to deploy peacekeepers in Africa.

Incidents where peace operations have been deployed in active conflict or where peace is only maintained during the deployment of peacekeepers have given rise to a greater appreciation for the political dimension of peace agreements and post-conflict reconciliation, including in conflicts in Africa. The UN peacekeeping mission in South Sudan (established in 2011) has been mandated with a greater political role and lighter footprint than its predecessor. The mission is focused on building up state structures in governance, rule of law, and security sector reform, as well as conflict prevention, mitigation and resolution – tasks not commonly associated with traditional peacekeeping.[21]

The UN is also placing a greater priority on mediation and prevention. The gradual strengthening of the UN's Department of Political Affairs since Ban Ki-Moon became Secretary-General has highlighted increasing support among member states for its diplomacy and prevention activities.[22] Both the Security Council and the General Assembly have been actively involved in furthering efforts to enhance mediation activities and strengthen conflict prevention measures, particularly in Africa. Reports by the Secretary-General in 2008 and 2009 on conflict prevention and mediation, as well as the first ever report on the use of preventive diplomacy in

2011, focus on enhancing these mechanisms and support activities.[23] Recommendations include the strengthening of partnerships and better coordination with regional organizations, particularly the AU.

As the international community continues to grapple with how to respond effectively to the crisis in Mali and support its transitional authorities, there is consensus among the UN, the AU and the ECOWAS on the need for an inclusive and credible political process to guide its efforts.[24] Researchers and policymakers are also focusing increasingly on how to effectively support political settlements among elites and between elites and the broader population.[25]

This recognition comes in part from conflict-affected states themselves. The g7+ grouping of fragile states,[26] created in 2010, seeks to share experiences and articulate coordinated messages to the international community about international aid and support. African countries are 11 of the 17 members, with nine currently hosting a peace operation.[27] The g7+ has led efforts to strengthen national ownership of international support to fragile and post-conflict states and its New Deal articulates five peacebuilding and statebuilding goals, the first of which is to support inclusive political settlements.[28]

The increasing importance of innovative peace operation models in Africa

Multilateral peace and security efforts have also recently been bolstered by the use of new and newly refined tools for crisis management. Efforts to develop and deploy these tools have been driven by a combination of the factors identified in the previous section: large-scale peacekeeping operations are not feasible in many post-conflict environments because member states are unwilling to fund them, but also because they may be an inappropriate response to an underlying political crisis.

Three of the most important shifts in this regard have been increased interest in the use of civilian-led political missions, growing roles for regional initiatives, and stronger over-the-horizon security guarantees, including for inter-mission cooperation.

Political missions: a range of actors yielding mixed results

Political missions are civilian-led peace operations, without military components.[29] What differentiates political missions from peacekeeping and other peace operations, such as human rights missions, is their core task of political engagement in the form of good offices, mediation or facilitation.

Political missions are versatile operations, with a wide range of mandated tasks and functions that are deployed in varying shapes and sizes – ranging from a single envoy to field-based missions with thousands of staff. While these missions are deployed at different stages of a conflict's cycle, from prevention to mediation and from ongoing conflict to post-conflict settings, they rarely play a purely preventative role, in the sense of keeping conflict from breaking out where it has not yet occurred.[30] Yet, as discussed below, they can play an important role in preventing conflicts from reigniting or escalating by building national and regional capacities for conflict prevention or by engaging in mediation.

The AU has 14 liaison offices in the field, ten of which are in countries hosting another multilateral peace operation. While the efforts of these small offices are often below the radar, the offices provide the AU with representation on the ground and expand its information and monitoring capacity. They also extend the AU's ability to support the implementation of peace agreements.[31] The offices typically partner with other multilateral presences on the ground, particularly the UN. In Guinea-Bissau, for example, the Special Representative and head of the AU Liaison Office is working closely with the UN mission on the ground to harmonize international efforts to achieve a return to constitutional order following the April 2012 coup.[32]

ECOWAS also has a network of offices across West Africa. In addition to its four offices that are part of the ECOWAS Early Warning and Response Network (ECOWARN), these include offices of the Special Representatives of the President of the ECOWAS Commission. The latter assist member states in dealing with crisis situations, or provide support in post-conflict settings.[33] In 2012, Special Representatives were located in Mali, Côte d'Ivoire, Guinea-Bissau and Liberia.

The EU has country- and region-specific Special Representatives (EUSRs) for the Horn of Africa and Sudan, as well as an institutional Special Representative for the AU. EUSRs support the work of Catherine Ashton, the High Representative of the Union for Foreign Affairs and Security Policy, and give the EU an active political presence, helping it shape more effective security policy. In doing so, EUSRs provide good offices, engage in conflict resolution, mediation and facilitation, and cooperate closely with third parties, including international organizations such as the AU.[34]

With nine field-based missions, including two regional offices that range from 20 to almost 200 in total staff, the UN is the largest institutional player in Africa in deployment of political missions. Although political missions engage across various thematic areas, they can be roughly divided into five categories. First, envoys, special representatives and mediators are usually appointed to address a specific crisis and to provide political support to ongoing processes. In response to the 2012 military coups in Guinea-Bissau and Mali, for example, ECOWAS appointed mediators to work with national and international stakeholders to resolve the crises. Envoys often work in a joint institutional capacity for added political weight and legitimacy, as for example in the case of the Joint AU/UN Chief Mediator for Darfur; or in close cooperation, as in the case of

ECOWAS and UN envoys to Mali. Second, governance assistance missions, such as the UN Office in Burundi, have a primary focus on assisting authorities to strengthen key institutions and critical aspects of governance, such as security sector reform and the rule of law. Third, missions in support of peace processes, such as the UN Office in Somalia that assists in the implementation of the Djibouti peace agreement, can help the authorities in moving forward the political process. Fourth, integrated peacebuilding offices assist countries in peace consolidation in the post-conflict phase. In Sierra Leone and the Central African Republic, UN presences assist governments' peacebuilding efforts through the coordination of UN humanitarian and development actors on the ground. And fifth, regional offices, such as the UN offices for West and Central Africa, promote an integrated sub-regional approach to peace and security challenges, working closely with the respective regional organizations and actors in the UN system.[35] In addition to strengthening regional and sub-regional institutions' capacities, the presences also use their good offices to address crises, particularly in countries with no peace operation on the ground. For example, in 2012, in addition to responding to the developments in Mali, the Special Representative of the Secretary-General for the UN Office in West Africa, Said Djinnit, used his good offices function to reduce electoral tensions in Senegal and Togo.[36]

Due to their vastly different operating environments, mandated tasks and capacities, political missions have a mixed track record of delivering results. Precarious security situations and politically uncertain environments can hamper their engagement and effectiveness.[37] For example, while recent advances in stabilizing the security situation in Somalia have allowed the UN Political Office for Somalia (UNPOS) to relocate its headquarters to Mogadishu after 17 years of operating outside of the country, the mission in the Central African Republic (CAR) was forced to temporarily evacuate its non-essential staff amid the advance of an armed rebel coalition toward the capital in December 2012.

In their work, political missions largely rely on political leverage gained through the legitimacy of the respective mandating decision-making bodies.[38] The absence of a strong political framework or united support can thus hinder political missions' effectiveness. The consent of key conflict parties to a mission and their cooperation with it are also crucial for achieving political goals.[39] In 2009 in Burundi and in 2012 in Sierra Leone and Guinea-Bissau, the UN had to withdraw its special representatives at the request of the governments, as the governments' questioning of their partiality would have blocked political processes from moving ahead. In many cases the request for withdrawal is also interpreted as a signal to the UN that the host government no longer welcomes its political presence. However, seeking consensus among key actors can also lead to mandates with either an overly limited scope, or mandates that are too broad and loosely defined, making it hard for missions to achieve real gains.[40]

Political missions are not a panacea in conflict resolution. Some situations will require the presence of international military peacekeepers to prevent spoilers from unsettling situations of fragile peace and to protect civilians from violence. In addition, reviews of political missions illustrate that they are most likely to be effective alongside peacekeeping operations or when deployed as follow-on mechanisms to peacekeeping missions, once a certain level of security has been established.[41]

However, political missions have shown their resilience and effectiveness in a number of cases recently.[42] In Libya, the UN Support Mission successfully assisted in holding the first elections in over 40 years, and after gains in peace consolidation the UN missions in Sierra Leone and Burundi are expected to transition to smaller development presences in 2013. ECOWAS envoys, meanwhile, took the lead in mediation efforts in Mali and Guinea-Bissau that have led to the establishment of transitional governments. As large-scale military operations are likely to go into a drawdown phase in Africa over the short to medium term, political missions are expected to take on an increasingly prominent role.

Regional deployments and initiatives: strategic engagements to combat transnational threats

As noted above, transnational threats such as drug trafficking, organized crime, terrorism and piracy have gained visibility in Africa in recent years, particularly in the west and central sub-regions.[43] Persistent structural weaknesses including porous borders, weak rule of law and justice systems, widespread corruption, and socioeconomic problems such as high youth unemployment make countries in the region particularly vulnerable. In recognition of the interlinked nature of these threats, the international community has increasingly engaged in strategic international partnerships. Comprehensive approaches include engagement on regional initiatives that address the threats themselves and efforts to build up national capacities and robust institutions.

One of the most visible international engagements in Africa centres on efforts to combat the notorious rebel group the Lord's Resistance Army (LRA), which has conducted violent campaigns in regions straddling the borders of the CAR, the DRC and South Sudan since Uganda managed to eject it in 2005. In March 2012, the AU launched the Regional Cooperation Initiative for the Elimination of the LRA (RCI-LRA) in Juba.[44] The strategy aims to bolster the operational capacities of the countries affected by the LRA, to establish an environment conducive to the stabilization of the affected areas, and to facilitate the delivery of humanitarian assistance. Having assumed operational command in September, the RCI-LRA's military component, the Regional Intervention Force, is composed of soldiers from CAR, DRC, South Sudan and Uganda, numbering up to 5,000 at full deployment. The AU receives military and financial support for the strategy from international partners. In October 2011, the United States sent 100 military advisers to Uganda for intelligence and training support, and in March 2012, the EU pledged €9 million in humanitarian assistance to LRA victims.[45]

The RCI-LRA is further bolstered through the UN regional strategy for humanitarian, development and peacebuilding assistance to areas affected by the LRA. Endorsed by the Security Council in June 2012, the strategy has been developed by the UN Regional Office for Central Africa (UNOCA) in close collaboration with the AU. In addition to supporting the implementation of the RCI-LRA, the UN strategy will utilize the UN system to support the protection of civilians, to strengthen disarmament, demobilization and reintegration activities, to further the coordination of humanitarian assistance and child protection programs, and to give support to the affected countries in establishing state authority in their territories.[46]

The UN's regional political offices play an important role in promoting an integrated approach to peace and security challenges in Africa. Next to UNOCA, the UN Office for West Africa (UNOWA) works to promote good governance and to enhance regional capacities for conflict mediation, prevention and cross-border threats. UNOWA, for example, regularly convenes the heads of peace operations and UN agencies in the region to address growing cross-border challenges and to review implementation on a sub-regional strategy to combat threats such as mercenaries, cross-border movements of weapons and armed groups, and illicit trafficking.[47] UNOWA also supports ECOWAS and other regional entities in the design and implementation of counter-terrorism and anti-piracy strategies and supports regional efforts to combat illicit trafficking and organized crime through the West Africa Coast Initiative (WACI).[48]

Regional and intergovernmental organizations also take action on the ground to strengthen national governance capacities, further enhancing the comprehensive approach to security challenges. In Guinea-Bissau, for example, regional actors took the lead on security sector reform (SSR) efforts after the withdrawal of the EU SSR mission in September 2010. ECOWAS and the Community of Portuguese Language Countries (CPLP) developed an SSR strategy, while Angola deployed the Angolan Military Mission in Guinea-Bissau (MISSANG) in March 2011 to assist implementation of the ECOWAS-CPLP roadmap for SSR.

In April 2012, following the military coup, tensions spiked between MISSANG and the military junta, resulting in a request for the mission to depart. In response, ECOWAS, after consultations with the AU, deployed the Economic Community Mission in Bissau (ECOMIB), comprised of 629 soldiers and police officers from Nigeria, Burkina Faso, Togo and Senegal.[49] In addition to facilitating the safe withdrawal of MISSANG, ECOMIB has assisted in securing the transitional process and aided the implementation of the ECOWAS-CPLP SSR roadmap.

Regional, comprehensive approaches to tackling security threats have gained traction in recent years, particularly in West and Central Africa. Specific elements of these initiatives, such as joint problem-solving, confidence building across countries and strengthening good governance, can have significant benefits for conflict prevention in other areas as well. The World Bank's *World Development Report 2011*, for example, details how regional and global initiatives can reduce stresses on fragile states.[50] However, efforts are often marred by gaps in financial, human and organizational resources. The RCI-LRA strategy suffers from a lack of funding to secure sufficient logistical support, troops and equipment.[51]

James Cockayne and Camino Kavanagh point out that this strong focus on tackling transnational threats to the reform of justice and security institutions may have limited impact when not coupled with efforts to address the problems inherent in political systems dominated by predatory elites.[52] Guinea-Bissau's trajectory of successive military coups and the intimate relationship of the country's ruling elite with international drug syndicates[53] demonstrate the interlinked nature of these issues. Furthermore, regional initiatives may require cooperation between countries that have a history of tensions. This is the case with the states participating in the AU-LRA strategy. It remains to be seen whether the participating countries can overcome operational challenges related to shared military command. Efforts by regional actors can be affected similarly. In Guinea-Bissau, differences between ECOWAS and the CPLP in their approaches to re-establishing constitutional order have hindered progress on the transition process and the implementation of crucial reform efforts, including SSR.

Over-the-horizon guarantees: increasing peace operations' flexibility

In October 2012, UN Under-Secretary-General for Peacekeeping Hervé Ladsous stressed the need for UN peacekeeping operations to be increasingly flexible and nimble, particularly within the context of financial restraint.[54] One option to make peacekeeping arrangements more flexible is through over-the-horizon security guarantees. Based on a reliable commitment from an international or regional organization or bilateral partner, these security guarantees can include external forces providing a surge function to a peace operation during particularly tense periods, or can extend the security guarantee of a peacekeeping mission once it has drawn down. These security guarantees can also add flexibility, credibility and security to political missions that otherwise do not have a deterrent factor.[55]

A well-known bilateral over-the-horizon security guarantee is the United Kingdom's commitment to the Sierra Leone government to intervene militarily within 48 to 72 hours if a security crisis emerges in Sierra Leone. The commitment was made following the UK's successful military intervention against the armed group Revolutionary United Front in 2000, and it helped end the civil war.[56] Security guarantees can also work between peacekeeping missions. A recent example is the transfer of military and police capabilities as well as helicopter assets from UNMIL to the UN Operation in Côte d'Ivoire (UNOCI) between 2010 and 2012. The inter-mission cooperation agreement is based on a report by the Secretary-General on inter-mission cooperation and possible cross-border operations between the UN missions in Liberia, Côte d'Ivoire and Sierra Leone and the subsequent authorization by the Security Council through Resolution 1609 (2005).[57] The 2010–2012 transfer took place against the backdrop of heightened tensions and increased violence, and illicit activity along the border with Liberia after the 2011 elections in Côte d'Ivoire. The arrangement is likely to be of continued use, particularly along the volatile border area between the two countries, as UNOCI aims to reduce its troops by one battalion in the near future,[58] and UNMIL continues its troop reduction from 7,950 in September 2012 to 3,750 by July 2015.[59] This is particularly true for strategic assets such as military helicopters, which provide a deterrent value and can serve as force multipliers and supply rapid deployment capability, especially in difficult terrain.

As peacekeeping operations in Africa are expected to continue to draw down, bilateral partners and regional organizations are likely to be called upon increasingly to provide security guarantees as in-country risks may persist after missions leave or are replaced by civilian missions. In this regard, the development of AU and ECOWAS standby forces are an important step. However, over-the-horizon security guarantees do not come without challenges. For security guarantees to have a deterrent effect or to be put into action when a situation requires, they have to be part of a reliable commitment. Changes on the ground, including rapidly deteriorating security situations, disagreement over command and control, or political disunity within the deploying country or organization making the commitment, can jeopardize these deployments. Inter-mission transfers, meanwhile, can affect a mission's operational effectiveness, as unforeseen and fast-changing situations on the ground can necessitate the deployment of assets that may not be immediately available to the mission.[60] These arrangements can also only work if missions have sufficient capabilities and if their operational effectiveness is not already hampered by a lack of resources. In general, over-the-horizon security guarantees benefit from strong bilateral or institutional partnerships.

The importance of partnerships in Africa

Peace operations partnerships are not new, but have become an increasingly central feature of multilateral peace operations. Currently, approximately one half of all UN missions and two-thirds of all EU operations are deployed with a partner on the ground.[61] The AU, ECOWAS and the UN collaborated to respond to the multiple crises affecting West Africa in

2012 and 2013. These partnerships have also become more complex, and the relationships between organizations have evolved considerably over the past ten years. As the crises of the past few years indicate, these partnerships may be moving towards a more prominent role for regional and sub-regional organizations in crisis management and more modular forms of engagement, where organizations provide specialized assets or units in pursuit of finite political or security objectives.

The AU is currently participating in two Security Council–authorized peacekeeping missions, in Somalia and Darfur. In addition, as noted above, it fields liaison offices in a number of countries also hosting a peacekeeping or political mission. Because the majority of inter-organizational cooperation occurs between the AU and the UN, this section will focus primarily on this partnership.

Partnerships between headquarters

The AU is the only regional organization to regularly meet with members of the UN Security Council.[62] Beyond annual high-level meetings between the Security Council and the AU Peace and Security Council, the two organizations have a number of cooperation mechanisms covering strategic and operational collaboration. The Joint Task Force on Peace and Security was developed in 2010 to strengthen the strategic aspects of the partnership.

The capacities of the AU are the focus of a ten-year capacity-building program started in 2008. Following the launch of the program the UN opened the UN Office to the African Union in 2010, integrating a number of existing UN presences in Addis Ababa and strengthening the flow of information between the two organizations. The UN has also engaged in considerable activities to support the development of the African Standby Force, though the development of the brigades has been delayed in several regions.

The UN also provides training on a wide range of issues including planning, logistics and senior mission leadership development.[63] The UN and AU have increased their cooperation on prevention and mediation issues, with the UN's Department of Political Affairs assisting in building the AU's mediation capacities. However, the UN acknowledges that this is still a work in progress.[64] In assessing the organization's support to the AU's development, the UN's Office of Internal Oversight Services noted that given some limits to absorptive capacity and challenges in donor coordination, the support to the AU sometimes functioned as substitute capacity, at the expense of long-term capacity and skills development.[65] In addition to training support, the UN is also able to provide expertise to regional organizations. Most recently, at the request of the Security Council, the UN provided military and security planners to the AU and ECOWAS to assist in planning efforts for a military intervention force in Mali.[66]

Translating strategy into action: partnerships on the ground

The efforts to strengthen institutional links and capacities are all intended to improve the deployment and conduct of peace operations on the ground. Operations can be sequential, parallel, or fully integrated – or hybrid – missions.

Between the UN and African regional organizations the most frequent type of sequential operation involves the AU or ECOWAS acting as a first responder, sometimes in situations where a ceasefire has yet to be achieved, with the UN taking over follow-on responsibility for longer-term, wider-ranging peace operations. In 2003 the UN took over peacekeeping duties in Liberia from ECOWAS.[67] More recently, the AU Mission in Sudan transitioned to the hybrid AU-UN mission in Darfur. A number of sequential missions have suffered from challenges in the handover process, where logistical and supportive regulations can further impede already challenging and fast-moving processes.

As noted above, the majority of current peace operations are deployed in parallel with another mission. These partnerships take a variety of forms. In some cases, specialized military assets are deployed in the short term to assist a larger or longer-term mission in achieving a discrete security objective. In Sierra Leone in 2000 the UK deployed troops alongside the UN's peacekeeping mission. In the DRC the EU deployed Operation Artemis to assist in stabilizing Ituri province in the east. Most recently, France launched a short-term military mission in early 2013 in Mali to regain territory from Islamists and pave the way for the deployment of a UN-authorized, African-led operation.

Parallel operations can also run for medium- and long-term deployments, often operating with a division of labour. The EU's advisory and assistance mission for security sector reform in the DRC deployed in 2006 and has worked alongside the UN presence in the country. While the UN's peacekeepers have a broad mandate, the European Union Security Sector Reform Mission (EUSEC) focuses on reforming the Congolese army. The intention in Somalia was for AMISOM's operations to be turned over to UN peacekeeping sequentially once a degree of security and stability was established. While the UN Department of Field Support runs the UN Support Office for AMISOM, the mission runs in parallel with UNPOS, whose efforts focus on supporting the political process. In the current financial climate, it seems unlikely that the UN will take over the peacekeeping duties of AMISOM.

Somalia is not the only case of a political mission deploying alongside a military mission in Africa. As noted above, the majority of AU and ECOWAS envoys and special representatives are in countries with peacekeeping presences, while the UN Envoy for Western Sahara works in close cooperation with the UN Mission for the Referendum in Western Sahara. The UN Integrated Peacebuilding Office in Guinea-Bissau (UNIOGBIS) has been working alongside MISSANG and, after its replacement in mid-2012, with ECOMIB. In the Central African Republic, the UN Integrated Peacebuilding Office works in parallel with the Economic Community of Central African States' peacekeeping mission, MICOPAX. The mandates of UN regional offices often cover countries with a military mission. In West Africa, UNOWA provided good offices during the electoral crisis in Côte d'Ivoire; the UN's Regional Office in Central Africa is cooperating closely with the UN Organization Stabilization Mission in the DRC (MONUSCO) on LRA-related issues.

Integrated missions offer the promise of division of labour based on comparative advantage and stronger coordination between organizations.[68] In practice, integrated missions are still quite rare. The closest approximation comes in the form of UNAMID in Darfur, with joint strategic oversight and UN responsibility for command and control and backstopping the mission. Here the design of the mission was born of compromise rather than a strategic decision on how to allocate responsibility between organizations.

A 2011 report by the Secretary-General identified a number of lessons learned from operational and strategic cooperation, and joint operations on the ground, between the AU and the UN.[69] These include the need for harmonized policy and strategy, which require coordinated and joint planning as well as clear command and control structures. In addition, mechanisms for regular communications, including communications related to planning, are required for effective partnerships. The report also notes that the AU's lack of substantive staff has represented a challenge for its planning capacity, but points to recent planning recruits as a positive step. Finally, positive partnerships between the UN and the AU require an intelligent division of labour that delivers real operational benefits for all actors involved and that includes strengthened mechanisms for getting the needed resources – material, human and financial – on the ground quickly. As Almut Wieland-Karimi and Tobias von Gienanth note, there is a natural complementarity to AU and UN operations in the field:

> The AU possesses unrivalled local knowledge and legitimacy. Its member states have also shown the political will to authorise operations in high-risk environments. There exists, however, a considerable gap between the organization's willingness and its ability to act. The AU has neither a predictable funding mechanism nor the capacities to independently sustain its missions. The UN, on the other hand, has unique experience and abilities to plan, deploy, and support large-scale peace operations. Crucially, it also has access to a reliable source of funding in the form of its assessed contributions. What it lacks is the political will to intervene in on-going conflicts: UN peacekeepers can only go where there is "a peace to keep".[70]

Partnership challenges and possibilities

As intimated in the above quote, there are a number of important challenges and risks that underlie these increasingly complex partnerships. First, these organizations admit that cooperation is often ad hoc and driven by emergency action during crises, without a fully developed strategic vision of the partnership.[71] Despite regular meetings, if institutions have not codified the purpose of the cooperation, it may be difficult to operationalize joint structures in a crisis.

A related challenge is that organizations deploying missions are operating with different objectives, mandates and values for their intervention. Some of these challenges have been observed in the debates around the deployment of a peacekeeping operation to Mali (and its financing). The AU and UN's shared strategic oversight of the hybrid mission in Darfur is intended to strengthen the coordinated vision of the mission, but the organizations have at times differed in their reading of the situation. In these situations the head of mission can end up with two sets of guidance,[72] a problem when political messaging needs to be clear. When organizations disagree about the appropriate course of action, it can complicate efforts on the ground. Differences between some African states and Western countries on the response to the uprising in Libya in 2011 were magnified in the UN Security Council vote to authorize the NATO air campaign. Also in 2011 in Côte d'Ivoire, as Laurent Gbagbo refused to accept electoral defeat by Alassane Ouattara, the AU initially sought a political power-sharing arrangement while the UN firmly backed Ouattara's electoral victory.[73] It is likely that these differences on the appropriate political course of action extended the acute crisis.

Third, at the operational level, multiplying organizations necessarily adds challenges to coordination and coherence, already manifold in international support to post-conflict states. Institutionally this is also an issue: multiple organizations provide support to the development of AU bodies, including the African Standby Force, which raises the question of whether these multiple channels for organizational support are sufficiently coordinated and coherent.

While it is difficult to predict with certainty how peace operations partnerships will evolve, Richard Gowan and Jake Sherman identify four possible options for future cooperation between organizations.[74] First, joint mission support frameworks, in which organizations share logistical and other supporting mechanisms, could lay the foundation for a division of labour that would provide the strongest supportive assets to a joint or modular mission. Second, organizations with particular military skills could deploy in the short term to supplement a longer peace operation on the ground, as in the case of US support to anti-LRA activities. Similarly, third, as missions take on a broadening array of civilian tasks, specialized civilian expertise could be loaned or shared among organizations.

For instance, the UN could provide expertise on police reform to support a policing mission fielded by the AU or the EU. Finally, when organizations agree to cooperate on a mission, joint planning frameworks, including assumptions and objectives, could prove to be an important component of co-deployment. This would force discussion and agreement on the goals and priorities of the mission prior to deployment, reducing a number of the risks identified above.

Conclusion

While larger-scale peacekeeping operations continue to be the primary form of international conflict management in Africa, alternative models, including political missions, regional deployments, and over-the-horizon security guarantees, are gaining in importance as tools for crisis response in Africa. Critical to the success of these new or newly refined peace operation models are strengthened partnerships between the institutional actors that are engaged in peacekeeping activities on the continent.

Collaboration is not without risk: notwithstanding more collaborative approaches to mission planning, international organizations still operate with distinct goals and assessments of tradeoffs. In Mali, for example, ECOWAS is primarily concerned with regional stability whereas the EU's priority is to ensure that al-Qaeda does not gain a foothold in a region so close to its borders.

However, even if organizations are able to develop a shared strategic vision of the objectives of a specific peace operation, this does not automatically translate into coherent action at the operational level. To ensure that planned peace operations are providing the maximum support for stability, the organizations fielding them will need to ensure agreement both on the overall objectives and on the operational means for their achievement.

Notes

1 Mission strength is as of 31 October 2012. Center on International Cooperation (CIC), *Annual Review of Global Peace Operations*, Boulder CO: Lynne Rienner Publishers, 2013.
2 World Bank, *World Development Report 2011: Conflict, Security and Development*, Washington DC: World Bank, 2011, pp. 49–66.
3 Fund for Peace, *Failed States Index 2012*, available at www.fundforpeace.org/global/?q=fsi-grid2012.
4 CIC, *Annual Review*, p. 9.
5 "Report of the Secretary-General on Somalia", United Nations (UN), S/2013/69, 31 January 2013, para. 87 and 88, pp. 19–20.
6 See for example "Security Council Presidential Statement Calls for System-Wide UN Action to Combat Transnational Crime – Drug Trafficking, Piracy, Terrorism – in West Africa, Sahel", UN, 21 February 2012, available at www.un.org/News/Press/docs/2012/sc10546.doc.htm.
7 CIC, *Annual Review*, p. 2.

8 In February 2013, EU member states agreed to the first ever cut in the EU's budget, limiting spending to €960 billion between 2014 and 2020. See for example "EU Budget Deal: First Ever Cut in Brussels' Spending", *Euronews*, 8 February 2013, available at www.euronews.com/2013/02/08/eu-budget-deal-first-ever-cut-in-brussels-spending/.
9 See for example C. Lynch, "US and Europe Fight Over Cuts in Peacekeeping", *Foreign Policy*, 10 October 2011, available at http://turtlebay.foreignpolicy.com/posts/2011/10/10/us_and_europe_fight_over_cuts_in_peacekeeping.
10 "July 2012 Monthly Forecast, Sudan/Darfur", Security Council Report, 29 June 2012, available at www.securitycouncilreport.org/monthly-forecast/2012–07/lookup_c_glKWLeMTIsG_b_8191997.php.
11 "Special Report of the Secretary-General on the United Nations Mission in Liberia", UN, S/2012/230, 16 April 2012, para 46 and 35.
12 "Letter dated 16 October 2012 from the Secretary-General Addressed to the President of the Security Council", UN, S/2012/772, 17 October 2012.
13 See for example B.L. Pascoe, "Rediscovering Preventive Diplomacy: A View from the United Nations", Remarks at the Brookings Institute, 26 July 2010, available at www.un.org/wcm/content/site/undpa/main/peacemaking_prevention.
14 "Review of Arrangements for Funding and Backstopping Special Political Missions", Report of the Secretary-General, UN, A/66/340, 12 October 2011.
15 For a background on the discussions around the funding and backstopping of political missions at the UN, see R. Gowan, " 'Less Bound to the Desk': Ban Ki-moon, the UN, and Preventive Diplomacy", *Global Governance* 18, 2012, pp. 398–399.
16 See UN Security Council Resolution 2036, 22 February 2012, and "The EU Increases its Support to Peace and Security in Somalia", European Commission, 6 March 2012.
17 Author interviews with an EU expert.
18 See V.P. Fortna, *Does Peacekeeping Work? Shaping Belligerents' Choices after Civil War*, Princeton NJ: Princeton University Press, 2008, p. 116.
19 That is the case, for example, with the UN operation in the DRC, which has been in the country for over 12 years, and the UN mission in Liberia, first deployed in 2003.
20 M.J. Gilligan and E.J. Sergenti, "Do UN Interventions Cause Peace? Using Matching to Improve Causal Inference", *Quarterly Journal of Political Science* 3, 2008, pp. 89–122.
21 Safer World, "UNMISS: A Second Chance for UN Peacekeeping in South Sudan", *South Sudan Monitor*, August 2011.
22 Gowan, " 'Less Bound to the Desk' ", pp. 387–404.
23 See "Report of the Secretary-General on the Implementation of Security Council Resolution 1625 (2005) on Conflict Prevention, Particularly in Africa", UN, S/2008/18, January 2008; "Report of the Secretary-General on Enhancing Mediation and its Support Activities", UN, S/2009/189, 8 April 2009; and "Preventive Diplomacy: Delivering Results, Report of the Secretary-General", UN, S/2011/552, 26 August 2011.
24 UN News Centre, "UN Peacekeeping Chief Stresses Need for Flexibility as Missions Face New Challenges", 22 October 2012, available at www.un.org/apps/news/story.asp?NewsID=43351#.URF5regj4Tk.
25 T. Parks and W. Cole, "Political Settlements: Implications for International Development Policy and Practice", *The Asia Foundation*, July 2010.
26 Since its establishment in April 2010, the group has grown from its original seven member states to 17 across Asia, Africa and the Pacific. For a list of member countries, see www.g7plus.org/members/.

27 These are Burundi, Central African Republic, Côte d'Ivoire, the DRC, Guinea Bissau, Liberia, Sierra Leone, Somalia and South Sudan.
28 International Dialogue on Peacebuilding and Statebuilding, *A New Deal for Engagement in Fragile States*, November 2011.
29 Some political missions have Military Experts on Mission (MEMs) that are engaged in an advisory capacity. Some missions, such as the UN Assistance Mission in Iraq, have a small contingent of guards.
30 The UN has only deployed one preventive mission in Macedonia in 1999. See CIC, *Building on Brahimi – Peacekeeping in an Era of Strategic Uncertainty*, New York: CIC, April 2009, p. 19.
31 See for example "African Union and International Partners Sign a Joint Financing Arrangement on Support for Sustaining and Strengthening African Union Liaison Offices", African Union (AU), 12 November 2011, available at www.au.int/en/sites/default/files/Communique%20-%20Signing%20of%20JFA%20for%20AU%20Liaison%20Offices%20_eng_-11–11–11%20_3_%20.-1.pdf.
32 See for example, "Report of the Secretary-General on the Restoration of Constitutional Order in Guinea-Bissau", UN, S/2012/887, 27 November 2012, para. 26, p. 6; and CIC, *Annual Review.*
33 For more on the role of the Special Representatives, see B.T. Afolabi, "Peacemaking in the ECOWAS Region: Challenges and Prospects", *Conflict Trends* 2, 2009.
34 For more information on the role of EUSRs, see C. Adebahr, "The EU Special Representatives as a Capability for Conflict Management", in R.G. Whitman and S. Wolff (eds), *The European Union as a Global Conflict Manager*, London: Routledge, 2012, pp. 155–168.
35 For a more in-depth description of political missions deployed by the UN, see A. Kugel, "No Helmets, Just Suits: Political Missions as an Instrument of the UN Security Council for Civilian Conflict Management", *International Policy Analysis*, Berlin: Friedrich Ebert Stiftung, March 2011.
36 See for example "Report of the Secretary-General on the Activities of the United Nations Office for West Africa", UN, S/2012/51029, June 2012, pp. 8–9.
37 R. Gowan and T. Dreisbach, "Taking Risks: Sustaining Political Missions in Unstable Environments", *Review of Political Missions 2012*, New York: CIC, 2012, pp. 12–16.
38 I. Johnstone, "Emerging Doctrine for Political Missions", *Review of Political Missions 2010*, New York: CIC, 2010, p. 22.
39 Consent of the parties and impartiality are two basic principles of UN peacekeeping that are also applied to peace operations more broadly; see UN, *United Nations Peacekeeping Operations: Principles and Guidelines [Capstone Doctrine]*, New York: United Nations Department of Peacekeeping Operations/Department of Field Support, 2008, p. 31.
40 Kugel, "No Helmets", p. 3.
41 See CIC, *Review of Political Missions 2010, 2011 and 2012*, available at www.cic.nyu.edu/politicalmissions/index.html.
42 For a more detailed overview of developments related to political missions see CIC, *Review of Political Missions.*
43 See for example "Special Research Report No. 1: Emerging Security Threats in West Africa", Security Council Report, 2 May 2011, available at www.securitycouncilreport.org/special-research-report/lookup-c-glKWLeMTIsG-b-6740225.php.
44 "The African Union-led Regional Cooperation Initiative for the Elimination of the Lord's Resistance Army Enters its Operational Phase", AU, 27 March

2012, available at www.peaceau.org/en/article/the-african-union-led-regional-cooperation-initiative-for-the-elimination-of-the-lord-s-resistance-army-enters-its-operational-phase.

45 Institute for Security Studies (ISS), *Peace and Security Council Report*, Issue 34, 4 May 2012, available at www.issafrica.org/pgcontent.php?UID=31476.

46 "Regional Strategy to Address the Threat and Impact of the Activities of the Lord's Resistance Army", UN, S/2012/48125, June 2012.

47 "Cooperation at All Levels is Crucial to Resolve Current Crises in West Africa", Twenty-fourth High-level Meeting of Heads of UN Peace Missions in West Africa, UN Office for West Africa, 8 October 2012, available at http://appablog.wordpress.com/2012/10/08/cooperation-at-all-levels-is-crucial-to-resolve-current-crises-in-west-africa-twenty-forth-high-level-meeting-of-heads-of-un-peace-missions-in-west-africa/.

48 Launched in 2009, WACI entails activities targeting capacity-building, at both national and regional level, in the areas of law enforcement, forensics, border management, anti-money-laundering and the strengthening of criminal justice institutions, contributing to peacebuilding initiatives and security sector reforms. The four WACI pilot countries are Côte d'Ivoire, Guinea-Bissau, Liberia and Sierra Leone. In 2012, the initiative was extended to include Guinea.

49 "600-strong ECOWAS Mission Deployed in Guinea-Bissau", *Xinhua News*, 29 May 2012, available at http://news.xinhuanet.com/english/world/2012–05/29/c_131616442.htm.

50 World Bank, *World Development Report 2011: Conflict, Security and Development*, Overview, Washington DC: World Bank 2011, p. 35.

51 "Report of the Secretary-General on the Activities of the United Nations Regional Office for Central Africa and on Areas Affected by the Lord's Resistance Army", UN, S/2012421, 11 June 2012, p. 8.

52 J. Cockayne and C. Kavanagh, "Flying Blind? Political Mission Responses to Transnational Threats", in CIC, *Review of Political Missions 2010*, New York: CIC, 2010, p. 27.

53 See for example A. Frintz, "Drugs: The New Alternative Economy of West Africa", *Le Monde Diplomatique*, February 2013, available at http://mondediplo.com/2013/02/03drugs.

54 UN News Service, "UN Peacekeeping Chief Stresses Need for Flexibility as Missions Face New Challenges", 22 October 2012.

55 CIC, *Building on Brahimi*, p. 24.

56 See for example "Sierra Leone: Belated International Engagement Ends a War, Helps Consolidate a Fragile Democracy", p. 9, in *A Diplomat's Handbook, Community of Democracies*, available at www.diplomatshandbook.org/index.html.

57 "Report of the Secretary-General on Inter-mission Cooperation and Possible Cross-border Operations between the UN Mission in Sierra Leone, the UN Mission in Liberia and the UN Mission in Côte d'Ivoire", UN, S/2005/1352 March 2005.

58 UN Security Council Resolution 2062, 26 July 2012.

59 UN Security Council Resolution 2066, 17 September 2012.

60 J. Sherman, A. Kugel and A. Sinclair, "Overcoming Helicopter Force Generation Challenges for UN Peacekeeping Operations", *International Peacekeeping* 19, 2012, p. 90.

61 A. Wieland-Karimi and T. von Gienanth, "Enabling United Nations and Regional Organizations Partnerships in Africa – Priorities for the Future", *International Forum of Challenges of Peace Operations Background Paper*, February 2012.

62 See M. Artiñano, "Peace Operations Partnerships: The UN Security Council and (Sub-)Regional Organizations", Berlin: Center for International Peace Operations, March 2012.

63 Wieland-Karimi and von Gienanth, "Enabling".

64 "Report of the Secretary-General on United Nations-African Union Cooperation in Peace and Security", UN, S/2011/805, December 2011.

65 "Thematic Evaluation of Cooperation between the Department of Peacekeeping Operations/Department of Field Support and Regional Organizations", Office of Internal Oversight Services, UN, A/65/762, February 2011.

66 UN Security Council Resolution 2071, 12 October 2012.

67 This was the second time such a handover occurred, though this time the relationship between the UN and ECOWAS was significantly less contentious than collaboration in Liberia in the 1990s. For further information see A.S. Bah and B.D. Jones, "Peace Operations Partnerships: Lessons and Issues from Coordination to Hybrid Arrangements", *Annual Review of Global Peace Operations 2008*, New York: Lynne Rienner Publishers, 2008.

68 This terminology is distinct from that of UN integrated missions that seek to unite the various UN presences on the ground.

69 UN, S/2011/805.

70 Wieland-Karimi and von Gienanth, "Enabling".

71 UN, S/2011/805.

72 *Ibid.*

73 See R. Gowan and J. Sherman, *Peace Operations Partnerships: Complex but Necessary Cooperation*, New York: CIC, March 2012, p. 3.

74 *Ibid.*

2 An evolving model of African-led peace support operations?

Lessons from Burundi, Sudan (Darfur) and Somalia

Jide Martyns Okeke[1]

Introduction

Since its establishment in 2002, the AU has demonstrated its vision and aspirations in conflict management. One of the most notable aspects in which the AU has been able to translate its pursuit of peace in Africa into practice is through peace support operations. The history and practice of traditional peacekeeping first arose from the missions authorized and primarily implemented by the UN. The actors, mandates and missions have significantly changed and expanded since the beginning of the twenty-first century, following the security challenges of the immediate post-Cold War era. Regional organizations such as the AU, ECOWAS, the North Atlantic Treaty Organization (NATO) and the EU have become more involved in peace operations. Their mandates have also evolved from merely observing peace (notably the 1956 UN Emergency Force in Egypt, UNEF 1) to more complex multidimensional, integrated stabilization operations requiring extensive civilian protection. Such expansion has been described as part of a liberal interventionist agenda that has been constructed in terms of a Responsibility to Protect (RtoP).[2]

Since 2003, the AU has mandated and deployed peace missions to Burundi, Comoros, Darfur (Sudan), Somalia, Mali, and the Central African Republic. These interventions have led to suggestions that there is an evolving African vision of peace partly reflected through the practice of African-led peace support operations.[3] Such a *pax Africana* does not discount the primacy of the UN, which continues to play important roles in the legitimization, partnership and support of African-led PSOs. Yet is it timely to declare that there is an African-led model of PSOs? Is Africa's leadership adequate to sustain the current African-led approach to PSOs? What are the current and future difficulties that are likely to confront an institutionalized African model for PSOs? This chapter seeks to address these questions with the aim of shedding light on the issue of "African solutions to African problems". A PSO is defined here as

> the expeditionary use of uniformed personnel (police and/or military) with or without UN authorization, with a mandate or

> programme to: assist in the prevention of armed conflict by supporting a peace process; serve as an instrument to observe or assist in the implementation of ceasefires or peace agreements; or enforce ceasefires, peace agreements or the will of the UN Security Council in order to build stable peace.[4]

This definition provides a general conception of the composition, functions and objectives of PSOs, although limiting the composition of PSOs to uniformed personnel fails to capture the importance of civilians as an integrated part of contemporary peace missions. This definition, however, is useful in interrogating the complex nature of contemporary PSOs, especially in Africa where these missions operate amid ongoing conflicts. Importantly, it provides the requisite conceptual guidance for ascertaining the changing nature of PSOs, specifically within the context of an ostensibly African-led model of PSOs in response to Africa's conflicts. Indeed there has been important normative and institutional transformation since the establishment of the AU. In particular, the conception and institutionalization of the African Peace and Security Architecture (APSA) as contained in the *Protocol Relating to the Establishment of the Peace and Security Council* provides the mechanism for the prevention and response to conflicts.

This chapter argues that African-led peace support operations reflect an ad hoc process that is almost entirely dependent on external resourcing. An extension of this argument is the overriding political determinants of the pattern of current PSOs, heavily guided by state consent justified on the basis of respect for sovereignty. This is contrary to the normative commitments of AU member states to the principle of sovereignty as a responsibility contained in Article 4(h) of the AU's Constitutive Act. This principle allows member states to act unilaterally (that is, without the consent of the target state), including through the use of force to protect civilians from mass atrocities. Such normative underpinning reinforces the protection mandate as an essential part of contemporary PSOs. Using the empirical context of AU-led missions in Burundi, Darfur and Somalia, this chapter draws the following conclusions: first, all these missions were set up as ad hoc operations that were (in)voluntarily transferred (Burundi), that were transformed (Darfur) or that continue to receive support from the UN (Somalia). Second, these missions were or continue to be heavily dependent on donor support. This seems to be unsustainable, especially when there are other emerging security priorities. For example, the 2013 French military intervention in Mali constrained the resources available for sustaining the hard-won achievements of the AU Mission in Somalia (AMISOM). Third, there seems to be little political will on the part of AU member states to institutionalize PSOs. This is evident in the delays in the full operationalization of the African Standby Force (ASF). The ASF is a component of the APSA that was intended to achieve a permanent structure, in collaboration with Regional Economic Communities (RECs) and Regional Mechanisms (RMs), that would allow for the rapid deployment of peace support missions. Despite considerable support by international partners for the full readiness capacities of the ASF, repeated delays have characterized its full operationalization. Such delays are substantially reflected in the failure to implement work-plans contained in the ASF Roadmaps. The reluctance of some influential African states to embrace the ASF's full implementation will remain its most profound challenge.

This chapter is divided into three parts. The first section provides an assessment of African-led PSOs within the empirical context of Burundi, Darfur and Somalia. It considers the mandate, actors and actions of these missions as a way of contextualizing the African model of PSOs. The second section provides an analysis of the trends that can be observed in the three case studies under consideration. It examines the ASF to determine whether its full operationalization is ever achievable. The final section draws conclusions about trends in African-led peace support operations.

From "saving strangers"[5] to "helping neighbors": African-led peace support operations

There has been a paradigm shift in the way African institutions seek to prevent and respond to peace and security challenges in Africa. This is most discernible in the increasing prominence of African-led PSOs on the continent. This section reviews three cases of PSOs that have been driven by African states acting through the AU. These are the AU Missions in Burundi (AMIB), in Sudan (AMIS) and in Somalia (AMISOM). There are other examples of AU-led PSOs such as in Comoros (2004 and 2007–2008). Rather than giving an exhaustive review of all peace operations led by African regional institutions and the AU in particular, this chapter adopts these case studies to demonstrate how the normative and institutional transformation following the establishment of the AU has created the political legitimacy for a more interventionist approach to conflict management. This does not imply that the AU has been successful in the institutionalization and practice of its peace operations. As Alex de Waal argues, albeit contentiously, the significance of AU-led operations is less because of their concrete achievements than because of the symbolic intentions and aspirations of the AU and its regional institutions.[6]

The withdrawal of Cold War powers from developing countries, especially in Africa, profoundly contributed to and led to limited or sometimes deficient international responses to the proliferation of intra-state wars. Accordingly, there were African-led attempts to engage in interventions in response to these conflicts, often with little support from the international community. It is within this context that the ECOWAS Monitoring Group

(ECOMOG), for example through the leadership of Nigeria, was involved in peace operations in Sierra Leone and Liberia. These interventions were significant, not least because of their "politicized" attempts to protect civilians;[7] they were an exception rather than a rule. This is because the Charter of the Organization of African Unity (OAU) upheld in its rigid forms the principle of non-intervention and the inviolability of sovereign territories. The OAU based its conflict management efforts primarily on preventive diplomacy and peacemaking strategies.[8] These were predicated on the establishment of the 1993 OAU Mechanism for Conflict Prevention and Management. The latter structure served as an important foundation for the legitimization of African-led missions (notably AMIB) prior to the establishment of the APSA. Criticism persists that the OAU was at best a "club of dictators" and was ineffective, and therefore that it failed to promote peace and security in Africa.[9] Yet the achievements of the OAU in the pursuit of decolonization and the dissolution of the apartheid regime in South Africa are widely acknowledged.

It has been a decade since the OAU was transformed into the AU. In these years, there have been important attempts in the formulation of norms and the establishment of institutions. First, the AU Constitutive Act was a watershed achievement because of its introduction of a legal basis for intervention. Article 4(h) of the AU Constitutive Act particularly underscored the "right of the Union to intervene in a Member State pursuant to a decision of the Assembly in respect of grave circumstances, namely: war crimes, genocide and crimes against humanity".[10] Such legal provision for intervention is a departure from the OAU's historical position, which was based on the respect of traditional sovereignty and non-intervention. It also represents an unprecedented milestone in the enshrinement of the interventionist principle as a part of regional and international institutions. Second, the AU has advanced and built upon its intervention framework through other legal instruments that allow for the practice of intervention where possible. In 2002, for example, the Protocol Establishing the Peace and Security Council (hereafter referred to as the Protocol) was conceptualized and endorsed by AU member states. The Protocol sets out an institutional framework for the prevention of, and response to, conflicts and crisis situations. It is within this framework that the APSA was conceived and can be understood. The APSA is composed of the Peace and Security Council (PSC), a non-permanent 15-member body that operates at the level of the Heads of State and Government, Ministers of Foreign Affairs, and Permanent Representatives to the AU. The PSC remains the primary decision-making organ addressing the prevention of, and response to, conflicts. However, it is supported by the AU Commission Chairperson and other structures of the APSA, such as the Panel of the Wise, the Continental Early Warning System, the African Standby Force (ASF), the Military Staff Committee and the Peace Fund. All these supporting structures are at various stages of full operationalization. In PSOs, these supporting structures (and the ASF in particular) are intended to work closely with the PSC in the formulation of policies, prevention (for instance through early deployment) and direct responses to crises (peace enforcement). Official AU documents suggest that the ASF will attain full operational status by 2015.[11]

Third, despite the fact that the APSA is not yet fully operational, there have been direct efforts by the AU in the deployment of PSOs. This is evident in AMIB, AMIS and AMISOM. Like similar interventions led by the UN, for example, these deployments were and are not without some challenges. The rest of this section provides a background to the actors and mandates of these three AU-led PSOs, and suggests lessons that may be learned.

African Union Mission in Burundi (AMIB)

It has been more than a decade since the Arusha Agreement, which formally ended hostilities between the Tutsi and Hutu groups. Yet a recent study suggests that Burundi is regressing in its post-conflict transition as evidenced in "the government's authoritarian drift and the resumption of political violence".[12] The importance of Burundi in the evolution of a putative African-led PSO mechanism stems from the 2003 AU peace mission referred to as the AU Mission in Burundi (AMIB). The 2000 Arusha Agreement made provision for the establishment of an international peacekeeping force. Specifically, Article 8 of Protocol V of that agreement stated that immediately following the signature of the Agreement, the Burundian Government would submit to the UN a request for an international peacekeeping force.[13] An AU-led peace mission was subsequently made admissible following the 2002 Ceasefire Agreement between the Transitional Government of Burundi and the Burundi Armed Political Parties and Movement. Both parties agreed that "verification and control of the ceasefire may be conducted by a UN mandated mission, or an African Union (AU) [mission]".[14] This provision led to the establishment of AMIB in April 2003, a process that was strongly influenced by the charismatic leadership of South Africa's President Nelson Mandela.[15]

The establishment and mandate of AMIB was endorsed by African states during the 91st Ordinary Session of the OAU Central Organ of the Mechanism for Conflict Prevention, Management and Resolution. It is important to note that the deployment of AMIB was a temporary measure pending the authorization by the UN Security Council of a fully-fledged UN mission. The AMIB had a protection mandate, which was to allow political representatives of parties involved in the agreement to join the transitional government. AMIB was also deployed to facilitate the delivery of humanitarian assistance to refugees and internally displaced persons (IDPs).[16] In terms of a long term post-conflict reconstruction and development agenda, AMIB was mandated to provide technical assistance to the Demobilization, Disarmament and Reintegration (DDR) process. The overall intended outcome of AMIB was stated in the 91st Communiqué of the Ordinary Session of the OAU Central Organ of the Mechanism for Conflict Prevention, Management and Resolution. The Communiqué noted that "AMIB will have fulfilled its mandate after it has facilitated the implementation of the ceasefire agreements and the defence and security situation in Burundi is stable and well-managed by newly created national defence and security structures".[17]

The particularly special aspect of AMIB was that it was the first time that the AU would deploy a PSO. It was conceived as an integrated mission composed of military, police and civilian components. But as in other interventions, there was an essential need for a pivotal state to lead the process of AMIB's deployment. Through President Nelson Mandela and President Jacob Zuma, South Africa acted as a Chief Mediator in the Burundian peace processes. In relation to AMIB, South Africa demonstrated its commitment through its rapid and largest deployment of troops, while Ethiopia and Mozambique were also part of the troop-contributing countries (TCCs), with an Ethiopian Brigadier-General appointed as the Deputy Force Commander. However, the contributions and support from these TCCs were delayed and largely dependent on funding from the United States and the United Kingdom. Arguments have been made that minimal commitments shown by Ethiopia and Mozambique, not least other AU member states to AMIB, could be partly attributed to the dominance of South Africa in the establishment and deployment of this peace mission.[18] There are still widespread speculations about the unspoken interests of South Africa as a leading nation in AMIB. At the same time, one cannot discount the pan-African vision of Mandela and Thabo Mbeki, who were pushing the New Partnership for African Development as the next phase in the political and economic transformation of Africa.[19]

Assessments of AMIB's performance have drawn mixed conclusions. On the one hand, some analysts have argued that it was a success story in the history of peace missions in Africa. According to Boshoff *et al.*, even though there were constraints on resources, AMIB "had the internal capacity and willingness to do its best under difficult circumstances".[20] In addition, one of the most significant aspects of AMIB is that it acted as an important foundation for the deployment of the UN Mission in Burundi (ONUB). The initial conceptualization of AMIB was to function as an entry point for ensuring a ceasefire and creating conditions for deployment of a UN mission.[21] Accordingly, the deployment of ONUB in May 2004 could be regarded as a partial fulfilment of the AMIB mandate. Despite these achievements, AMIB was characterized by some shortcomings. There were instances of a lack of proper reintegration of IDPs and refugees into the society. For example, the DDR program failed to increase the capacity of disengaged combatants which created the potential of some returning to their rebel and criminal activities as a means of survival. Besides, AMIB did not fully achieve its intended mandate of a ceasefire and an improvement in the security situation in the entire country. Yet credit should be given to the peace operation for creating a precedent for the deployment of other AU-led missions in crisis situations.

African Union Mission in Sudan (AMIS)

While AMIB appeared to be a traditional peacekeeping mission, the AU Mission in Sudan was more challenging, because it required a robust enforcement posture in order to prevent or respond to further mass atrocities. In 2003, there was an escalation of violence in Darfur following an armed rebellion led by the Justice and Equality Movement and the Sudan Liberation Movement/Army against the government of Sudan. The latter responded disproportionately using its security apparatus, including the notorious Janjaweed militia group, which used various strategies including "scorched-earth" tactics in crushing the rebellion. The outcome of this was large-scale civilian deaths that amounted to crimes against humanity, and massive displacements of population. Between 2003 and 2008, it was reported that there were 300,000 deaths and almost 2.5 million IDPs in Darfur.[22] This is why the crisis in Darfur has been variously described as "genocide", "genocidal intent", "ethnic cleansing" and "war crimes and crimes against humanity".[23]

The severity of this crisis and the complicit involvement of the Government of Sudan led to increased pressure on regional and international actors to react. Regrettably, permanent members of the UN Security Council (UNSC) were not willing to use coercive measures to respond to the Darfur crisis for different unrelated reasons. For the Western powers, notably the US, France and the UK, their involvement in military interventions in Iraq and Afghanistan made it less appealing to become involved in another costly peace mission. A subset of this reduced appetite for intervention was that there was also a perception that a military intervention in Darfur would lead to a setback in the hard-won 2005 Comprehensive Peace Agreement. This agreement marked the formal end of hostilities (although it was a precarious situation) in long-running wars between the Government of Sudan (GoS) and South Sudan. On the other hand, Russia and China had strong commercial ties with Khartoum, especially in the extraction of oil and arms sales, and would have vetoed a possible UNSC Resolution urging military intervention.[24]

The establishment of AMIS was part of the peace process initiated by the AU. In particular, the signing of the 2004 Humanitarian Ceasefire Agreement (sometimes referred to as the N'djamena Agreement) provided for the establishment of AMIS. It introduced the creation of a team of military observers to monitor the ceasefire. In addition, the agreement made provision for a small contingent of armed forces with a mandate to primarily protect military observers. Hence AMIS was originally conceived as an observer mission and a protection force regrettably not for civilian protection, but for ensuring the safety of the military observers. AMIS was deployed in 2004 with 132 observers and a protection force of 300. This deployment proved insufficient to address the security situation, especially because parties in the conflict were consistently violating the N'djamena Agreement. An AU-led assessment team concluded that this was because AMIS lacked an integral combative service support unit to deal with the security situation in Darfur.[25] This situation eventually led to considerable expansion of AMIS to 7,000 troops, including police contingents, in July 2005. This deployment was drawn from African states, namely Nigeria (eight battalions), Rwanda (three battalions), Senegal (one battalion), and South Africa (one battalion). At the same time, logistical support, especially in terms of the Air Movement Cell, was provided by the EU, NATO and the US, through the Darfur Integrated Task Force.[26] The funding of this mission was also largely through these donor states.

There have been strong criticisms against AMIS. The primary pitfalls were its limited operational capacity, due to inadequate equipment on the ground, and the absence of strong leadership by the AU needed for sustained success. Also, there was the suspicion that the presence of AMIS was to the advantage of the GoS, because it prevented the possibility of a stronger UNSC sanctioned force. Such a perception was buttressed by failed attempts to sanction a UN force to support AMIS as provided for in UNSC Resolution 1706 (2006). The transformation of AMIS into a joint operation by the AU and the UN, referred to as the UN-AU Mission in Darfur (UNAMID), has sometimes been construed as evidence that AMIS "died a death of a thousand cuts in matters big and small".[27] Also the establishment of UNAMID was not a smooth process, in particular due to administrative, political and operational frictions between the AU and the UN.[28] However, it fostered a necessary dimension and a new direction in the AU-led peace operations through the establishment of hybrid or joint operations. This process has inspired aspects of the current AU-led mission in Somalia, as will be explained below.

African Union Mission in Somalia (AMISOM)

On 30 September 2012, the AU Commission announced that AMISOM had pushed al-Shabaab, the main radical Islamist group in Somalia, away from Canjeel (a southern Somali town), and as a result the AU troops were just 5 km away from the port city of Kismayo.[29] This was one of a series of AMISOM's recent advances towards a strategic end state of depleting the military capacity of al-Shabaab and restoring Somali political and security institutions. The persistent insecurity in Somalia is historically linked to the 1991 collapse of its central government, then led by Siad

Barre. As a result, "successive generations of Somali leaders have engaged in corrosive political and economic practices that have aggravated the conflict and helped thwart the restoration of peace and security in the country".[30] In addition, the tragic US-led military operation in Somalia in 1993 considerably diminished the leadership of the international community in further direct engagement in the crisis. The regional security of the Somalian crisis, especially in the alleged role of Eritrea in sustaining instability, inspired a military incursion by Ethiopia, an influential state in the Horn of Africa, with the support of the US.

The legal basis for AMISOM was initiated by UNSC Resolution 1725, adopted in December 2006, which authorized "IGAD and Member states of the African Union to establish a protection and training mission in Somalia". This was an important antecedent in the establishment of AMISOM by the AU Peace and Security Council in January 2007. AMISOM was initially authorized for a period of six months but has been repeatedly renewed since its inception. It had three main mandates, namely to provide support to the Transitional Federal Institutions in their efforts towards the stabilization of the situation in the country and the furtherance of dialogue and reconciliation; to facilitate the provision of humanitarian assistance; and to create conditions conducive for long term stabilization, reconciliation and development in Somalia. The expected strategic end state is to deplete the power of al-Shabaab, pirates and regional security threats, to build the capacity (especially security) of Somali institutions, and to implement post-conflict peace building programs.

AMISOM has been sustained by military and police contributions from African states. Support for AMISOM and the Transitional Federal Government (TFG) has also been provided by the Ethiopian Defence Forces. In October 2011, the Kenyan Defence Forces (KDF) launched attacks against al-Shabaab from the south-west in support of the TFG. Although there was a lean civilian component to the mission, there has been an increasing drive to expand the number and mandate of civilian officers. This partly reflects the recorded military successes by AMISOM and the desire to move towards the robust implementation and consolidation of the political strategy, especially in the areas of constitution-making, outreach and reconciliation, good governance, and parliamentary reforms and elections. These elements are part of the implementation of the 2011 Roadmap, which was supposed to be fully achieved by August 2012. With an imperfect transition following the parliamentary elections, it is likely that there will be a need for long-term engagement.

Indeed, like previous interventions, AMISOM has been largely dependent on external support. The EU provides one of the largest funding contributions to the mission, estimated to be about €16 million per month.[31] There has also been increased support from non-traditional donors including Turkey, Japan, Saudi Arabia and China to ensure sustained engagement by AMISOM. The political and financial commitment of the UN is also significant. As previously mentioned, the initial basis for an African-led mission in Somalia was sanctioned by the UN. This seems like a continuation of, though not necessarily a similarity to, the joint operations between the AU and the UN as manifested in Darfur. The UN has also sought to establish offices in Somalia, such as the UN Political Office for Somalia (UNPOS) and UN Support Office for AMISOM (UNSOA). The latter is mandated to provide AMISOM with logistical support up to the ceiling of 12,000 uniformed personnel. This has been considered to be limited and inadequate, especially given the desire to integrate the KDF into AMISOM. Besides, separate offices created by the UN have been regarded as problematic, as they limit coherence in the command, control and coordination architecture of the whole of AMISOM.[32]

AMISOM may continue to make progress in the fulfilment of some of its mandate, especially in its military strategy over al-Shabaab, which offers a ray of hope in the political transition. However, the absence of predictable funding to ensure continuity for the mission remains a major challenge. With dependence on external support, there are already indications that the current assistance to Somalia may suffer important setbacks, especially given the French-led military operation in Mali. Besides, the military successes have not necessarily been succeeded by Quick Impact Projects in so-called liberated territories, which would provide a way of delegitimizing the rhetoric of al-Shaabab in the local population. This is partly because of the disconnection between the military operation and the political roadmap. Other logistical challenges include the inadequacy of air assets, transport, mobile medical services, and supply and combat engineers. Several analysts have applauded this intervention as an important part of the evolution of African-led peace operations.[33] The final section of this chapter provides a critical assessment of the so-called Africanization of peace operations as the next phase of peace operations in Africa.

Trends in the Africanization of peace operations

The above case studies provide an empirical context upon which analysis can be based, and regarding which both rhetoric and reality can be assessed in regard to African leadership in peace missions. At least five trends can be identified. First, the practice of African-led PSOs has been primarily tied to the principle of consent by the target state. Article 4(h) of the AU Constitutive Act provides for the possibility of military intervention sanctioned by the AU Assembly without the consent of the state if necessary. In the case of Darfur, in particular, where there seemed to be substantive evidence that the GoS was complicit and directly responsible for alleged war crimes, the AU still failed to act in the absence of the authorization of the Sudanese government. In fact, AU member states acknowledged that atrocities were committed by the GoS when they refused to allow President Omar al-Bashir to take up the chairmanship of the AU in 2005, thus extending the tenure of Olusegun Obasanjo, the former Nigerian President. The prospects of an unauthorized military intervention are made more difficult when the target state is an influential power within the AU Assembly. Sudan, for example, not only dictated to the AU how the peace mission in Darfur should proceed, but also used its allies within the UNSC to influence decisions, especially in respect to possible implementation of unauthorized intervention (such as UNSC Resolution 1706 (2006)). The fact that powerful African states are often the suppliers of resources (personnel, finance and logistics) to the AU means that it would either not have sufficient capacity or would experience severe political difficulties if it considered intervening in a big state.

Second, and related to this, African-led PSOs have been largely driven by a lead state. Proponents of the theory of hegemonic stability have often underscored the importance of the leadership of a hegemon or pivotal state possessing the required capacity and resources to drive the international system.[34] This has been historically evident in earlier interventions by African states (notably ECOWAS's intervention in Liberia and Sierra Leone in the 1990s) and remains a strong basis for AU-led interventions. In the cases reviewed here, leadership was provided by South Africa in the case of AMIB; Nigeria, Rwanda and Senegal for AMIS; and Uganda, Burundi, Ethiopia and recently Kenya in AMISOM. These core countries have often driven the actual practice of PSOs, which is grossly inadequate and certainly requires more involvement from the AU's 54 member states.[35] In the event that these core countries are either unwilling to or become incapable of contributing troops, logistics and/or financial resources to a specific peace mission, such a mission is likely to encounter some challenges. For example, despite having the biggest military force in West Africa and having fulfilled its troop contribution to the African-led International Support Mission in Mali (AFISMA), Nigeria may continue to be cautiously involved in that mission in the north of Mali against armed opposition groups, and may not be willing to provide a pre-commitment guarantee for future deployment in the prevention of and response to mass atrocities.

Third, there is an evolving operational synergy between the AU and the UN in peace support operations. AMIB deployed as an interim mission pending the deployment of ONUB; the transition from AMIS to UNAMID marked a new beginning in joint (hybrid) operations between the UN and the AU; while the UN has been working in close support of AMISOM. The 2007 establishment of the UN Office to the AU has increased the likelihood that PSC decisions can be closely monitored and reported to UN headquarters in order to feed into UNSC resolutions. For example, UNSC Resolution 2036 (2012), which sought to increase the AU troop level in Somalia, was an outcome of a technical assessment carried out jointly by the AU and the UN. The UN Security Council further acknowledged the work of the AU PSC in relation to the AMISOM strategic concept. In addition, the UN through UNPOS and UNSOA has continued to provide support packages to AMISOM, especially with the aim of ensuring its expansion. Notwithstanding this, the relationship between the AU and UN is an imperfect partnership with significant administrative, operational and political difficulties. In particular, the relationship between the UN Security Council and Secretariat on the one hand, and the PSC and AU Commission on the other hand, has remained largely unsystematic. This was acknowledged in the 2008 Prodi report, which highlighted the fact that while "the UNSC supports stronger cooperation between the UN and regional organizations, it has not considered the issue in a systematic way".[36] This is not to discount the issue that limited capacity within the AU Commission and a lack of political will by AU member states often undermine the search for a strategic and political coherence and partnership.

Fourth, most PSOs have been largely dependent on donor support. The heavy reliance of the AU on traditional and non-traditional donors has been widely discussed and acknowledged. The peace operations considered demonstrated that donors were directly responsible for sustaining these missions. The EU provides the largest support to the APSA support program. In addition, the Joint Financing Agreement between the AU and some international partners (Denmark, Norway, Sweden, the UK and the EU) provides significant support towards the salaries of staff within the AU Peace and Security Department. The AU Partner Group on AMISOM, comprising 14 donor states including India and China, is the foundation upon which the mission is able to sustain its manpower (including troop allowances), training, and operational costs (such as transport and equipment). Without such support, there would be little progress and at worst the complete absence of this mission. Therefore, the question of sustainability and predictability arises: with new security demands and unexpected budget cuts, there could be major setbacks in the progress of the mission. Furthermore, the deployment of AFISMA led to the withdrawing of resources (human and financial) from existing missions such as AMISOM. Besides, donor support can be sometimes delayed due to lengthy approval requests in the midst of an emergency situation.

Finally, an overriding challenge to the continuity of a putative African-led peace operation is the lack of activation of a permanent operational structure for missions. The examples under consideration have demonstrated that the missions are primarily ad hoc, without a permanent institutional basis. The ASF, which is expected to provide such an institutional foundation for peace operations, is expected to be fully operational by 2015. The remainder of this section provides an assessment of the ASF in order to review its strengths and gaps in the process towards its full operationalization. Such analysis further contributes to the discourse on whether there is a real momentum towards the institutionalization of African-led PSOs.

African Standby Force: is full operationalization ever achievable?

The original conception of the ASF as contained in the 2002 Protocol Relating to the Establishment of the Peace and Security Council of the AU (hereafter referred to as the Protocol) was based on the idea of a continental brigade. Article 13 of the Protocol simply mentions "a force composed of multidimensional contingents, with civilian and military components in their countries of origin ready for deployment at appropriate notice". It seems the initial ASF vision was therefore to synergize the military and civilian capacities of AU member states into a sort of continental army. This vision was conceived by Kwame Nkrumah (1963) and later promulgated (albeit cautiously received by African states) by Muammar Gaddafi on the eve of the establishment of the AU.[37] The Protocol did not provide a clear division between the components of the ASF, particularly in that it merged the police dimension as part of the civilian composition. It was the 2004 Policy Framework on the ASF adopted by the AU Assembly during the third Ordinary Summit that provided further clarity about the composition, chain of command and operationalization of the ASF. First, it provided for the establishment of five regional brigades in consonance with the official regional representation of the AU (North, South, East, West and Central). These regional brigades, which are subsets of RECs/RMs, should be ready for deployment within 30 days if the need arises. Second, the policy framework also differentiated between the roles of the military, police and civilians as part of the ASF's multidimensional composition.

Since its establishment, three phases or roadmaps have been identified and implemented towards full operationalization of the ASF.[38] The timeline for the first roadmap was until the end of June 2005, but continued until the end of 2006 with some aspects carried over to 2008. This phase was primarily intended to establish the military policy framework and working tools of the AU Strategic-level Headquarters. As a result, the main achievement of this phase was the production of five policy documents on the ASF's doctrine, training, logistics, command and control, and standard operating procedures. The second roadmap (2005–2010) was intended to achieve further consolidation of the key goals of phase I, but centred on capacity development that would allow for the AU to manage complex peacekeeping operations on a permanent basis. This Roadmap II culminated in the 2010 ASF Command Post Exercise (CPX) (often referred to as the AMANI exercise) to determine its operational readiness. Unfortunately, there were several gaps identified in the CPX which meant that the full operationalization of the ASF would be deferred to 2015. These issues include the military dominance of the exercise planning and conduct, which significantly undermined the concept of ASF multidimensionality. This was reinforced by the fact that military terminologies (such as "Wash-up", "battle rhythm") were mostly used during the exercise. In addition, the management structure of the AU Peace Support Operation Division (PSOD) was deemed structurally deficient as a functional HQ. There was also no meorandum of understanding between the AU and RECs on the ASF, and the absence of legal modalities for deployment poses a serious problem to the operationalization of the ASF.[39]

Some of these highlighted problems inspired Roadmap III, adopted by the AU Assembly in October 2011 with the aim of achieving full operationalization by 2015. This phase seeks to achieve three main objectives. The first is to improve the management structure of the PSOD through the establishment of four pillars (policy development unit, capability development unit, plans and operations unit, and mission support unit). Second, in order to accommodate emerging security threats, the ASF is being operationalized to cope with new priorities such as maritime safety and security through the establishment of a Maritime Information and Coordination Cell. There are also attempts to mainstream the protection mandate in the ASF through the publication of draft AU guidelines for protection of civilians (PoC) which have been finalized but are yet to be adopted by AU member states. Third, there is increased momentum towards the development of the less developed civilian dimension of the ASF.[40] For example, through the support of the German government, the development and reconfiguration of the AU Civilian Standby Roster is being finalized.

Despite this ostensible progress, there is considerable scepticism about the full operationalization of the ASF. The regional brigades are at various stages of development, with the North African Standby Brigade being the least developed and with further setbacks following the North African uprisings. Even where regional brigades are making a great deal of progress, there are concerns that influential states within the region may be reluctant to commit their troops to a regional force. A notable example is the Eastern Africa Brigade, where there has been slow progress in ensuring that states like Ethiopia provide the necessary leadership. In addition, there is no legal framework guiding the interaction between the AU Commission and the RECs/RMs, especially in decisions about the possible deployment of a brigade. Above all, the progress made towards the operationalization of the ASF has been largely dependent on donor support. It has been suggested that the EU has provided €4 billion towards the operationalization of the APSA, which includes €1 billion for the operationalization of the ASF.[41]

With these challenges, there are renewed debates on either an early operationalization of the ASF, including its rapid deployment capability (RDC), or the establishment of a transitional arrangement prior to operationalization. On 25 January 2013, the AU Assembly endorsed the decision by the PSC that the AU Commission should review and submit a report on the difficulties encountered in the early operationalization of the ASF. Subsequently, the AU Commission appointed Professor Ibrahim Gambari to lead an independent team of experts in the assessment of the ASF. The outcome of the Gambari panel will have important ramifications for the ASF and its RDC. It may lead to either the continuation of the operationalization of the ASF, with a specific action plan for its partial or full operationality by 2015, or an endorsement of a transitional military mechanism that will potentially be able to deploy in the prevention and response to mass atrocities (technically described as Scenario VI under the ASF doctrine) within fifteen days. Currently, however, the ASF remains at a crossroads with uncertainties over its full operationalization.[42]

Conclusion

The establishment and institutionalization of African-led PSOs have achieved mixed results. This chapter has provided an assessment of emerging African-led PSOs or what has sometimes been described as the Africanization of peace support operations. Locating this analysis within the empirical context of the AU Missions in Burundi, Darfur and Somalia, some important conclusions were made. First, progress has been registered in the intentions and aspirations evident in the AU's deployment of peace missions. Through its normative and institutional transformation, the AU through its peace and security architecture is now able to sanction peace operations. This is a clear departure from the principles of the sacrosanct nature of sovereignty and inviolable territories that characterized the OAU. Second, the new interventionism of the AU has inspired progressive partnerships with the UN, which remains the largest contributor to global peace operations. Although the emergent AU-UN partnership is problematic in some ways, the transfer (Burundi), joint (Darfur) and support (Somalia) missions are indicators of innovative approaches that can be adopted in future peace operations. Despite this, this chapter has argued that it is rather too early to conclude that there is an African-led peace support regime that is based on institutionalized practice. Current missions have remained ad hoc, and there is much uncertainty over whether the ASF will ever be fully operational. In addition, the overarching dependence and concomitant lack of political will by African states on closing the resource gap means that peace operations in Africa may be implemented by Africans, but will most certainly be governed by the growing expansion of external actors' involvement.

Notes

1 The views expressed in this paper are primarily based on the author's personal views and previous research endeavor. Accordingly, he wishes to express his gratitude to the Institute for Security Studies (ISS), Addis Ababa office, where the first draft of this article was written.

2 See D. Chandler, "The Responsibility to Protect: Imposing the 'Liberal Peace'?", *International Peacekeeping* 11, 2004, pp. 59–81; F.M. Deng, *Sovereignty as Responsibility: Conflict Management in Africa*, Washington DC: Brookings Institution Press, 1996.

3 See A. de Waal, "Contesting Visions of Peace in Africa: Darfur, Ivory Coast, Libya", *Limerick Papers in Politics and Public Administration* 1, University of Limerick, 2012, pp. 1–16.

4 P.D. Williams, "Lessons Learned from Peace Support Operations in Africa", *Africa Security Brief* 3, March 2010, p. 2.
5 For a comprehensive overview of the literature on "saving strangers", see N. Wheeler, *Saving Strangers: Humanitarian Intervention in International Society*, Oxford: Oxford University Press, 2000.
6 de Waal, "Contesting Visions".
7 See A. Adebajo and C. Landsberg, "Back to the Future: UN peacekeeping in Africa", *International Peacekeeping* 7, 2000, p. 175.
8 See T. Murithi, "The African Union's Evolving Role in Peace Operations: The African Union Mission in Burundi, the African Union Mission in Sudan and the African Union Mission in Somalia", *African Security Review* 17, 2008, pp. 70–82.
9 *Ibid.*
10 "Constitutive Act of the African Union Adopted by the Thirty-Sixth Ordinary Session of the Assembly of Heads of State and Government, Lome", African Union (AU), 11 July 2000, available at www.africa-union.org/root/au/aboutau/constitutive_act_en.htm, accessed 7 May 2013.
11 "The African Stand-By Force (ASF): Plan of Action for Roadmap III (2011–2015)", AU Commission: ASF Civilian Dimension – Community of Practice, 21 March 2012, available at www.civilian.peaceau.org/index.php?option=com_docman&task=cat_view&gid=48&Itemid=61&lang=en, accessed 20 November 2012.
12 "Somalia report of the Monitoring Group on Somalia and Eritrea Submitted in Accordance with Resolution 2002 (2011)", UN, S/2012/544, 13 July 2012, available at www.un.org/sc/committees/751/mongroup.shtml, accessed 11 November 2012.
13 "Arusha Peace and Reconciliation Agreement for Burundi", Arusha, 28 August 2000, p. 93, available at https://peaceaccords.nd.edu/site_media/media/accords/Arusha_Peace_Accord.pdf, accessed 7 May 2013.
14 F. Agoagye, *The African Mission in Burundi: Lessons Learned from the First African Union Peacekeeping Operation*, Pretoria: ISS, July 2004, p. 9.
15 *Ibid.*
16 For example, see Agoagye, *African Mission*; Murithi, "African Union".
17 "Communiqué of the Seventh Ordinary Session of the Central Organ of the Mechanism for Conflict Prevention, Management and Resolution at Heads of State and Government Level", AU, Addis Ababa, 3 February 2003, available at www.africa-union.org/news_events/Communiqu%E9s/Communique_E9_20_Eng_3feb03.pdf, accessed 20 October 2012.
18 See A. Peen Rodt, "The African Union Mission in Burundi: The Successful Management of a Violent Ethno-Political Conflict?", *Ethnopolitics Papers* 10, May 2011, p. 18.
19 See *South Africa's Peacekeeping Role in Burundi: Challenges and Opportunities for Future Peace Missions*, Occasional Paper Series 2, Durban, South Africa: ACCORD, 2007.
20 H. Boshoff, W. Vrey and G. Rautenbach, *The Burundi Peace Process: From Civil War to Conditional Peace*, Monograph 171, Pretoria: ISS, 2010, p. 69.
21 Agoagye, *African Mission*, p. 14.
22 O. Degomme and D. Guha-Sapir, "Patterns of Mortality rates in Darfur Conflict", *The Lancet* 375, 2010, pp. 294–300.
23 See for example M. Kapila, *Sudan: Ethnic Cleansing in Darfur (Note to Mr. Riza)*, RCHC/SUD/Note 39, Khartoum: UN Integrated Regional Information Networks (UNIRIN), 22 March 2004; International Criminal Court (ICC), *Outreach Report 2009*, The Hague: ICC Public Information and Documentation Section, Outreach Unit, 2009; International Commission of Inquiry on Darfur, *Report of*

the International Commission of Inquiry on Darfur to the United Nations to the Secretary-General, Geneva, 25 January 2005.

24 See Agoagye, *African Mission.*

25 "Conclusions of the Third Meeting of the Military Staff Committee", Meeting of the Military Staff Committee of the Peace and Security Council, AU, 25 April 2005, available at www.africa-union.org/.../CEM%20Conclusions%20%203e%20reunion, accessed 20 November 2012.

26 *AU Press Release: The First Rwandan Battalion has been Fully Deployed to Darfur*, Addis Ababa, 26 July 2005, available at http://reliefweb.int/report/sudan/sudan-darfur-integrated-taskforce-ditf-information-update-no-5-current-status-military, accessed 11 November 2012.

27 J. Flint and A. de Waal, *Darfur: A New History of a Long War*, African Arguments, London: Zed Books, 2008 (revised edition), p. 178.

28 R. Gowan and J. Sherman, "Peace Operations Partnerships: Complex but Necessary Cooperation", *ZIF Policy Briefing*, Berlin: Centre for International Peace Operations (ZIF), March 2012.

29 Voice of America (VOA), "Al Shabab Withdraws from Kismayo", 28 September 2012, available at www.voanews.com/content/somalia/1517209.html, accessed 11 October 2012.

30 "Somalia Report of the Monitoring Group on Somalia and Eritrea Submitted in Accordance with Resolution 2002 (2011)", UN, S/2012/544, 13 July 2012, available at www.un.org/sc/committees/751/mongroup.shtml, accessed 11 November 2012, p. 5.

31 Interview with an anonymous EU staff member, Berlin, 15 September 2012.

32 Interview with an anonymous AMISOM personnel member, Addis Ababa, 10 October 2012.

33 For example, see de Waal, "Contesting Visions", pp. 1–16; Williams, "Lessons Learned".

34 See Robert Keohane, "The Theory of Hegemonic Stability and Changes in International Economic Regimes, 1967–1977", in O.R. Hosti, R.M. Siverson and A.L. George (eds), *Change in the International System*, Boulder CO: Westview Press, 1980, p. 132; D. Myers, "Threat Perception and Strategic Response of Regional Hegemons: A Conceptual Overview", in D. Myers (ed.), *Regional Hegemons: Threat, Perception, and Strategic Response*, Boulder CO: Westview Press, 1991.

35 Williams, "Lessons Learned", p. 16.

36 "Identical letters dated 24 December 2008 from the Secretary-General Addressed to the President of the General Assembly and the President of the Security Council", UN Secretary-General Report, General Assembly, Sixty-third session, UN, A/63/666–S/2008/813, 31 December 2008.

37 K. Nkrumah, *Africa Must Unite*, Accra: PANAF Publishers, 1963.

38 The ASF Framework document called for the establishment of the ASF in two phases up until June 2010. Due to the repeated delays, full operationalization of the ASF has now been extended to 2015, therefore requiring a third implementation phase.

39 Interview with staff of the AU Peace Support Operations Division, Addis Ababa, 10 October 2012.

40 See Agoagye, *African Mission.*

41 Interview with a Senior EU Delegation to the African Union, Addis Ababa, 10 October 2012.

42 See "Communiqué of the 353rd African Union Peace and Security Council, PSC/AHG/COMM/2.(CCCLIII)", AU, 25 January 2013, available at www.peaceau.org/en/article/communique-of-peace-and-security-council-353th-meeting-at-the-level-of-heads-of-state-and-government, accessed 10 February 2013.

3 EU peacekeeping in Africa

Towards an indirect approach

Alexander Mattelaer and Esther Marijnen

Introduction

It has only been a decade since the EU became active as a peacekeeping actor. Yet in this short timeframe it has undergone a significant evolution. The EU's Common Security and Defence Policy (CSDP) originally aimed to provide European states with an organizational vehicle for full spectrum crisis management – or even "the progressive framing of a common Union defence policy".[1] This objective remains part of the official discourse. In practice, however, the CSDP gradually developed into a platform for a limited number of niche tasks in international security. These notably include small-scale civilian and military capacity-building missions. In addition, the European Commission developed a number of financial instruments aimed at enabling offshore security assistance, such as the African Peace Facility and the Instrument for Stability. This European choice for specializing in diplomatic action, conflict mediation and high-end security assistance implies that the brunt of international peacekeeping efforts will continue to lie with the UN and regional arrangements other than the EU. The trend towards an indirect approach in the EU's role in international peacekeeping has major ramifications for Africa.

The EU's experimental role in African security is not easy to understand. It is characterized by a mixed heritage, blending the practices of former colonial powers with those of neutral states. It also relies upon an uneasy but pragmatic division of labour between the European institutions and the member states. This chapter seeks to take stock of the EU's track record as a peacekeeper in Africa, to describe the broad trend from direct to indirect engagement, and to assess the different explanations that can be put forward in interpreting this trend. The overall conclusion that can be drawn is that the EU will continue to be engaged in African security based on a strategy of "affordable influence". While political and financial constraints increasingly push the EU to play only an enabling role in African peacekeeping, the EU is trying to maintain its political leverage. Such a posture is intended to shape the broad dynamics in the African strategic environment rather than delivering specific political outcomes.

This argument is structured as follows. The first section offers an overview of the EU's experimental track record as an organization able to mount crisis management operations. The second section is devoted to analyzing the shift from direct to indirect engagement. This analysis covers the evolving political context, the recent trends in CSDP missions and the incorporation of financial instruments. The third section is devoted to a review of six different narratives that help explain this shift. These range from African ownership, cost-effectiveness and long-term sustainability to protecting the *chasse gardée*, lowering the CSDP level of ambition and the concept of crisis management losing its political salience. In the conclusion we consider the interplay between these explanatory narratives and put forward the notion of "affordable influence".

The EU's experimental track record

The EU's crisis management structures were born out of frustration with the European inability to handle the violent disintegration of the former Yugoslavia.[2] Yet this particular origin was only part of a broader European disillusionment with UN peacekeeping in the 1990s. The UN missions in Somalia, Rwanda and Bosnia left deep scars in European defence establishments, pertaining in particular to command and control arrangements. While having recourse to NATO structures offered a credible stopgap as far as the management of the Balkan wars was concerned, various political constraints prevented the Atlantic Alliance from becoming the default framework for European peacekeeping ambitions. As such, the EU's development as a security actor followed an experimental course.

What eventually became the EU's CSDP was politically conceived as a trade-off between multiple member states.[3] At the Saint Malo summit in 1998, France and Britain struck a compromise about increasing European defence efforts. For London, this represented an opportunity to spur the development of military capabilities in Europe. It was hoped that this would in turn allow for more equitable burden-sharing in the transatlantic context. For Paris, the Saint Malo deal constituted the fulfilment of a long-standing desire to set up a framework for autonomous European military operations. As this bilateral consensus was Europeanized at the Cologne summit in 1999, the emphasis on expeditionary capabilities and interventionism was tempered by Germany and the Nordic European states.[4] This caused the CSDP to be configured as a mechanism not only for military crisis management, but also for civilian stabilization efforts. Paradoxically, it was the civilian strand of CSDP action that experienced the highest growth rate in the ensuing years. The EU's strategic posture also became firmly anchored in a broader framework that stressed the primacy of the UN Security Council as ultimate arbiter in international peace and security.[5]

This delicate political balancing act also translated into operational terms. The establishment of the CSDP blended different strategic cultures. Colonial legacies stressing early response, military robustness and political pragmatism had to accommodate neutrality constraints and a more principled approach towards the making of foreign policy. Nowhere was this as visible as in the early EU operations in Africa. Whereas France had already advocated Europeanizing some of its African initiatives since the early 1990s – including controversial undertakings such as *Opération Turquoise* in Rwanda in 1994 – the eventual EU operations assumed an altogether distinct form. As French and Swedish special forces landed in the eastern DRC in 2003, it rapidly became clear that the EU's crisis management efforts would be geared towards complementing UN peacekeeping with more robust capabilities or with specific expertise.[6]

Although Operation Artemis – arguably the most aggressive EU operation to date – was by and large a French operation conducted under European flag, it set a critical precedent for the EU's later endeavours.[7] EU operations would not be designed as stand-alone undertakings, but would rely on a division of labour between various international organizations. In the DRC, the EU offered temporary military support to the UN Mission in the Congo in stressful conditions (in 2003 and again in 2006). The EU also set up civilian missions tasked with police assistance and security sector reform mandates. In Darfur, the EU at first provided logistic support to the AU. Later on, it set up its own mission in eastern Chad to contain the regional spill-over effects of the conflict. Interestingly, the EU in Chad provided the military entry force whereas the UN took charge of police capacity-building.

This organizational division of labour not only emerged as a matter of operational practice but also became politically and doctrinally espoused. In 2003, the EU and the UN officially endorsed a joint declaration in crisis management, outlining the model of bridging operations *à la* Artemis and stand-by forces *à la* EUFOR RD Congo. The UN's Department of Peacekeeping Operations (UNDPKO) even drafted doctrinal guidance for joint UN-EU planning.[8] The emergence of the political discourse about "integrated peacekeeping" or "comprehensive crisis management" bears witness to the deeply engrained thinking about organizational cooperation – even if this promise of comprehensive action is seldom fulfilled in the field.

While observers disagreed over the deeper meaning of these developments, the fact that the EU was rapidly becoming a trend-setting peacekeeping organization was for a while undisputed. Although some – not altogether incorrectly – perceived the invisible hand of the Elysée in the EU's various Africa endeavours, the majority of scholarly writings embraced the idea of the EU offering a more high-end platform for peacekeeping in the broader European neighborhood.[9] Although the EU's operational endeavours were endowed with only modest objectives – thus increasing their chances for internally defined mission success – the simple fact that none of them had so far ended in disaster provided grounds to present the EU's peacekeeping experimentation as a political success story in Brussels' corridors.[10]

From direct to indirect engagement

Despite all this experimenting, the European appetite for large-scale missions on African soil has decreased considerably. Individual member states are equally reluctant to deploy their forces in UN operations. One can therefore speak of a broader phenomenon of "mission fatigue" that plagues the peacekeeping ambitions of the EU and its member states. The EU's role in African peacekeeping is ever more characterized by an indirect approach. In the wider peacebuilding discourse of which these efforts are part, this is reflected in the growing prominence of the "security-development nexus".[11]

Shifting political discourse

This section puts the trend towards an indirect approach in a broader political context by deconstructing the EU's discourse vis-à-vis African security. The EU has a long-standing relationship with Africa. As a result of the colonial legacies of several member states, the EU is more strongly connected to the African continent than any other external actor. For historical reasons, the US has by and large perceived Africa as a European responsibility.[12] This European engagement was originally built around development assistance and framed as being "apolitical" and limited to the provision of development aid. This engagement started evolving when the end of the Cold War heralded a boom in international peacebuilding activities. Within the literature on the "liberal peace debate", one can identify three historical waves of peacebuilding discourses: top-down liberal-democratic peacebuilding, bottom-up civil society peacebuilding, and security-sector-focused statebuilding.[13]

One can easily detect the spirit of these different discourses in the EU's engagement in Africa. It is above all in the third wave that one can find the roots of the CSDP: the notion of so-called failed states was being gradually incorporated in the grand narrative of European policy-makers. The 2003 European Security Strategy framed state failure as one of the five key threats the EU faced. While development assistance remained at the core of the political discourse, conflict management with military means gradually became a more prominent component of the EU's policy towards Africa.[14] The origin of Operation Artemis probably cannot be understood without considering the historical timeframe. Launched just after the start of the Iraq War, it was deliberately modelled as a different, more multilateral model of statebuilding. The EUFOR Chad/CAR operation took this practice even further by working closely with the NGO community. In the regional strategies the EU adopted for the Sahel and Horn of Africa regions, the fight against terrorism was highlighted as a priority.

These successive discourses do not exclude and replace each other but rather constitute different components of a *practical peacebuilding* meta-narrative.[15] This meta-narrative qualifies as an attempt to bridge the gap between the emphasis on civil society and social justice that emerged in the mid-1990s, and the old focus on state security institutions, which regained currency in recent years. As a result of these two contesting perspectives, security and development concepts underwent a rhetorical merger. In the EU arena, this translates into a pragmatic discourse that flexibly accommodates elements of all three discursive waves. When analysing any set of conclusions from the Council of the EU, one cannot avoid stumbling across these different discourses used in an overlapping fashion. This is hardly surprising given the fact that such documents must reflect the political ideas of 27 member states. This pragmatic discourse arguably manifests itself most clearly in the idea of the "security-development nexus", stressing the twin ideas that underdevelopment can lead to violence and that insecurity precludes development. The newest addition to the vocabulary concerns the "comprehensive approach", i.e. the ambition to synchronize different policy instruments into a coherent crisis response. By stretching the semantic limits of both development and security discourses, all policy areas can be treated as interlinked. This pragmatism provides the political context for both the evolution of the CSDP proper and the expansion of the EU's toolkit with financial peacebuilding instruments.[16]

Shifting operational posture

As far as its own operational activity is concerned, the EU initially experimented with concepts that can collectively be referred to as "robust peacekeeping". Such a posture was reliant on both politically strong mandates and operational excellence. Politically strong mandates consisted of delegating the authorized use of force further downward than is customary in peacekeeping operations. Operational excellence was based on higher tactical mobility, technological sophistication, and experimenting with extensive civil-military coordination. Although such a robust posture turned out to be reasonably effective in operational terms, the EU has in recent years been limiting itself to advisory missions geared towards building up local security capacity of a civilian as well as a military nature. While these advisory missions are small and significantly cheaper, their operational effectiveness is as yet unclear.

Some of the earlier EU military operations – most notably Artemis and EUFOR Chad/CAR – had clear-cut peacekeeping mandates. They conformed to the peacekeeping principles of neutrality, impartiality, and consent from the host state.[17] EU forces as such constituted a substitute for UN or regional peacekeepers. Yet these forces displayed remarkable military prowess for peacekeepers. In both the DRC and Chad, EU peacekeepers, upon arrival and also afterwards, engaged in skirmishes during which both parties were shooting to kill.[18] Through the availability of close air support, they disposed of clear escalation dominance. This robust character was part of their political mandate as well as their strategic posture based on deterrence.

In political terms, these operations had the overarching aim of contributing to a safe and secure environment. In order to deliver upon that objective, the agreed rules of engagement delegated the authorization for the use of force downwards to the lowest possible level (i.e. to the individual soldier for small arms fire, to the operation commander for the use of air strikes). The legacy of the Yugoslavia and Rwanda operations is clear: European defence establishments did not want to deploy troops without wide authority for self-defence or to depend on a political decision for escalating the level of violence. If EU soldiers came under threat – as repeatedly happened – it would immediately trigger an armed response.

Strategically, these operations relied on a logic of deterrence. The presence of a military force – and the implicit threat of retaliation – was intended to influence the cost-benefit calculations of local conflict parties. The military credibility of the force – communicated through frequent patrolling and joint exercises showcasing fighting prowess – ensured that there was no doubt over who would have the upper hand in any conceivable engagement. As far as the military stabilization of the operational areas was concerned, this proved to be remarkably effective: European peacekeepers were typically challenged at the start of an operation, but rapidly demonstrated their determination not to be intimidated and subsequently went about their business unopposed. Of course, this did not automatically translate into a "safe and secure environment" – which depends on more factors than military stability alone – but it resulted in positive security trends. The main problem, however, is that the stability bought by a logic of deterrence is limited in duration: all depends on the continued presence and credibility of the military threat. In all cases, the handover of security responsibility to UN or local forces led to questions over the sustainability of the realized security gains.[19]

It is in this context that one finds the roots of the more recent CSDP operations. In order to make security gains sustainable, local security forces must be able to "hold the fort". The key challenge therefore resides not so much in realizing greater security but in fostering indigenous capacities for delivering on that objective. All recent CSDP operations in Africa therefore concentrated on such capacity-building tasks: the training of Somali recruits on behalf of AMISOM (European Union Training Mission, EUTM Somalia), the strengthening of maritime capacities in the Horn of

Africa states (European Capacity Building Mission, EUCAP Nestor), the training of the Nigerien Gendarmerie and National Guard (EUCAP Sahel Niger) or the airport security strengthening mission in South Sudan. Most recently, the EU deployed a training mission to reform and reinforce the Malian National Army (EUTM Mali) in a follow-up to the French Operation Serval.[20]

In operational terms, capacity-building missions are at heart an educational undertaking. They mostly draw on senior cadre personnel from EU member states to instruct the nascent security sector in target countries. Such missions typically confront two major obstacles. On the one hand, it is often complicated to recruit adequate numbers of EU personnel – as experienced cadres are in short supply and may not always have sufficient incentives to leave their home services behind. On the other hand, these "educational" missions operate over a long time span. They need to be sustained for multiple years in order to yield measurable effect. Given that the EU only recently started experimenting with such missions, the verdict on their operational impact is still unknown.

These capacity-building operations nonetheless have considerable political appeal. They entail a significantly lower level of resources, typically involving only dozens of trainers and advisors rather than thousands of soldiers. At the same time, the avoidance of front-line security duties makes them more palatable as they entail only modest levels of risk. Thus these operations address some of the thorny issues of the earlier, more robust operations that jeopardized European cohesion: their financial cost and political risk. Yet this in itself does not qualify as a good explanation for the overall trend. While cost and risk considerations may complicate the decision-making leading to robust operations, one would expect that low-cost and low-risk capacity-building missions would be comparatively easy to agree on. This, however, is emphatically not the case. Even very small civilian missions (such as both EUCAP missions or the aviation security mission in South Sudan) turn out to be divisive in political terms. All the recent operations have been on the drawing board for extended periods and have been redesigned repeatedly in order to accommodate the concerns of various member states.[21] Questions must therefore be asked regarding how broader explanations can help in making sense of the trend towards indirect engagement. Before this, however, the non-CSDP part of the EU's peacekeeping profile must also be considered.

Broadening the toolkit

The growing prominence of capacity-building efforts does not come out of the blue. Years ago, the EU engagement in African crisis situations had already come to include financial support for regional peacekeeping solutions and the development of local capacity. This was discursively built around the notions of "African solutions for African problems" and "an equal partnership". Besides the AU, the EU also works together with various sub-regional economic communities, such as the South African Development Community (SADC) and the ECOWAS.

To institutionalize the growing will of the EU to cooperate with African countries and the AU, the EU in 2004 set up the African Peace Facility (APF) as a financial vehicle enabling the EU to sponsor AU capacity-building, peacekeeping operations and early response mechanisms. From a political perspective, the APF allows the EU to contribute to specific crisis responses while avoiding direct military involvement. The structural financial contribution for the APF comes from the European Development Fund, which is managed by the European Commission. Since its inception, the EU has already committed over one billion Euros to this instrument.[22] APF-financed interventions must be requested by the AU or an African sub-regional organization, but must also be approved by the EU's Political and Security Committee before the European Commission can release the funds. The AU Mission in Somalia (AMISOM) arguably qualifies as the best example of a mission carried out by the AU but supported by the EU through the APF. As the EU Special Representative for the Horn of Africa has pointed out, EU development aid is effectively used to fund a war against al-Shabaab.[23]

The EU's Instrument for Stability (IfS) constitutes another important financial vehicle for contributing to African security. This tool was designed to address a number of thematic security and development challenges that were not adequately covered by the traditional (geographical) development programs.[24] The IfS, which includes both a long-term and a short-term component, is used frequently to respond to crisis situations. In practical terms, this means that the EU makes funds available for a diverse range of initiatives of third partners (NGOs, regional organizations and the UN) as well as of its own structures (i.e. programs set up by delegations, special representatives or CSDP missions). As development aid and conflict sensitivity are not always systematically integrated, the EU presents the IfS as a flexible mechanism to fill the various gaps not covered otherwise. A good example is the so-called Counter-Terrorism Sahel program, which aims to strengthen local capacities and improve regional cooperation for fighting terrorism and organized crime in the Sahel. It constitutes de facto a financial complement to the EUCAP Sahel engagement under the CSDP flag. On a more general level, the ongoing discussions on how to "operationalize" the EU's comprehensive approach also feature proposals to allow for greater flexibility of its funding lines in support of its CSDP missions.[25] In this sense, the EU's changing political discourse, its own operational posture and its increasing financial toolkit march hand-in-hand in the same direction.

Interpreting the trend

As the EU and its member states move away from direct peacekeeping activities and instead focus on more indirect methods of tackling security problems in Africa, the obvious question to ask is what factors can help explain this trend. This section seeks to present an overview of various explanatory narratives. We put forward six of these, namely: (1) the growing preference for African ownership; (2) a recalculation of cost-effectiveness; (3) the increasing concern with long-term sustainability; (4) a shift toward deterring other actors from making inroads into the African continent; (5) the lowering of the EU's CSDP ambitions; and (6) the decreasing salience of military crisis management itself. It is clear that these explanations are situated on different levels. Some of them concern specific policy choices, yet others relate more to the strategic context. Also, it needs to be made clear that these explanations are not necessarily mutually exclusive but may overlap.

Towards African ownership

As far as political discourse is concerned, the EU is keen to avoid accusations of neo-colonialism and therefore promotes the mantra of "African solutions to African problems". Shortly after the EU's first experiences in CSDP, the emphasis increasingly shifted to highlighting the responsibility of African countries themselves to tackle the conflicts on the continent. This resulted in an increased focus on regional economic communities. From the perspective of EU donors these served the double purpose of economic and political integration. A more ambitious project was the establishment of an African Peace and Security Architecture, which constituted one of the key deliverables of the African Peace Facility discussed earlier.

However, the validity of the mantra of African ownership can be discussed at two different levels. On the one hand, the proclaimed equal partnership between the EU and the AU is not as equal as the discourse would suggest. As long as the EU is the main financial contributor to the APF and one of the key providers of capacity-building and training programs, it has a significant degree of influence over the design of the resulting peacekeeping missions. In its position of paymaster, the EU can frequently articulate its concerns and priorities – be it through its Special Representative to the AU or in the frequent dialogues held between EU institutions and their AU counterparts. On the other hand, one can also question the very notion of "African solutions to African problems". Many African scholars are openly critical of this slogan and insist that Europeans in many cases carry responsibility for these problems, for example in the involvement of some EU member states in supplying weapons to conflict-prone regions.[26] Moreover, it can be said that crises in

Africa are not only an African problem but increasingly have an impact beyond the continent, as illustrated by the problem of piracy threatening shipping lanes.

Cost-effectiveness

Since the end of the Cold War, European levels of defence spending have stagnated in absolute terms and decreased relative to gross domestic products and in terms of purchasing power. Furthermore, the current fiscal condition of most EU member states does not bode well for the future of defence budgets. Diverse factors such as the ageing of European societies and the Eurozone crisis are causing most European states to cut back even further on defence, leading to an uncoordinated freefall of European military capabilities.[27] The most visible outcome of this trend is the push towards multinational defence cooperation (labelled as "pooling and sharing" in the EU context or "smart defence" in the NATO context). A secondary outcome is that European defence establishments are increasingly concerned with the cost-effectiveness of crisis management efforts. The deployment of large numbers of European forces over extended periods – as happened in the Balkans or in Afghanistan – is increasingly being seen as a political non-starter due to the financial implications of such a course of action.

In order to illustrate this with numbers, one only needs to consider that the Chad operation – the largest EU military deployment in Africa to date – cost approximately one billion Euros in total, with €120 million common costs being distributed through the Athena mechanism and the remainder on a "costs lie where they fall" basis.[28] The much smaller capacity-building missions, by contrast, operate on a yearly budget of a few million Euros each. The EU advisory and assistance mission for security reform in the DRC (EUSEC RD Congo), for example, runs on a budget of €11 million a year, whereas the EUCAP Sahel Niger and EUCAP Nestor missions have an annual financial reference amount of €8.7 and €22.88 million, respectively.[29] Of course, this is hardly surprising when one considers the numbers of personnel and material involved: the cost of more ambitious endeavours goes up exponentially.

In this light, it is revealing that in the context of the Libyan crisis in 2011 all member states conspicuously refrained from talking publicly about putting boots on the ground. The contingency scenarios drafted by the EU military staff for dealing with instability in the post-Gaddafi era envisaged military options requiring between 30,000 and 120,000 troops.[30] It is not hard to guess why policy-makers – already embroiled in difficult financial discussions on a near daily basis as a result of the Eurozone crisis – were deeply reluctant to discuss such options. The somewhat odd focus on border security assistance for Libya cannot be understood without taking into account the price tag inherent in other options.[31]

Concerns over cost-effectiveness must also take into account the intended effects. Recent scholarship into the motivational logic behind CSDP operations suggests that the EU is above all concerned with a domestically-driven urge to "do something" in reaction to various crises rather than deliver a pre-defined effect in terms of addressing the crisis itself or balancing other international actors.[32] If one accepts the notion that EU crisis management is all about reactive pragmatism, then one can also see why capacity-building is increasingly appealing. Given that the more ambitious operations have hardly delivered decisive outcomes but have only satisfied the urge to "do something", the same effect can be achieved cheaply as well. Whether a mission involves only a few dozen or multiple thousands of personnel is of little importance if showing the European flag is the overriding concern driving decision-making. In such an explanatory narrative, capacity-building missions simply offer the best value for money. Should these capacity-building efforts deliver the hoped-for effects over the longer term, this argument becomes even stronger.

Long-term sustainability

The concern over cost-effectiveness can be interpreted differently. Given that deterrence-based stability is costly to sustain over the long-term, the appeal of capacity-building over time increases because it can be portrayed as an investment in some sort of "exit strategy". The very idea of local capacity-building to a large extent originated in the debates over how to wind down the stabilization missions in the Balkans. The EU took this logic one step further by experimenting with capacity-building not in *follow-up* to large-scale military stabilization missions, but *instead* of them. The building up of local security structures can in this light be portrayed as going to the root causes of instability: the relative absence of strong state structures.

Critical observers often lament the lack of progress made by the majority of capacity-building endeavours or the fact that more capable security forces constitute a double-edged sword.[33] The ultimate effect of providing security assistance is highly uncertain: EU funding or training does not necessarily render local security forces immune to the temptation to commit human rights violations. Political embarrassment is hard to avoid when a security sector reform mission is followed by a coup d'état a few years down the road – as happened in Guinea Bissau, for instance. Yet such criticisms fail to take one crucial element into account: that of political leverage.

All security assistance programs constitute a platform for maintaining engagement, and therefore buy a limited amount of political leverage. Training missions typically buy a stake into local command and control chains and foster personal networks and relationships. Funding programs represent a very rudimentary control mechanism over the way a state finances its security structures. The coup d'état in Mali in March 2012, for example, was swiftly stopped in its tracks by cutting nearly all development assistance.[34] Educational programs in the field of peace and security allow for the creation of a framework to shape doctrines and institutions. It should perhaps be remarked that EU activities in this domain are often complementary to programs offered by other actors. As such they are only part of a more complex web of influence networks.[35] This makes it complicated to identify the actual political leverage of the EU relative to other actors.

Security cooperation does not amount to full control over how this support is being put to use by local stakeholders, but rather represents a gamble.[36] The risk of such assistance backfiring – in terms of public relations or otherwise – is always present. But it buys the proverbial "finger in the pie" at a limited cost. It represents the middle ground between complete disengagement, which would entail giving up influence altogether, and direct hands-on engagement that is fiscally unsustainable. The fact that security assistance can be sustained over years or even decades therefore qualifies as a decisive factor. Capacity-building based on a "light but long footprint" therefore seems to be the way of the future. As this may entail implicit support for unsavoury regimes, critical questions over the democratic legitimacy and human rights track record of the supported regimes are part and parcel of this narrative.

Deterring external interference

If one leaves behind the confines of politically correct discourses about the EU's engagement with Africa in favour of traditional *Realpolitik*, still other explanatory narratives come to mind. Michael Kluth, for example, argues that the EU's security focus vis-à-vis sub-Saharan Africa is rapidly shifting from an interventionist role to a deterrence posture aimed at keeping rising powers such as China out of the European *chasse gardée*.[37] In Kluth's analysis, European powers such as France and the United Kingdom push European military cooperation as a means to preserve their "custodianship" over the African continent. The shift to capacity-building must be read as a way of sub-contracting stabilization responsibilities to regional actors such as the AU so that European military efforts can be re-oriented towards investment in long-range war-fighting capabilities.

It is of course debatable whether the recent decisions of European states to acquire new submarines, aircraft carriers or combat aircraft should be read purely in terms of their Africa policies. Naval and air platforms are by their very nature flexible security tools: a frigate can hunt pirates in the Indian Ocean just as well as it can patrol the Arctic waters. Yet it is hard to deny that European interest in maintaining such platforms is increasing precisely as the budgetary context is making their acquisition more difficult. At the same time, a growing awareness exists that China's economic interests in Africa are accompanied by a more strategic dimension.[38] Taking these elements together one can construct a narrative that the shifting focus towards capacity-building and security assistance efforts is part of a broader trend of increasing geopolitical competition. Africa is, in Kluth's analysis, nothing more than a specific geographic theater over which the Europeans want to keep control.

Needless to say, this narrative runs counter to all official political discourses. Yet the extreme version described above can be watered down into more moderate language. Such a version could stress the idea that the increasing level of international competition pushes the EU to be continuously seeking new ways to increase its visibility on the international stage. Given that the EU can more easily agree on decisions pertaining to Africa than on the Middle East, for example, it can be expected to continue to launch security initiatives in response to African crises. In this sense, EU missions in Africa "are in effect more about EU experimenting with its own capabilities than about Africa".[39]

Lowering CSDP ambitions

Looking at the CSDP from the perspective of power politics, Luis Simon has convincingly argued that the level of ambition of the EU's CSDP has effectively decreased throughout its existence.[40] The drift towards "soft" crisis management – a focus that originated in a context of American global hegemony – is in his view leading to a situation of "strategic atrophy" from which Europeans urgently need to wake up. If one adopts this frame of reference, the shift from direct to indirect security engagement acquires yet another connotation. Here capacity-building acquires its relative prominence from the simple fact that it is the only task of which Europeans are still capable.

There is considerable empirical evidence supporting such a view. The EU's original ambitions of being able to conduct robust military interventions through its own rapid reaction corps have been quietly abandoned. Even the rather small and distinctly unambitious EU battlegroups have – as a result of their non-deployment – proven to be paper tigers. Moreover, the crisis in Libya in 2011 dealt the CSDP a near-mortal blow: the EU was collectively unable to address the very type of challenge it had been preparing for since the start.[41] This was at the outset a problem of political unity (the German abstention in the UN Security Council), but the ensuing air campaign under NATO leadership also brought to light the increasingly desperate state of European military establishments. Without extensive US support and resupplies, European states are likely to have been materially unable to complete the operation. Finally, the limited degree of European support for the French intervention in Mali early in 2013 does not bode well for CSDP either. Frustration about the slow response time of the EUTM Mali mission is palpable, and the 2013 French *Livre Blanc* even goes as far as calling integrated European defence efforts "illusory".[42]

Among EU member states there is an ongoing debate over what the CSDP should be about. Some favour more ambitious goals for the CSDP – culminating in the ability to conduct high-intensity military operations without US support. Others play down this power-maximizing orientation in favour of a more humanitarian vision of European foreign policy. As the political decision-making in the Foreign Affairs Council operates on the basis of consensus, the lowest common denominator wins.

Indirect security assistance and capacity-building missions in this light qualify as policy options that are on the one hand clearly within the material reach of European states, and on the other hand within political reach in terms of finding consensus. The planning for the EUCAP Sahel mission is illustrative in this regard: whereas the original proposal was to send hundreds of military trainers to Mali, the only consensus that could be reached was to send a handful of civilian advisers to Niger.[43] The eventual decision to set up EUTM Mali could only be reached as the country was spiralling towards implosion during the course of 2012, inviting a unilateral French intervention. Even now, the EU trainers are precluded from engaging in combat operations and mentoring Malian forces in the field. In any case, the shift to the indirect approach in this analysis must be read as a function of growing political constraints that hamper more ambitious engagement.

The end of crisis management

The preceding narratives have a Eurocentric bias in common. Yet the shift from direct peacekeeping to indirect security assistance also corresponds to broader trends. It is not only in Europe that peacekeeping is going out of fashion to some extent: similar trends towards sub-contracting to local parties and indirect assistance can be observed elsewhere as well. A final narrative that must therefore be considered is that we are witnessing a general "turning away" from peacekeeping and crisis management. The idea that lies at the heart of this analysis is that the peacekeeping boom that characterized the past two decades is close to topping out and may have passed its peak. In this view the remarkable growth rate of peacekeeping and crisis management efforts was bound up within a specific historical timeframe characterized by US hegemony and the relative absence of geopolitical competition. As this post-Cold War era comes to a close, a process of strategic reprioritization is taking place that may refer crisis management once again to the fringes of the security policy debate. The idea that external actors can "manage" crises and conflicts in a foreign environment is increasingly contested.[44] The EU's changing role in international security must therefore be interpreted accordingly.

The end of the Cold War coincided with a dramatic increase in peacekeeping and with its growing legitimization. Whereas the world numbered approximately 11,000 UN peacekeepers in 1989, this increased to a first high in 1994 of approximately 78,000 and ultimately peaked in 2010 with a grand total of over 100,000 uniformed UN personnel. The Bosnian War arguably provided the turning point in the organizational as well as conceptual expansion of the traditional peacekeeping concept into that of crisis management. First NATO and the EU transformed into organizational platforms for military and civilian crisis management. Soon afterwards, non-Western regional organizations followed suit. According to the figures collected by the Center on International Cooperation, the grand total of UN, NATO, regional and ad hoc deployments of military peacekeepers surpassed the 250,000 watermark in 2010 and continued growing at a reduced pace in 2011.[45]

Few historical trends last indefinitely. As the West is facing increasing fiscal as well as geopolitical challenges, one can reasonably expect the peacekeeping output of the Western-led international order to suffer accordingly. The EU's shift towards an indirect approach in African peacekeeping in this light is but one manifestation of the growing fatigue of the international order that was designed in the aftermath of World War II. The various narratives outlined earlier therefore do not so much represent descriptions of articulate policy choices made by European decision-makers, but should rather be thought of as different translations of a broader macro-historical trend. In this analysis, it is not so much the Europeans that are shifting their policy preferences, it is rather the world itself that is changing and forcing all actors to accommodate new realities. Just as the post-Cold War order of the 1990s and 2000s allowed the crisis management business to bloom, the more contested world order of the 2010s may foster different phenomena in international security. The emergence of a lively debate over a naval arms race developing in East Asia is but one example of this trend.[46] The growing prominence of security assistance missions can be read as the last gasp of the old crisis management model, but also as a new model for the future. In this analysis, it is as yet not possible to make this distinction: the direction of the macro-historical trend only becomes clear in retrospect.

Conclusion

Multiple competing narratives exist for explaining the EU's changing role in African security. As a union of 28 member states with different security cultures, the EU cannot really be accused of the naked pursuit of its interests. The role played by the EU as a major donor of development assistance and humanitarian aid, in combination with its political discourse stressing democratic values and the rule of law, makes it hard to characterize the EU as anything other than what it claims to be: a peace project that seeks to export its model mainly by the power of attraction. And yet at the same time, it is equally difficult to reconcile the actions of its member states with the discourse of the EU as a whole. A discrepancy exists between the long-term engagement of the EU as an institution and some of the short-term imperatives of crisis management as undertaken by the member states. Both qualify as constitutive components of the EU's role in Africa and therefore need to be accommodated in a pragmatic discourse.

The overall picture that emerges from the sum of the different analytical prisms outlined above is that of an intertwining of political and financial constraints on EU action in Africa. These combined constraints push the EU to focus on an enabling role in African peacekeeping. Instead of seeking to lead peacekeeping operations, the EU is content to support other organizations playing this role. It does so through a combination of financial assistance, training programs and capacity-building missions – only intervening directly as a matter of last resort. (As the French intervention in Mali shows, the last resort may also entail operating under a national flag, albeit with political and logistical support from partners.) The key idea that seems to capture this preference for indirect engagement is that of "affordable influence". European states – and the European institutions they created – loathe giving up their role as major players on the world stage and in African security.

Affordable influence in this context means engaging in depth with the evolution of the African security architecture within the remit of the available means and without trying to fully control the system. At the same time, the EU tries to steer the process politically and has to "approve" all the interventions. Squeezed by austerity, European defence establishments must play to their strengths while preserving resources for an uncertain future. In political terms, the EU has to abandon any pretention of being able to deliver specific political outcomes – be it ending long-standing conflicts or reaching the millennium development goals. What is politically important, however, is to remain engaged and to contribute to shaping the overall security context on the African continent. This entails a constant search for public visibility of European actions and a continuous assessment of how the EU can maintain a degree of political leverage vis-à-vis African governments and institutions.

It is not entirely clear what this means for the future. What is certain is that the EU's role in Africa is constantly evolving. The trend towards capacity-building engagement, premised on the idea of affordable influence, is not sure to last indefinitely either. As the EU itself is going through a period of internal political turmoil, past trends may not be a good indicator of future events. Yet the continued African demand for peacekeeping expertise and the European ability to supply the same mean that this saga will continue for the foreseeable future.

Notes

1 Treaty on European Union, Article 42.

2 See, e.g., J. Howorth, *Security and Defence Policy in the European Union*, Basingstoke: Palgrave Macmillan, 2007. It is probably no coincidence that the EU embraced the notion of "crisis management" rather than "peacekeeping" – suggesting that the political intent is broader than peacekeeping alone. For present purposes, however, we shall use these labels interchangeably: the role of the EU as a peacekeeper is effectively buried within its crisis management discourse.

3 See, e.g., L. Simon, "CSDP, Strategy and Crisis Management: Out of Area or Out of Business?" *The International Spectator* 47, 2012, pp. 100–115.

4 Cf. P.V. Jakobsen, "Small States, Big Influence: The Overlooked Nordic Influence on the Civilian ESDP", *Journal of Common Market Studies* 47, 2009, pp. 81–102.

5 See "A Secure Europe in a Better World: European Security Strategy", Brussels: European Council, 12 December 2003.

6 Cf. e.g., A. Novosseloff, "EU–UN Partnership in Crisis Management: Developments and Prospects", New York: International Peace Academy, June 2004.

7 Cf. S. Ulriksen, C. Gourlay and C. Mace, "Operation Artemis: The Shape of Things to Come?" *International Peacekeeping* 11, 2004, pp. 508–525.

8 Cf. UNDPKO/DFS, "Guidelines for Joint UN-EU Planning Applicable to Existing UN Field Missions", New York: UNDPKO Policy Evaluation and Training Division, 13 June 2008.

9 For some examples of writings stressing the theme that France continuously seeks to Europeanize its Africa policy, see, e.g., P. Berg, "EUFOR Tchad/RCA: The EU Serving French Interests", in M. Asseburg and R. Kempin, *The EU as a Strategic Actor in the Realm of Security and Defence*, Berlin: Stiftung Wissenschaft und Politik, 2009, pp. 57–69; B. Charbonneau, "What Is So Special about the European Union: EU–UN Cooperation in Crisis Management in Africa", *International Peacekeeping* 16, 2009, pp. 546–561; F. Mérand and H. Rakotonirina, "La force européenne au Tchad et en Centrafrique: le baptême du feu", *Politique africaine* 114, 2009, pp. 105–125.

10 Cf. A. Rodt, "EU Performance in Military Conflict Management", in R. Whitman and S. Wolff (eds), *The European Union as a Global Conflict Manager*, London: Routledge, 2012, pp. 169–188.

11 Cf. M.W. Doyle and N. Sambanis, "International Peacebuilding: A Theoretical and Quantitative Analysis", *The American Political Science Association* 94, 2000, pp. 779–801.

12 See G.R. Olsen, "Conflict Management in Africa: American and European Union Policies Compared", paper presented at the 50th ISA convention, New York, February, 2009.

13 See J. Heathershaw, "Unpacking the Liberal Peace: The Dividing and Merging of Peacebuilding Discourses", *Millennium* 36, 2008, pp. 597–621.

14 See Olsen, "Conflict Management".

15 Heathershaw, "Unpacking", p. 613.

16 Cf. S. Görtz and A. Sherriff, "1st Among Equals? The Instrument for Stability and Conflict Prevention and Peacebuilding in the EU's New Financial Perspective", *ECDPM Briefing Note* 39, Maastricht and Brussels: European Centre for Development Policy Management (ECDPM), May 2012.

17 It can of course be remarked that no military operation is ever neutral in a strict sense of the word – that no party would benefit or suffer from it – but that is another matter. For a discussion, see A. Mattelaer, "The Strategic Planning of EU Military Operations – The Case of EUFOR Tchad/RCA", *Working Paper* 5, Brussels: Institute for European Studies, 2008, p. 19.

18 Multiple interviews with EU member state officials, October–November 2010.

19 Cf. A. Mattelaer, *The Politico-Military Dynamics of European Crisis Response Operations: Planning, Friction, Strategy*, Basingstoke: Palgrave Macmillan, 2013, pp. 75–77; and B. Seibert, *Operation EUFOR Tchad/RCA and the European Union's Common Security and Defense Policy*, Carlisle: Strategic Studies Institute, 2010, pp. 41–42.

20 See, e.g., B. Rouppert, "EUTM Mali: Une mission déployée dans l'urgence dans un contexte de conflit ouvert", Brussels: GRIP, April 2013.

21 Multiple interviews with EU member state and European External Action Service (EEAS) officials, November 2010 – November 2012; cf. A. Mattelaer, "Reviewing the EU's Crisis Management Procedures", *IES Policy Brief* 2012/04, Brussels: Institute for European Studies, 2012.

22 See "Annual Report 2011: The African Peace Facility", Brussels: European Commission, 2011.

23 See "Turning the Tide on Piracy, Building Somalia's Future: Follow-up Report on the EU's Operation Atalanta and Beyond", London: House of Lords European Union Committee (3rd Report of Session 2012–2013), 21 August 2012, p. 24.

24 Cf. Görtz and Sherriff, "1st Among Equals?".

25 Multiple interviews with EEAS officials, January–March 2013.

26 Roundtable discussion with African scholars on Africa, EU Partnership on Peace and Security, Institute for European Studies, Brussels, 10 October 2012.

27 Cf. T. Valasek, "Surviving Austerity: The Case for a New Approach to EU Military Collaboration", London: Centre for European Reform, 2011; J. Gordon, S. Johnson, F.S. Larrabee and P.A. Wilson, "NATO and the Challenge of Austerity", *Survival* 54, 2012, pp. 121–142.

28 See, e.g., D. Helly, "The EU Military Operation in the Republic of Chad and in the Central African Republic (Operation EUFOR Tchad/RCA)", in G. Grevi, D. Helly and D. Keohane (eds), *European Security and Defence Policy: The First 10 Years (1999–2009)*, Paris: EU Institute for Security Studies (EUISS), 2009, pp. 339–351.

29 All figures are drawn from the EEAS website or the Council Decisions creating the missions.

30 Interview with EEAS official, 10 June 2011.

31 Cf. e.g., N. Gros-Verheyde, "Eubam Libya sur les rails", *Bruxelles 2*, 17 May 2013.

32 See B. Pohl, *"But We Have To Do Something": The Drivers Behind EU Crisis Management Operations*, PhD Thesis, Leiden: Leiden University, September 2012.

33 See, e.g., R. Egnell and A. Grissom, "Military Diffusion through Training and Mentoring: Building Forces in our Image", paper presented at the 54th ISA Convention, San Francisco, April 2013.

34 See "Council Conclusions on Mali/Sahel", Luxembourg: EU Foreign Affairs Council, doc 8772/12, 23 April 2012. EU actions in this regard complemented other sanctions adopted by ECOWAS.

35 One only needs to consider for instance the dynamic interplay between French-led and EU-led training initiatives in sub-Saharan Africa. See, e.g., J. Caballero, "Les Ecoles Nationales à Vocation Régionale: Une Contribution à la paix, la stabilité & la sécurité en Afrique subsaharienne", available at www.operationspaix.net/DATA/DOCUMENTTEXTE/4708.pdf.

36 Cf. e.g., C. Guicherd, "L'investissement de l'UE dans la sécurité collective en Afrique centrale: un pari risqué", *Occasional Paper* 95, Paris: EUISS, 2012.

37 See M. Kluth, "The European Union and Sub-Saharan Africa – From Intervention towards Deterrence?", *African Security Review* 22, 2013, pp. 19–29.

38 Cf. A.K. Stahl, "The Impact of China's Rise on the EU's Geopolitical Reach and Interests in Africa", *European Foreign Affairs Review* 16, 2011, pp. 427–446.

39 See A. Vines, "Rhetoric from Brussels and Reality on the Ground: The EU and Security in Africa", *International Affairs* 86, 2010, p. 1091.
40 See Simon, "CSDP, Strategy".
41 See J. Howorth, "CSDP and NATO Post-Libya: Towards the Rubicon?", *Security Policy Brief* 35, Brussels: Egmont Institute, 2012.
42 Cf. J.-Y. Le Drian, "Discours devant le think-tank 'Notre Europe' ", Brussels, 15 May 2013, available at www.defense.gouv.fr/ministre/prises-de-parole-du-ministre/prises-de-parole-de-m.-jean-yves-le-drian/discours-devant-le-think-tank-notre-europe; *Livre Blanc: Défense et Sécurité Nationale,* Paris: Direction de l'information légale et administrative, 2013, p. 61.
43 See L. Simon, A. Mattelaer and A. Hadfield, "A Coherent EU Strategy for the Sahel", Brussels: European Parliament (DG EXPO), 2012, pp. 28–29.
44 Cf. D. Chandler, "Resilience and Human Security: The Post-interventionist Paradigm", *Security Dialogue* 43, 2012, pp. 213–229.
45 Center on International Cooperation, *Annual Review of Global Peace Operations 2012,* Boulder CO: Lynne Rienner, 2012, p. 6.
46 Cf. e.g., G. Till, *Asia's Naval Expansion: An Arms Race in the Making,* Adelphi 432–433, London and New York: International Institute for Strategic Studies and Routledge, 2012.

4 Whose money funds African peace operations?

Negotiating influence and autonomy with external partners

David Ambrosetti and Romain Esmenjaud

Introduction

This chapter addresses the financial dimension of African peace operations. Its objective is to identify the different forms of financial arrangements that make African peace operations possible, and to raise some of the main political issues associated with each of them. Four types of such arrangements will be discussed: (1) when African states deploy military missions with their own financial resources; (2) when financial support is offered on a voluntary and ad hoc basis by non-African partners, not only through bilateral channels, but also through multilateral mechanisms set by regional organizations such as the EU; (3) when African-led operations are funded by the assessed contributions to the UN peacekeeping budget; and (4) when African troop-contributing countries (TCCs) are given the institutional and financial cover of a formal UN-commanded peace operation.

This taxonomy is the result of an inductive method, founded on an exploratory, inevitably selective, investigation among case studies – some very recent, others less so – on which the authors have worked. While it does not pretend to cover all the imaginable options, this taxonomy does allow us to address the most lively debates in relation to the funding of peace operations. The question of African ownership is one of the controversies which are of concern to both practitioners and academics. Indeed, one cannot miss the situation of dependency that characterizes the African peace and security architecture, as well as the consequences of this situation for the limited freedom of action African states and organizations have in their endeavors.[1]

Going beyond the idea of a mere opposition between two categories of actors (Africans vs. non-Africans) trying to claim ownership over the management of peace missions, this chapter analyzes the contextual negotiations, involving both African (be they regional organizations or states) and external actors, which have given rise to the existing funding arrangements. Importantly, the result of these discussions is always unpredictable, which means the division of labour between organizations is not based on their comparative advantages,[2] but rather on the basis of compromises made on a case-by-case basis.

At first glance, our fourfold taxonomy fails to offer clear-cut, exclusive categories that avoid mutual overlapping. For instance, one may ask why funding by regional multilateral institutions on a voluntary and ad hoc basis is distinguished from funding by the UN, which, after all, is just another multilateral institution? Is it the regional nature of the first that is making the difference here? Or is it that support through the EU may allow some European states to gather support for particular African states, whereas the UN does not offer this kind of multilateral institutional cover for state-to-state relations? In fact, each of the mechanisms offers varying room for manoeuver to the parties involved. For instance, when an external donor state opts for financial support on a bilateral basis, it can suspend it or refuse to renew it later on. Alternatively, when the UN budget is mobilized to take charge of the funding of others' peace operations (here, an African regional organization), it is seriously reducing the donors' leverage on the mission. In the end, organizations shall here be thought of as providers of resources, be they political (legitimacy) or financial, to states wishing to deploy peace missions.

Throughout our empirical investigation, we have encountered some – rare – instances where African states have themselves funded their peace operations. By starting with a discussion around those examples, we will be able to better understand the conditions under which African states have displayed readiness to mobilize their own resources and a desire to act autonomously. But the situations where African actors find it more interesting or valuable to resort to the UN or external partners are much more common, despite the calls from the big donors for a stronger African financial contribution. This contradicts the idea of African ownership, which implies African funding for African missions ("he who pays the piper calls the tune", as practitioners say).

Why, in most cases, African actors show no interest in financial ownership and rely on the resources of others is the question policy-makers keep asking every time a new mission is established. It is hoped that our discussion on those four types of financial arrangements may offer some useful insights in dealing with this question. Examining each of these types successively will shed light on some underlying political stakes for the different actors involved.

African operations funded by African actors

This first model refers to cases where African actors have funded their own peace interventions, or those of their "brothers" from the continent. This unusual scenario has mainly taken place in a context where African regional powers were exposed to the risk of destabilization in their vicinity and, more precisely, under the threat of interferences by rival powers (be they African or extra-African).

The first mission ever deployed by an African organization took place in Chad in late 1981,[3] where the sending of troops from Zaïre, Senegal and Nigeria was largely funded by France and the United States (US). But this experience was preceded by two others, much less dependent on Western partners, and much less addressed in the literature. First, in March 1979, Nigerian troops were sent to Ndjamena to supervise a truce between the Chadian parties that was signed in Kano the same month. Through this initiative, Lagos hoped to stabilize the situation in this neighbor country and pave the way for the withdrawal of the French troops, which had been present in the country since independence. Refusing some of the aid offered by France, Lagos displayed a true willingness to remain independent. After Nigerian troops had to withdraw on the request of Chadian authorities, Nigeria, together with Libya, pushed for the sending of another operation comprising troops from Guinea, Togo and Congo, whose main objective was again to replace French soldiers. Only Congolese troops were deployed thanks to Algerian air transportation support. Those troops, which never went out of their barracks and were lacking all kinds of resources including funding, withdrew as soon as the fighting broke out again in early 1980.

The history of the project of an all-African defence force was also largely shaped by such reactive postures. Among the many proposals to establish such an intervention capacity, one can mention Kwame N'Krumah's famous projects of a Defence Force in the early 1960s, Sierra Leone's African Defence Organization (1965), Nigeria's African Defence System (1970), or the project of a Defence Force of the Organization of African Unity (OAU) discussed between 1978 and 1981.[4] It must be emphasized, however, that most of these projects were put forward as a reaction to initiatives by external actors. For instance, attempts at destabilizing African countries by Portugal, both in 1970 and 1974, were followed by discussions on reinforcing pan-African cooperation.[5] Likewise, in the late 1970s and early 1980s – when the OAU probably moved closest to the creation of such a force[6] – debates followed the April 1978 Franco-African Summit, where Senegalese President Léopold Sédar Senghor was given the mandate to study the possibility of establishing an African multilateral intervention capacity.[7] In the end, none of these projects was translated into reality. Beyond disagreement around the very role such a force should play – whether it should defend the regimes in power or, rather, the states of Africa as a whole[8] – not only the required resources, but also the political will to mobilize them, were missing. Many of the projects actually resembled "window-dressing" initiatives through which their promoters could get pan-African credentials. While being reluctant to publicly challenge the relevance of such a tool, many states were actually comfortable with relying on the support from their external patrons, most often their former colonial masters.

The recent turn towards African regional organizations has partly changed the face of these experiences of autonomy, yet the major features

– the presence of a regional power interested in maintaining the status quo in a context of regional competition – remain. These cases are still, however, the exception. During the 1990s, Nigeria followed a strategy of regional military activism in Liberia and Sierra Leone under the auspices of the ECOWAS, and with the implicit support of the UN Security Council (UNSC). The UK and the US offered financial and technical assistance to the ECOWAS Monitoring Group (ECOMOG, the military force created by Nigeria, Ghana, Guinea, Mali and Sierra Leone) when the crisis was still confined to Liberia. Initially close to the two regimes and hostile to the "revisionist" forces led by Charles Taylor (in Liberia) and Foday Sankoh (in Sierra Leone), Nigeria assumed for eight years the bulk of the financial (and political) costs of this mission. This was so until 2000–2001, when the UN headquarters in New York and the UK took a firmer lead on the new UN Mission in Sierra Leone (UNAMSIL, created in 1999). The latter also benefited from a massive deployment of the Guinean army against the insurgent elements. Two concomitant dynamics drove that Nigerian military involvement. First, the Nigerian authorities felt they were challenged by these rebellions that intended to topple political friends (Liberian President Samuel Doe and Sierra Leonean President Joseph Momoh were close to Nigerian President Ibrahim Babangida), and that were suspected of receiving support from rival neighbors (from Muammar Gaddafi of Libya, Blaise Compaoré of Burkina Faso, and Félix Houphouët-Boigny of Côte d'Ivoire). Second, Nigerian partners within the UNSC were encouraging initiatives from sub-regional powers aimed at preserving stability and political status quo. At that time sending peace missions in internal conflicts was not (yet) the "normal" thing to do in most UN members' views, and decision-makers in Washington were anxious to avoid an inflation of the UN budget that would have deepened their contribution arrears to the organization.[9] Abuja progressively worked at demonstrating that it could assume the role of a credible peacekeeping force in the region, particularly when President Sani Abacha was denounced by human rights organizations for executing the writer Ken Saro-Wiwa.[10]

More recently, Nigeria again displayed its capacity to induce ECOWAS into action by sending troops to Guinea-Bissau. In June 2012, breaking with the organization's inertia vis-à-vis the crisis in Mali, Nigeria, Senegal and Burkina Faso sent about 550 troops to participate in the reform of Guinea-Bissau's armed forces. The sending of this force, whose presence is funded autonomously with the exception of external transportation support, again represents a reaction to the infringement of a rival power in Nigeria's backyard. The ECOWAS troops indeed replaced soldiers from Angola, which had been deployed in Guinea-Bissau under the umbrella of the Community of Portuguese Language Countries.

Apart from the action of other regional powers such as South Africa, which intervened in Lesotho in 1998 without requesting any external support, examples of genuine African funding ownership are very scarce.

One can note that in January 2013, the AU for the first time decided to participate in the funding of an African mission through its own budget. However, the US$50 million of promised aid to the African-led International Support Mission to Mali (AFISMA) was only to cover a small part of the budget of the mission (assessed to be close to US$1 billion). Besides, this promised contribution was to be partly mobilized by recovering arrears from AU member states.[11] In the same vein, the Economic Community of Central African States (ECCAS) is funding only about 30 percent of MICOPAX, the mission deployed in the Central African Republic (CAR).[12]

In this context, it should be asked whether African states are simply not interested in gaining real ownership over their operations. One common argument to justify Africa's dependence on external actors, regularly referred to by African leaders in particular, is resource scarcity. For instance, the former South African Minister of Foreign Affairs, Nkosazana Dlamini-Zuma, justified her country's request for UN financial support for AU operations on the basis of the existing gap between the commitments made by the organization and the resources at its disposal.[13] Indeed, even resource-rich Nigeria found it very difficult to sustain its military engagement in Liberia and Sierra Leone, which has cost some US$4 billion to the government in Abuja.[14] However, the mobilization of resources is also the result of political will and choices. As an example, Ethiopia has been able to intervene in Somalia in several instances outside the framework of any regional or international organization. As we have seen with Nigeria in Chad, then in Liberia and Sierra Leone, or with Ethiopia in Somalia, specific contexts of regional competition affecting an African power may have created a context conducive to African financial ownership in military interventions.

Otherwise, the limitation of Africa's financial contributions to peace operations is better understood when keeping in mind that most peace missions are called for by external actors as much as by Africans themselves. This is the subject of our second section.

African operations financially supported by external actors

When African troops are not part of a UN mission, their presence in peace operations has most often been funded by the voluntary contributions of external donors. We have identified this model, for instance, in Chad (1981–1982), the CAR (1997–1998; 2002 to date), Côte d'Ivoire (2002–2004), Burundi (2003–2004), Darfur (2004–2007) and Somalia (2007 to date).We will first retrace the forms taken by this kind of partnership, before addressing its political implications (who depends on whom and what are the political effects?).

African peace operations as division of labour between Africans and donors

External support may be provided directly to the troop contributors or to the regional or sub-regional organizations in charge of the operation. In the context of the OAU mission in Chad, out of fear that direct aid to the organization might compromise its independence, donors (i.e., France and the US) were asked to offer support to the participating states on a bilateral basis. Today, while bilateral aid remains significant when it comes to material and logistical requirements, financial support is generally managed at the level of the mandating organization, which can thus assert its control over the operation. In recent operations (CAR and Mali), ad hoc financial cells have been established to channel the aid to the operations. Such units, which include representatives of the donors, also allow for more transparency in the administration of support, thereby helping to overcome the suspicions of mismanagement (or corruption) that have emerged in the operations in Darfur and the CAR.[15]

While aid from individual states was predominant in the past, most contributions nowadays are channelled through regional organizations. NATO, for instance, offered logistical support to the AU operation in Darfur (2005–2007), while the EU has become the main (financial) partner of African organizations. Through the African Peace Facility (APF), an instrument of the European Development Fund, the EU has been taking charge of the greatest share of the budget of the missions in the CAR, Darfur and Somalia.[16] For some time, Western countries have tried to encourage other donors to participate in the funding of African operations, with very little success. At this stage, only Turkey has responded to the call to support the AU Mission in Somalia (AMISOM). Moreover, the Turkish US$1 million contribution remains relatively small given the needs of the operation, which has become the largest ever deployed by an African organization (17,000 soldiers), and to which the EU contributes no less than €19 million a month.[17]

African peace operations are therefore most often the result of a specific division of labour between African and non-African, in fact Western, actors, where the former provide the human resources and the latter the financial, technical and material (equipment) ones. Without this external voluntary funding, the AU could not have become such a big player in peace operations. Yet this direction was not obvious when the AU undertook its first full-fledged peacekeeping mission in Burundi (African Mission in Burundi, AMIB) in 2003. At that time, the AU did not respond to a strong lobbying from external donors. The initiative came from inside, from South Africa. It stemmed from Nelson Mandela's appointment as facilitator to the Arusha peace negotiation (1999–2000) and the subsequent deployment of a South African Protection Support Detachment to Burundi in October 2001. Burundi would eventually become a test for the AU in the eyes of Pretoria. The UK then directly supported Ethiopia as an AMIB contributing country, while South Africa bilaterally supported Mozambique and, as the leading nation, delivered the logistical support needed by the force as a whole. The EU then used its new APF to cover the allowances paid by the AU to the troops. It was the first time that partners offered direct support to the AU's peace and security activities.[18]

The situation repeated itself with the AU mission in Darfur (AMIS), established in 2004. However, external actors, mainly Western countries, exerted intensive lobbying to get the AU to deploy the operation. Their support included the prospect of takeover by the UN, despite Khartoum's hostility. These partners would also become providers of funding. The most spectacular contribution came from the APF, which alone brought €305 million to the AMIS funding, out of €440 million dedicated to the Facility between 2004 and 2007.[19] The US, the UK and Canada also provided AMIS with important contributions, while African financial support remained insignificant.[20]

A noticeable limitation of the EU Peace Facility is that it cannot, in principle, fund expenditures with clear military aims (military training and equipment, etc.). As in Burundi, in Darfur the main part went to fund AMIS soldiers' allowances. Bilateral contributions by other partners – including EU states – then complemented the APF support by providing war-fighting capacity-building, ammunition and weapons. Significantly, partners did not rely on the permanent structures in charge of logistical support for peace operations (Peace Support Operation Division), and opted for the creation of a Darfur Integrated Task Force (DITF) as an ad hoc transmission belt (including funding) between them and the AU Department for Peace and Security. Interestingly, though, the DITF office was placed in Addis Ababa outside the AU headquarters (at Adams Pavilion, a few meters away from it).

These levels of funding did not help turn AMIS into a success. They revealed the structural weaknesses of the AU support services in peace operations: their low ability to absorb an important, but irregular, flux of financial support and to transform it into operational efficiency.[21] Beyond the Darfuri situation, the deficiencies have more generally been concerned with staffing and logistics within the Peace and Security Department of the AU Commission, and the inefficient Military Staff Committee.[22] These shortcomings were identified by an external audit commanded by the AU in December 2007 on the staff resources of the organization. It drove the AU and its partners to launch large recruitment projects for the AU Department for Peace and Security, with the contribution of external experts and consultants.[23]

AMIS also reflected the negative impact of too direct a dependency on external voluntary contributions, which followed their own tempos, and often overlapped with one another. In the end, the AU suffered from the political sensitivity of Western governments – particularly during electoral periods in the US and the UK – to well-organized lobbies calling for more robust intervention in Darfur or, at least, for a takeover by a UN mission even without Khartoum's approval.[24] Eventually, Sudan, the AU and UN leaderships, as well as external partners, agreed in November 2006 on a UN-AU joint mission, UNAMID.

Are African actors simply not interested in autonomy?

In most cases mentioned above, African operations have resembled subcontracted interventions or actions by proxies. African peace operations have often resulted from the initiative of non-African powers unwilling to intervene themselves, but eager to get a stabilizing force deployed. From the outset, they have then encouraged African states to contribute troops by promising them financial and material support. France has displayed its ability to induce African allies to participate in peace operations on several occasions, either as a way to replace its own soldiers, for instance in 1997 in the CAR, or as a complement to its own action, for instance in Mali.[25]

Of course, such a division of labour has political implications in that African troop contributors are not in a position to act autonomously. In particular, the level and nature of external support largely shapes the characteristics of peace missions (size, mandate, duration, etc.). For instance, the AU has for a long time asked for an increase in AMISOM's numbers of troops, claiming as early as October 2010 that 20,000 personnel were needed. This request was only – partly – accepted in February 2012, after the UNSC adopted Resolution 2036 authorizing the deployment of 17,000 troops, and donors (the EU in particular) accepted that they would increase their support.[26]

But this is only part of the story. Decisions are usually taken through a lengthy and difficult dialogue between all parties, in which Africans still maintain strong leverage. Aware that their action fits into the agenda of Western states and of the donors' unwillingness to intervene themselves, the actors of the continent can manipulate their partners through a kind of blackmail ("if you don't pay, we will withdraw and create a security vacuum"). In this way, African actors have sometimes decided to intervene on their own, and later "send the bill" to their traditional backers. In January–February 2013, the rapid and autonomous deployment of Chadian forces to Mali through Niger was welcomed by the international community. Later President Déby made it clear, however, that he expected his country to be reimbursed for its action.

Beyond this, African contributing countries can also find immediate benefits to this division of labour. First and foremost, contributing troops gives access to a sort of "geopolitical rent", as the case of AMISOM illustrates. Through an analysis of Uganda's involvement in this operation, Jonathan Fisher allows us to support the claim that the funding of African operations reflects what we would call a pattern of extraversion. By developing an image of regional peacemaker in Somalia, Uganda increased its leverage on the international scene and thereby succeeded in nuancing the diplomatic condemnations of its destabilizing military involvement in the Democratic Republic of Congo (DRC) since 1998.[27] In this sense, Museveni follows the path of other regimes that have bet on their relations with Western partners (Meles' Ethiopia and Kagame's Rwanda), primarily in Washington and London, to ensure their consolidation as sub-regional powers.

The calculations made by the regimes in Burundi and Kenya, whose troops joined the Ugandan units in late 2007 and mid-2012 respectively, are similar. It has been pointed out that Burundian President Pierre Nkurunziza has gained, if not a reputation as a peacemaker (like his predecessor Pierre Buyoya), at least international indulgence regarding the management of Burundi's internal affairs, while his democratic credentials have recently been called into question by non-governmental organizations.[28] Suspicions around Burundian acquisitions of military equipment with (EU-funded) soldiers' allowances also shed light on the potential financial advantages associated with the participation in peace missions. Besides this controversial point, some donors in Bujumbura felt recently that the Ministry of National Defence was getting used to the millions of dollars it was receiving from AMISOM sponsors, and was counting on them for its regular functioning as a structural rent, rather than as a temporary, contextual situation that would require anticipation.[29] More broadly, for the national armies of war-torn states, contributing to a peace operation offers access to training programs and equipment that may help enhance their professionalism, efficiency and discipline. In the eyes of political elites, it provides soldiers with a well-paid occupation that may keep them from interfering in national politics.[30]

Regarding Kenya, participation in AMISOM resulted from the integration of the soldiers that intervened in Somalia in October 2011. Through this move, and as Kenyans are still largely acting autonomously, Nairobi was able to externalize the funding of its military presence in Somalia, though its intervention actually reflected a purely national decision. Following the kidnapping of Westerners in northern Kenya, earlier in 2011, Operation Linda Nchi ("Protect the Nation") was undertaken to create a buffer zone between the two countries, so as to prevent the spread of Somalia's instability towards the south.[31]

Examining the motivations of contributors in other missions does not challenge such patterns of extraversion. The case of Kenya in Somalia can indeed be seen in parallel with that of Chad in the CAR. By placing its troops under the (theoretical) authority of MICOPAX, Ndjamena was able to get funding and legitimacy for its action in this country. The disorder in this neighboring state has threatened to spread into the southern part of Chad, where its oil fields are located. Rwanda's contribution to the operation in Darfur offers another case worth mentioning. As argued by

Danielle Beswick, "while Rwanda's contribution to peacekeeping may be altruistic, it also serves to reinforce the present regime by highlighting its moral authority and 'saviour' role in recent Rwandan history".[32] Kigali's leverage has become so great that it could even threaten to withdraw its troops from the AU-UN mission in Darfur as the UN High Commissioner for Human Rights was to issue, in 2010, a report on the human costs of Rwandan involvement in Eastern Congo.[33]

This section has presented some of the forms taken by ad hoc external support to African TCCs and has thereby shed light on some of the political interests bringing African states to accept institutional arrangements that make them rely on the goodwill of donor countries. The patent limits observed in the efficiency of this model – described both above and below – have led to the establishment of two alternative options. Both are introduced below.

African operations funded by the UN: a model which is gaining ground

Complaining about the lack of predictability in the aid provided on a voluntary basis, African states and organizations have for a long time asked for the support of the UN, and in particular of its peacekeeping budget. They consider such aid would only be fair considering that their interventions are made on behalf of the "international community" as a whole.

In 2008, South Africa, then a non-permanent member of the UNSC, put the issue of UN support to African operations on the agenda of the Security Council. The report issued by the so-called "Prodi panel" (December 2008), created following South Africa's initiative, endorsed the idea of funding African peace operations through UN assessed contributions, though under very strict conditions. With the explicit approval of the UNSC, the contribution of UN member states could be mobilized for a period of up to six months, after which the UN would take over the mission.[34] Large contributors to the UN budget such as Japan and many Western states, including UNSC permanent members, opposed this idea on the grounds that it would explicitly allow the UN to finance an operation which is not under its control. The creation of a voluntary trust fund aimed at reinforcing the capacity of African organizations – another option put forward in the report – was then deemed more appropriate.[35]

Contextual calculations by Western states have, however, led them to trump their own doctrinal preferences, i.e., their refusal to mobilize the UN budget for operations which would not be under UN command. The Prodi Report's recommendation – to resort to assessed contributions from the UN budget to fund African operations – has been put into practice in several cases, sometimes in an even more extensive way. UN support was first mobilized in the transition period between AMIS and the AU-UN Hybrid operation in Darfur (UNAMID). "The logistical support package" put in place for AMISOM, created in March 2009 and enlarged in several instances,[36] constitutes a valuable complement to bilateral support that covers military equipment and the payment of soldiers' allowances by the APF. As in Darfur, the package was initially conceived as a strictly transitory measure. During the transition period from the Bush to the Obama administration (late 2008 to early 2009), the US State Department showed – for a short period of time – some flexibility on the possibility of having UN blue helmets in Somalia. Other UNSC members endorsed this package as a way to alleviate the pressure from the AU regarding the immediate deployment of a fully-fledged UN mission.[37] In the end, given the lack of consensus regarding the creation of a UN operation, the package was, as of April 2013, still offering crucial support to AMISOM.

If UNSC members underlined that the mechanism in Somalia had been established on "an exceptional basis and owing to the unique character of the mission",[38] recent events have confirmed that decisions are actually taken on a case-by-case basis, depending on political and financial interests of the time. In the early 1980s, France, which was recently the most vocal opponent to the establishment of a "support package" in Somalia, endeavoured in vain to obtain UN support to the OAU operation in Chad.[39] Even more interestingly, Paris recently asked for the reproduction of this model in Mali, where it has been opposed by the US.

In the end, this section tells us two things. First, it illustrates – once more – the fact that funding arrangements and inter-institutional cooperation mechanisms result from political negotiations rather than doctrinal or ideological concerns. Second, it makes clear that African states are gradually increasing their leverage in their relations with donors. Of course, Western states still keep the upper hand on decisions regarding the mobilization of UN resources, since the mechanism described above is in no way automatic. But with the multiplication of precedents, donors will find it increasingly difficult to refuse its reproduction.

UN takeover: rewarding troop-contributing countries and sharing the burden

The previous section demonstrated that funding arrangements may take a particular form in the context of a transition from an African-led to a UN-led operation. The latter manifestly stands high in the scale of legitimacy, for it gives the political responsibility of the operation to the universal international organization mandated to ensure peace and security worldwide. But is a UN operation then still an African operation? In principle, the answer is negative. A takeover by the UN formally means a shift in the political chain of command to the benefit of the UN Secretariat and the UNSC.

In practice, this depends on how influential African actors remain within the UN Secretariat. No one would seriously suggest that a UN peace mission in Africa can result from an exclusively African initiative to the sole benefit of particular African states, considering the weak positions African members hold in the UNSC.[40] Yet a UN takeover does not induce a complete loss of control on the part of these contributing states' military chiefs of staff. They usually keep a firm grip on the operational and tactical choices of their national contingent. Notably, the UN Secretariat's political ability to command depends not only on the UNSC members' political support, but also largely on who holds the leading UN positions in the field (Special Representative of the Secretary-General, SRSG; Force Commander; and their deputies). The Secretariat is thus inclined to appoint an SRSG and/or a Force Commander who belong to the main TCCs of the operation.

What is important here is not to assess the degree of "Africanity" or African ownership of UN operations on the continent, but rather to better understand the politics behind the transformation of African operations with African contingents into UN missions, which gives the African troops already deployed in the field a new institutional envelope. Indeed, through this takeover solution, partners provide African TCCs with new opportunities. Intervening states are offered new logistical conditions for their soldiers, an actual financial rent through the distribution of UN-funded troops' allowances, constancy and predictability in the funding of the operation, training and material support for the national armies concerned, and a new legitimacy (a UN mandate and a larger international diplomatic support). In this sense, the re-hatting with blue helmets gives external partners an original instrument to ensure high-quality financial support for African TCCs.

When is the UN to take over an African operation? In 2004, the "Burundi model" formalized a fairly efficient division of labour between the stakeholders, according to which the UN was to take over after the situation has been stabilized by a regional organization. Many other UN operations in Africa since the end of the Cold War have followed this scheme. This includes MINUAR (French acronym for the *Mission des Nations Unies pour l'assistance au Rwanda*) in 1993, MINURCA (French acronym for the *Mission des Nations Unies en République centrafricaine*) in 1998, UNAMSIL (UN Mission in Sierra Leone) in 1999, UNOCI (UN Operation in Côte d'Ivoire) in 2007, UNAMID (Darfur) in 2007 and, most recently, MINUSMA (French acronym for the *Mission multidimensionnelle intégrée des Nations Unies pour la stabilisation du Mali*). As suggested above, the takeover often leans on a special relationship between African contributing countries and influential members of the UNSC. Regarding Darfur, one can mention the strong involvement of Washington and London in 2006 in order to obtain the transformation of the AU mission into a UN operation, and the diplomatic support they have granted to Kigali as a major troop contributor to these two successive missions. The position of lead country, acknowledged and sanctioned by UN diplomats and bureaucrats, offers a good empirical entrance for those who try to grasp the relationship between partners and African contributing countries from a sociological perspective. It shows that success in peace operations also lies in a large number of tasks, routine practices and informal norms that need to be assumed by a member state in a rather consensual way.[41]

In the eyes of external partners, proposing a UN takeover is often considered to be a way of proposing a new funding model for the operation. Not only does it satisfy African actors' request for regular and predictable funding, but it can also alleviate their own financial responsibility. Among donors, the case of the US may be considered separately, given the extent of its assessed contributions to the UN budget for peace operations (27 percent). But when a "middle power" such as France or the UK secures the UN takeover of an African mission, which they had been funding bilaterally or through regional mechanisms like the APF, they can significantly reduce their share of the burden. For instance, France's assessed contribution reaches 19.5 percent of the APF, compared to 7.56 percent in the UN peacekeeping budget. Even if UN peace operations are known to be more expensive than African-led missions, the transformation into a UN mission then still means money savings for Paris or London at the expense of the other major contributors to UN operations (particularly the UNSC permanent members, Japan, the Western European countries – notably Germany, Italy and Spain – Canada and South Korea). In these circumstances, one understands better why France pushed for a UN takeover in Mali as it did in 1998 in CAR.

When the takeover of an African operation by the UN is under discussion, such financial concerns are of course balanced with other considerations, including doctrinal ones. In particular, out of fear of putting the credibility of the UN at risk,[42] it remains difficult for states, especially UNSC members, to send blue helmets to theaters exposing them to high risks of visible failure. The so-called Brahimi Report made it clear that UN operations should be sent when certain conditions are met, including the existence of a ceasefire (i.e., a peace to keep), and of a political process which the soldiers are to support. But in times of budget restrictions, it is more likely than ever that financial considerations will trump such doctrinal concerns. In this way, France is sometimes suspected of having described the security situation in Mali in a rather "rosy" way so as to facilitate the creation of a UN operation and thereby a partial withdrawal of its troops.

Conclusion

African governments have rarely displayed any eagerness to invest financial resources into integrated political-military arrangements that would allow Africa to reach the "security kingdom"[43] its member states pretend to be aiming at. Financial ownership – or lack thereof – has certainly much to do with the material means available. However, African authorities taking the initiative to call for military operations and raise external funds have not been, as far as we could assess, much more frequent than African pledges for direct financial contribution to such operations. What is also lacking, many would argue, is political will. This question is probably where donors nurture their main disappointments vis-à-vis the African political class and constitutes the crux of the problem. This is the question we have intended to address through an examination of the existing financial arrangements that exonerate African actors from funding their own mechanisms for peace and security.

Demonstrations of political will have existed and still exist, though. Several African operations have been initiated by the actors of the continent. In the early years of the OAU, assertiveness by African actors largely stemmed from a wish to demonstrate pan-Africanist ambitions and gain anti-imperialistic credits, with little operational follow-up. Political will was also displayed by particular sub-regional powers concerned by a foreign military presence in their vicinity (Nigeria with the French presence in Chad), or by insurrectional movements affecting the stability of their spheres of influence (Nigeria with Liberia and Sierra Leone). South Africa's and Uganda's leadership roles in Burundi and Somalia respectively offer more recent examples of African assertiveness.

Lack of political will, however, transpires in the weaknesses of the institutional arrangements that African states have created, or rather not created, to offer planning and visibility in the logistical and funding dimensions of their operations. While they have not themselves initiated the creation of the mission, external actors have been requested to bring their financial and material support so as to fill the gaps left by African actors. The UN's aid, in particular, is called for by the leaders of the continent, for in their eyes it does not present the same level of sensitivity as the direct financial involvements of foreign states into their business. In this context, many African rulers demand closer connection between the UN and the African regional organizations in matters of logistical and financial support.

Understanding the existing financial arrangements underlying African peace operations – as this chapter has argued – can be done only by looking at the political relationship between external donors and TCCs, and more precisely by examining the patterns of extraversion shaping the policies of African states. As we have seen, the participation of African actors in peace operations, as it is developing today, is most often based on some sort of geopolitical rent, or even purely financial motivations. Some may argue that such an extraversion strategy might play a constructive role in the long term, by facilitating the emergence of strong African states disposing of efficient military capabilities. One may wonder, however, whose security such states are likely to promote.

Notes

1 R. Esmenjaud, *L'africanisation et l'appropriation africaine des opérations de paix: Etude politique et historique à travers les missions africaines au Tchad (1979–1982), en RCA (1997 à nos jours) et au Darfour (2004 à nos jours),* PhD thesis, Graduate Institute of International and Development Studies, Geneva, 2012; P.A. Kasaija, "The African Union (AU), the Libya Crisis and the notion of 'African solutions to African problems'", *Journal of Contemporary African Studies* 31, 2013, pp. 117–138; B. Franke and S. Gänzle, "How 'African' is the African Peace and Security Architecture? Conceptual and Practical Constraints of Regional Security Cooperation in Africa", *African Security* 5, 2012, pp. 88–104.

2 For instance, the UN is said to be more efficient in the field of post-conflict peacebuilding, compared to regional organizations, which are often considered more able as far as peace imposition is concerned.

3 The 1978 interventions in Shaba are sometimes associated with the OAU, although this is an error. For Chad, see T. Mays, *Africa's First Peacekeeping Operation: The OAU in Chad, 1981–1982,* Westport CT: Praeger, 2002.

4 B. Franke, "A Pan-African Army: The Evolution of an Idea and its Eventual Realisation in the African Standby Force", *African Security Review* 15, 2006, pp. 1–16.

5 In 1971, Portugal supported a coup attempt against Guinean President Sekou Touré; in 1974, it attacked the newly independent state of Guinea-Bissau.

6 In July 1979 the OAU heads of states endorsed the principle of the creation of a pan-African force, and in April 1981 the Defence Commission endorsed a "Protocol establishing an African Defence Force".

7 This initiative had the aim of giving a formal institutional cover to initiatives such as the African interventions in Shaba (1978), which received strong support from France and the US.

8 R. Esmenjaud, "Africa's Conception of Security in Transition: The Continent's Approach to Multilateral Interventions, from N'Krumah to the African Standby Force", in Tim Murithi (ed.), *Handbook of Africa's International Relations,* London: Routledge, 2013, pp. 115–124.

9 This context is notably depicted by J. Woods, "US Decision-making During Operations in Somalia", in W. Clarke and J. Herbst (eds), *Learning From Somalia: The Lessons of Armed Humanitarian Intervention,* Boulder CO: Westview, 1997, p. 152, quoting Herman Cohen, former US Assistant Secretary of State for African Affairs (1989–1993).

10 F. Olonisakin, *Reinventing Peacekeeping in Africa: Conceptual and Legal Issues in ECOMOG Operations,* The Hague: Kluwer Law International, 2000, pp. 142, 160–164; F. Olonisakin, *Peacekeeping in Sierra Leone: The Story of UNAMSIL,* Boulder CO: Lynne Rienner, 2008, pp. 29–31.

11 In the end, the transformation of the African mission in Mali into a UN mission has made this contribution unnecessary.

12 Interview with an EU official, Paris, January 2013.

13 "6092nd meeting", UN Security Council, S/PV.6092, 18 March 2009, p. 9.

14 F. Olonisakin, *Peacekeeping in Sierra Leone,* p. 44.

15 "Des euros 'évaporés' par millions au Darfour", *Libération,* 16 July 2007.

16 For instance, the EU is paying 70 percent of the MICOPAX budget.

17 Interview with an EU official, Paris, January 2013.

18 Interview with a senior officer of the Peace Support Operation Division (PSOD) within the Department for Peace and Security of the AU Commission, Addis Ababa, October 2008. This military officer was in charge of the Darfur dossier since the beginning in 2004.

19 N. Pirozzi, *EU Support to African Security Architecture: Funding and Training*

Components, Occasional Paper, Paris: European Union Institute for Security Studies (EUISS), 2009, p. 26.

20 As with the other AU missions thus far, AMIS could not count on the AU member states' contributions to the Peace Fund, which the organization had created in 2004 to fund its peace missions; *ibid.*

21 J. Cilliers, "Force africaine en attente: État des progrès accomplis dans sa mise en place", Article 160, Pretoria: Institute for Security Studies (ISS), March 2008, pp. 13–14. These difficulties are clearly demonstrated through the case study of the AU in Darfur, according to C. Guicherd, *L'UA au Soudan: Enseignements pour la force africaine en attente*, New York: International Peace Academy, March 2007, pp. 16–19; and A. Ekengard, *The African Union Mission in Sudan (AMIS): Experiences and Lessons Learned*, FOI Report, Swedish Defence Research Agency, Division of Defence Analysis, Stockholm, August 2008, notably pp. 36–39 and 40–41.

22 Audit of the AU, submitted by the High Level Panel to the President of the AU, 27 December 2007.

23 Interviews with two officers of the EU delegation following the activities of the partner group for peace and security matters, and with the team leader of the UN DPKO/AU Peacekeeping Support Team in Addis Ababa, November 2008.

24 D. Lanz, "Why Darfur? The Responsibility to Protect as a Rallying Cry for Transnational Advocacy Groups", *Global Responsibility to Protect* 3, 2011, pp. 223–247.

25 The *Mission de Surveillance des Accords de Bangui* (MISAB) was deployed in the Central African Republic in 1997. Its presence allowed the French troops to withdraw in 1998.

26 "More EU Funding to Increase AMISOM Troop Strength", European Commission, 23 February 2012, available at http://brussels.cta.int/index.php?searchword=Rondos&option=com_k2&view=itemlist&Itemid=54, accessed 12 January 2013.

27 J. Fisher, "Managing Donor Perceptions: Contextualizing Uganda's 2007 Intervention in Somalia", *African Affairs* 111, 2012, pp. 404–423. Concerning the extraversion of African rulers, see J.-F. Bayart, "Africa in the World: A History of Extraversion", *African Affairs* 99, 2000, pp. 217–267.

28 International Crisis Group (ICG), *Burundi: A Deepening Corruption Crisis*, Africa Report 185, 21 March 2012.

29 Interviews with two top managers of security sector reform programs in Burundi, Bujumbura, December 2011 and November 2012.

30 Fisher, "Managing Donor Perceptions", p. 418.

31 ICG, *The Kenyan Military Intervention in Somalia*, Africa Report 184, 15 February 2012, p. 3.

32 D. Beswick, "Peacekeeping, Regime Security and 'African Solutions to African Problems': Exploring Motivations for Rwanda's Involvement in Darfur", *Third World Quarterly* 31, 2010, p. 752.

33 Eventually, Rwanda could not prevent the publication of the report, but it obtained the right to insert in the report itself its own responses and interpretations on the incriminated facts.

34 "Report of the AU-UN Panel on Modalities for Support to AU Peacekeeping Operations", UN, S/2008/813, 31 December 2008.

35 For instance, see the statement of the French Permanent Representative to the UN, S/PV.6092, 18 March 2009, p. 25.

36 The package covers the costs of various elements (oil, air transportation, water, etc.) and, since March 2012, helicopters, arms and vehicles.

37 The AU requested the deployment of a UN mission from the very creation of AMISOM. In January 2007 (Ugandan troops were deployed in March only), the Peace and Security Council requested the UNSC to consider the sending of a

UN force after the expiration of the six-month mandate granted to AMISOM. "Peace and Security Council Communique", AU, PSC/PR/Comm(LXIX), 19 January 2007, para. 14.

38 UN Security Council Resolution 2036, 22 February 2012.

39 See R. Esmenjaud, *L'africanisation.*

40 These weak positions are due to their non-existent weight in the UNDPKO budget, the predominance of the P-5 (or even the Western P-3) in the drafting of the UNSC resolutions (which, despite this, concern Africa in some 65 to 70 percent of the cases), and the lack of military liaison officers, civil staff and institutional memory in many African permanent missions to the UN.

41 D. Ambrosetti, "The Diplomatic Lead in the United Nations Security Council and Local Actors' Violence: The Changing Terms of a Social Position", *African Security* 5, 2012, pp. 63–87.

42 M. Barnett, "The UN Security Council, Indifference, and Genocide in Rwanda", *Cultural Anthropology* 12, 1997, pp. 551–578.

43 A. Adebajo, *The Curse of Berlin: Africa after the Cold War*, London: Hurst and Co., 2010.

Part II

States' policies

5 China's peacekeeping efforts in Africa

Assessing the contributions, future prospects, and challenges

Ian Taylor

Introduction

Since 1990, China has contributed over 7,000 peacekeepers to UN peacekeeping operations, and Chinese peacekeepers have served in places such as the Democratic Republic of Congo (DRC), Liberia, and Sudan. In 2012, China was sending more peacekeeping personnel abroad than any other permanent member of the UN Security Council (UNSC). As of December 2012, China was sending 1,815 peacekeepers (military and police) to UN operations. This made China fifteenth overall in the ranking of contributors (the next permanent member of the UNSC was France, sending 919 people and ranking Paris at twenty-sixth; the United States was fifty-seventh, sending 111 peacekeepers).[1] Importantly, three-quarters of all Chinese personnel deployed under the UN serve in Africa.

The number of Chinese military personnel sent on peacekeeping operations (PKOs) has been growing in recent years and has become a major development in Sino-African relations, as many of the Chinese peacekeepers are deployed on the African continent. However, China's stance on peace operations is closely tied to its attitude on state sovereignty, and this limits the type of interventions that Beijing is prepared to sanction vis-à-vis its role in peacekeeping missions. The most remarkable feature of China's "flurry of UN peacekeeping" efforts in the post-Cold War era has been its focus on the "domestic political scene" of the countries where the Chinese contribute to peace operations.[2]

This chapter discusses why and how this has played out as China has become more and more involved in peacekeeping operations in Africa. It seeks to look at why Beijing is involved in PKOs, the evolution of this involvement, and the challenges facing China as it becomes an important player in PKOs, with reference to its role in sub-Saharan Africa.

Discussion of China's PKO role in Africa needs to be situated within a central tenet of Chinese foreign policy post-1949, i.e., the normative principles of state sovereignty and non-interference. Though this position is shifting somewhat, as Beijing's growing involvement in peace operations demonstrates, this remains fundamental. China's valorization of sovereignty springs from its experiences in the nineteenth century and the early twentieth. This "Century of Humiliation", in popular Chinese parlance, lasted from the First Opium War in 1839 to the triumph of the Chinese Communist Party (CPC) in 1949 – when, according to Mao Zedong, the Chinese people stood up *(zhongguo renmin zhancilai le).* China guards its sovereignty as a correlative of "regaining" its "rightful place" in international affairs:[3] "The attainment of ... great-power aspirations ... draws upon strong emotions, linked to nationalist sentiments, traditional cultural ethnocentrism, and a deeply rooted sense of injustice at the hands of ... (especially) Western countries".[4]

In addition, China has traditionally emphasized the right of states to resolve issues among themselves, in keeping with its resistance to outside involvement in affairs it perceives as strictly domestic, such as those of Tibet and Taiwan.[5] As Pang Zhongying notes,

> Central to Chinese concerns is the changing nature and context of peace operations – with the potential for mission creep and the move to "coalitions of the willing" – and the implications [these] would have for international involvement in China's key internal affairs relating, for example, to Taiwan, Tibet, and Xinjiang.[6]

However, we should emphasize that the rhetoric contained in official Chinese pronouncements "has led many observers to reach the premature conclusion that Beijing opposes all forms of intervention and is wedded to an antiquated approach to sovereignty".[7] In fact, it is possible to discern a subtle shift in China's position regarding state sovereignty.[8] Consider, for instance, the evolution of four of its official guidelines on legitimate intervention. These state that intervening bodies must first proceed with respect for the concerned state's sovereignty. Second, they must gain the authorization of the UN. Third, they must secure an invitation from the concerned state. Finally, they should use force only when all other options have proven ineffective.[9] This set of necessary conditions demonstrates that Beijing has softened its hard-line stance on state sovereignty and non-interference.

Yet the Westphalian notion that interference requires an invitation holds, even in the event that the host government has embarked on widespread and systematic killing or territorial cleansing. By implication, such governments can veto intervention. In the past, when foreign troops intervened in the affairs of a state at the behest of its government, China based its opinion of the legality of the action on whether the official request corresponded to the genuine desires of "the people" as it saw them. This qualification, of course, permitted China to decide legality on the basis of political expediency. China has now effectively abandoned this position and currently focuses on a legalistic interpretation of state sovereignty in the face of intervention. The will of the people is not part and parcel of China's diplomacy or decision-making process in this regard.

Perhaps to avoid such potential conundrums, China has become quite adept at pursuing a strategy of non-participation or abstention from Security Council debates and votes on peace operations. For the Chinese, traditional peacekeeping is "organized and deployed directly by the UN with the consent of all parties".[10] "All parties" in this context refers to state actors. In contrast, the new forms of PKOs as envisioned by the 2000 Brahimi Report urge consent from the host government but not necessarily from all the parties involved. Thus far, Beijing has felt a degree of comfort in this, as the 2002 Chinese Defence White Paper illustrates: "China supports the active measures taken by the UN Secretariat in this regard and welcomes the progress made by the UN General Assembly and the Security Council in deliberating the Brahimi Report on Reforming the UN's Peacekeeping Operations".[11] This move has had implications for the evolution of China's peacekeeping commitments in Africa and elsewhere.

The evolution of China's involvement in peace operations

There have been four phases in the evolution of Beijing's attitude toward peace operations. The first phase, lasting from 1971 to 1980, was characterized by inactivity if not outright hostility with respect to such missions. The second phase reflected a gradual change in attitude from 1981 to 1987. The third period, from 1988 to 1999, saw China cooperate in some UN peace operations, in particular in Africa, while issuing a fair number of challenges toward others. The fourth period, from 1999 onwards, is marked by greater Chinese participation, despite some remaining reservations on certain issues.

Aloof and rejectionist, 1971–1980

In the first phase, China avoided playing any role in UN peacekeeping missions and did not even contribute to their costs. We should remember, however, that China was the object of the first US-led enforcement mission sanctioned by the Security Council in 1951, in the context of the Korean War. Thereafter Beijing saw all UN interventions as superpower chicanery aimed at weaker states within the international system. This suspicion – compounded by the memory of the Korean War – lasted well past the era of Mao. Indeed, in 1990, Foreign Minister Qian Qichen stated that Beijing's reluctance to support the enforcement mission in Iraq sprang from the fact that "the Chinese people still clearly remember that the Korean War was launched in the name of the United Nations".[12] Consequently, "most of such UN actions were seen as interference in countries' internal affairs and as the undesirable result of US–Soviet hegemonic power competition".[13] What is more, the People's Republic of China (PRC) was emerging from the Cultural Revolution at the time, so issues of Chinese diplomatic capacity within the UN system cannot be underestimated.

Conversely, upon joining the UN in 1971, China was often accused of free riding on the international community and avoiding its global responsibilities as a permanent member of the Security Council. Indeed, China was charged with being a group of one, not interested in contributing to world order but reaping all the benefits thereof.[14] It was not until the 1980s that Beijing's overall attitude toward the UN began to evolve. Interestingly, however, when China did begin to play a more active role, some in the West feared that it would represent the more conservative, old-fashioned opposition to those in favour of the evolving form of peacekeeping, which was more forceful and involved potential interference in the domestic affairs of recipient nations.

While the traditional peacekeeping initially favoured by China may still have its place after Brahimi – for example, in such conflicts as the Ethiopian-Eritrean border war – it would not really work in contemporary civil wars, as exemplified by Darfur. Given that Chinese foreign policy has long been predicated on the Five Principles of Peaceful Coexistence, which include a strong normative commitment to non-interference, Beijing's increasing willingness to play an active role in peacekeeping missions is indeed intriguing. It has certainly begun to shape an aspect of China's Africa policy hitherto ignored by most commentators.

Initially, upon entering the UN, China maintained its vehement opposition to all peacekeeping operations, refusing to take part in Security Council votes on resolutions pertaining to peace operations and going so far as to refuse to pay the peacekeeping contributions expected of it as a member of the Security Council. Contributing troops to peace operations was certainly out of the question. As Fravel put it, "Based upon Mao's theory of just war, China viewed peacekeeping as an act of superpower 'power politics', a pretext deployed to justify US or Soviet intervention in the affairs of small states".[15]

Gradual involvement, 1981–1987

As China's modernization project was continuing apace, China started to vote in favour of peacekeeping resolutions, such as an extension of the UN mission in Cyprus in 1981. Beijing also began to disburse its annual peacekeeping contribution from 1982 onwards. It thereafter supported every resolution on UN peace operations from 1981 to 1990.[16] This policy change originated from the adoption of an "independent foreign policy of peace" *(duli zizhu de heping waijiao zhengce)* which the CPC inscribed into the PRC's revised constitution at the Twelfth National Congress in 1982 and which reflected policymakers' awareness that China needed a stable and peaceful world in which to realize its plans for economic development and modernization. As Xia stated,

> "Peace" mean[t] that China began to formulate its foreign policy from the viewpoint of whether it [was] beneficial to international and regional peace instead of [to the pursuit of] military superiority, while "independence" mean[t] that China began to formulate its foreign policy according to its national interests and the common interests of peoples of all the countries in the world.[17]

This included maintaining "equidistant" relations with the United States and the Soviet Union as well as a "more positive [attitude toward] UN affairs" in general.[18]

Equally, the policy allowed China to pose as a counterbalance to the superpowers in the name of the developing world, where peace operations were most likely to take place. However, Beijing was still "stak[ing] out a particularly narrow interpretation of the international community's right to intervene ... predicated upon an interpretation of sovereignty as a virtually sacred right of states".[19]

China's strategic presence in Africa, 1988–1999

In this context, however, the third period of China's policy was marked by a strategic engagement in PKOs on the African continent and an expansion of China's presence there. During the 1990s, Beijing reluctantly began to accept the development of trends in international politics that militated against their hard-line stance. According to a *China Daily* article by Wu Miaofa of the China Institute of International Studies dated 29 May 2007, China changed its tack for three key reasons. First, Beijing became conscious of the fact that UN peacekeeping operations were "an important means of maintaining international peace and security", for although "many of the long-standing conflicts [could not] be permanently resolved by peacekeeping efforts alone ... peacekeeping [could] alleviate crises and provide strong support for developing countries suffering from a lack of allies as well as their own weaknesses". Second, Wu noted that a Chinese analysis of peacekeeping operations "carried out from 1948 to 2000 showed that a total of 54 missions concerning 52 countries mostly involved developing nations". Since "some developing countries also joined peacekeeping operations, including seven African, six Asian, and six Latin American nations", and since "quite a few commanders of peacekeeping troops were from developing countries", China was, in Wu's view, motivated to change its policy by its self-image as the de facto leader of the developing world. Finally, Wu argues that:

> As one of the permanent members of the UN Security Council, China reassessed its position in the international system and concluded: despite undesirable aspects, the current international order [could] drive the growth of productivity; it remain[ed] a long-term task to

> build a new international political and economic order; [and thus] China should join other developing countries in pushing the international political and economic order in a more sensible direction. This included using the UN peacekeeping mechanism.[20]

As China's economic and political clout continues to grow, Chinese policymakers are also gaining confidence, which enables them to commit to selective involvement in international affairs. Peacekeeping is no exception.

The Chinese are also interested in gaining experience by participating in the UN and its peace operations. Drew Thompson identifies several important benefits that China derives from taking part in UN operations.[21] First, participation enhances Beijing's authority not only in regions where Chinese peacekeepers operate but also on the UNSC and among other voting members of the UN, not least those representing Africa – who are thus all the more likely to continue providing useful support in times of difficulty.

Second, China's reputation as a responsible world power is enhanced by involvement in peace operations. As "the most self-conscious rising power in history … [it] is desperate to be seen as a benign force".[22] Third, by participating in peace operations, China increases its strategic presence in regions, particularly within Africa, whose resources may prove crucial for meeting China's energy needs.

Furthermore, as noted earlier, China is also filling a noticeable vacuum left by Western members of the UNSC who contribute financially to peace operations but generally shy away from committing significant troop numbers. As Bonny Ling notes, "This has undoubtedly enhanced China's strategic positioning at the UN, especially since peacekeeping is the single most high-profile element of any UN activities on the ground".[23]

China took part in its first UNPKO in 1988, having joined the UN Special Committee on Peacekeeping Operations (also called C-34) shortly after UN peacekeeping forces had received the Nobel Peace Prize.[24] The following year it sent non-military personnel to observe Namibia's general elections, and in 1990, it sent five military observers to join the UN Truce Supervision Organization in the Middle East. Later, in 1993, Beijing approved the UN Transitional Authority in Cambodia (UNTAC), not only financing a good part of the operation but also sending in a military unit. These moves represented a "significant departure from [China's] past behaviour in multilateral diplomacy for collective security purposes".[25] In fact, "since the early 1990s, the Chinese [have] consistently finessed the meaning of these principles [regarding sovereignty] in order to create a rhetorical space for [their] acquiescence in various 'Western'-sponsored UN operations",[26] as a way to break out of the temporary diplomatic isolation encountered after Tiananmen Square in 1989.[27]

Nevertheless, China remained cautious in its attitude toward peacekeeping, restating its opposition to the use of force whenever it overrode the sovereignty of a state. Beginning in the mid-1990s, "Beijing saw problems as the lines between peacekeeping and peacemaking became fuzzier; as expansion was accompanied by civilian missions concerned with human rights, refugees, and inspections; and as these missions had less-than-complete support from host nations".[28] Consequently, China's

> involvement in UNTAC was not repeated in subsequent missions. This was partly due to [its] attitude toward the principles of state sovereignty and its concern about the use of force in peacekeeping operations. These issues only served to highlight the emerging contradictions and ambiguities with regard to China's position on the nature of peace operations.[29]

As a result, China opposed features of Operation Provide Comfort in Iraqi Kurdistan, the UN Protection Force in Yugoslavia, Operation Turquoise in Rwanda, and Operation Restore Democracy in Haiti – all by abstaining from the Security Council resolutions to authorize or expanding them.[30] China was clearly taking a rearguard action against contemporary peace operations insofar as they involved military enforcement, while supporting traditional peacekeeping operations. It was, to all intents and purposes, a stance against "mission creep", which China believed meant that "the United Nations was becoming an instrument of 'hegemonism' ".[31]

In the run-up to the first Gulf War (1990–1991), Beijing was supportive of Chapter VII resolutions concerning Iraq, though it expended a great deal of energy working to take out recommendations specifying military force. When the UNSC did approve Resolution 678 (1990), entailing the deployment of all necessary means including military force, China abstained. However, as part of its effort to rebuild its international image post-1989, Beijing continued to support traditional peacekeeping missions such as the 1994 UN Operation in Mozambique (ONUMOZ), which it saw as demonstrating the efficacy of traditional peacekeeping. As a Chinese commentary put it:

> The experience of ONUMOZ has proved that as long as the two parties to the conflict are sincere about resolving their problems through negotiations and unswervingly implement the agreements reached by the parties, it is highly possible for them, with the help of the international community, to end yesterday's suffering and open up a new vista.[32]

However, China had more difficulty determining what to do when said parties resisted the implementation of peace agreements.[33] China has in general opposed deviation from Chapter I (Article 4 of which opposes the use of force "against the territorial integrity or political independence of any state") and Chapter VI of the UN Charter, which requires, from peacekeeping operations, impartiality of the forces, the consent of the parties involved in the dispute, the non-use of force except in self-defence, and the prior agreement to a ceasefire between the parties concerned. These remain the legal basis for China's support for peacekeeping operations, and, naturally, their violation forms the basis for Chinese opposition.[34] In this context, though, one of China's first peacekeeping roles in Africa involved support of the US-led United Task Force (UNITAF) and its UN Operation in Somalia (UNOSOM). UNOSOM was organized to monitor the ceasefire between warlords, despite the fact that they were still engaging in violence and that humanitarian assistance was under threat from looting and abuse by their militias.

It was the interception of humanitarian aid that led to the authorization of the UNITAF mission under Chapter VII of the UN Charter. China supported UNITAF but made clear that it considered the situation exceptional, as anarchy was raging in the absence of any government in Mogadishu – a key point as far as China was concerned. Beijing's position was influenced by the fact that it

> did not want to be perceived as obstructionist by casting vetoes on Somalia-related UNSC resolutions and hindering humanitarian assistance. This was especially true since it already had a bad image abroad, especially in the West, following the 1989 Tiananmen incident.[35]

Once UNITAF had completed its mission, Beijing supported UNOSOM II, again under Chapter VII, and again on the grounds that Somalia constituted a temporary exception and that "normal" peacekeeping operations should be resumed as soon as possible. However, once fighting between UN troops and Somali militias began – culminating in the infamous Black Hawk Down incident – China backtracked. The *Beijing Review* asserted that

> the torturous experience in Somalia has taught the lesson that peacekeeping must be limited to peacekeeping. The internal affairs of one country can be solved only by the people of that country. The efforts of the international community can only be helpful or supplementary.[36]

Assistant Minister of Foreign Affairs Li Zhaoxing likewise stated that "the fundamental and effective way to settle the Somali question is by peaceful means. Resort to coercive military actions will only serve to complicate matters".[37] The implication of these comments was that without active participation and commitment by the affected populations, the role of external PKOs was limited at best.

Crucially, the Mogadishu debacle resulted in a de facto refusal by Washington to get involved in efforts to stop the 1994 genocide in Rwanda.

While the United States and other Western powers have been (rightly) lambasted for resisting calls to intervene, criticism of China, which was equally resistant to getting involved, has been muted.[38] China abstained from the subsequent vote on the resolution establishing the French-led Operation Turquoise. This was despite the fact that the resolution authorizing the Chapter VII mandate emphasized the temporary and unique nature of the mission, on the grounds that the mission did not have the approval of all parties involved in the fighting – granting the *genocidaires* an implicit veto on the vote to stop their butchering.

In May 1997, China agreed in principle to contribute to the UN Department of Peacekeeping Operations (DPKO). However, that same year, it was active in warning against the intrusion into the domestic affairs of African countries under the guise of peace operations; it backed the establishment of the UN Observer Mission in Angola in 1997, but expressed concern that the military element of the mission might get drawn into issues that should by rights concern other UN departments: Wang Xue Xian, China's UNSC representative, stated at the time that "as a principle, the Security Council should not get involved in those activities which fall under the terms of reference of other United Nations bodies" and that "China had reservations on certain elements of the draft resolution and on aspects of the observer mission's mandate".[39]

China had similar concerns with the UN Mission in the Central African Republic (MINURCA), which aimed to stabilize and restructure the republic's military. In a vote to extend MINURCA's mandate in 1999, China's UNSC representative, Lin Chengxun, while supportive, observed that although

> the mission had played a great role and ... demonstrated that the Security Council could do concrete work for African countries and people ... reforms, especially the restructuring of the armed forces, [are] the internal affairs of a country. Therefore, the Council should not intervene too much in that area.[40]

The events in Kosovo in 1998 and 1999 particularly worried Beijing, as NATO's air campaign served to flag to Chinese policymakers the dangers of non-UN-mandated interferences in domestic affairs. Beijing was absolutely against the NATO campaign, deeming the whole exercise deeply problematic if not ominous. Indeed, after the Chinese embassy in Belgrade was hit by NATO missiles on 7 May 1999, indignant, anti-Western nationalism proved difficult to contain. As Dreyer put it,

> The view from China's capital was that the United States – the main organizer and contributor of the coalition – was bent on enforcing its vision of proper global order on the rest of the world, even if the attainment of this goal required armed aggression.[41]

As Tony Saich notes, "By and large, China is an empire with a Westphalian concept of the nation-state trying to operate in an increasingly multilateral world".[42] This view of sovereignty has arguably often eclipsed China's perception of its responsibilities as a global power.

Peacekeeping as a tool of China's broader African agenda, 1999–present

The Kosovo campaign served as a positive catalyst for changes in China's policies, as "the shock of [it] and especially the embassy bombing compelled Chinese strategists to seek new ways to ensure Chinese influence over the methods and processes of international intervention".[43] This shift helps explain China's support for a 1999 mandate for the UN Mission in Sierra Leone (UNAMSIL) to implement a disarmament, demobilization, and reintegration program, support elections, and smooth the transfer of aid to the country.[44] UNAMSIL was authorized under Chapter VII to ensure the safety of its personnel and to defend civilians but acknowledged the rights and responsibilities of the government of Sierra Leone, which in turn fully supported the mission. Thus China was likewise more than willing to support it. Protecting the distribution of humanitarian aid and patrolling strategic locations within Sierra Leone were clearly compatible with China's stance on peacekeeping.

In subsequent African missions, China collaborated on operations in the DRC, Liberia, Côte d'Ivoire, Burundi, and Sudan (see below), since they all explicitly limited military force to the defence of UN personnel and civilians in impending danger and "interference" in domestic affairs was not an issue. In short, China agreed to peacekeeping operations with elements of peace enforcement, provided they were carefully restricted.

However, as the UNSC has adopted an increasingly broad interpretation of what constitutes a threat under Chapter VII, China's position has become increasingly complicated.[45] Beijing still insists on securing the blessing of the host country before authorizing operations based on human rights infringements. Thus China unambiguously supported the UN Mission in the Democratic Republic of Congo (MONUC), which was created with Kinshasa's approval after the signing of the Lusaka Ceasefire Agreement in 1999. MONUC was authorized under Chapter VII to take the necessary measures to improve security in North and South Kivu and the Ituri district, where the UNSC had identified serious human rights abuses. Importantly for China, the Congolese government was a key signatory of the original agreement for the cessation of hostilities in DRC and hence a willing host nation of MONUC – however limited in practical terms its reach may have been in the areas in question. China's position relied on the literal definition of "host nation" *(dangshi guo)* used in its Defence White Paper of 2002 (a revision of the 1998 White Paper), namely "the state that is a party".[46] This definition suggests that the consent of all parties to UN involvement is not absolutely necessary, a qualification that is important "where state authority is either highly disputed or effectively non-existent", as in the case of DRC.[47]

In stark contrast is the case of Darfur, where Beijing opposed initial efforts to involve outsiders in improving the security conditions. Thus, whereas the UN Mission in Sudan had functioned in southern Sudan since early 2005, it took considerable efforts – often in the teeth of Chinese opposition – for a mission to be sent to operate in Darfur. Initially, only a somewhat lacklustre effort by the AU was allowed by Khartoum, with Beijing continually backing up the Sudanese refusal to allow a more intrusive and fully international mission. This continued even after it became clear that the AU's ability to defend Darfurians was negligible, as Beijing continued to insist it would back peacekeeping operations only with an invitation from the host country.[48]

However, from late 2006 Beijing began to exhibit an increased willingness to engage with the international community on Darfur and started to apply pressure on Khartoum to modify its behavior and engage in a political process for the peaceful resolution of the Darfur conflict. This policy change was mainly due to overwhelming international criticism of China's role in Sudan and the increasing reputational costs that Beijing was experiencing by being closely associated with Khartoum. Subsequently, in late July 2007, Beijing voted for UNSC Resolution 1769 that created a hybrid UN-AU Mission in Darfur (UNAMID). While it was the case that China at times went along with the Sudanese government's opposition to its full implementation, in mid-June 2008 Hu Jintao strongly urged Sudan to cooperate in allowing the deployment of peacekeeping forces into Darfur as part of UNAMID, clearly indicating that the limits of Chinese patience had been reached. Indeed, in a meeting with Sudan's vice-president, Ali Uthman Muhammad Taha, Hu was reported to have used unusually frank language in calling on Khartoum to try harder to settle the conflict in Darfur.[49] This was in the context whereby 26,000 peacekeepers were supposed to have been deployed in Darfur, but no more than half that number had arrived on the ground by mid-2008, mainly due to intransigence by Khartoum. According to one report:

> Hu's comments and their prominent publication ... are part of an increasingly open Chinese diplomatic campaign to persuade Sudanese leaders to cooperate more with international efforts to end the fighting in Darfur. ... China has come under criticism from human rights activists for failing to pressure Khartoum forcefully enough [and] the official portrayal of [the] meeting was seen as a departure from China's usual style of quiet diplomacy and ritual proclamations of friendship.[50]

Thus there has been a clear movement in China's position on peacekeeping operations – one which has departed from the hard-and-fast defence of sovereignty and non-interference which is usually characterized as marking out Chinese foreign policy.[51]

Rationale for China's presence in African peacekeeping operations

Raising China's profile

China has long been circumspect about intervening in other countries' affairs even when sanctioned by the UN and remains suspicious that the UNSC authorizes Chapter VII mandates too readily.[52] However, as Beijing has emerged as an economic superpower it has been compelled to embark on a change of direction in some aspects of its foreign policy. One such shift is from an absolute refusal to support peace operations under any circumstances, to a permanent commitment to doing so. China is now a major contributor of UN peacekeepers, most of whom are in Africa. It also maintains two training facilities for peacekeeping personnel – one in Nanjing, in Jiangsu province, and the other in Langfang, in Hebei. Furthermore, in August 2007 it was announced that Major-General Zhao Jingmin would be appointed force commander for the UN Mission in Western Sahara, making him the first Chinese national to head a UN mission.[53]

In many ways, Beijing has had international leadership pushed upon it. As China's economy has exponentially expanded and its trade profile has increased across the globe, expectations that Beijing would (and should) play a greater role in international relations have been almost axiomatic. Furthermore, in considering questions of domestic security, "China has gradually realized that peacekeeping missions can help to secure a peaceful international environment, which works in China's national interest as the country begins to build a sound external environment for its long-term economic growth and social development".[54]

China's increased profile, particularly in Africa, has led to criticism – including charges of neo-colonialism – which Beijing's makers of foreign policy are attempting to counteract. Acutely aware of its global reputation, China is taking part in peace operations as one way to project a more benign and even positive image. As Dai Shao'an, vice-director of the Peacekeeping Affairs Office of the Ministry of Defence, has put it,

> wherever they go or whatever they do, [Chinese peacekeepers] always bear in mind that they are messengers of peace, representing China.... To win hearts and minds, you need to devote your own hearts and minds, and that is exactly what our peacekeepers are doing.[55]

A Chinese academic agrees that

> active participation [in peace operations] is a demonstration of China's commitment to the UN and its security functions as mandated by the UN Charter. It is not only useful for serving China's moral cause or fulfilling its international responsibility in the post-Cold War era. It also provides an arena in which China can learn to interact with the international community in ways commensurate with its status as a rising power.[56]

Playing a role in Africa is particularly important for China, explains Elizabeth Economy from the Council on Foreign Relations, as it attempts to reassure the world that it is not motivated solely by its need for resources: "It has a number of reputational risks. Being seen as a force for peace and security is an important and good first step".[57]

Beijing is now steadily constructing a reputation for being at the forefront of conflict resolution in Africa – even if the numbers it actually contributes to various peace operations is small.[58] In fact, China has been relatively successful in projecting a positive diplomatic image vis-à-vis peace operations in Africa, earning the praise of various African commentators. Liberian president Ellen Johnson-Sirleaf, for instance, commended China for supporting Liberia in its peacekeeping, asserting that "Liberians will never forget the friendship of Chinese peacekeeping soldiers".[59]

Interestingly, it was the Chinese who urged other nations to support the deployment of peacekeepers to Somalia during a UNSC mission to Addis Ababa in June 2006 – "the first time [China] had taken the lead in the fifteen nation council in promoting foreign intervention to resolve a conflict thousands of miles from its own borders".[60] According to Chinese reports, African governments pressed China to raise the issue with the Council. However, Princeton Lyman – a former US ambassador with expertise on Sino-African ties – has a more prosaic view, namely that China is seeking to score diplomatic points by supporting vital regional allies such as Ethiopia, which had itself sent thousands of troops to Somalia to protect the official interim government.[61]

There are of course tangible rewards for the Chinese military in taking part in peacekeeping operations. For Thompson,

> The PLA [People's Liberation Army] and PAP [People's Armed Police] ... directly benefit from involvement in UN peacekeeping operations. First, participation enhances training and skills that promote the modernization of the PLA and PAP. Second, deployment provides the opportunity to field-test equipment and methods, gain firsthand experience in the field, and assess the capabilities of other nations deploying or supporting the mission. Third, as China's gross domestic product rises, [its] share of UN contributions increases, arguing for greater involvement in operations and greater reimbursement for deployments from UN coffers.[62]

Indeed, speaking at the closing ceremony of the four-day PLA Peacekeeping Work Conference in Beijing in June 2007, Major-General Zhang Qinsheng, deputy chief of the general staff of the PLA, revealed that

> active participation in the UN peacekeeping operations is ... an important measure to display China's image of being a peace-loving and responsible big country and likewise an important avenue to get adapted to the needs of the revolution in military affairs in the world and enhance the quality construction of the army.[63]

Thus it happily meets a key criterion of Chinese political engagement with Africa – namely that China is seen as a friend of the continent – which means that China's visibility in African peace operations is only likely to grow.

The way forward: between conservatism and the necessity to engage

It appears that an increasingly important aspect of China's African policy involves peacekeeping. Where it will lead remains open to question. The lack of strategic trust between China and many Western countries with regard to military involvement – including peacekeeping – around the world, not least in Africa, is problematic.[64] China is highly sceptical about the motives behind much Western interest in peace operations and understandably rejects US leadership at the UN and US interpretations of international relations.[65] China has always couched its concerns in terms of hegemony, and there is little evidence to suggest it will do otherwise in future. Indeed, following the NATO military strikes against the Federal Republic of Yugoslavia in the spring of 1999, one Chinese commentator wrote, that "Hegemonism and power politics are still developing, and there will be no peace under heaven in the twenty-first century".[66] Wang Jincun, a senior researcher at the Chinese Academy of Social Sciences, similarly asserted in an article titled "Global Democratization – Camouflage of US Hegemony" that

> what deserves more attention is that the United States, not yet satisfied with its Cold War achievements, seeks to gain more advances through military means.... The military interference by the United States in Iraq, Somalia, Haiti, and Bosnia-Herzegovina, the bombing against Sudan and Afghanistan, and especially the on-going air strikes against Yugoslavia serve as prominent examples.[67]

The Chinese share the prevalent suspicion among developing countries regarding the motives behind potential interventions by foreign powers, especially the United States and ex-colonial powers. Thus they often take the position that "in interventions carried out in the name of 'humanitarianism' ... what the interveners themselves were concerned about [was] not humanitarianism per se but their own interests".[68] Interestingly, in so doing, they echo Peter Baehr's claim that "'humanitarian intervention' is a misnomer. It would be far better to speak of the use of military force for (allegedly) humanitarian purposes".[69] But such analyses – whether by Chinese or Western commentators – fail to generate insight into the rationale behind any given intervention. What is required in each case is an investigation into the claims that motivated the intervention and a methodical scrutiny of the endorsement of so-called humanitarianism. Both are sadly lacking.

A Chinese source, quoting a former deputy permanent representative to the UN, Shen Guofang, reminds us of Beijing's central tenet with respect to peacekeeping, namely that it should always observe "the principles of respect for state sovereignty, non-interference in internal affairs, fairness and neutrality, [and] non-use of force except for self-defence [as well as obtaining] prior consent from parties concerned".[70] Ambassador Zhang Yishan, at the 2006 Session of the Special Committee on Peacekeeping Operations, reiterated that any UN mission must "fully respect the views of the parties concerned and strictly preserve neutrality".[71] The Chinese government once described the Special Committee as an attempt to create "a US-controlled headquarters of international gendarmes to suppress and stamp out the revolutionary struggles of the world's people".[72] While such rhetoric has been muted in the post-millennium years, the suspicion that Washington seeks to use the UN as a vehicle to project its interests and policies is still held by Beijing – and resonates in many African capitals as well.

China's stance on peace operations is intimately bound up with its position on state sovereignty – both of which have, however, evolved over time.

> China's attitudinal change to peacekeeping can be seen as part of the process of state socialization ... [P]articipation is an important learning or socializing process [for any] member of an international community. As this learning process continues, we should see a less passive and more active China that needs to craft its own strategies for participation in international affairs in the future.[73]

According to Allen Carlson, "this process ... aptly labelled 'norms diffusion' ... led to the emergence within China of more open, flexible interpretations of sovereignty's role in international politics".[74] However, there are limits to Beijing's flexibility.

Paradoxically, the more Beijing becomes enmeshed in global activities, the more it perceives pressures that need to be managed. In fact, it could be argued that Chinese policy toward UN peace operations is largely decided by Beijing's evolving assessment of the global security situation in relation to its national interests as much as by new thinking on sovereignty:

> China's enhanced national strength and its improved status within the international environment provide [the] ... resources and political currency that enable it to adopt an active policy on [UN peace operations]. The aims of such a policy are to sustain its core national interests – including the maintenance of its role as a responsible power, strengthening the UN regime, and sharing common concerns regarding peace and security.[75]

Conclusion

Beijing's increasing acceptance of international responsibility, as defined by transnational actors such as the UN and as reflected in Beijing's emerging status as a contributor to peace operations, indicates broader changes in China's political economy. As the Chinese economy becomes more and more integrated into, and influenced by, the global capitalist system, the CPC is able to identify new, if indirect, sources of political legitimacy. This trend has spurred a "domestic hunger in China for global linkages [that has] brought down institutional impediments to transnational relations and weakened the state's control over its citizens, resources, and sovereignty".[76]

A peaceful international environment is attractive in this regard. Hu Jintao's concept of *hexie shijie* or "harmonious world"[77] is grounded in the recognition that an interdependent peaceful order is a precondition for China's development.[78] This new understanding of the international milieu, which relies on flexible definitions of state liability and legitimacy, reflects not only the transformation in Beijing's international relations,[79] but also that of the Chinese state itself: "Such thinking serves as a guideline for China's active participation in international efforts and contribution to international peace and security", including UNPKOs.[80] While the Chinese remain leery of intervention, they now also accept it as part of the post-Cold War world order. In this sense, "China is no longer so much of an outlier when compared with other states in the international system".[81] However, this "cautious acceptance and incremental evolution" in Beijing's attitude toward UNPKOs is a function of Chinese policymakers' attempts to control the terms of intervention, however imprecise they may be.[82] This fact makes the study of Chinese contributions to peace operations on the continent particularly important.

Beijing is resistant to processes whose definitions of sovereignty are out of its control – particularly if they are being shaped by Western powers.[83] As Rosemary Foot has pointed out,

> The nature of the international regime in question, especially its level of intrusiveness and the extent to which it might erode strategic independence, threaten political control, or actually enhance China's power, has influenced Beijing's compliance and involvement for

> reasons that have become familiar in studies of Chinese foreign policy behaviour.[84]

In short, Beijing is flexible on sovereignty as long as it is in a position to help define the terms of the debate, but not while they are decided by Washington or by a General Assembly vote that it cannot veto. This stance was clear with respect to the Darfur issue.

In other words, the PRC is strongly against the establishment of new norms on such issues. As for international humanitarian law, "China complies as best it can when it is in its interest to do so but [otherwise] uses whatever techniques at its disposal to resist intrusion into its domestic arena".[85] On this score, "whether China is significantly different ... from other countries is doubtful".[86]

The reality of Chinese self-interest has important implications not only for China's involvement in peace operations in Africa but also, sometimes unfortunately, for African peoples – Darfurians being the most recent and graphic example. Controlling the terms of the debate on sovereignty in ways that protect Chinese interests remains key to China's stance on intervention and, by extension, peacekeeping. Thus, while China has moved away from absolute repudiation of peace operations to a more responsible point of view that allows limited peace operations, it continues to insist on the express permission of the recipient state or host government.[87] Given the instability of many African states, such insistence is highly problematic and in Sudan certainly delayed the sending of peacekeepers to Darfur long after they were needed.

Yet responsibility for Africa's domestic conflicts lie more with Africa than with China, a fact that may have an interesting impact on the development of Chinese policies toward sub-Saharan Africa in particular:

> As China becomes involved in volatile regions in its peacekeeping, Beijing will be drawn into conflicts and post-conflict situations and will be forced to think through a coherent policy regarding how such conflicts start and why. This will inevitably have implications for how Beijing regards the make-up of African states.[88]

In sum, we might say that China's attitude toward peace operations has finally been normalized, such that "the contribution of personnel [to UNPKOs is] more of a routine action ... than an exceptional policy move".[89] How Beijing navigates the African milieu as its involvement in peace operations in Africa deepens will be of great interest to observers of Sino-African relations.

Notes

1 See UN website, www.un.org/en/peacekeeping/resources/statistics/contributors_archive.shtml, accessed 5 March 2013.
2 A. James, "Internal Peace-Keeping: A Dead End for the U.N.?", *Security Dialogue* 24, 1993, p. 359.
3 R. Elegant, *The Centre of the World: Communism and the Mind of China*, London: Methuen, 1963.
4 M. Swaine, *China: Domestic Change and Foreign Policy*, Santa Monica CA: RAND, 1995, p. 84.
5 Interview with Shu Zhan, Chinese ambassador to Eritrea, Asmara, Eritrea, 29 June 2006. See also P. Zhongying, "China's Changing Attitude to UN Peacekeeping", *International Peacekeeping* 12, 2005, pp. 87–104.
6 Zhongying, "China's Changing Attitude", p. 88.
7 A. Carlson, "More than Just Saying No: China's Evolving Approach to Sovereignty and Intervention", in A. Johnston, and R. Ross (eds), *New Directions in the Study of China's Foreign Policy*, Stanford CA: Stanford University Press, 2006, p. 218.
8 Interview with He Wenping, Chinese Academy of Social Sciences (CASS), Beijing, 18 September 2007.
9 A. Carlson, "Helping to Keep the Peace (Albeit Reluctantly): China's Recent Stance on Sovereignty and Multilateral Intervention", *Pacific Affairs* 77, 2004, pp. 9–27.
10 Z. Li, "Some Reflections on International Intervention", in *International Intervention and State Sovereignty*, Beijing: China Reform Forum, 2003, p. 209.
11 *White Paper on China's National Defence*, Beijing: Information Office of the State Council, 2002.
12 Quoted in S. Kim, "China's International Organizational Behavior", in T. Robinson and D. Shambaugh (eds), *Chinese Foreign Policy: Theory and Practice*, Oxford: Oxford University Press, 1995, p. 423.
13 W. Jianwei, "Managing Conflict: Chinese Perspectives on Multilateral Diplomacy and Collective Security", in D. Yong and W. Fei-ling (eds), *In the Eyes of the Dragon: China Views the World*, Lanham MD: Rowman and Littlefield, 1999, p. 70.
14 Kim, "China's International Organizational Behavior".
15 M.T. Fravel, "China's Attitude Toward UN Peacekeeping Operations Since 1989", *Asian Survey* 36, 1996, p. 1104.
16 S. Morphet, "China as a Permanent Member of the Security Council, October 1971–December 1999", *Security Dialogue* 31, 2000, pp. 151–166.
17 X. Liping, "China: A Responsible Great Power", *Journal of Contemporary China* 10, 2001, p. 18.
18 Zhongying, "China's Changing Attitude", p. 90.
19 Carlson, "More than Just Saying No", p. 221.
20 *Ibid.*
21 D. Thompson, "Beijing's Participation in UN Peacekeeping Operations", *Jamestown Foundation China Brief* 5, 2005.
22 *Christian Science Monitor*, 27 June 2007.
23 B. Ling, "China's Peacekeeping Diplomacy", *China Rights Forum* 1, 2007, p. 48.
24 S. Staehle, "China's Participation in the United Nations Peacekeeping Regime", MA thesis, Elliott School of International Affairs, George Washington University, 2006.
25 Jianwei, "Managing Conflict", p. 76.
26 Carlson, "More than Just Saying No", p. 218.
27 See D. Roy, *China's Foreign Relations*, London: Macmillan Press, 1998, pp. 147–148.

28 B. Gill, *Rising Star: China's New Security Diplomacy*, Washington DC: Brookings Institution Press, 2007, p. 116.
29 Zhongying, "China's Changing Attitude", p. 91.
30 Carlson, "More than Just Saying No", p. 224.
31 Gill, *Rising Star*, p. 116.
32 Quoted in Y. Choedon, "China's Stand on UN Peacekeeping Operations: Changing Priorities of Foreign Policy", *China Report* 41, 2005, p. 43.
33 Interview with Pentagon official, Washington DC, 5 April 2007.
34 Interview with Zhou Yuxiao, Chinese ambassador, Monrovia, 20 November 2009.
35 H. Wenping, "The Balancing Act of China's Africa Policy", *China Security* 3, 2007, p. 29.
36 Quoted in Fravel, "China's Attitude", p. 1114.
37 Quoted in *ibid.*, pp. 1113–1114.
38 Interview with British diplomat, Addis Ababa, 15 May 2007.
39 Quoted in "Security Council Establishes UN Observer Mission in Angola (MONUA) Mandated to Assist Angolan Parties to Consolidated Peace", UN Security Council, Press Release, SC/6390, 30 June 1997.
40 Quoted in "Security Council Extends Central African Republic Mission Until 15 November", UN Security Council, Press Release, SC/6651, 26 February 1999.
41 J. Dreyer, *The PLA and the Kosovo Conflict*, Carlisle PA: Strategic Studies Institute, 2000, p. 3.
42 T. Saich, *Governance and Politics of China*, Basingstoke: Palgrave, 2001, p. 275.
43 B. Gill and J. Reilly, "Sovereignty, Intervention and Peacekeeping: The View from Beijing", *Survival* 42, 2000, p. 48.
44 Staehle, "China's Participation", p. 41.
45 Interview with a Pentagon official, Washington DC, 5 April 2007.
46 *White Paper on China's National Defence.*
47 Gill and Reilly, "Sovereignty", p. 44.
48 Interview with a Chinese diplomat, Addis Ababa, 15 May 2007.
49 *Washington Post*, 13 June 2008.
50 *Ibid.*
51 Interview with Zhou Yuxiao, Chinese ambassador, Monrovia, 20 November 2009.
52 Interview with Shu Zhan, Chinese ambassador, Asmara, 29 June 2006.
53 *Xinhua*, 28 August 2007.
54 Zhongying, "China's Changing Attitude", p. 97.
55 *China Daily*, 24 July 2007.
56 Zhongying, "China's Changing Attitude", p. 87.
57 Quoted in the *Washington Post*, 24 November 2006.
58 Interview with military attaché, Western embassy, Addis Ababa, 15 May 2007.
59 *People's Daily*, 1 February 2007.
60 *Washington Post*, 24 November 2006.
61 *Ibid.*
62 Thompson, "Beijing's Participation", p. 9.
63 *PLA Daily*, 22 June 2007.
64 Interview with military attaché, Western embassy, Addis Ababa, 15 May 2007.
65 Interview with Shu Zhan, Chinese ambassador to Eritrea, Asmara, 29 June 2006.
66 *Liaowang*, 17 May 1999.
67 *Xinhua*, 27 May 1999.
68 Qin Xiaocheng, "Reflections on 'Globalization' and State Sovereignty", in *International Intervention and State Sovereignty*, Beijing: China Reform Forum, 2003.

69 P. Baehr, "Humanitarian Intervention: A Misnomer", in M. Davis, W. Dietrich, B. Scholdan and D. Sepp (eds), *International Intervention in the Post-Cold War World: Moral Responsibility and Power Politics*, Armonk NY: M.E. Sharpe, 2004, p. 34.
70 *People's Daily*, 21 October 1999.
71 *Xinhua*, 27 February 2006.
72 Quoted in R. Foot, *The Practice of Power*, Oxford: Oxford University Press, 1995, p. 239.
73 Zhongying, "China's Changing Attitude", p. 98.
74 Carlson, "More than Just Saying No", p. 218.
75 *Ibid.*, p. 14.
76 D. Zweig, *Internationalizing China: Domestic Interests and Global Linkages*, Ithaca NY: Cornell University Press, 2002, p. 268.
77 *China Daily*, 16 September 2005.
78 See Y. Sienho, "Towards a Harmonious World: The Roles of the International Law of Co-Progressiveness and Leader States", *Chinese Journal of International Law* 7, 2008, pp. 99–105.
79 Z. Quansheng *Interpreting Chinese Foreign Policy: The Micro-Macro Linkage Approach*, Oxford: Oxford University Press, 1996.
80 H. Yin, *China's Changing Policy on UN Peacekeeping Operations*, Stockholm: Institute for Security and Development Policy, 2007, p. 54.
81 Carlson, "More than Just Saying No", p. 234.
82 *Ibid.*, p. 224.
83 Interview with Shu Zhan, Chinese ambassador to Eritrea, Asmara, 29 June 2006.
84 R. Foot, "Chinese Power and the Idea of a Responsible State", *China Journal* 45, 2001, p. 14.
85 K. Lee, "China and the International Covenant on Civil and Political Rights: Prospects and Challenges", *Chinese Journal of International Law* 6, 2007, p. 452.
86 R. Peerenboom, "Assessing Human Rights in China: Why the Double Standard?", *Cornell International Law Journal* 38, 2005, n. 18.
87 Interview with Zhou Yuxiao, Chinese ambassador, Monrovia, 20 November 2009.
88 Interview with Naison Ngoma, African Union official, Addis Ababa, 15 May 2007.
89 Carlson, "More than Just Saying No", p. 230.

6 Indian peacekeeping and the performance of the United Nations Mission in the Democratic Republic of Congo

Zachariah Mampilly[1]

Introduction

In 1908, Winston Churchill, then the undersecretary of state for the colonies, visited East Africa. During his tour of the region, he praised the role of Sikh soldiers within Britain's imperial army, complimenting their "honourable part in the conquest and pacification of these East African countries".[2] Though India has long had direct ties to Africa, prior to their deployment as part of the British Royal Army, there had never been an instance of Indian military personnel fighting anywhere on the African continent.[3] This changed during the second half of the nineteenth century when Indian soldiers were frequently stationed throughout the Indian Ocean rim – from Burma and Malaya in the east to Kenya and Sudan in Africa – to quell nativist challenges to the empire's dominion claims.[4]

This chapter examines recent Indian peacekeeping efforts in Africa, drawing on the experiences of Indian peacekeepers in the Democratic Republic of Congo (DRC). What determines the success or failure of Indian peacekeepers in Africa? The chapter argues that Indian troops succeed in peacekeeping operations when commanders on the ground are empowered to make decisions regarding civilian protection. However, since peacekeeping is central to India's own ambitions within the UN and other international forums, peacekeeping missions are rarely designed to decentralize the command structure. There is an unavoidable tension as debates unfolding at the international level affect the performance and capacity of Indian contingents at the local level.

New Delhi has long invested in promoting goodwill among African states by participating in UN peacekeeping operations. As part of a broader push to build stronger ties to African countries, India has redoubled its commitment to peacekeeping efforts over the past decade, and in the views of many in the UN peacekeeping system, the capacity of Indian military contingents makes them essential to any peacekeeping effort on the continent.

Yet remarkably little is actually known about how Indian troops perform on the ground. This chapter examines the actual performance of Indian peacekeepers in Africa. The focus is on the period from 2008 to 2012, during which India reached a nadir in its performance in Congo followed by several important reforms that led to considerable praise. Though India participates in a wide variety of missions across the continent, the DRC case is significant as it is the most high-profile of India's deployments abroad and represents India's largest investment in an African peacekeeping operation thus far.

The chapter demonstrates that India's strategy of using peacekeeping as a tool to push for its broader foreign policy agenda has a significant impact on the success or failure of international peacekeeping missions in Africa. India, alongside South Africa and Brazil, has been pushing for greater influence over the evolution of peacekeeping and humanitarian intervention.[5] We examine how ongoing debates at the UN headquarters in New York, triggered by disagreements with the three UN Security Council permanent members (Great Britain, France, and the United States) over the application of the Responsibility to Protect (RtoP) in the Libyan conflict, and encapsulated most recently in the debate over "Responsibility while Protecting", affect peacekeeping performance in Africa. As with the role of Indian soldiers during the colonial period, there is an increasing sense that the Indian role in peacekeeping missions has been primarily the provision of labour without the capacity to influence the decision to intervene or the nature of the mandate in the first place. As India seeks to exert its rising influence internationally, the question of peacekeeping mandates and to what degree India is able to define them is increasingly shaping the outcome of peacekeeping missions in Africa.

Research for this chapter was conducted during a trip to North Kivu in the DRC in March of 2012 (and builds on an earlier visit in 2009). During two weeks in the country, interviews were conducted with peacekeepers associated with the mission in North Kivu (both civilian and military), members of the UN, especially those affiliated with the Department of Peacekeeping Operations (DPKO) in the DRC, outside observers of the mission drawn from local think tanks and NGOs working in the region, and local Congolese civilians affected by the mission.

Indian peacekeeping in Africa

India has had several motivations for its involvement in African peacekeeping. During the Cold War, its primary concern was to bolster the UN as a neutral institution through which the countries of the Third World could articulate claims to equity within the international system. In addition, involvement in peacekeeping missions was seen as a resource both to improve the capacity of the Indian military and to secure lucrative mission reimbursements. More recently, the country has sought to use peacekeeping to bolster its claim for a seat on the UN Security Council (UNSC), as detailed in a later section.

India does have a long history of peacekeeping in Africa. Though the country first became involved with peacekeeping to uphold the Korean Armistice Agreement of 1953, its role was limited to providing medical support. India also played a minor role in resolving the crisis in the Suez Canal in 1956. But its first major involvement in a complex peacekeeping operation was as part of the UN Operation in Congo from 1960 to 1964. The Congo intervention was unique in that it was the first UN operation in a domestic conflict versus the inter-state wars that defined peacekeeping efforts throughout most of the Cold War. India deployed a large contingent of soldiers including an air force bomber detachment.[6] That mission took heavy casualties and India lost 39 men.

Up to 2009, over 100,000 Indians had served in 43 operations around the world, with 130 losing their lives during their deployments abroad.[7] In early 2013, India was the third largest contributor of troops: 7,840 personnel were deployed, operating in nine of the 14 UN peacekeeping operations globally, with the bulk concentrated in South Sudan (1,983) and the DRC (4,032). This put India behind only Pakistan and Bangladesh in total numbers.[8] The country touts its longstanding record of contributing to various missions across Africa including in Somalia, Mozambique, Angola, Sierra Leone, and more recently, the DRC and Sudan/South Sudan. In many of these cases, including the DRC and currently South Sudan, India was the largest troop contributor to the missions. In Somalia, India had operational responsibilities for a third of the country, the largest ever held by a UN contingent.[9] India's total number of troops represents more than double the amount of peacekeepers deployed by the five permanent members of the Security Council.[10]

Positions abroad are highly sought after by Indian officers and troops. According to officers interviewed in Goma, positions in peacekeeping missions provide an opportunity to gain field experience that is highly valued upon their return to India. Every year, 15,000 troops are selected for a first interview, with 5,000 eventually deployed to various missions following a "pre-induction training" at the Centre for United Nations Peacekeeping in New Delhi. Most troops have little awareness of Africa but receive a series of briefings prior to departure, where they learn the background of the specific mission, the activities of Indian troops, and a general history of the country. Once in country, life is often difficult for the troops, who work six days a week and are prohibited from socializing with the local population due to DPKO restrictions.

Troops interviewed in North Kivu stated that it was "not an easy life over here", while complaining that the "UN is never concerned about the working life of peacekeepers – he's like a slave". Indian troops have been at the centre of a number of sexual scandals in different African countries, a fact often attributed to the difficult and isolating working conditions.[11] As one officer dismissively explained in response to a question about prostitution, "Soldiers have no outlets".

Despite the lacklustre performance of many missions with large Indian contributions, the country does possess several unique competencies that it touts in relation to its African peacekeeping efforts. In addition to its history of peacekeeping and the fact that officers know English (making them accessible to all UN employees), the country also possesses the capacity to provide well-trained troops accustomed to operating in a diverse array of terrain. This is generally credited to the extensive number of operations in which the military engages domestically, often in environments comparable to African conflict zones.[12] More importantly, unlike other leading troop-contributing countries such as Pakistan and Bangladesh, India possesses "standalone capability" to support a peacekeeping operation on its own. Its history as one of the leading arms buyers – in 2012, the largest in the world – also means that Indian troops are familiar with state-of-the-art equipment including a wide variety of weapons and systems supplied by all the major arms-producing countries such as the United States, the United Kingdom and importantly, due to the lack of interoperability between their systems and those of the Western powers, Russia.

India also provides regular training to African military officers. Currently, Indian army training teams are operating in six countries including four in Africa. In addition, the country's military academies regularly host African officers in India, especially in recent times from Kenya, Mauritius, Namibia, Nigeria, South Africa, Sudan, Tanzania, Zambia and Zimbabwe.[13] As a result of these initiatives, the country is often preferred by many African governments due to their familiarity with the Indian military.

Indian peacekeeping performance in the Democratic Republic of Congo

The UN Mission in the Democratic Republic of Congo (known here by its French acronym MONUC) began in 1999 when the Security Council authorized a Chapter VI peacekeeping mission with 500 military observers to help monitor the shaky Lusaka ceasefire agreement. Recognizing its inadequacy, in February 2000, the Council authorized a relatively small Chapter VII mission of 5,537 troops to help oversee the faulty peace process in the DRC.[14] By July of 2007, it had ballooned to over 22,000 uniformed personnel (not including civilian staff) at an annual cost of over US$1 billion per year, the largest military force in the history of peacekeeping operations. These personnel were drawn from over 60 countries.

In July of 2010, MONUC changed its name to the Stabilization Mission in the Democratic Republic of Congo (MONUSCO) to reflect a perceived shift from a conflict to a post-conflict context. For 2012 to 2013, MONUSCO's budget is estimated at slightly under US$1.4 billion.[15] India's contribution of between 4,000 to 5,000 troops to the Congolese mission(s) makes it the largest contributor to the largest peacekeeping mission in the world.[16] Yet the vast size of the DRC means that only one soldier is responsible for every 1,100 civilians. Put in geographic terms, this means that each Indian soldier is responsible for patrolling 12 square kilometers of territory in North Kivu.[17]

Based in Goma with multiple bases scattered throughout North Kivu, India has been central to the Congolese mission, as it is the only troop contributor willing *and* able to provide air support and other advanced military gear.[18] In 2003, the country deployed the Indian Aviation Contingent (IAC-1) to North Kivu, a unit that included four Mi-25s (one squadron), a Russian-built attack helicopter, and five Mi-17 transport helicopters (one squadron) split between bases in Goma and Bunia. This gave the Indian peacekeepers both the ability to patrol very remote parts of Congo, and the capacity to provide air support against combatants that frequently resorted to guerrilla tactics to undercut the mission's ground forces.

The performance of Indian troops in the DRC has involved a number of setbacks over the first decade of the mission, followed by a brief yet noticeable improvement in their performance beginning in late 2008. Prior to 2008, Indian peacekeepers and MONUC in general had weathered a variety of criticisms related to their performance, both from local Congolese and from international observers. Foremost among these was a consistent inability to carry out the mission's mandate of civilian protection. In addition, the mission has been accused of corruption, sexual misconduct, and favouritism towards the various anti-government militias operating in the region. Indian peacekeepers have also been accused of extensive involvement in the region's illicit trade in natural resources, especially gold.[19] A number of reasons have been offered for these failures, ranging from the complexity of the mandate to the relatively small size of the force, but misbehavior on the part of the troops has been a consistent concern.

Responding to multiple claimants from a variety of sources, a preliminary investigation by the UN's Office of Internal Oversight (OIOS) in February of 2008 listed 44 allegations of misbehavior between late 2005 and October 2007, with investigators collecting substantial evidence on at least ten of the accusations. Among these were accusations of gold smuggling, sexual trafficking and abuse of local women, information sharing and weapons trading with the militias that still render eastern DRC a dangerous place, unlawful detention of Congolese citizens, and the illicit use of MONUC equipment and resources.[20] Although the report received coverage in the national and international media including the BBC, it never led to a comprehensive investigation by OIOS. Despite the lack of formal prosecutions, MONUC came in for harsh criticism from national and international sources, much to the chagrin of Indian government officials, who felt the country was being unfairly blamed for the failure of the mission.[21] A low point was reached when Congolese civilians, encouraged by local politicians, pelted rocks at all four MONUC bases in Goma in

2008.[22] One such attack north of Goma resulted in an Indian officer being critically wounded.

The Kiwanja massacre and the rise of locally-driven peacekeeping

The nadir of the Indian experience was reached at the local, national and international level in late 2008, following a series of events that, on 4–5 November, led to the deaths of at least 150 civilians in a little over 24 hours, less than half a mile away from a MONUC base in the town of Kiwanja. In response to what has become known as the Kiwanja Massacre, which led to many negative reports regarding Indian performance, a number of reforms were enacted that significantly improved Indian peacekeeping performance by empowering local level commanders.

In August of 2008, fighting recommenced between the forces of the National Congress for the Defence of the People (CNDP) led by Laurent Nkunda, a Congolese Tutsi leader initially supported by Rwanda, and the national army, despite a ceasefire agreement signed between the two in January of the same year. The Congolese army launched an offensive, but was overwhelmed by CNDP forces with the rebels quickly capturing the towns of Rutshuru (and its smaller neighbor Kiwanja) and Masisi. CNDP leaders informed MONUC that they were in control and appointed their own territorial administrator, Jules Simpenzwe. Indian peacekeepers were blamed for being sympathetic to the CNDP and allowing them to take over by September of 2008, and relations between them and local Congolese officials deteriorated even further.[23] According to Human Rights Watch, "crowds in North Kivu stoned MONUC and UN vehicles, erected barricades to impede their movement, and demonstrated outside MONUC bases. Congolese army soldiers were seen organizing such 'popular' actions and participating in them".[24] The consequences of the demonstrations were significant, including injuries to 20 peacekeepers and damage to at least 25 vehicles.

Things only deteriorated from this point. On 4 November 2008, a group of Mai Mai soldiers, nativist militias suspicious of the CNDP's pro-Tutsi bent, launched a surprise attack on Kiwanja.[25] Numbering over 200 strong, Mai Mai forces were initially effective and able to briefly retake the town. On the morning of 5 November, the CNDP counter-attacked and by 2pm had regained control. Members of the CNDP under the command of its military chief, Bosco Ntaganda, then went from door to door in Kiwanja looking for young men and boys who were accused of collaborating with the Mai Mai. Many were summarily executed. Older men and women were also killed and a large number of women were raped or sexually assaulted. By the time it was over, around 150 people lay dead, most killed intentionally by combatants (including Mai Mai forces) while others died in the course of the fighting itself.

The 2008 Human Rights Watch report blamed MONUC for relying too heavily on the Congolese army, the *Forces Armées de la République Démocratique du Congo* (FARDC) – with which it was meant to engage in joint operations but had often had difficult relations – to fulfil its primary mandate of civilian protection. Many civilians actually fled to the MONUC base, which was staffed with about 120 troops, seeking refuge, but peacekeepers instead focused on "assuring the security of humanitarian workers, a foreign journalist, and a group of military observers, rather than protecting the civilian population".[26]

When the attack took place, Indian troops were manning the base, but had begun to be rotated out to be replaced by a Uruguayan contingent. As a result, during this period, Indian troops had especially poor logistics with limited access to a single interpreter speaking French and Kiswahili, North Kivu's lingua franca. In addition, there was a shortage of equipment and men, and confusing commands emanated from the MONUC command in Goma, according to the Indian commander of the base, Lt. Col. H.S. Brar.[27] The rotation of contingents also meant that the base lacked useful military intelligence or even the capacity to analyse any intelligence they did have.[28] In addition, MONUC's attention was focused on protecting the provincial capital, Goma, with its large expatriate population, not Rutshuru.

In fairness, the mission also faced a number of challenges that would have been hard to overcome regardless of its other failings. Only about a third of the mission, or 6,000 troops, were based in North Kivu during MONUC's battles with Nkunda as compared to the 10,000 strong CNDP force. In addition, Nkunda's reliance on hit-and-run tactics had a significant impact on MONUC forces, which were dispersed widely through the territory and hence susceptible to such attacks.[29] The mission's complex mandate, of protecting civilians while disarming rebel fighters *and* policing buffer zones separating insurgents from Congolese troops, also hindered their ability to fulfil their obligations.

The condemnation of MONUC's performance was universal, especially once it became known that most of the contingent remained unaware of the massacre until after it was over.[30] Indian troops took the bulk of the blame and the government chafed at the extensive and often brutal criticism, especially considering the casualties suffered by the Indian contingent as a result of the fighting with Nkunda's forces.

The response to the Kiwanja massacre demonstrates the dramatic disconnect between policies pursued at the national and international level and the ability of commanders to adjust their behavior at the local level. At the national level, in November 2008, the Congolese government asked Indian troops to leave the country, only changing their tune in response to US prodding in early 2009. At the international level, India first threatened to cancel new deployments due to the negative coverage of both the Kiwanja massacre and the sex abuse scandals.[31]

But at the local level, the Indian contingent in North Kivu implemented a number of reforms that drastically improved the performance of peacekeepers and were hailed as a model for other peacekeeping missions, as detailed below. Three weeks before the CNDP pulled out of the ceasefire in mid-2008, Bipin Rawat, an Indian Major-General, was appointed as the Commander of all UN troops in North Kivu.[32] At the same time, an ex-Oxfam employee and human rights lawyer from Ethiopia, Hiroute Guebre Selassie, was appointed as the civilian head of the UN peacekeeping force in North Kivu. Following the Kiwanja massacre (for which they received little blame as the CNDP crisis had begun just three weeks into their tenure), the civilian and military commands were brought together by Rawat and Guebre Selassie to take stock of the mission. It was quickly recognized that the overarching problem for MONUC was that though the mission's ostensible focus was meant to be on protection of civilians, there was no specific strategy in place to do so.[33] Instead, too often, civilian protection was subsumed by a variety of other confusing mandates emanating from different sites.

The central issues identified during the evaluation process included the "information vacuum" that characterized relations between the peacekeepers and local communities; the lack of direct mechanisms for civilians to report abuses directly to the military command; the inability of populations to organize to protect themselves; and the lack of civilians to work within the base to network and ensure communication with the local community.[34] In addition, a number of military challenges were identified such as the lack of appropriate weaponry, including all-terrain vehicles to traverse the difficult road network in North Kivu; a shortage of armoured vehicles to offset the insurgents' ability to use heavy weaponry; insufficient night-flying equipment for the helicopters; confusing directions from the head office in Goma that required the base in Rutshuru to divert resources to alternate agendas beyond the prime mandate of civilian protection; and constrictive rules of engagement that required MONUC troops to announce their presence with verbal warnings and shots fired in the air prior to engaging the rebels, hence denying the mission the element of surprise.[35]

To rectify these shortcomings, a number of changes were made that either rejuvenated existing DPKO practices or sought to devise new approaches. Working together, the civilian and military teams introduced a number of reforms including the creation of Joint Protection Teams that brought together various UN military and police personnel with MONUC Civil Affairs, Human Rights, and Child Protection staff operating from within the mission's forward military bases; Early Warning Systems for which the Indian contingent paid for mobile phones to distribute to civilians to alert peacekeepers to disturbances; Community Alert Networks which provided a way for local civilians to contact the base via a basic closed cellular network 24 hours a day; Community Liaison Assistants

(CLAs), which empowered existing Congolese translators to serve as the eyes and ears of the mission by operating within the community to gather information, a MONUC innovation; and a renewed focus on Quick Impact Projects, which were civilian outreach campaigns in which the bases organized games and vocational training and provided other gifts to local communities with money provided by the mission.[36]

In addition, Indian and South African contingents in North Kivu attempted to broaden their presence in the province by employing Standing Combat Deployments, in which approximately 30 to 35 troops are temporarily deployed to vulnerable towns without UN bases with the goal of stabilizing the situation, restoring civilian confidence in the mission, and providing a sense of security.[37] The mission also began utilizing additional foot patrols, including night patrols, in order to foster more direct connections with local communities. Numerous informants in Goma praised the Indian contingent for doing more of this than contingents from other countries.

Most importantly, the mission adopted a more decentralized structure allowing commanders to make decisions outside of their strict military remit. This reform was important as the behavior of individual peacekeepers on the ground is often determined by the initiatives of their specific commander.[38] By empowering commanders to engage in locally targeted actions that could generate goodwill, the mission also sought to alleviate the widely held perception that the peacekeepers were too sympathetic to renegade militias. The reform process was bolstered by UNSC Resolution 1856 of 22 December 2008, which renewed MONUC's mandate for an additional year and called for the mission to attach the highest priority to the protection of civilians, a first for a UN peacekeeping mission.[39] In addition, both Guebre Selassie and Rawat took their campaign to the international media, strongly criticizing the structure and mandate of the mission and seeking to garner support for the changes they hoped to implement.[40]

Though it is difficult to offer a comprehensive assessment of the perceptions of civilians living in North Kivu, at the international level the reforms were widely praised. For example, the 2009 *United Nations Peace Operations Year in Review* touted the reforms and even went as far as suggesting that they could lead to a "phased troop drawdown" of MONUC forces in 2010.[41] As Guebre Selassie proudly explained, "It was born here, initiated here, piloted here and now it is the best practices of DPKO". She was not alone in this view. An anonymous DPKO consultant who was preparing a comparative study of ongoing peacekeeping missions explained that as a result, "Every village has the perception that the contingent is on their side", and that the mission had become a "standard setter" for DPKO. Outside of the UN system, Aloys Tegera of the Pole Institute suggested that reforms helped the mission "to freeze the conflict situation", though he went on to compare the situation to a boiling pot, suggesting that MONUC's reforms "put a lid on it, but cannot touch what is inside ... it is too hot".[42] A report by Refugees International suggested that as a result of the reforms, "MONUSCO is at the forefront of innovative tactics to protect civilians".[43]

Return to the status quo? Geopolitical developments and the neutering of the local peacekeeping initiative

Despite the clear improvement in performance in 2009 and 2010, and especially that of the Indian contingent, the story of peacekeeping in North Kivu province is not one of unmitigated success since the 2008 reforms. According to one close observer of the mission, at the "end of 2011 and beginning 2012, all the good practices developed previously were abandoned by MONUSCO". As a result, there have been a number of setbacks since, including the killing of three Indian peacekeepers in Kirumba camp in North Kivu in August of 2010, and more threateningly the rise of the March 23 (M23) insurgency under the command of the CNDP's Bosco Ntaganda since early 2012. After the initial success of the reforms, why did the mission abandon them so quickly?

What is distinctive about MONUC's performance in the aftermath of the Kiwanja massacre was that local commanders were empowered, albeit briefly, to determine their approach to community relations. In other words, commanders on the ground were able to exert a degree of influence in relation to how the operation fulfils its mandate, thereby bringing about performance improvements. This was a departure from the usual norm in which commanders on the ground are simply responding to directives coming from above. However, peacekeeping remains an essentially political pursuit, one defined by the struggle of states for influence within international bodies, and a return to the status quo was inevitable. In other words, national and international agendas continue to trump local initiatives.[44] This gap between the debates occurring and decisions made in New York or Kinshasa versus the reality of the local conditions peacekeepers face on the ground structurally favours the international body.

In 2011, the intervention in Libya set the stage for a standoff that allowed the Indian government to reassert its primacy over the nature of the mission's mandate, with direct consequences for peacekeeping performance in North Kivu. On 17 March of 2011, the Security Council passed Resolution 1973 establishing a no-fly zone in Libya and authorizing the use of force for the protection of civilians. Ten countries including the United Kingdom, France and the United States, the so-called P-3, voted in the affirmative, with five countries including India, Brazil, Germany and two permanent members, China and Russia, abstaining after strained negotiations.

The actual conduct of the Libya campaign further incensed the abstaining Council members. Once the campaign began, it became clear that the

P-3 countries, which retain the power to draft Security Council resolutions, were pushing for a regime change, a position that the abstainers felt went outside the boundaries of the mandate itself. Though the intervention could not be stopped once it had begun, the Libyan war triggered a broader debate about one of the central questions driving peacekeeping missions in the contemporary period, the meaning and practice of the evolving international norm of the Responsibility to Protect (RtoP).

The concern for India was whether its participation in peacekeeping missions was merely designed to advance the agendas of Western powers or was truly in line with historical Indian foreign policy values and objectives. In other words, was India's contribution to peacekeeping merely an echo of colonial Indian troops bolstering the British Empire or the symbol of a rising power claiming its rightful place within the global community? As one leading Indian foreign policy figure suggested, RtoP is perceived by many developing countries "as yet another attempt by the more powerful members of the developed world to impose their value systems on the weaker states".[45] For India, blindly supporting RtoP through its contributions to peacekeeping missions while allowing the P-3 to retain control over defining peacekeeping mandates produced a deep sense of unease. Many in the foreign policy establishment felt that Indian troops were again being deployed to bolster the foreign policy preferences of Western powers. As the Indian Permanent Representative to the UN, Hardeep Singh Puri, bluntly put it, "The principle of RtoP is being selectively used to promote national interest rather than protect civilians".[46]

The basic tension for India is its role in contributing troops to peacekeeping missions – often undertaken without the country playing a direct role in devising the mandate – and its historic support for the centrality of sovereignty in the current international order, particularly when it is perceived as being abrogated by more powerful states. During the Cold War, reflecting its limited strength as a middling global power, India could participate on the basis of being a good citizen within the global community. Support for peacekeeping operations even helped bolster India's claim to non-alignment and its historical emphasis on the importance of the UN as a politically neutral space for the countries of the Third World. But the end of the Cold War and the subsequent politicization of the humanitarian discourse mean that India can no longer participate in "neutral" humanitarian interventions without contradicting many of its central and long-standing foreign policy positions, including respect for state sovereignty, independence and territorial integrity of states, and peaceful settlement of disputes with the use of force being the last resort.[47]

India sought to retain some commitment to its principles by retaining ties to the Gaddafi regime after it was clear that the Western powers were intent on its removal, even inviting a Libyan delegation to attend the second Africa-India Forum Summit held in Addis Ababa in May 2011. During the summit, India's External Affairs Minister, S.M. Krishna, met on the sidelines with Libya's Foreign Minister, Abdal al Latti al Obedi, expressing regret for the NATO-led airstrikes and urging an immediate ceasefire. The declaration that ended the conference chastised NATO, calling for its efforts to remain "within the spirit and letter of those resolutions". It also urged both parties to the conflict to strive for a political solution and expressed support for the marginalized African Union (AU) High-Level Ad hoc Committee initiative and the AU roadmap for the peaceful and consensual resolution of the conflict.[48]

The leverage the Indians have to push for a greater voice within the Security Council around peacekeeping missions has been its capacity and willingness to deploy aerial power, a key component of the missions in Sudan and the DRC. Towards this end, parallel to the debate unfolding around Libya and RtoP, in July of 2011, India began threatening to withdraw its four remaining Mi-35 helicopters from MONUSCO (as well as helicopters delegated to the United Nations Mission in Sudan) when its contract ended on 4 July, unless troop-contributing countries were given a greater say in designing peacekeeping missions, much to the chagrin of the P-3. One close observer of the Council noted that the debate was the "most acrimonious" she had ever witnessed.[49]

With few exceptions, notably South Africa and Ukraine, no other country has the capacity or the will to provide helicopters consistently, which makes the Indian threat a substantive one.[50] Although the government claimed that it faced a domestic need for the helicopters to fight its internal Maoist insurgency – a position bolstered by a damning Comptroller and Auditor General report that suggested that operational shortages faced by the Indian Army in its battle with domestic insurgents were directly linked to its participation in UN missions – it was widely perceived as a power play by the Indian government to assert more influence over the direction of future peacekeeping mandates.[51] Leading Indian voices have long called for leveraging India's contributions to peacekeeping in order to "insist on adequate representation at the UN Headquarters and on decision-making mechanisms there".[52] India's Deputy Ambassador to the UN, Manjeev Singh Puri, also spoke openly about the need for "more consultation" with key troop-contributing countries about the mandate of peacekeeping missions.[53]

At the same time, India was about to serve its term as President of the Security Council, during which the Council was set to host an "Open Debate on Peacekeeping" at the country's urging, rendering its threat far more resonant. In addition, both Brazil and South Africa, India's rising power allies through groupings such as IBSA (India, Brazil and South Africa) and BRICS (Brazil, Russia, India, China and South Africa), were also rotating members of the Council with similar misgivings about the Libyan intervention. With the IBSA countries in agreement, both China and Russia would feel compelled to agree.[54] Prior to the debate in August, India circulated a memo entitled, "Peacekeeping: taking stock and preparing for the future". In the memo, India highlighted the importance of host government consent and RtoP's implications for state sovereignty, calling for peacekeeping missions to be treated as a "partnership" between the Security Council, the General Assembly and the troop-contributing countries, rather than the preserve of the P-3. In addition, the memo repeated India's longstanding concern that peacekeeping mandates continued to underestimate the resources necessary, with troop-contributing countries bearing the bulk of the blame when these missions failed.[55]

In September 2011, Brazilian President Dilma Rousseff introduced the idea of a "responsibility while protecting" (RwP) to regulate future RtoP missions during her speech to the UN General Assembly. That November, Brazil circulated a concept note arguing that RtoP, as became apparent during the Libyan intervention, needed to be supplemented with an additional set of principles and procedures under the rubric of RwP. The two key proposals made by the Brazilians with the support of the BRICS, especially the IBSA grouping, included a set of criteria requiring that last resort, proportionality, and a balance of consequences should be taken into consideration before the use of force is authorized, and a monitoring-and-review mechanism to ensure that Security Council mandates are seriously debated by all the members, and not just the P-3.[56] One reading of the proposal is that the Council would have greater operational control over Western military operations, including those orchestrated by NATO forces, an idea which was anathema to the P-3.[57]

Effects on peacekeeping in Africa

The overall effect of this debate has been to weaken the capacity of Indian peacekeepers on the ground in the DRC and Sudan, leading directly to increased civilian suffering. Stung by the lacklustre response from the P-3 to its initiatives to reform peacekeeping, the Indian government has reduced its support for the DRC mission while undercutting the capacity of commanders on the ground to have operational control over the mission. For example, the MONUSCO Force Commander, Lt. Gen. Chander Prakash, explicitly withdrew support for foot patrols and other reforms designed to increase interaction between peacekeepers and civilians after being appointed to the position in 2010.[58] In line with India's complaints about the mismatch between mandates and resources, Prakash began parroting, in a variety of venues, the official Indian position that resource shortages undermined the capacity of the mission to adequately fulfil its mandate of civilian protection.[59] This was despite the fact that most of the reforms instigated by Indian commanders in North Kivu did not require additional financial outlays.

Most importantly, despite agreeing to return its helicopter to North Kivu, the Indian government decided to replace the eight Mi-25/35 attack helicopters and nine Mi-17 transport helicopters deployed to the missions in the DRC and Sudan with six light utility helicopters manufactured in India (Chetak and Cheetah). Beyond the net reduction in the number of helicopters, the Indian-made helicopters have significantly less military capacity than the Russian-made Mi's and can only undertake surveillance, observation, search and rescue, medical and reconnaissance missions.[60] By late 2011, the situation became so dire that Secretary-General Ban Ki-Moon even drafted a letter to the Council warning that lack of helicopters has made the situation "critical" and called for members to "think outside the box" to cover the shortfall.[61] Ukraine offered four Mi-24 attack helicopters in March of 2012 and South Africa provided some transport helicopters to cover the shortfall, but neither has been willing to make the long-term commitment necessary to retain MONUSCO's aerial advantage.

In March of 2012, a group of ex-CNDP soldiers loyal to Bosco Ntaganda mutinied from the Congolese Army. Claiming that the government had failed to implement the 23 March 2009 peace agreement with the CNDP, the group adopted the moniker M23 for itself. In a striking repeat of events that took place in 2008, M23 quickly set about taking control of large territories in North Kivu, including the towns of Bunagana on the Ugandan border, and marched on to Rutshuru and Rugari despite the presence of an Indian contingent at the Kiwanja base. M23's advance led to a massive humanitarian crisis that MONUSCO has appeared incapable of stopping. Both the rebels and government forces are accused of numerous war crimes since fighting began, including the summary executions of civilians, mass rapes, and forced recruitment including children, directly leading to the displacement of hundreds of thousands of people.[62] Though most Congolese Tutsi remain wary of the movement, fearing its clear ties to the Rwandan government and its seeming economic (rather than political) focus, attacks by nativist Mai-Mai forces against the Banyamulenge persist, and may have the effect of driving the community into the arms of the insurgents.

It is impossible to know to what degree the weakening of the Indian contribution to MONUSCO allowed this new insurgency to take hold in North Kivu. However, available evidence suggests that the mission has been affected by the shift in approach and lacks the capacity to effectively prevent M23 from attacking civilians, despite the group possessing significantly less military power than its predecessor, the CNDP.[63] As the International Crisis Group notes, the failure to prevent M23's rise is related to the "militarily passive" behavior of MONUSCO and demonstrates the "ineffectiveness" of the mission.[64] Relations with Congolese civilians have also severely declined, and both local and national political leaders have again criticized the mission's performance, a dramatic turnaround from the praise showered on it following the post-Kiwanja reforms.[65]

In July 2012, following the recapture of several towns by joint FARDC/MONUSCO teams, a ceasefire was agreed between M23 and the Congolese government. Yet fighting has continued intermittently, leading the

UN to announce the creation of a 3,000-strong "Intervention Brigade" with the explicit intention of strengthening MONUSCO's offensive abilities.[66] In a first for a UN peacekeeping mission, the brigade, staffed primarily with contributors from other African nations, was empowered to carry out targeted offensive operations against armed groups and achieved considerable success routing out the forces of M23 in November 2013.

Conclusion

Indian contributions to peacekeeping are an integral component of UN peacekeeping missions and serve an important role in promoting the country's foreign policy objectives. As part of its broader push in to Africa, peacekeeping remains central to India's ambitions to strengthen its ties to the continent. The country's involvement in peacekeeping is also central to its efforts to garner greater status within international bodies by generating support from among African countries for its campaign for a permanent seat on the Security Council. This strategy has even borne fruit outside of the continent, as evidenced by US President Barack Obama's statement in support of an Indian seat during which he cited the country's involvement in peacekeeping as a key reason for American support.[67]

Yet the country risks squandering this goodwill by politicizing its peacekeeping efforts at the expense of the performance of specific missions. In particular, the DRC case demonstrates that India may undermine any goodwill by ignoring the judgment of those best suited to improve the performance of its peacekeepers, i.e. its own commanders on the ground. The key lesson from India's involvement in the DRC is that the performance of peacekeeping missions, particularly in relation to civilian protection, is likely to be undermined when the country views peacekeeping merely as a tool through which to advance its broader foreign policy objectives. Instead, the country should seek to divorce its individual decisions regarding peacekeeping allocations from the larger geopolitical context. Failing to do so may undermine its own objectives as actions undertaken to generate goodwill instead promote animosity due to weak performance on the ground.

There are several lessons to be drawn from the Congolese case, and in particular India's role within it, for peacekeeping in Africa. First, UN peacekeeping, particularly in regards to protection of civilians, is more effective when local commanders are empowered to make decisions regarding civilian outreach. This is in line with much recent scholarship on the DRC, and civil wars more generally, that stresses the importance of micro-dynamics on patterns of violence.[68] It only follows that if violence in complex civil wars like those in the DRC and Sudan is driven by primarily local-level factors then solutions must also emphasize local-level initiatives.

Second, despite the above, national and international dynamics will always trump local initiatives. Regardless of the performance of local commanders, international and national political dynamics are far more determinative of the performance of peacekeepers than local dynamics. Decisions about how resources are allocated flow from the top down, often ignoring bottom-up concerns, and leading to irresolvable mismatches between peacekeeping mandates and how resources are allocated on the ground.

Finally, the ongoing transformations of the geopolitical system are likely to have lasting impacts on the structure and performance of future peacekeeping initiatives. The rise of the IBSA countries in particular will require the P-3 to cede some degree of control over the design of peacekeeping mandates, a position it is likely to reject. As the debate around RwP demonstrates, the prior division between troop-contributing countries and those that pay for the missions, in which the former cede any influence over the design of peacekeeping mandates, is no longer stable. Increasingly, countries such as India are not only demanding a say in devising the mandates of peacekeeping operations, but also have the leverage to affect the performance of missions, for better or worse.

Notes

1 The author is grateful to Severine Autesserre, Bruce Heilmann, Issa Shivji, Marco Wyss, and Thierry Tardy for their comments. He also appreciated the excellent research assistance of Kartik Kapoor. Earlier versions of this chapter were presented at the conference on International Peacekeeping in Africa in Zurich, Switzerland, 2012, and the conference on India in Africa in Dar es Salaam, Tanzania, 2013.

2 W. Churchill, *My African Journey*, Toronto: William Briggs, 1909, p. 49.

3 In contrast, African soldiers were frequently valued members of the armies of various South Asian kingdoms during the pre-colonial period, either as slave warriors or as mercenaries.

4 S. Bose, *A Hundred Horizons: The Indian Ocean in the Age of Global Empire*, Cambridge MA: Harvard University Press, 2006, pp. 123–147.

5 The three countries are the sole members of the India, Brazil, South Africa Dialogue Forum (IBSA) that was founded in 2003 to push for reforms of major international institutions.

6 N.K. Pant, "India's Peacekeeping Missions", Article 340, Institute of Peace and Conflict Studies, 23 March 2000.

7 T.S. Chinna, "For the Honour of India: A History of Indian Peacekeeping", *Journal of the United Service Institution of India* 576, 2009.

8 "Missions Detailed by Country", UNDPKO, 2013, available at www.un.org/en/peacekeeping/contributors/2013/jan13_5.pdf, accessed 20 February 2013; "Country contributions detailed by mission", UNDPKO, 2013, available at www.un.org/en/peacekeeping/contributors/2013/jan13_3.pdf, accessed 20 February 2013; "Ranking of Military and Police Contributions", UNDPKO, 2013, available at www.un.org/en/peacekeeping/contributors/2013/jan13_2.pdf, accessed 20 February 2013.

9 India Strategic, "India to Continue Supporting UN Peacekeeping Operations", 2011, available at www.indiastrategic.in/topstories172.htm, accessed 23 May 2013.

10 C. Lynch, "India's Withdrawal of Helicopters from Congo Points to Wider Trend", *Washington Post*, 14 June 2011.

11 B. Mutumayi, A.K. Sen and S. Datta, "The Peacekeeper's Child: Sexual misconduct by Indian soldiers and officers on UN duty in Congo raises disturbing questions", *Outlook*, 8 August 2011, available at www.outlookindia.com/article.aspx?277848, accessed 23 May 2013.
12 India Strategic, "India to Continue".
13 *Ibid.*
14 A Chapter VI mission is limited to non-coercive functions such as conciliation, mediation and fact-finding, while a Chapter VII mission is authorized to use economic interventions and military coercion.
15 "MONUSCO Facts and Figures", UNDPKO, 2013, available at www.un.org/en/peacekeeping/missions/monusco/facts.shtml, accessed 20 February 2013.
16 The United Nations–African Union Hybrid Operation in Darfur (UNAMID) has slightly more troops than MONUSCO currently, but is a joint UN-AU mission rather than a sole UN mission. "Missions Detailed by Country", UNDPKO.
17 D. Smith, "Etiquette, Deference, Tradition and Tea amid an Unsung Tour of Duty", *Guardian*, 3 February 2010.
18 Lynch, "India's Withdrawal".
19 Human Rights Watch, "UN: Tackle Wrongdoing by Peacekeepers: Letter to Secretary-General Ban Ki-Moon", 30 April 2008, available at www.hrw.org/news/2008/05/01/un-tackle-wrongdoing-peacekeepers, accessed 23 May 2013.
20 *Ibid.*
21 Lynch, "India's Withdrawal".
22 M. Faul, "Congo Conflict Shows Flaws in UN Force", *Independent*, 31 October 2008.
23 This has been a consistent criticism of MONUC's behavior and has been bolstered by a number of untoward incidents. For example, in 2008, a drunk Indian colonel was recorded as praising Laurent Nkunda's fighting abilities, according to a United States cable released by Wiki Leaks (cited in Lynch, "India's Withdrawal").
24 Human Rights Watch, "Killings in Kiwanja: The UN's Inability to Protect Civilians", New York, December 2008, p. 22.
25 *Ibid.* Mai Mai are officially independent of the national army, but are often deployed by it to do the "dirty work" against the Democratic Forces for the Liberation of Rwanda (referred to by its French acronym FDLR,) in the words of one high ranking MONUSCO civilian officer.
26 Human Rights Watch, "Killings in Kiwanja", p. 2.
27 L. Polgreen, "A Massacre in Congo, Despite Nearby Support", *New York Times*, 11 December 2008; S. Wambua, "Revisiting DR Congo's Massacre Site", *Al Jazeera*, 24 May 2012.
28 Human Rights Watch, "Killings in Kiwanja", p. 22.
29 Faul, "Congo Conflict".
30 Wambua, "Revisiting".
31 *Asian Age*, cited in China View, "India Cancels New UN Peacekeeping Mission in Congo over Scandal", 9 March 2009, available at http://news.xinhuanet.com/english/2009–03/09/content_10975745.htm, accessed 23 May 2013.
32 This position is distinct from and subservient to the mission's overall Force Commander, which at the time was held by a Senegalese general.
33 Interview with Hiroute Guebre Selassie, Goma, 7 March 2012.
34 Interview with Selassie; Polgreen, "Massacre in Congo".
35 Polgreen, "Massacre in Congo"; D. Blair, "UN Commander says Hands are Tied in Congo", *The Telegraph*, 17 November 2008.
36 Interview with Selassie; anonymous UNDPKO Consultant, Goma, 8 March

2012; Refugees International, "DR Congo: Support Community-Based Tools for MONUSCO", 2011, available at www.refintl.org/policy/field-report/drc-support-community-based-tools-monusco, accessed 23 May 2013.

37 Refugees International, "DR Congo", p. 3.
38 Interview with anonymous MONUSCO civilian official, Goma, 7 March 2012.
39 J. Reynaert, "MONUC/MONUSCO and Civilian Protection in the Kivus", International Peace Information Service, 2011, available at www.ipisresearch.be/publications_detail.php?id=327, accessed 23 May 2013.
40 Blair, "UN Commander"; M. Kelemen, "In Congo, U.N. Official Sees Limits Of Diplomacy", *National Public Radio*, 15 December 2008, available at www.npr.org/templates/story/story.php?storyId=98293184, accessed 23 May 2013.
41 UNDPKO, "MONUC: A Watershed Year for the Protection of Civilians", in *United Nations Peace Operations Year in Review 2009*, New York, pp. 27–30.
42 Interview with Aloys Tegera, Goma, 7 March 2012.
43 Refugees International, "DR Congo".
44 S. Autesserre, *The Trouble with the Congo: Local Violence and the Failure of International Peacebuilding*, New York: Cambridge University Press, 2010.
45 S. Nambiar, "Robust Peacekeeping Operations, Rapid Deployment Capability of the UN: An Indian Perspective", *Journal of the United Service Institution of India* 566, 2012.
46 V. Prashad, "Syria, Libya and Security Council: Interview with Hardeep Singh Puri, Permanent Representative of India to the United Nations", *Frontline* 29, 10–23 March 2012.
47 K. Kumar, "India's Past Year at the UN Security Council", *IDSA Comment*, Institute for Defence Studies and Analyses, 7 February 2012.
48 S. Varadarajan, "India, Africa call for End to Libya Bombing", *The Hindu*, 26 May 2011.
49 Interview with Kirsten Hagan, Oxfam, Goma, 6 March 2012.
50 Interview with Hagan (Oxfam); Lynch, "India's Withdrawal".
51 Pragmatic Euphony, "Indian Helicopter Back in UN Peacekeeping", 8 September 2011, available at http://pragmatic.nationalinterest.in/2011/09/08/indian-helicopters-back-in-un-peacekeeping/, accessed 23 May 2013.
52 Nambiar, "Robust Peacekeeping".
53 *The Hindu*, "India withdrawing helicopters from U.N.'s Congo Mission", 16 June 2011.
54 Interview with Hagan (Oxfam).
55 What's in Blue, "Peacekeeping Debate Preparations", 12 August 2011, available at www.whatsinblue.org/2011/08/peacekeeping-debate.php, accessed 23 May 2013.
56 G. Evans, "R2P and RWP After Libya and Syria", Global Centre for the Responsibility to Protect, Rio de Janeiro, 23 August 2012, available at www.globalr2p.org/publications/161, accessed 23 May 2013.
57 T. Wright, "Brazil Hosts Workshop on 'Responsibility While Protecting'", Brookings, 12 August 2012, available at www.brookings.edu/research/opinions/2012/08/29-brazil-responsibility-while-protecting-wright, accessed 23 May 2013.
58 Interview with anonymous human rights worker.
59 Relief Web, "General Chander Prakash explains MONUSCO's contingency plan for the next six months", 26 September 2011, available at http://reliefweb.int/report/democratic-republic-congo/general-chander-prakash-explains-monusco%E2%80%99s-contingency-plan-next, accessed 23 May 2013.
60 Pragmatic Euphony, "Indian Helicopter".
61 Ban Ki-Moon, "Letter Dated 20 September 2011 from the Secretary-General Addressed to the President of the Security Council", UN, S/2011/589, 20

September 2011. The letter states that the lack of helicopters will have multiple consequences including the following:

> Joint operations with the Congolese Armed Forces have had to be postponed, investigations of allegations of mass human rights violations have had to be delayed, and some deployments to protection hot-spots have had to be deferred. Getting essential supplies to United Nations troops in far-flung, volatile areas has also been extremely difficult.

62 Human Rights Watch, "DR Congo: M23 Rebels Committing War Crimes", 11 September 2012, available at www.hrw.org/news/2012/09/11/dr-congo-m23-rebels-committing-war-crimes, accessed 23 May 2013.

63 According to the International Crisis Group (ICG), M23 has less than a fifth as many troops at its disposal as did the CNDP, though substantive rumours of Ugandan and Rwandan military involvement compensate for this weakness. ICG, "Eastern Congo: Why Stabilisation Failed", *Africa Briefing* 91, 4 October 2012, p. 11.

64 ICG, "Eastern Congo", pp. 9–13.

65 *Ibid.*, p. 11.

66 "DR Congo Hails UN Attack Force", BBC World News, 29 March 2013, available at www.bbc.co.uk/news/world-africa-21976255, accessed 23 May 2013.

67 B. Obama, "Remarks by the President to the Joint Session of the Indian Parliament in New Delhi, India", The White House, 8 November 2010, available at www.whitehouse.gov/the-press-office/2010/11/08/remarks-president-joint-session-indian-parliament-new-delhi-india, accessed 23 May 2013.

68 S. Kalyvas, *The Logic of Violence in Civil War*, New York: Cambridge University Press, 2006; Autesserre, *The Trouble with the Congo*.

7 *Primus inter pares?*

France and multi-actor peacekeeping in Côte d'Ivoire

Marco Wyss[1]

Introduction

At the height of the so-called post-electoral crisis in Côte d'Ivoire, on 6 April 2011, the conservative French newspaper *Le Figaro* ran the headline "In Côte d'Ivoire and in Libya, Obama is satisfied with the secondary roles".[2] In a similar vein and also referring to Côte d'Ivoire and Libya, as well as Afghanistan, the *New York Times* ran an article the same day with the headline "France's Role in Three Conflicts Displays a More Muscular Policy".[3] Thus, in spring 2011, while the conflict in Libya and France's role therein featured most prominently in the media, the muscular French intervention in Côte d'Ivoire did not go unnoticed. Although the French Licorne Force operated alongside UN troops in the final assault on pro-Gbagbo forces, it had a decisive impact on the outcome of the crisis. The French military intervention finally allowed the *Forces Républicaines de Côte d'Ivoire* (FRCI) to arrest Laurent Gbagbo, and Alassane Ouattara to take the reins of power according to the certified results of the December 2010 presidential elections.[4] France thus appeared as the "kingmaker" in the post-electoral crisis.

It was not the first time that France had played an influential role in the Ivorian crisis. Since 2002 it had repeatedly intervened as a peace-broker, peacekeeper and peace-enforcer. The French acted, however, alongside the UN, the African Union (AU), the Economic Community of West African States (ECOWAS), and individual regional and sub-regional powers. The question thus arises of whether France was only "first among equals" or, in light of its prominent role in the Ivorian crisis, the predominant external actor in the Ivorian theatre, and thereby hampered sub-regional, regional and international peacekeeping efforts. Although the French forces were placed, from 2003, under a UN mandate, and operated first in partnership with ECOWAS and then with UN troops, they nevertheless maintained their operational autonomy and remained under national command. Consequently, France's security role in Côte d'Ivoire ran contrary to the military disengagement, as well as the "multilateralisation" of crisis management and "Africanisation" of peacekeeping, which Paris had advocated and professed to follow since the mid-1990s, and which had been confirmed by the government of Nicolas Sarkozy;[5] and especially since in theory, France's strategic re-orientation corresponded perfectly to regional and sub-regional crisis management aspirations. Under the slogan of "African solutions to African problems", both the AU and ECOWAS have become increasingly active in peacekeeping over the last two decades.[6]

This chapter assesses whether the French were "more equal", and substituted themselves for the AU and ECOWAS, or whether they shouldered the burden in the face of African inaction. It will also be questioned whether through its interventions, Paris betrayed its multilateral strategy and, as a corollary, discredited the UN Operation in Côte d'Ivoire (UNOCI) or, on the contrary, provided essential support to the struggling UN. In light of the UN's peacekeeping overstretch, a significant and relatively independent French military role in Côte d'Ivoire could be beneficial and alleviate some of the pressure from the UN.[7] Yet Paris could also have pursued hidden neo-colonial intentions, and thereby have a harmful impact on the Ivorian crisis. Côte d'Ivoire is not just any of France's former African colonies; instead, since decolonisation it has enjoyed a privileged place in the so-called French *pré carré* (backyard) in Francophone sub-Saharan Africa. It is the second largest economy in West Africa after Nigeria. In Côte d'Ivoire France has large investments, a permanent military base, and the largest expatriate community south of the Sahara.[8]

This chapter argues that France was the predominant actor in the Ivorian theatre and, through its interventions, has strongly influenced the Ivorian crisis up to this very day. French military action was not, however, solely driven by strategic interests, but was also rendered possible by the African community's lack of means and political impasse. On the other hand, while the French forces provided essential support to the UN and helped prevent more bloodshed, they also undermined the credibility and impartiality of the international community. These arguments are based first on a brief analysis of the French role in relation to the African actors and the UN from the 2002 coup d'état onwards, and then on an examination of the same actors during the post-electoral crisis. The chapter concludes with an assessment of the impact of the French policy on the Ivorian crisis, and on the aftermath of the post-electoral episode.

Reluctant arbitrator

As Côte d'Ivoire faced its first coup d'état in 1999, France stuck to its newly proclaimed non-interventionist policy. But as the Ivorian crisis unfolded in earnest in 2002, the French stepped in through a military intervention. Initially intended to protect French nationals, Operation Licorne rapidly evolved into an interposition force and, as a consequence, France became the arbitrator between the warring factions. Although the French used their diplomatic clout to receive international legitimacy and support from the UN, they had by 2004 already run into serious trouble, and had to leave the initiative to African actors, whose previous inefficiency had provoked France's forceful intervention in the first place.

In 1999, as General Robert Gueï overthrew President Henri Konan Bédié and took the reins of power in Côte d'Ivoire, France refrained from intervening. In line with its new African policy, Paris explained its inaction on the basis of the maxim of non-interference. Advised by Michel Dupuch, a former French Ambassador in Côte d'Ivoire and a friend of the toppled president, French President Chirac had first been tempted to come to the help of Bédié. Prime Minister Lionel Jospin, by contrast, was against intervention. It therefore seems that Chirac was not willing to risk the "cohabitation" to save a controversial president, while Gueï did not seem to be an uneasy partner for France.[9] By 2002, France could not and did not want to remain on the sidelines of the unfolding Ivorian crisis. Meanwhile, Laurent Gbagbo had acceded to the presidency after winning the elections of 2000, which he himself described as "calamitous", and from which Bédié and Alassane Ouattara (because of his "doubtful nationality") had been excluded.[10]

Only two years into his presidential term, on 19 September 2002, Gbagbo was confronted with a coup d'état and simultaneous attacks against Abidjan, Bouaké and Korhogo.[11] Although the *Mouvement Patriotique de Côte d'Ivoire* failed to conquer Abidjan and to topple Gbagbo, it took control of the northern part of the country. Joined by two other rebel groups from the West, the *Mouvement Patriotique Ivoirien du Grand Ouest* and the *Mouvement pour la Justice et la Paix*, it turned into a full-blown insurrection under the name of *Forces Nouvelles* (FN). It called on the president to step down, and requested free and fair elections, as well as an end to the xenophobic concept of *ivoirité*, which discriminated against foreigners and Ivorian people of mixed parenthood.[12] In this civil-war-like situation, France intervened rapidly, albeit with the initial aim of protecting and evacuating its citizens.[13]

It was the beginning of what would become the most significant French military operation in Africa since the Cold War, made possible by prepositioned forces on the continent, and the defence and military cooperation agreements with Côte d'Ivoire.[14] Yet despite these agreements, France did not come to the help of Gbagbo, who had asked for military support against what he considered to be a foreign-sponsored rebellion.[15] Although Ouagadougou's support for the rebellion could hardly be discarded, the Elysée refused to intervene on Gbagbo's side on the grounds that there was no discernible foreign involvement. But it was rather that France was not willing to arbitrate between its Burkinabe and Ivorian allies,[16] and did not want to risk its image by supporting the regime of a controversially elected president. A direct intervention in an African civil war also appeared too risky. Moreover, it has also been argued that France refrained from helping Gbagbo "as a way of punishing him for his anti-French sentiments and strong African nationalist rhetoric".[17] Regardless of the real motivations, the Ivorian President felt betrayed and voiced his anger against the French in the media and the streets.[18] Following the difficulties encountered by ECOWAS in the handling of the Ivorian crisis, however, the French forces became increasingly involved in Côte d'Ivoire.

The ECOWAS heads of state were worried by the strong destabilising potential of another civil war in their region, and therefore rapidly took care of the Ivorian crisis. In their extraordinary summit of late September 2002, they decided to mediate between the conflicting parties, and to send a peacekeeping force. While their mediation efforts were largely successful – not least thanks to the help of France – and led to a ceasefire agreement, the West African peacekeeping force encountered significant delays. On ECOWAS's request, the French Licorne Force thus changed its role and shouldered the responsibility of overseeing the ceasefire. Despite the arrival of the ECOWAS Mission in Côte d'Ivoire (ECOMICI) by spring 2003, Licorne's peacekeeping role became permanent. Largely financed and equipped by France and other Western states, ECOWAS was unable to deploy sufficient troops, and on the ground ECOMICI remained dependent on operational and logistical French support.[19]

Similarly, ECOWAS failed in its negotiations, started in October 2002 in Lomé, of having a political issue to the crisis. As an influential actor and the guarantor of the ceasefire, Paris took over and brokered in January 2003 the Linas–Marcoussis Accords, which foresaw – among other things – a transitional government composed of both conflict parties, free and fair elections, and changes to the eligibility criteria of the president.[20] Paris aspired, however, to international legitimacy and desired to present itself as a third party to the conflict. Therefore, it worked from its privileged position as a UN Security Council permanent member to have both the accords and its military role approved by the international organisation. On 4 February 2003, Security Council Resolution 1464 endorsed the Linas–Marcoussis Accords and authorised *a posteriori* the deployment of ECOMICI and the Licorne Force.[21] Meanwhile, France also wanted to secure a UN commitment on the ground, not only for the sake of international legitimacy, but also to reduce the incurred costs from its own operation and the support to the ECOWAS mission. The French Government again used its influential position within the UN system to push through, first, the establishment of the UN Mission in Côte d'Ivoire in spring 2003, and then UNOCI in early 2004.[22]

But whereas the West African troops were absorbed by UNOCI, the French forces remained autonomous and under national command in a relatively loose partnership with UN troops. For financial and practical reasons, the Security Council allowed France to retain control over its Licorne Force, of which the first *raison d'être* was to serve national interests – mainly the protection of French citizens – but which could simultaneously claim to serve the international community.[23] This was certainly not what Gbagbo had had in mind when in November 2003 he criticised ECOMICI's dependency on the Licorne Force, and had therefore called for a UN operation in Côte d'Ivoire.[24] With France at the origin of the Security Council resolutions, the Ivorian President considered the UN missions to be in the service of the French to oversee a situation they had created to his detriment.[25] Indeed, although the French interposition protected Gbagbo from renewed insurgent attacks, in combination with the Linas–Marcoussis Accords, it also undermined his power by legitimising the armed rebellion, and Ouattara – who at the height of the crisis had found refuge in the French embassy – reappeared as a potential contender for the presidency in Côte d'Ivoire.[26]

The dramatic events of 2004 further discredited the impartiality of the Licorne Force and, by association, UNOCI in the eyes of the presidential camp. Despite the Accra Accord of July 2004, through which the conflict parties agreed on a roadmap to implement political reform and disarmament, the peace process had stalled by the autumn. In November, the *Forces Armées Nationales de Côte d'Ivoire* attacked the FN, and in an aerial bombing they also killed nine French soldiers and an American.[27] President Chirac reacted by ordering the destruction of the Ivorian Air Force, which in turn sparked riots that targeted Europeans and in particular French people. The French and UN forces were overtaken by these events, and in addition to the evacuation of French citizens, the Licorne Force killed – depending on the source – between 20 and 64 civilians in an attempt to suppress the violent protests.[28] Even though France and the UN remained thereafter important actors in the Ivorian theatre because of their troops, they had to leave the floor to African initiatives, which were by and large favoured by Gbagbo.

In spring 2005, thanks to the mediation of South African President Thabo Mbeki, Gbagbo, Ouattara and the FN leader Guillaume Soro renewed their commitment to the principles of the Linas–Marcoussis Accords. Progress in the political and security situation remained insufficient, however, to hold the presidential election as foreseen in October 2005. Despite important diplomatic efforts by ECOWAS, the AU, and the UN, the election had to be repeatedly postponed. But in spring 2007, the political stalemate seemed to have been overcome with the Ouagadougou Agreement, brokered by Burkinabe President Blaise Compaoré, between Gbagbo and Soro, which foresaw elections in 2008 and installed Soro as Prime Minister.[29] This regional and inter-Ivorian agreement further reduced the position of France and the UN, which thus began to review their role in Côte d'Ivoire.[30]

UNOCI's achievements were rather modest, and were mainly limited to the interposition mission, for which the support of the Licorne Force was essential. But because of their sometimes forceful interventions, the impartiality of the French forces and, by association, of the UN, was questioned.[31] Nevertheless, the French intervention at the beginning of the crisis had certainly been decisive in avoiding more bloodshed, and was rendered necessary because of the West African inability to rapidly mobilise and deploy an operational peacekeeping force. France played a predominant role in the management of the Ivorian crisis both on the ground and within the UN. This, however, made UNOCI appear suspect not only in Côte d'Ivoire, but also in the Security Council, which hesitated to provide the UN operation with the necessary means to fulfil its mission.[32] France left its imprint on the crisis from the beginning, and because of its traditional military might in Africa and Côte d'Ivoire, and political weight in the UN system, it was "more equal" than the African and UN actors. France's role was only reduced after the violent events in 2004 and, especially, after the Ouagadougou Agreement. It seemed as if the African actors had gained some equality – the question was how long for.

The post-electoral crisis

After the Ouagadougou Agreement, France was pushed into a supporting role in the Ivorian crisis and, in contrast to his predecessor, Sarkozy did not seem particularly interested in sub-Saharan Africa and wanted to reform French African policy altogether. Moreover, the Ivorian crisis had not turned into a Rwandan-like civil war, and Operation Licorne became an increasingly heavy financial burden. Paris thus began planning the military withdrawal from its former colony for the moment that the presidential election would provide the crisis-torn country with some stability.[33] But instead of peace and a French withdrawal, the long-awaited election of 2010 brought about renewed civil strife, a certain African paralysis, a significant French re-engagement, and an insecure country where reconciliation remains a distant ideal.

Ivorian and African impasses

After years of waiting and consecutive postponements, the Ivorian presidential elections could finally be held in autumn 2010. Gbagbo won the first round of 31 October with 38.3 per cent of the votes, against Ouattara and Bédié, who obtained 32.1 and 25.2 per cent of the votes respectively. But in sharp contrast to his expectations, the rallying of Bédié to Ouattara's cause in the second round of 28 November left its mark. According to the Independent Electoral Commission (IEC), Ouattara won with 51.1 per cent of the vote against Gbagbo, who had received 45.9 per cent. But the incumbent President refused to accept his defeat and had the President of the Constitutional Council invalidate the votes of seven northern regions, and declare himself the winner with 51.4 against 48.5 per cent for Ouattara. As an unintended consequence, on 3 December, both candidates were sworn in as President.[34]

Outside of Côte d'Ivoire, however, France, the United States, the EU, the AU and ECOWAS recognised Ouattara's victory and called on Gbagbo to accept his defeat.[35] With the exception of China and Russia, as well as South Africa and Gbagbo's African allies including Angola, all relevant international actors condemned the incumbent president, and adopted sanctions against him and his entourage.[36] Gbagbo was not willing to give in to the international pressure. Hence the mediation efforts by ECOWAS and AU representatives, such as Mbeki, were doomed to fail. Ouattara, however, refused to renounce his victory, and against the background of indiscriminate violence by pro-Gbagbo forces, his followers took up arms and the country again began to slip into civil war.[37]

From the beginning and led by Nigeria, ECOWAS asserted its right to play a key role in the resolution of the crisis. At its extraordinary summit of 24 December 2010, it threatened Gbagbo that it would "take other measures, including the use of legitimate force" if he did not make a "peaceful exit".[38] But even though the ECOWAS Chiefs of Staff met to examine the possibility of intervention, this initiative did not lead to a peace operation, mainly because of the disagreements between the organisation's various members. The Nigerian President, Goodluck Jonathan, was the main advocate for a West African peacekeeping force, through which he hoped to strengthen the international position of his country. In this undertaking, he was supported by the President of Burkina Faso, Blaise Compaoré, who feared the sudden and uncontrolled return of millions of Burkinabe nationals; the President of Senegal, Abdoulaye Wade, who saw the economic interests of the Senegalese diaspora in Côte d'Ivoire threatened by Gbagbo; and the President of Sierra Leone, Ernest Koroma, who upheld the flag of democracy. Their initiative for an interposition force was, however, opposed by Gambia, which refused to participate; Liberia, which feared destabilisation and a massive influx of refugees; Guinea, which was absorbed by domestic affairs; and, above all, by Benin, Ghana and Togo, which pretended to be neutral, but were close to Gbagbo.[39] In addition to their individual interests, Gbagbo's threats against their citizens living on Ivorian soil certainly also dissuaded certain West African states from resorting to force.[40] It was probably because of these inter-African disagreements that the UN Security Council did not comply with Nigeria's request to authorise an intervention by ECOWAS. Anyway, this organisation did not have the necessary financial and, especially, military means to rapidly mobilise and deploy an effective peacekeeping force.[41] The option of an interposition force was thus rapidly discarded, and on 10 February 2011, ECOWAS re-emphasised the need for a political solution to the crisis.[42]

At the regional level, the inter-African disagreements were even stronger than within the sub-region. The AU encountered difficulties in adopting a common position towards the post-electoral crisis, and the military option was never seriously considered. In particular, Angola and

South Africa, joined by Cape Verde, Uganda, Togo and Zimbabwe, voiced their opposition to a military intervention, which was favoured by Burkina Faso, Kenya, Nigeria and Senegal.[43] As a loyal ally, Angolan President José Eduardo dos Santos lent his political, military, and financial support to Gbagbo.[44] The biggest stumbling block to a common position was, however, the great regional power, South Africa. At the onset of the crisis, it was part of the decision of the AU's Peace and Security Council (PSC), which endorsed the ECOWAS position that called on Gbagbo to step down.[45] But by late January 2011, South African President Jacob Zuma questioned the electoral results advanced by the IEC and certified by the international community, and stated that it was too early to declare a winner. The governing party in South Africa, the African National Congress, traditionally adopted a staunchly anti-imperialist position because of its particular historical experience. Zuma and his party colleagues were thus open to the rhetoric of the Gbagbo camp, which accused the international community of being manipulated by a neo-colonial France.[46]

As a consequence, South Africa supported Gbagbo diplomatically, and outside of the AU even tried to rally China and Russia to his cause. This initiative failed, however. While Russia was largely absent from the Ivorian theatre, China had been part of the electoral certification process, and was thus not willing to support the South African standpoint.[47] Without significant support from its elder BRICS partners, and largely isolated in the AU's PSC, Pretoria reviewed its position. On 10 March 2011, the PSC recognised Ouattara's victory without reservations and requested Gbagbo's departure.[48] Seemingly, Paris had also contributed to this shift, because during Zuma's state visit to France in early March, Sarkozy had tried to convince the South African leader to change his position.[49] The final African consensus did not, however, imply an "African solution", and the field was left to France.

French comeback

From the start of the post-electoral crisis, Paris deployed its vast diplomatic network at all levels, and influenced the European, international and African positions for the recognition of Ouattara and sanctions against Gbagbo. This strategy proved especially effective in Brussels and Côte d'Ivoire itself, where France's European partners blindly followed the French initiatives.[50] In reaction, the Gbagbo camp accused Ouattara of being a foreign stooge in the service of French neo-colonial interests, and labelled the crisis as a "'war of second independence' against an all-powerful France and its Western and African allies".[51] Moreover, Gbagbo ordered the French and, by association, the UN forces, to leave what he still considered to be his country.[52] But Paris clearly won this trial of strength. Together with its African and European allies, as well as the United States, it pushed a resolution through the Security Council that not only prolonged UNOCI's and Licorne's mandates, but also called on the incumbent president to step down.[53]

Gbagbo remained defiant, and rejected this and the following resolutions on Côte d'Ivoire by arguing that they had been written by France.[54] Although the French authorship of the resolutions could hardly be denied, Paris countered this criticism by emphasising its commitment to multilateralism, and its preference for an "African solution" to the conflict through the mediation or an intervention by the AU or ECOWAS. Sarkozy also insisted on the impartiality of the Licorne Force, and declared that it was not up to French soldiers to intervene in Ivorian internal affairs.[55] But in light of the absence of an "African solution" and the mounting violence in Côte d'Ivoire, the French President began to prepare the ground for a military intervention with the support of ECOWAS and, especially, Nigeria.

Despite their failure to establish a West African consensus for a peacekeeping force, Nigeria and its allies remained convinced that the use of force might be necessary. Against a background of increasing violence by pro-Gbagbo forces against the civilian population, on 25 March 2011, they gained the approval from their organisation for a resolution, which called on the UN Security Council "to strengthen the mandate" of UNOCI, to enable "the Mission to use all necessary means to protect life and property, and to facilitate the immediate transfer of power to Mr. Alassane Ouattara".[56] Strengthened by this appeal and the AU recognition of Ouattara as the legitimate Ivorian President of early March, and spurred by the Libyan intervention, France began to lobby the UN Security Council for a tougher position on the Ivorian crisis. This diplomatic offensive was successful, because, thanks to African – and above all, Nigerian – support, the French overcame Chinese and Russian opposition.[57] On 30 March 2011, the Security Council voted unanimously in favour of Resolution 1975, which recognised Ouattara as the legitimate president, condemned Gbagbo's refusal of a peaceful solution, and authorised UNOCI and the French Licorne Force "to use all necessary means to carry out its mandate to protect civilians ... including to prevent the use of heavy weapons against the civilian population".[58]

Only a few days later, France and the UN went from words to deeds. The French and UN forces did not limit themselves to the simple protection of civilians, but also supported the pro-Ouattara forces. Initially, the FRCI did not seem to be in need of external support. After a rapid offensive, which encountered little resistance, they arrived in Abidjan in late March.[59] But in the streets of the economic and de facto capital of Côte d'Ivoire, they encountered stiff resistance by Gbagbo loyalists in early April.[60] At exactly this juncture in the conflict, the French and UN forces entered the battle for Abidjan. After taking control of the airport in order to enable the evacuation of foreigners, French and UN helicopters attacked Gbagbo's residence, the presidential palace, the military camps of Agban and Akouédo, the barracks of the Republican Guard, and the antenna of the Ivorian radio and television network. The intervention of the Licorne Force and UNOCI came at the express request of the UN Secretary-General, and was officially intended to neutralise the heavy weapons, which had been used against the civil population.[61] This French and UN military activism immediately attracted criticism from China and Russia.[62]

The intervention was not decisive, however, and soon thereafter the FRCI even lost the initiative against Gbagbo's forces. But the Licorne Force and UNOCI struck once more. After skirmishes during the evacuation of the Japanese Ambassador, the French shelled the presidential residence on 7 April. Despite criticism from within the AU, three days later, the French and UN forces launched their decisive offensive.[63] On 10 April, French and UN helicopters fired missiles at the presidential residence and palace, and at the positions of pro-Gbagbo forces in Cocody. The French also employed their light tanks in this assault, which lasted until dawn of the following day, and finally allowed the FRCI to reap the fruits of victory and arrest Gbagbo.[64]

If in the end the pro-Ouattara forces were victorious, it was thanks to the UN and, above all, French forces. Before the intervention of UNOCI and the Licorne Force, the FRCI's military situation was becoming increasingly untenable, if not desperate, and could have led to defeat – at least in Abidjan. The fact that the combined French and UN strikes had been decisive has not only been admitted by Western diplomats in Côte d'Ivoire, but also within the higher echelons of the FRCI.[65] Meanwhile, it is also highly questionable whether UNOCI could have defeated the pro-Gbagbo forces on its own. During the entire post-electoral crisis, the UN troops rather distinguished themselves through their inability to protect the civilian population.[66] From a military point of view, the UN troops were by and large powerless, and had to rely on their French colleagues. The Licorne Force possessed not only superior equipment and military hardware, which allowed it to fight during the night, but also more professional and better trained soldiers.[67] It is thus not surprising that UNOCI required the support of the French troops, whose strikes were decisive in the battle for Abidjan.[68]

France thus played a major role in the dénouement of the post-electoral crisis, and even though the civil war would probably not have turned into a war of genocide, its intervention stopped the bloodshed.[69] But through its actions, the Licorne Force also supported the FRCI, which had – like Gbagbo's troops – committed war crimes, especially in the west of the country.[70] The French intervention also allowed Ouattara, who had been in frequent contact with his friend President Sarkozy during the crisis and had asked for Licorne's support, to seize the reins of power. According to the Gbagbo camp, the French intervention thus confirmed that Ouattara stood in the service of France, which wanted to reconquer its neo-colonial role in Côte d'Ivoire.[71] The French role in the crisis was also criticised by Russia and by the African states which had opposed military intervention to begin with. They accused both the French and UN forces of having exceeded their mandate by entering the fight on the side of the FRCI, instead of confining their action to the protection of civilians.[72] Thabo Mbeki went so far as to write that France's intervention was "consistent with *Françafrique* policies, which aim to perpetuate a particular relationship with its former African colonies".[73] The Françafrique analogy was also made by French socialist members of parliament.[74] The accusation of the former South African president was certainly ideologically tainted, and the criticism by French socialists was a leftover from their party's past friendship with Gbagbo. Yet it is beyond doubt that Licorne and UNOCI did not restrict themselves to the protection of civilians, but sided with one party to the conflict.[75]

Hangover

The disputed intervention by the Licorne Force and, to a lesser degree, UNOCI, ended the post-electoral crisis, and produced not only winners but also losers. Moreover, at the time of writing, the Ivorian crisis is still ongoing and French and UN troops have remained in Côte d'Ivoire. Because of the daunting security challenges and a resurgence of violence in Côte d'Ivoire, the Security Council prolonged their mandate for another year in July 2011 and then again in July 2012 – with a renewed emphasis on disarmament, demobilisation and reintegration and on security sector reform.[76] Although Licorne's strength has been reduced to approximately 450 troops[77] operating from its base in Port-Bouët since April 2011, it remains a significant security actor on Ivorian soil. It continues to play a deterrent role through its continued, albeit less numerous, patrols in Abidjan and, more importantly, through its role in security sector reform. The Licorne Force intervenes in the training and reconciliation of the Ivorian Armed Forces, which are supposed to be comprised both of pro-Ouattara and pro-Gbagbo forces.[78] Paris has therefore also posted a military advisor to the presidential palace in Abidjan.[79]

Yet in their current role, the French forces wear a second hat. On the one hand, they act in support of UNOCI under a UN mandate, and on the other, they train and advise the Ivorian military under the umbrella of the new Franco-Ivorian defence agreement. The latter replaces the old agreement of 1961, and was signed during Ouattara's first visit as a Head of State to France in late January 2012, as he came to Paris "to thank President Sarkozy and his government for the intervention conducted in April 2011".[80] The new agreement – in contrast to the previous one – does not include the protection of the incumbent president, and is supposed to be more transparent in being presented to the French and Ivorian parliaments.[81] However, it could also be argued that France seized the spoils of victory and, with the active collaboration of Ouattara, has reasserted its influential role in Côte d'Ivoire. In the aftermath of the post-electoral crisis, representatives of French companies accompanied Prime Minister François Fillon to Côte d'Ivoire to seize new business opportunities, and Sarkozy himself came to Ouattara's presidential inauguration.[82]

Meanwhile, Gbagbo was extradited and now faces trial in The Hague, and some of his allies are still detained without formal charges or are standing trial in Côte d'Ivoire for their role during the post-electoral crisis. The victors, by contrast, are not, despite alleged war crimes, worried by the brunt of justice. Instead, ex-rebel leader Soro and his *Comzones* have been propelled to the highest echelons of the Ivorian state. Moreover, the FRCI and those who claim to be part of it continue to be in charge of domestic security. They often abuse their power and commit exactions on the civil population, especially on those they identify as Gbagbo supporters. Although Ouattara has announced that he will bring the FRCI into line, he has not equipped the police forces with the necessary means to control the situation. The Ouattara government does not trust the police, and in light of the recent deadly attacks on the FRCI, increasingly fears a coup by Gbagbo loyalists. The security situation in Côte d'Ivoire remains fragile: the reinsertion of the numerous former rebel fighters, who enjoy the power provided by their weapons, is difficult; there are, depending on the estimate, tens or even hundreds of thousands of small weapons in circulation in Côte d'Ivoire; and after violent incidents in the West of the country, anonymous and deadly attacks have also reached Abidjan.[83]

Thus, the decisive French intervention in the post-electoral crisis brought only a temporary end to the violence in Côte d'Ivoire. And instead of national reconciliation, it allowed for the establishment of a regime that practices victor's justice, distributing the spoils of victory among its comrades-in-arms. Moreover, in agreement with Ouattara, the French have regained a privileged position in Côte d'Ivoire. This situation strengthens the Gbabgo camp in its accusations that the current president stands in the service of France, and allows it to nurture thoughts of revenge against the pro-Ouattara forces, whose victory depended on French and, to a lesser degree, UN assistance.

Conclusion

Since the 2002 coup d'état, France has been "more equal" than other actors and has played a primary role in the Ivorian crisis. Through its military interventions, which reached their peak in the post-electoral crisis, it has strongly influenced the destiny of its former colony. Paris did not seek it, but endorsed this role because of the delayed and inefficient deployment of the West African peacekeeping force. During the post-electoral crisis, France was already present on the ground, and intervened in light of the absence of an "African solution". Consequently, France did not take the place of the African community, but its intervention was rendered possible through the inaction of and the disagreement within ECOWAS and the AU. But due to its traditional military presence in Côte d'Ivoire, as well as its initial intervention to protect French nationals, France was destined to become an important actor in the Ivorian crisis in one way or another.

Through its dominant role, France has also been able to influence the peace process in Côte d'Ivoire, where it has a large expatriate community, as well as strategic and economic interests. Paris thus attended not only to its financial but also to its national interests more broadly when it used its influential role in the UN Security Council for the establishment of a UN operation and at the same time preserved the autonomy of its forces. Nevertheless, the continued French military presence was also desired by the UN, which faced financial and material constraints in peacekeeping. Moreover, in the management of the Ivorian crisis and especially during the 2011 post-electoral crisis, the support of Licorne was essential for UNOCI, which was by and large powerless. But the other side of the coin was that the French role in the Ivorian crisis both within the UN Security Council and on the ground discredited UN impartiality. The forceful intervention of French troops in the dénouement of the post-electoral crisis confirmed the views of the Gbagbo camp and its allies that France pursued its neo-colonial interests under the cover of the UN and international legitimacy. Even though the French forces once again helped to put an end to the bloodshed, the influential role of the former colonial power in the Ivorian crisis is a burden for national reconciliation in Côte d'Ivoire, which remains in a state of crisis.

Notes

1 The author is grateful to Fredrik Nordin for his research assistance in preparing this chapter.

2 L. Mandeville, "En Côte d'Ivoire et en Libye, Obama se contente des seconds rôles", *Le Figaro*, 6 April 2011, p. 7.

3 S. Erlanger, "France's Role in Three Conflicts Displays a More Muscular Policy", *New York Times*, 6 April 2011, p. 4.

4 A. Nossiter, S. Sayare and D. Bilefsky, "Leader's Arrest in Ivory Coast Ends Standoff", *New York Times*, 12 April 2011, p. 1.

5 M. Wyss, "The Gendarme Stays in Africa: France's Military Role in Côte d'Ivoire", *African Conflict & Peacebuilding Review* 3, 2013.

6 U. Engel and J. Gomes Porto (eds), *Africa's New Peace and Security Architecture: Promoting Norms and Institutionalizing Solutions*, Farnham: Ashgate, 2010; C.I. Obi, "Economic Community of West African States on the Ground: Comparing Peacekeeping in Liberia, Sierra Leone, Guinea Bissau and Côte d'Ivoire", *African Security* 2, 2009, pp. 119–135.

7 D.S. Tull, *Die Peacekeeping Krise der Vereinten Nationen*, Berlin: Stiftung Wissenschaft und Politik, 2010.

8 S. Smith, "La politique d'engagement de la France à l'épreuve de la Côte d'Ivoire", *Politique africaine* 89, 2003, p. 114; M. Bovcon, "Françafrique and the Regime Theory", *European Journal of International Relations*, 19, 2013, p. 13.

9 B. Charbonneau, *France and the New Imperialism: Security Policy in Sub-Saharan Africa,* Aldershot: Ashgate, 2008, p. 158; D. Kroslak, "France's Policy Towards Africa: Continuity or Change?", in I. Taylor and P.D. Williams (eds), *Africa in International Politics: External Involvement on the Continent,* London: Routledge, 2004, p. 79.

10 T. Hofnung, *La crise ivoirienne: De Félix Houphouët-Boigny à la chute de Laurent Gbagbo,* Paris: La Découverte, 2011, pp. 49–62.

11 M. McGovern, *Making War in Côte d'Ivoire,* Chicago: University of Chicago Press, 2011, pp. 15–19.

12 C. Gramizzi and M. Damian, *La crise ivoirienne: De la tentative de coup d'Etat au gouvernement de réconciliation nationale,* Brussels: GRIP, 2003, pp. 10–14.

13 M. Bovcon, "France's Conflict Resolution Strategy in Côte d'Ivoire and its Ethical Implications", *African Studies Quarterly* 11, 2009, p. 6.

14 R. Utley, "Franco-African Military Relations: Meeting the Challenges of Globalisation", *Modern & Contemporary France* 13, 2005, p. 33.

15 J.-J. Konadjé, *L'intervention de l'ONU dans la résolution du conflit intraétatique ivoirien,* thesis, Université de Toulouse le Capitole, 2010, pp. 94–95.

16 R. Banégas and R. Otayek, "Le Burkina Faso dans la Crise Ivoirienne: Effets d'aubaine et incertitudes politiques", *Politique africaine* 89, 2003, p. 74.

17 C. Ero, "UN Peacekeeping in West Africa", in A. Adebajo (ed.), *From Global Apartheid to Global Village: Africa and the United Nations,* Scottsville, South Africa: University of Kwa-Zulu-Natal Press, 2009, p. 297.

18 L. d'Ersu, "La crise ivoirienne, une intrigue franco-française", *Politique africaine* 105, 2007, p. 89.

19 Bovcon, "France's Conflict Resolution Strategy", p. 9; Gramizzi and Damian, *La crise ivoirienne,* pp. 21–23; Obi, "Economic Community", pp. 128–129; H. Sada, "Le conflit ivoirien: enjeux régionaux et maintien de la paix en Afrique", *Politique étrangère* 68, 2003, pp. 237–239; H. Serequeberhan, "Le réengagement français dans les conflits africains et le défi ivoirien", *Annuaire français de relations internationales 2005* vi, 2006, pp. 324–326.

20 République française, "Texte de l'Accord de Linas–Marcoussis", Ministère des Affaires étrangères – France Diplomatie, 24 January 2003, available at www.diplomatie.gouv.fr/fr/pays-zones-geo/cote-d-ivoire/colonne-droite-1347/documents-de-reference/article/accord-de-Linas–marcoussis, accessed 3 October 2012. On peacemaking in the Ivorian crisis see A.B. Bah, "Democracy and Civil War: Citizenship and Peacemaking in Côte d'Ivoire", *African Affairs* 109, 2010, pp. 597–615.

21 UN Security Council Resolution 1464, 4 February 2003.

22 UN Security Council Resolution 1479, 13 April 2003; UN Security Council Resolution 1528, 27 February 2004; Konadjé, *L'intervention,* pp. 106, 277.

23 P. Weiss, "L'Opération Licorne en Côte d'Ivoire", *Annuaire français de relations internationales 2004* v, 2005, p. 323.

24 "Message de S.E.M. Laurent Gbagbo, Président de la République de Côte d'Ivoire, au Conseil de sécurité", 10 November 2003, Official Document System of the UN, available at http://documents-dds-ny.un.org/doc/UNDOC/GEN/N03/612/17/pdf/N0361217.pdf?OpenElement, accessed 9 August 2012.

25 A. Adebajo, *UN Peacekeeping in Africa: From the Suez Crisis to the Sudan Conflicts,* Boulder CO: Lynne Rienner, 2011, p. 162; Ero, "UN Peacekeeping", p. 299.

26 Charbonneau, *France and the New Imperialism,* pp. 148, 161–164; Smith, "La politique d'engagement", pp. 118–119.

27 McGovern, *Making War in Côte d'Ivoire,* pp. 21–22.

28 M. Bovcon, "French Repatriates from Côte d'Ivoire and the Resilience of Françafrique", *Modern & Contemporary France* 17, 2009; Bovcon, "France's Conflict Resolution Strategy", 11.

29 See Bah, "Democracy and Civil War"; and M.I. Mitchell, "Power-sharing and Peace in Côte d'Ivoire: Past Examples and Future Prospects", *Conflict, Security & Development* 12, 2012, pp. 171–191.

30 M. Bovcon, "Françafrique and the Regime Theory", pp. 19–20; McGovern, *Making War in Côte d'Ivoire*, pp. 22–24.

31 X. Zeebroek, *Côte d'Ivoire: La paix malgré l'ONU*, Brussels: GRIP, 2008, pp. 12, 17.

32 G. Yabi, "Côte d'Ivoire", in B. Antonini (ed.), *Security Council Resolutions Under Chapter VII: Design, Implementation and Accountabilities*, Madrid: Fride, 2009, p. 115; G. Piccolino and J. Karlsrud, "Withering Consent, but Mutual Dependency: UN Peace Operations and African Assertiveness", *Conflict, Security & Development* 11, 2011, p. 456.

33 McGovern, *Making War in Côte d'Ivoire*, p. 211.

34 "Africa", *Strategic Survey* 111, 2011, pp. 291–292.

35 A. Nossiter, "Both Rivals in Ivory Coast Vote Take Presidential Oath of Office", *New York Times*, 5 December 2010, p. 8.

36 R. Banégas, "Post-Election Crisis in Côte d'Ivoire: The Gbonhi War", *African Affairs* 110, 2011, p. 458.

37 T.J. Bassett, "Winning Coalition, Sore Loser: Côte d'Ivoire's 2010 Presidential Elections", *African Affairs* 110, 2011, p. 479; A. Nossiter, "In Ivory Coast, a Second Government Takes Shape", *New York Times*, 5 December 2010, p. 6; "Africa", p. 292.

38 "Extraordinary Session of the Authority of Heads of State and Government on Côte d'Ivoire, Final Communiqué", ECOWAS, 24 December 2010, available at www.ecowas.int/publications/en/communique_final/session_extra/Communique_Final_CI_election.pdf, accessed 4 October 2012.

39 Interview with Western diplomat, Abidjan, 22 May 2012; interview with Western diplomat, Abidjan, 24 May 2012. See also B. Rouppert, *La Côte d'Ivoire un an après: Rétrospective sur cinq mois de crise électorale, ses impacts et ses questionnements*, Brussels: GRIP, 2012, pp. 20–21.

40 M. Fofana, "Des Forces nouvelles aux Forces républicaines de Côte d'Ivoire", *Politique africaine* 122, 2011, p. 165.

41 Interview with Western diplomat, Abidjan, 23 May 2012. See also Hofnung, *La crise ivoirienne*, p. 163; Rouppert, *La Côte d'Ivoire*, p. 21.

42 "Press Statement by the President of the ECOWAS Commission on the Current Crisis in Côte d'Ivoire", ECOWAS, 10 February 2011, available at http://news.ecowas.int/presseshow.php?nb=015&lang=en&annee=2011, accessed 13 August 2012.

43 Interview with Western diplomat, Abidjan, 23 May 2012. See also A. Kappès-Grangé, "Côte d'Ivoire: Désunion africaine", *Jeune Afrique* 2613, 6–12 February 2011, pp. 30–33.

44 "Zedu veille sur son petit frère 'Laurent'", *La Lettre du Continent*, 23 December 2010; "Luanda vole au secours de Gbagbo III", *La Lettre du Continent*, 13 January 2011.

45 "Communique of the 252nd Meeting of the Peace and Security Council", AU, 9 December 2010, available at www.africa-union.org/root/au/Conferences/2010/december/Communiqu%C3%A9%20of%20the%20252nd.pdf, accessed 4 October 2012; "Final Communique on the Extraordinary Session of the Authority of Heads of State and Government on Côte d'Ivoire", ECOWAS, 7 December 2010, available at http://news.ecowas.int/presseshow.php?nb=188&lang=en&annee=2010, accessed 4 October 2012.

46 Interview with Western diplomat, Abidjan, 24 May 2012.

47 Interview with Western diplomat, Abidjan, 22 May 2012; interview with Western diplomat to the UN, New York, 19 June 2012.

48 "Communique of the 265th Meeting of the Peace and Security Council", AU, 10 March 2011, available at http://au.int/en/dp/ps/sites/default/files/2011_mar_10_psc_265theeting_cotedivoire_communique_en.pdf, accessed 14 August 2012.
49 V. Darracq, "Jeux de puissance en Afrique: le Nigeria et l'Afrique du Sud face à la crise ivoirienne", *Politique étrangère* 2, 2011, pp. 366–368. See also B. Charbonneau, "War and Peace in Côte d'Ivoire: Violence, Agency, and the Local/International Line", *International Peacekeeping* 19, 2012, pp. 518–519.
50 Interview with Western diplomat, Abidjan, 24 May 2012; interview with EU diplomat, Brussels, 22 June 2012.
51 G. Piccolino, "David against Goliath in Côte d'Ivoire? Laurent Gbagbo's War against Global Governance", *African Affairs* 111, p. 2.
52 A. Nossiter, "Ivory Coast President Orders U.N. to Leave", *New York Times*, 19 December 2010, p. 12.
53 "6458th meeting", UN Security Council, S/PV.6458; UN Security Council Resolution 1962, 20 December 2010.
54 A. Nossiter, "Diplomacy Again Falls Short in Tense Ivory Coast Standoff", *New York Times*, 4 January 2011, p. 4.
55 N. Guibert and N. Nougayrède, "Côte d'Ivoire: la France veut éviter d'être entraînée dans une crise militaire", *Le Monde*, 21 December 2010; J.P. Rémy, "Côte d'Ivoire: la médiation africaine marque le pas", *Le Monde*, 6 January 2011, p. 6.
56 "Resolution A/RES.1/03/11 of the Authority of Heads of State and Government of ECOWAS on the Situation in Côte d'Ivoire", ECOWAS, 25 March 2011, available at http://news.ecowas.int/presseshow.php?nb=043&lang=en&annee=2011, accessed 4 October 2012.
57 T.J. Bassett and S. Straus, "Defending Democracy in Côte d'Ivoire", *Foreign Affairs* 90, 2011; A.J. Bellamy and P.D. Williams, "The New Politics of Protection? Côte d'Ivoire, Libya and the Responsibility to Protect", *International Affairs* 86, 2011, p. 833; Darracq, "Jeux de puissance", p. 372.
58 See UN Security Council, S/PV.6508, 30 March 2011; UN Security Council Resolution 1975, 30 March 2011.
59 Interview with high-ranking officer of UNOCI, Abidjan, 23 May 2012.
60 Interview with Western diplomat, Abidjan, 22 May 2012.
61 Interview with high-ranking officer of UNOCI, Abidjan, 23 May 2012. See also T. Portes, "L'assaut 'final' contre les pro-Gbagbo a commencé", *Le Figaro*, 5 April 2011, p. 7; A. Nossiter, "U.N. and France Strike at Ivory Coast Strongman's Bases and Residence", *New York Times*, 5 April 2011, p. 8.
62 S. Erlanger, "France's Role in Three Conflicts Displays a More Muscular Policy", *New York Times*, 6 April 2011, p. 4; L. Mandeville, "En Côte d'Ivoire et en Libye, Obama se contente des seconds rôles", *Le Figaro*, 6 April 2011, p. 7.
63 Interview with high-ranking officer of UNOCI, Abidjan, 23 May 2012. See also S. Sayare, "Gbagbo Loyalists Regain Ground in Ivory Coast", *New York Times*, 10 April 2011.
64 A. Nossiter, "France and U.N. Hit Ivory Coast Strongman's Home and Palace", *New York Times*, 11 April 2011, p. 4; T. Berthemet, "Amère fin de partie pour Laurent Gbagbo", *Le Figaro*, 12 April 2011, p. 6.
65 Interview with high-ranking officer of the FRCI, Abidjan, 24 May 2012; Interview with Western diplomat, Abidjan, 23 May 2012; interview with Western diplomat, Abidjan, 22 May 2012.
66 Adebajo, *UN Peacekeeping*, p. 160.
67 Interview with officer II of the Licorne Force, Abidjan, 22 May 2012; interview with Western diplomat, Abidjan, 22 May 2012.
68 Interview with high-ranking officer of the FRCI, Abidjan, 24 May 2012; interview with Western diplomat, Abidjan, 23 May 2012.
69 Interviews with Officers I and II from the Licorne Force, Abidjan, 22 May 2012;

interview with Western diplomat, Abidjan, 22 May 2012. See also S. Straus, "'It's Sheer Horror Here': Patterns of Violence During the First Four Months of Côte d'Ivoire's Post-Electoral Crisis", *African Affairs* 110, 2011, pp. 481–489.

70 Human Rights Watch, "Côte d'Ivoire: 'They Killed Them Like It Was Nothing': The Need for Justice for Côte d'Ivoire's Post-Election Crimes", New York: October 2011; J.-C. Djereke, "What Hides Behind the Question of Child Soldiers in Côte d'Ivoire?", *Peace Review* 24, 2012.

71 C. Boisbouvier, "Pourquoi la France y est allée", *Jeune Afrique* 2622, 10–16 April 2012; P. Rousselin, "Libye, Côte d'Ivoire: Sarkozy à la manœuvre", *Le Figaro*, 9 April 2011, p. 2; M. McGovern, "The Ivorian Endgame: Can Ouattara Rebuild a Shattered Country", *Foreign Affairs*, 14 April 2011, available at www.foreignaffairs.com/articles/67728/mike-mcgovern/the-ivorian-endgame?page=show.

72 M. Semo, "La stratégie risquée de Sarkozy l'Africain", *Libération*, 12 April 2011, p. 5; S. Erlanger, "French Colonial Past Casts Long Shadow Over Policy in Africa", *New York Times*, 17 April 2011, p. 10; Bellamy and Williams, "The New Politics of Protection?", pp. 825, 835.

73 T. Mbeki, "What the World Got Wrong in Côte d'Ivoire", *Foreign Policy*, 29 April 2011, available at www.foreignpolicy.com/articles/2011/04/29/what_the_world_got_wrong_in_cote_d_ivoire, accessed 8 October 2012.

74 K. Simonen, "*Qui s'excuse s'accuse* ... An Analysis of French Justifications for Intervening in Côte d'Ivoire", *International Peacekeeping* 19, 2012, p. 369.

75 A.J. Bellamy and P.D. Williams, "Local Politics and International Partnerships: The UN Operation in Côte d'Ivoire (UNOCI)", *Journal of International Peacekeeping* 18, 2012, p. 268; A. Mehler, "From 'Protecting Civilians' to 'For the Sake of Democracy' (and Back Again): Justifying Intervention in Côte d'Ivoire", *African Security* 5, 2012, p. 212.

76 See UN Security Council, S/PV.6584, 18 July 2011; UN Security Council Resolution 2000, 27 July 2011; UN Security Council, S/PV.6808, 18 July 2012; UN Security Council Resolution 2062, 26 July 2012.

77 République française, "Les forces françaises en Côte d'Ivoire", Ministère de la Défense, 4 October 2012, available at www.defense.gouv.fr/operations/cote-d-ivoire/dossier/les-forces-francaises-en-cote-d-ivoire, accessed 8 October 2012.

78 Interview with Western diplomat, 24 May 2012; interview with officers I and II of the Licorne Force, Abidjan, 22 May 2012; interview with Western diplomat, Abidjan, 22 May 2012. See also T. Koepf, "The Problems of French-led Peace Operations in Francophone Sub-Saharan Africa", *International Peacekeeping* 19, 2012, p. 337.

79 Interview with high-ranking officer of the FRCI, Abidjan, 24 May 2012. See also L. Varenne, *Abobo la Guerre: Côte d'Ivoire: terrain de jeu de la France et de l'ONU*, Paris: Mille et Une Nuits, 2012, p. 207.

80 "Ouattara: 'Rendre la démocratie irréversible en Côte d'Ivoire'", *Le Monde*, 26 January 2012, p. 3; T. Berthemet, "Alassane Ouattara reçu en ami à l'Elysée", *Le Figaro*, 27 January 2012, p. 6.

81 Interview with Western diplomat, 24 May 2012; interview with Western diplomat, Abidjan, 22 May 2012.

82 T. Hofnung, "La Françafrique revient aux affaires", *Libération*, 23 May 2011, p. 10; "Offensive française à Abidjan", *Libération*, 16/17 July 2011, p. 6; Varenne, *Abobo la Guerre*, pp. 205–207.

83 Interview with Western diplomat, Abidjan, 24 May 2012; interview with Western diplomat, Abidjan, 22 May 2012; interview with high-ranking officer of the FRCI, Abidjan, 24 May 2012. See also International Crisis Group (ICG), "Côte d'Ivoire: Faire baisser la pression", *Rapport Afrique* 193, 26 November 2012; Amnesty International, *Côte d'Ivoire: The Victors' Law*, London, February 2013; Human Rights Watch, *A Long Way from Reconciliation*, New York, November 2012.

Part III

Case studies

8 When the neighbors keep a foot in the door

Regional interventions and peacekeeping missions in the Democratic Republic of Congo and Somalia

Judith Vorrath

Introduction

The disaster of the UN operations in Somalia between 1992 and 1995 and the failure to respond to the Rwandan genocide in 1994 had an enormous impact on how international peace operations have evolved. These two contexts of armed violence have subsequently produced protracted crises reaching beyond state borders, and an international response including peacekeeping missions. The UN Organization Mission in the Democratic Republic of Congo (DRC) (MONUC; since 2010 UN Organization Stabilization Mission in the DRC, MONUSCO) and the African Union (AU) Mission in Somalia (AMISOM)[1] faced the situation that initially "there was little peace to keep". But both contexts were also characterized by complex regional conflict formations, "a set of transnational conflicts that form mutually-reinforcing linkages with each other across state borders".[2] This chapter argues that this regional dimension is as important to an understanding of outcomes of peace processes as the interaction of the international and the local spheres commonly stressed by the critical peacebuilding literature.[3] Thus, it focuses on how different peacekeeping missions relate to the regional level and deal with the challenge of continuing regional interference.

The transnational links of conflicts have been widely acknowledged and frequently been addressed by peace initiatives in the Great Lakes region as well as the Horn of Africa. However, they have continuously posed serious problems for the two missions since their deployment. The most obvious factor was the repeated interference by neighboring countries who "tried to keep a foot in the door" to preserve their own interests and spheres of influence. The respective countries, mainly Ethiopia and Kenya in Somalia, and Rwanda and Uganda in the DRC, usually justified interventions by citing security concerns, or simply denied them. The interference has taken on direct and indirect forms ranging from the deployment of troops to the support for local proxies on Congolese and Somali territory. Often these have been unilateral actions, sometimes undertaken in consultation with the respective (transitional) government; but they were not, at least not initially, an integral part of the international peacebuilding project.

Possible responses by peacekeeping missions to these interventions range from outright opposition to acceptance or even cooperation. At first sight, the benchmark for deciding how to deal with intervening (neighbor) states seems quite clear. However, international law provides only limited guidance on how to deal with regional interventions of the kind described above. First, often non-state actors are involved as local proxies for regional states. Overall, such labels as "state" and "non-state" are quite fluid and can generally have relatively little meaning in contexts where peacekeeping missions are deployed. Second, those direct interventions by neighbor countries that are authorized by the (transitional) government of the country concerned can still undermine the mandate of a peacekeeping mission, for example in relation to tasks such as disarmament or the protection of civilians. And finally, peacekeeping missions may not be in a position to respond to the violation of international law standards, due for example to their mandate or to limited resources. Therefore, the response of peacekeeping missions to regional interference is a complex affair. Additional difficulties mostly stem from two points. On the one hand, missions themselves become easily entangled in regional conflict formations. They are placed in the midst of the formation and interact with it. It is practically impossible for a mission to sustain a neutral stance – no matter how hard actors on the ground try to do so. On the other hand, regional states are often as much the solution as they are the problem in peace processes. Thus, the response by peacekeeping missions is always a difficult balancing act of diplomatic and operational considerations.

While these points refer to peacekeeping missions in general, their responses can differ depending on how the mission is positioned vis-à-vis the regional conflict formation. Naturally, this position depends on the setup of the mission itself. It is commonly assumed that regional organizations such as the AU are in a better position than the UN for effectively addressing armed conflict with a strong regional component. The alleged comparative advantage of "African solutions to African problems" entails a better knowledge of the context as well as stronger incentives, as member states are more directly affected. Some even see that there is an opportunity for regional organizations, such as the AU, to challenge the liberal peacebuilding policy pursued by the UN, among others.[4] So, are responses made by peacekeeping missions to regional interference strongly driven by the mission's organizational setup, or rather by other factors? The aim of this chapter is to place peacekeeping missions in Africa in the context of regional conflict formations. While many works have focused on how missions interact with the "local", this chapter is about how they interact with the "regional", sometimes acting through the "local", and sometimes on its own terms.

Regional conflict formations in the Great Lakes and the Horn of Africa

Both the DRC and Somalia are at the core of regional conflict formations involving severe and persistent armed violence. They combine a complex mix of relevant background factors such as colonialism, transnational ethnic groups, decades of political exclusion and dictatorship, regional rivalries, and global influences. The various conflicts within the two regions are strongly linked and dynamics set in motion in one country have a visible influence in others. The core parameters of these regional conflict formations, up to the point when the peacekeeping missions MONUC and AMISOM were deployed, are introduced in the following subsections.

Congo's conflicts and "Africa's world war"

The Rwandan genocide and the steady decline of the Congolese state, culminating in its near collapse in the 1990s, are commonly seen as the main drivers leading to the Congo wars and subsequent violent conflict. Against a background of local conflicts around land, ethnic identity and citizenship in North and South Kivu in Eastern DRC, the regional dimension clearly emerged at the beginning of the 1990s with the civil wars in neighboring countries. At some point, armed groups from Burundi, Rwanda, Uganda and Angola were on Congolese territory, posing a security threat to their countries of origin.

The most important factor was the emerging Rwandan "state in exile" in refugee camps in Eastern DRC,[5] after the takeover of power by the Tutsi movement Rwandan Patriotic Front (RPF) in July 1994 had ended the genocide. Components of the old Rwandan Hutu regime and the Interahamwe militias regrouped and recruited from among the large numbers of refugees, mostly unmolested and probably even supported by the Mobutu government. Thus, tension with Rwanda under the RPF government was constantly rising and finally reached a peak in the first Congo war of 1996–1997.[6]

The link between the Rwandan civil war and local conflicts in the DRC was embodied by the emergence of the Alliance of Democratic Forces for the Liberation of Congo (AFDL), led by Laurent Kabila, in October 1996. As the regime in Kigali had a strong interest in intervening in order to dismantle the Hutu refugee camps, it not only supported the rebellion but effectively planned and directed it. Uganda got involved as well after the Allied Democratic Forces (ADF), a rebel movement opposing the Ugandan government, also set up base on Congolese territory and attempts of dialogue with the Mobutu regime failed.[7] Finally, the AFDL and its allies ousted Mobutu in 1997 and Kabila became the new president.

Two main factors provided the background to another war that was soon to follow. First, despite the success of the alliance and massive attacks on refugee camps, the threat from the different armed groups was not eliminated. The Hutu extremists from Rwanda re-emerged under different names before finally evolving into the Democratic Forces for the Liberation of Rwanda (FDLR) in 2000. Second, the alliance that had mostly been held together by the members' enmity towards Mobutu proved to be rather fragile after his removal. Due to increasing criticism of the great influence of foreigners on the Congolese government, Kabila finally ordered all Rwandese troops to leave in July 1998. In making up for the loss in military strength Kabila also drew on former Rwandan army elements that he had initially helped to fight with his AFDL. Overall, the second Congo war turned yesterday's friends into enemies.[8]

But the second war also involved new regional players and has therefore been called "Africa's World War".[9] When Uganda and Rwanda turned against their former protégé, Angola and Zimbabwe stepped in and saved Kabila's regime. In the course of this war, the country eventually became divided into three different parts. Basically one was held by the Congolese government under Kabila, supported by his allies; one was controlled by the Rwandan government and local rebels of the Rally for Congolese Democracy (RCD-Goma), supported by Kigali; and a third part was held by the Ugandan Army, the allied Movement for the Liberation of the Congo (MLC), and from 1999 another local rebel faction. Furthermore, a new line of tension developed as Rwanda and Uganda increasingly turned against each other.[10]

In this situation of territories controlled by different transnational alliances, a ceasefire agreement was signed in Lusaka in 1999. Among the signatories were the Congolese government, outside powers and also, finally, the two main local groups involved. The agreement was drafted by the Organization of African Unity (OAU), the UN and the Southern African Development Community (SADC), of which the DRC had become a member in 1997. It acknowledged the internal and external dimensions of the conflict and requested the deployment of a robust UN peacekeeping force. Apart from the monitoring of the ceasefire, the task of tracking down and disarming all armed groups in the DRC was foreseen as part of the mission's mandate.[11] However, from the beginning the UN made clear that disarmament, demobilization, repatriation, resettlement and reintegration (DDRRR) would have to be voluntary, and MONUC adhered to this voluntary principle when it was set up.[12]

The first group of MONUC observers arrived in the Congo in late 1999, but renewed fighting between government and rebel forces threatened to prevent the deployment of the foreseen 5,537 UN troops in 2000. The real turning point came in January 2001, when Laurent Kabila was assassinated by one of his bodyguards and the installation of Kabila's son Joseph as new Congolese president revived the peace process. MONUC finally started the first significant troop deployments with Moroccan troops arriving in Kisangani.[13]

Somalia's "anarchy" and regional rivalry

The conflict in Somalia was effectively triggered by the fall of the Barre regime in 1991, but evolved around a number of local and regional factors. While internally the importance of clan-based ties came to the fore, the fact that ethnic Somalis were living in all neighboring countries, and the idea of a Greater Somalia, provided the background for the regional conflict formation. The local dynamics unfolded in a way that led to the clan-based warfare in late 1991 and early 1992, while none of the factions was able to establish central authority.[14] A ceasefire was negotiated between the two main belligerents in Mogadishu, and the UN Operation in Somalia (UNOSOM) was deployed. However, by 1995 the international efforts had largely failed; the second UNOSOM mission withdrew and foreign aid generally declined.[15]

Against the background of these local and international dynamics, the regional dimension of the conflict took on two central features. First, different political initiatives to settle conflicts in Somalia were promoted by regional states, often becoming an expression of regional rivalries. Second, several countries of the region also intervened militarily inside Somalia – directly or by supporting proxies. The first path with competing peace talks led to a division of Somalia between two broad political coalitions by the late 1990s. While Ethiopia promoted a decentralized, federal Somali state at the Sodere Conference in 1996–1997, Egypt countered this attempt with the 1997 Cairo Conference, bringing together those factions that had boycotted Sodere in order to establish a much more centralized Somali state. Somalia remained in a state of "neither war nor peace",[16] even after another peace process convened by Djibouti. While this initiative managed to install a Transitional National Government (TNG) as the first internationally recognized Somali authority since 1991, another alliance backed by Ethiopia opposed the process. In the regional formation, Djibouti and Egypt continued to support the TNG, and Ethiopia and Kenya opposed it. This led to an intensification of fighting as several countries backing the two factions provided weapons, thus violating the 1992 UN embargo.[17]

Even before, and parallel to, ongoing negotiations, neighboring states had interfered in different ways. Ethiopia supported some of the groups in the north that fought the Barre regime, as it was opposed to the Somali government. Later on, Ethiopia felt threatened by the emergence of an armed Islamist group and directly attacked its camps in the border area during 1997. Moreover, the confrontation between Ethiopia and Eritrea in 1998 was replicated in the Somali conflict theater since Eritrea supported proxies opposed to armed forces aligned with Ethiopia.[18]

Finally, a broader regional initiative by the Intergovernmental Authority on Development (IGAD) raised hopes of a more coherent and adequate regional response. However, Eritrea questioned the process as a whole, while Kenya and Ethiopia promoted a federalist Somali state.[19] After lengthy talks, a ceasefire and, finally, a new Transitional Federal Government (TFG) were established in October 2004. Even though the TFG was recognized by the UN as the new legitimate Somali government, in the region it was largely seen as an Ethiopian proxy.[20]

Overall, the internal support base of the TFG was weak, and it has largely been kept alive by international support. The core of this support was the continuing Ethiopian involvement. IGAD did not manage to set up a mission to secure the TFG against the threat from the Union of the Islamic Courts (UIC), which had ousted a US-backed group of warlords from Mogadishu in April 2006, and was able to establish some order in the area. Thus, it was again Ethiopia that intervened unilaterally in 2006 initially with 2,500 troops.[21] Ethiopia justified its intervention with the threat posed by an extremist Jihadist group, but also the pan-Somalia agenda of the UIC.[22] More importantly, the Ethiopian agenda was very much in line with interests of crucial international players, namely the US. While the AU, like the European Commission and the Arab League, called for the deployment of a UN peacekeeping force, the US supported the invasion in December 2006 as part of the war on terror. Ethiopia's intervention was approved by the TFG, but was only later backed by the AU.[23]

The outcome of the intervention was a clear manifestation of the regional conflict formation, despite the quick expulsion of the UIC from Mogadishu. First, the UIC leadership left for Eritrea, and along with other opposition figures, established the Alliance for the Re-Liberation of Somalia (ARS) against the Ethiopian occupation.[24] Second, Eritrea itself suspended its IGAD membership in protest over what it saw as an exclusive promotion of Ethiopian interests and continued support for Islamist forces inside Somalia. This led to the imposition of sanctions against Eritrea by the UN Security Council in 2009, which had been called for by the AU.[25] Third, the severe humanitarian crisis in 2006, due to the escalation of violence, reinforced the perception of the Ethiopian forces as foreign invaders.[26] Given the inability of IGAD to step in, the urgent need to facilitate the withdrawal of the Ethiopian troops, and the unwillingness to deploy an international force in this insecure environment, AMISOM was established in 2007.[27] However, Ethiopian forces remained in the country and it was not before January 2009 that AMISOM became the main external protection of the TFG.

Like MONUC in the DRC, the AU mission faced a regional conflict formation often following the logic of "the enemy of my enemy is my friend". In both contexts the weakness of central state authority and (real and imagined) threats posed by different armed groups provided the background for neighbors getting involved. No viable political settlement for the local and regional dimensions of the conflicts was reached at the time the missions were deployed.

The relationship of the peacekeeping missions with the respective (transitional) governments was strongly driven by the official recognition of their legitimacy and the dependence on their consent for deployment. Furthermore, missions were assigned the task of protecting transitional institutions. Overall, the statebuilding agenda was central to international engagement in both cases. The relation to neighbor states proved to be more complicated. Peacekeeping missions could hardly ignore continuing interference. But they had difficulties responding to it as they were facing complex and largely unresolved conflict formations. Moreover, as much as regional interference had been a problem, at times it also had the potential to provide solutions for the peace missions' manifold challenges.

A continuing balancing act: MONUC/MONUSCO and regional intervention

The international peacekeeping operation in the DRC shifted in its responses to regional intervention over time. In the beginning MONUC mostly observed and reported foreign interference. In a second phase, after the official end of the second Congo war, it tried to contain direct regional intervention, but struggled to address proxy warfare and achieve effective disarmament. Finally, MONUC shifted to forced disarmament of foreign armed groups that remained a threat and pretext for regional interventions. However, the mission remained something of an "active bystander" to neighbors' interference when they concluded secret agreements with the Congolese government to undertake military operation inside the DRC and continued to support local proxies. Finally, yet another turn occurred with the establishment of an Intervention Brigade under MONUSCO command that largely was a response to the regional setting. Generally, MONUC/MONUSCO was forced to take on a more active role in dealing with the regional conflict formation as interference by neighboring states repeatedly undermined its goals and credibility.

An observer to regional intervention

MONUC had been deployed between 30 November 1999 and 30 June 2010 before being transformed into MONUSCO. Under a Chapter VII mandate the mission's tasks included monitoring and developing an action plan for the implementation of the ceasefire, supervising and verifying the disengagement of the parties' forces, facilitating humanitarian assistance, protecting UN and co-located personnel and facilities and, most importantly, protecting "civilians under imminent threat of physical violence".[28] Yet MONUC had a difficult start. All the signatories delayed the implementation of the Lusaka agreement. Even the relatively small number of foreseen peacekeepers could not be deployed for over two years. This period was also marked by the continuing presence of Rwandan and Ugandan forces on Congolese territory. The two neighbors also adapted to the new circumstances, first by an increasing reliance on local Congolese proxies, and later by agreements signed with the Congolese government on the withdrawal of their troops. Both moves can be explained as an attempt to avoid isolation as a "spoiler" in international peace efforts.

As a result, the Ugandan Army provided arms to the MLC, and the RCD-Goma remained strongly linked to the Rwandan government. The Congolese government was also hesitant in helping MONUC in its DDRRR efforts since it used many of the "negative forces" to counter Rwandan influence.[29] On the other hand, Rwanda officially withdrew its forces in October 2002 based on an accord with the DRC government that also foresaw the disarmament of the remaining Rwandan Hutu rebels in the DRC. A similar agreement was finalized with Uganda in September the same year.[30] With its rather low profile at the time and a low presence in the east of the country, where violence increasingly took place, MONUC was placed in a difficult position. Furthermore, the UN policy was still characterized by a hesitation to openly condemn Uganda's and Rwanda's involvement in the DRC, due to the failure during the Rwandan genocide and the subsequent refugee crisis.[31] In this situation, the mission was left with little leverage to systematically address the interference by neighbors, but at least was there to verify violations of the ceasefire and the withdrawal of foreign troops.[32]

Eventually, the withdrawal of Rwandan and most Ugandan troops from the DRC rendered negotiations to bring the war to a final conclusion possible. The Inter-Congolese Dialogue, facilitated by the South African government, finally brought together the most important actors inside the DRC. When the Sun City agreement was signed in December 2002, it provided for the setup of a multi-party transitional government and democratic elections. Indeed, Joseph Kabila was sworn in as transitional president for two years alongside four vice-presidents, one from the government, one from the unarmed political opposition, and one each from the MLC and the RCD-Goma.[33] The latter point was particularly important as the former proxies of neighboring Uganda and Rwanda were now officially part of the Congolese government.

Struggling with proxy warfare in Ituri and the Kivus

It soon turned out that the settlement established by the Sun City agreement was not the end of regional interference. In Ituri, Ugandan troops were still present in early 2003, and in the Kivus, Rwanda had started to align with new proxies. In the light of previous experiences, MONUC had started to increase in size, and the new head of the mission decided in July

2003 to take a more proactive role and redeploy most of MONUC's troops to the main trouble spots in the east.[34]

However, before this decision took effect, another round of escalation occurred in Ituri. In March 2003, the Ugandan army occupied the regional capital Bunia after Rwanda started to align with a former proxy of Uganda in the area. When Uganda withdrew its forces in May in an uncoordinated manner, MONUC could not control the situation and militias entered the town, killing and looting. A contingent of UN troops tried to respond, but was not able to fill the vacuum.[35] The UN Security Council therefore authorized an Interim Emergency Multinational Force of the EU, led by France. This EU force, with its "Operation Artemis", was able to stabilize the situation by dislodging Rwanda's proxy and seizing weapons to such a degree that MONUC's new Ituri brigade could be installed by early September 2003 with troops increased to almost 11,000.[36]

The situation in the other main theater of conflict, the Kivus, deteriorated seriously in the first half of 2004, when fighting over the city of Bukavu left hundreds dead. A number of Tutsi officers had refused integration into the national army after the Sun City agreement, and now challenged the Congolese government. Among them was General Nkunda, who had strong links to the Rwandese government.[37] General Nkunda's forces approached Bukavu, and MONUC troops essentially let them pass into town. This passivity shocked the local population, and anti-UN riots broke out in many Congolese cities including Kinshasa. The whole peace process was seriously called into question as the Congolese government deployed thousands of troops to the east, the Rwandan government accused the DRC of preparing an invasion, and the RCD-Goma leader in the transitional government resigned. The UN warned neighboring countries and the DRC against fighting another war. Finally, under intense international pressure and following negotiations by MONUC, Nkunda withdrew his forces from Bukavu in June.[38]

However, the regional dimension of the conflict soon came to the fore again, this time with a direct Rwandan intervention. MONUC had already reported the presence of more than one hundred Rwandan troops in South Kivu in April 2004. Even though Kigali denied this involvement, representatives repeatedly stated that they would directly intervene due to the continuing threat of the FDLR. When this happened (again) in November 2004, MONUC – alongside other actors including the US and the EU – reacted by stating that the UN would not accept this interference and would react in a very firm way. An additional MONUC brigade was deployed to North Kivu, and in December the UN Security Council ordered Rwanda to withdraw any forces it might have in the east of the DRC.[39]

Overall, two developments characterized this period. First, effective peacebuilding in the DRC was still severely hampered by the regional framework. The core issue of the regional conflict formation at the time remained the presence of the FDLR and of opposing Rwandan proxies on Congolese territory. While the FDLR no longer posed such a strong security threat to Rwanda, it provided at least a pretext for frequent intervention.[40] Second, while the response to direct regional interference was relatively straightforward, MONUC faced difficulties in responding to the threat by proxies. The mission became more robust as it was authorized to use "all necessary means" to fulfil its mandate and got more military personnel in the second half of 2003.[41] Another step was the extension of MONUC's mandate to the entire territory of the DRC and again an increase in the number of peacekeepers in October 2004.[42] Yet these moves came after MONUC's credibility had already been seriously compromised by events in Bunia and Bukavu. Moreover, they hardly entailed a coherent approach for how to deal with regional interference by local proxies. In addition, a major problem remaining for MONUC was the stalled DDRRR process of (foreign) armed groups providing a pretext as well as a means for regional intervention.

Forced disarmament and the move towards enforcement

MONUC finally changed its policy on disarmament from voluntary to forced measures when nine Bangladeshi peacekeepers were killed in February 2005.[43] In trying to eliminate foreign armed groups, MONUC increasingly engaged in military operations. In June and October 2005, and in spring 2006, it launched campaigns with the Congolese military after ultimatums for the FDLR to disarm had passed. However, the results were very limited and by the time of the national elections of 2006, the issue had not been resolved.[44] MONUC was slightly more successful in responding to the reappearance of the Ugandan ADF in December 2005, again in cooperation with Congolese forces. However, Uganda threatened to intervene again directly in March 2006, since another notorious Ugandan rebel movement, the Lord's Resistance Army (LRA), had entered the DRC. Furthermore, General Nkunda undertook a new offensive in January 2006, and just before the elections he announced the creation of the National Congress for the Defence of the People (CNDP).[45]

In light of the limited success, MONUC fell back on the approach of negotiating with relevant actors, and brought together the Congolese, Rwandan and Ugandan armies in Kinshasa in May 2006 in order to address rising tensions over several unresolved issues.[46] In addition, MONUC negotiated with armed groups so that they would refrain from using violence during the electoral process, which they largely did. However, by engaging in bargaining with them, the UN mission had also indirectly legitimized the armed presence of these groups and their territorial claims.[47] Elections proceeded peacefully on the whole, but immediately after the Supreme Court had confirmed Kabila as the winner of the presidential contest, renewed violence occurred in North Kivu as

Nkunda's CNDP forces attacked Congolese Army units and approached the city of Goma. MONUC was able to stop the offensive, but the situation remained insecure.[48] Another crisis erupted in mid-2008, when a CNDP attack took the Congolese Army and MONUC by surprise, and the group captured several towns.[49]

At this point, a new pattern emerged in the relations of neighboring countries. As Nkunda became increasingly alienated from his Rwandan supporters and the Congolese Army failed to deal effectively with the CNDP, President Kabila and his Rwandan counterpart Kagame reached a secret agreement. There had been a joint communiqué between the two governments a year earlier, facilitated by the UN, the US and the EU. But this time the rapprochement had a real impact. Nkunda was arrested and brought to Rwanda, parts of the CNDP integrated into the Congolese Army, and Rwandan and Congolese forces undertook an offensive in North Kivu against the remaining FDLR. Similarly, the Ugandan and the Congolese armies (with the Sudan People's Liberation Army) undertook Operation Lightning Thunder against LRA camps in Congo in December 2008. Another sudden offensive occurred in June 2010 against the Ugandan ADF, undertaken by the Congolese Army.[50] MONUC had not been consulted and therefore was not involved in the planning and implementation of the different offensives. Despite the secrecy, particularly of the Congolese-Rwandan rapprochement, the UN did not openly oppose the plan and decided to associate with it in order to reduce the negative impact on the population.[51]

The success of the joint operations proved to be limited. A December 2008 UNSC Resolution had provided MONUC with the mandate for jointly planned operations with integrated Congolese Army brigades that had been trained by the mission. On this basis MONUC supported further offensives against the FDLR in March 2009 and again in January 2010, with assistance in planning, the provision of equipment, and logistical and military support. However, the joint operations further undermined MONUC's reputation as it was unable to control the campaigns of the national Congolese Army. Furthermore, the operations also led to FDLR retaliation against civilians, which further undermined MONUC as it failed to live up to its mandate.[52] Thus navigating between forced disarmament side by side with the Congolese military, containment of, but also negotiation with, proxy forces, and an "active bystander" role in secret regional agreements became a complex affair for MONUC.

Amid demands for its withdrawal by the Congolese government, MONUC was finally converted into the stabilization mission MONUSCO in 2010, by which time it had become the largest UN mission with 20,573 troops. But soon another wave of escalation proved that the regional conflict formation was very much alive. A mutiny by fighters integrated into the Congolese army based on the Rwandan-Congolese agreement led to the creation of the "March 23" rebel movement (M23) in the beginning of

2012. The renewed security threat by the group that, according to a UN report, has been supported by Rwanda and Uganda revealed again the limitations of dealing with regional interference. While there had clearly been increasing pressure on Rwanda at the diplomatic level, MONUSCO did not respond to the M23 takeover of Goma in November 2012, due to the limitations of its mandate. After a negotiated withdrawal of M23 from Goma in December, the situation remained fragile, as the rebels did not drop their demands and no lasting agreement was reached.

In this situation, the regional context for the setup of the international peace operation in the DRC proved decisive once more. On 28 March 2013, the UN Security Council authorized an Intervention Brigade under the command of MONUSCO consisting of up to 3,000 troops from South Africa, Tanzania and Malawi in order to contain, neutralize and disarm the M23 and other Congolese and foreign armed groups in targeted offensive operations.[53] This move towards peace enforcement strongly emanated from the regional context. On the one hand, the M23 takeover of Goma led to the realization that other options had to be explored, particularly in dealing with the foreign (backed) armed groups. On the other hand, the idea of a "neutral international force" for Eastern DRC had already been conceived of by regional states at a summit in July 2012 in Kampala. The International Conference on the Great Lakes Region and SADC, however, faced difficulties in putting together the force. The unclear relationship with MONUSCO was another serious concern; so, despite disagreement on the exact mandate of the brigade within the UN, the Security Council finally took action.

As part of a comprehensive approach, the "Peace, Security and Cooperation Framework for the DRC and the Region" was also signed on 24 February 2013 in Addis Ababa. Ten countries, including Rwanda and Uganda, committed themselves to non-interference in internal Congolese affairs and to refusing to tolerate or support armed groups, while the DRC's government promised reforms in the security sector as well as advancing decentralization and democratization.[54] Whether these measures will ultimately prove successful or not, they clearly are an expression of the important role of the regional dimension in the continuing Congolese crisis and its resolution.

Embracing the inevitable: AMISOM and regional intervention

AMISOM has responded in a very different way to regional interference. It usually (silently) accepted interventions whether they were authorized, unauthorized or pursued by proxies. There were more reservations regarding the involvement of Ethiopia because of its negative reputation inside Somalia. However, AMISOM relied on its military force in a kind of division of labour in combating Somali groups, mostly al-Shabaab.

Particularly since 2011, Ethiopian forces have intervened again to secure different areas before AMISOM ideally moves in and tries to replace them. Another response occurred with the integration of unilaterally intervening Kenyan forces into AMISOM. This may be a way to address regional interference, but also risks increasing frictions inside the mission. As with MONUC, the AU mission became more robust over time in response to threats inside Somalia. But in contrast to it, AMISOM developed a relatively clear approach of embracing regional interventions as largely inevitable and mostly conducive to its core goals. Due to the challenges of its peace enforcement profile, the mission basically accepted Ethiopian intervention, included Kenyan forces, and even promoted the use of proxy warfare itself. Furthermore, neighbors were backing the Somali governments and fighting the same enemy. Even though their interests may at times have been diverging from those of the AU mission, Ethiopia and Kenya were generally supporting the statebuilding project and the political process of the "Roadmap". Last but not least, the two countries have a strong influence in the AU and, particularly, in IGAD as its (sub-)regional pillar.

Getting AMISOM in and Ethiopia out

The initial mandate of AMISOM foresaw a deployment of only six months for short-term stabilization before takeover by a UN operation.[55] However, the evolution into a UN mission has not yet materialized, mostly due to the lack of a viable political framework and continuing insecurity. Like MONUC, AMISOM was set up where there was no real peace to keep.[56] The lack of an effective political process was even more severe than in the DRC. The UN Security Council thus called for a broad-based national reconciliation effort when authorizing the mission in February 2007.

The actual setup of the AU mission also proved to be difficult. Immediate neighboring countries were not barred from contributing troops by the respective resolution, but there clearly were reservations, particularly concerning Ethiopia, and Kenya did not want to be drawn into the conflict at the time.[57] Finally, Uganda was the first country to provide troops, allegedly in an effort to improve donor perceptions and its international profile more generally.[58]

Under a Chapter VII mandate, the official tasks of the peacekeepers are to provide security to the institutions of the TFG, to secure ports and airports to facilitate access to goods and humanitarian aid, and to help build security forces. The protection of civilians is not part of the mandate, but the AU Special Envoy to Somalia at the time claimed a certain responsibility to provide human security whenever possible due to provisions in the AU's Constitutive Act, particularly the principle of "non-indifference".[59]

The initial deployment of a first small group of AMISOM forces into Mogadishu in March 2007 did not essentially change the situation. The

UN therefore mediated talks in an attempt to broaden the basis of the TFG. The Djibouti mediation process from June 2008 to February 2009 ended with a timetable for Ethiopian withdrawal, and a new composition of the TFG that included the ARS and made the former Chair of the UIC the new president. The more radical offshoot of the UIC, al-Shabaab, portrayed the agreement as a betrayal, opposed the TFG and declared its support for al-Qaeda. This group, as well as Hizbul Islamiya forces, controlled much of southern Somalia.[60] As the presence of Ethiopian forces provided a unifying thread for various armed groups and civilians within Somalia, getting these forces out of Somalia became a pressing concern. Furthermore, as AMISOM was deployed alongside Ethiopian troops in 2007 and 2008, it came to be seen as an agent of Ethiopian interests and was increasingly the target of attacks.[61]

However, the official withdrawal of Ethiopian forces by January 2009 did not end opposition to the TFG and AMISOM. It did not lead to a security vacuum but further strengthened al-Shabaab, which openly rejected the presence of the peace mission.[62] All key actors such as the UN, the US and the EU invested heavily in the Somali statebuilding project, among other things by financing AMISOM and providing logistical support. The TFG and the AU peace mission to protect it relied heavily on external actors. Regional and international interests became further entangled as the US provided material and training support to countries neighboring Somalia, especially Kenya and Ethiopia.[63] As the TFG remained mostly ineffective, its regional and international recognition was the only real legitimacy it had at the time.[64]

AMISOM itself has sought different responses to the increasingly hostile situation inside Somalia. On the one hand, it became engaged in actual fighting in Mogadishu, and in doing so occasionally violated human rights and international humanitarian law.[65] The AU had also extended its forces considerably to 9,595 by September 2011.[66] On the other hand, AMISOM has tried to encourage the TFG to reach out to critical actors outside of Mogadishu and gain their support, for example the Somali Islamist group Ahlu Sunna Wal Jama'a (ASWJ), which is strong in the central regions and has prevented the advance of al-Shabaab to the north.[67]

However, it remained a serious challenge for the AU and the international community to de-link the security concerns of neighboring countries from the conflicts in Somalia.[68] In fact, this point has hardly been addressed in a systematic way. Ethiopia and Kenya have intervened directly and indirectly on several occasions since AMISOM's deployment. Ethiopia never really withdrew after 2009, but maintained a network of proxies and pursued a buffer zone strategy involving a network of proxy militias including the ASWJ inside Somalia. It also continued reconnaissance missions across the border.[69]

Kenya has recruited Somali youths from refugee camps as fighters, and also pursued the plan of a buffer zone on the other side of the border by creating an area controlled by friendly militias called "Jubaland". Kenya has stated security concerns, as its north-eastern province has been destabilized at times.[70] Yet Kenya has also had to deal with large waves of Somali refugees fleeing the conflict. Creating a buffer zone could thus also serve the purpose of providing a "safe area" inside Somalia to prevent more people from entering Kenya.[71] Whatever the real motivation was, Kenya tried to work with many different Somali allies over the course of 2011.[72] Overall, AMISOM was not only lacking the means to respond to the repeated regional interference. Due to an increasing al-Shabaab threat it had to rely on contributions by other forces, or at least discreetly embrace them. This position became obvious once more when the regional conflict formation materialized in another round of regional interventions.

Kenyan intervention and integration into AMISOM

In October 2011, Kenya intervened unilaterally with thousands of troops in the Juba Valley of Somalia. This was a new level of interference and "the biggest security gamble Kenya has taken since independence".[73] While some kind of direct intervention had been considered for years, the actual deployment of Operation Linda Nchi turned out to be poorly prepared. First, goals and potential risks of the intervention had not been coherently assessed. Kenyan officials outlined very different aims of the campaign, ranging from simply preventing cross-border threats by al-Shabaab to actually defeating the Islamist group.[74] Moreover, Kenyan forces ran into difficulties due to the unfamiliar terrain and the rainy season, which carried the risk of a lengthy presence on Somali territory that might antagonize public opinion.[75] Second, the intervention took place without prior approval of the relevant local, regional and international actors. The TFG only agreed to support the campaign after it had been going on for almost two weeks, and diplomatic tensions were visible at other levels, for example vis-à-vis Ethiopia. Western allies were also critical of the feasibility of the operation, and expressed only half-hearted support for it days after it had started. About a week after Kenyan troops entered Somalia, IGAD welcomed the offensive in a communiqué, but also called for enhanced coordination and the consideration of the integration of Kenyan forces into AMISOM.[76]

In light of these shortcomings and the strong burden of the operation, Kenya decided to integrate its forces into AMISOM. The AU approved their participation in December 2011 and in late February 2012, and the UN Security Council authorized an increase in troop strength from 12,000 to nearly 18,000.[77] At first sight the integration seemed to be in everybody's interest, particularly as the TFG and AMISOM have relied on the support of Ethiopia and Kenya and of different Somali clan militias in pushing back al-Shabaab in 2011. But the integration is also a serious challenge to the AU mission's functioning. Even before, the AU had little leverage over troop-contributing countries and found it difficult to make Uganda and Burundi adhere to AU rules and procedures. With Kenya's entry, the situation was further complicated and diverging views on the mission's mandate, as well as on command and control, quickly came to the fore. Furthermore, the integration was not the end of regional interventions outside of AMISOM as Ethiopian forces advanced into southern Somalia in late 2011 and early 2012.[78]

These recent developments had mixed implications. On the one hand, AMISOM managed to extend its control beyond Mogadishu and seized the port city of Kismayo in October 2012 together with Somali forces. It has been fully deployed since November 2012 with a strength of 17,709 troops.[79] Ethiopian troops helped the Somali government to capture additional areas, including the town of Baidoa.[80] On the other hand, apart from the fact that al-Shabaab is far from defeated – the remnants of it moved towards Northern Somalia, forged regional alliances and committed bomb attacks in Mogadishu, and infiltrated the Somali security apparatus – there is also the risk of regional fragmentation. The rivalry between Ethiopia, Kenya and Uganda may undermine the efforts to stabilize Somalia and create different zones of influence.[81] Moreover, looking more closely, the interests of neighbor countries and those of AMISOM and its international backers are not really congruent. Kenya and Ethiopia are not necessarily in favour of a stable central government in Somalia, but rather a decentralized federal state or even a weak confederal structure.[82] It was partly seen as a sign of strained relations with AMISOM and the Somali government when Ethiopia withdrew its forces from Hudur near the Ethiopian border in March 2013, leaving the town to al-Shabaab again.[83]

While the political process has moved forward slightly with the implementation of the Roadmap in the second half of 2012, followed by the partial lifting of the arms embargo by the UN Security Council in March 2013 and the decision to install a UN Assistance Mission in Somalia (UNSOM) by June 2013,[84] security remains volatile. Furthermore, it is AMISOM overall that remains stuck with the task of securing the process inside Somalia while also handling the regional dimension.

Conclusion

Regional interventions continue to confront MONUC/MONUSCO and AMISOM alike with difficult choices. In both conflict theaters, these missions became more robust over time. But this did not end the difficult balancing act of responding to neighbors "keeping a foot in the door". Moreover, there were important differences in how the two missions reacted to regional interventions. AMISOM tended to accept them as almost inevitable and more of a solution, at least for fulfilling its mandate. For MONUC/MONUSCO, on the other hand, regional interference was more of a problem, but the missions shifted between different responses – from passivity to more open opposition, partly depending on the kind of interference.

Certainly the different mandates and setups of the peacekeeping missions mattered. But the way international and regional agendas converged or clashed played an important role as well. In the DRC the most relevant neighboring countries ended up in opposition to the Congolese government, while in Somalia they supported the TFG and the subsequent government. As the statebuilding project has been core to international engagement in both cases, this fact had a decisive impact. In the DRC, MONUC and MONUSCO were often caught between local and regional aspirations. In contrast, a gap between internal and external conceptions of peacebuilding has emerged in Somalia.[85] The fact that AMISOM is a regional peacekeeping mission is relevant; yet what matters most is its specific role in battling al-Shabaab, its strong dependence on international and regional players and the resulting (superficial) convergence of agendas, not an alleged alternative approach of "African solutions".

Looking at the different responses to regional intervention over time, and the impact the missions had on the conflict formations and vice-versa, the general assumption that peacekeeping missions tend to freeze a conflict situation has to be questioned. In fact, it may be much more adequate to understand the deployment of a peacekeeping mission as the entry into a regional conflict formation that shapes its strategies and the behavior of the respective actors in turn. Furthermore, differences in these formations, and how they relate to the international as well as the local level, are clearly relevant to how peacekeeping missions respond to the challenge of neighbors' continuing intervention.

Notes

1 AMISOM is not a traditional peacekeeping mission, but it is still often labelled as such, even by the AU itself (see, e.g.: http://amisom-au.org/about/amisom-background/). Therefore, this chapter refers to AMISOM as a peacekeeping mission while still taking its specific character into account.
2 B. Rubin, A. Armstrong and G.R. Ntegeye (eds), *Regional Conflict Formation in the Great Lakes Region of Africa: Structure, Dynamics and Challenges for Policy*, Center on International Cooperation, New York University and The African Peace Forum, Nairobi, Kenya, 11–13 November 2001, p. 3.
3 R. Mac Ginty, "Hybrid Peace: The Interaction Between Top-Down and Bottom-Up Peace", *Security Dialogue* 41, 2010, pp. 391–412.
4 See K. Lidén, R. Mac Ginty and O.P. Richmond, "Introduction: Beyond Northern Epistemologies of Peace: Peacebuilding Reconstructed?", *International Peacekeeping* 16, 2009, pp. 587–598, 588.
5 At the time, the country was called Zaire.
6 G. Prunier, *Africa's World War: Congo, the Rwandan Genocide, and the Making of a Continental Catastrophe*, Oxford: Oxford University Press, 2009, pp. 4–5.
7 F. Reyntjens, *The Great African War: Congo and Regional Geopolitics, 1996–2006*, Cambridge: Cambridge University Press, 2009, pp. 57–60.

8 J.K. Stearns, *Dancing in the Glory of Monsters: The Collapse of the Congo and the Great War of Africa*, London: Perseus Running Press, 2011, p. 183; Reyntjens, *Great African War*, p. 201.
9 This expression has been used by US Assistant Secretary of State for African Affairs Susan Rice (see F. Reyntjens, "Briefing: The Second Congo War – More than a Remake", *African Affairs* 98, 1999, pp. 241–250, 247) and was later used in many analyses of the Congo Wars, most prominently by Prunier, *Africa's World War*.
10 F. Reyntjens, "Briefing: The Democratic Republic of Congo – From Kabila to Kabila", *African Affairs* 100, 2001, pp. 311–317, 311.
11 "Lusaka Ceasefire Agreement", DRC, 10 July 1999, p. 4.
12 M. Malan and J. Gomes Porto, "Introduction", in Malan and Gomes Porto (eds), *Challenges of Peace Implementation: The UN Mission in the Democratic Republic of Congo*, Pretoria: Institute for Security Studies (ISS), 2004, pp. 1–21, 13–14.
13 Prunier, *Africa's World War*, pp. 246–247, 266.
14 After the succession of Somaliland in 1991 and the declaration of the Puntland State of Somalia as an autonomous region in 1998, the southern part of Somalia was left essentially separated.
15 M. Bradbury and S. Healy, "A Brief History of the Somali Conflict", in M. Bradbury and S. Healy (eds), *Whose Peace Is It Anyway? Connecting Somali and International Peacemaking*, Accord 21, London: Conciliation Resources, 2010, pp. 10–14, 10–11.
16 *Ibid.*, p. 12.
17 D. Dehéz and B. Gebrewold, "When Things Fall Apart – Conflict Dynamics and an Order Beside the State in Postcollapse Somalia", *African Security* 3, 2010, pp. 1–20, 11.
18 Bradbury and Healy, "Brief History", p. 12.
19 K. Menkhaus, "Diplomacy in a Failed State", in Bradbury and Healy (eds), *Whose Peace Is It Anyway? Connecting Somali and International Peacemaking*, Accord 21, London: Conciliation Resources, 2010, pp. 16–19, 17–18.
20 Dehéz and Gebrewold, "When Things Fall Apart", p. 11.
21 Bradbury and Healy, "Brief History", pp. 13–14; Dehéz and Gebrewold, "When Things Fall Apart", p. 13.
22 T. Dagne, *Somalia: Current Conditions and Prospects for a Lasting Peace*, Congressional Research Service, 31 August 2011, p. 17; Dehéz and Gebrewold, "When Things Fall Apart", p. 10.
23 A. El-Affendi, "The Perils of Regionalism: Regional Integration as a Source of Instability in the Horn of Africa?", *Journal of Intervention and Statebuilding* 3, 2009, pp. 1–19, 10; A.S. Bah, "The Broader Horn of Africa: Peacekeeping in a Strategic Vacuum", *International Peacekeeping* 16, 2009, pp. 499–513, 503.
24 Bradbury and Healy, "Brief History", p. 14.
25 Dehéz and Gebrewold, "When Things Fall Apart", pp. 12–13; Human Rights Watch, *Harsh War, Harsh Peace Abuses by al-Shabaab, the Transitional Federal Government, and AMISOM in Somalia*, New York, April 2010, p. 61.
26 M. Bradbury, *State-building, Counterterrorism, and Licensing Humanitarianism in Somalia*, Briefing Paper, Feinstein International Center, Somerville MA: Tufts University, September 2010, p. 7.
27 S.A. Dersso, *Somalia Dilemmas: Changing Security Dynamics, but Limited Policy Choices*, ISS Paper 218, Pretoria, October 2010, p. 13.
28 UN Security Council Resolution 1291, 24 February 2000.
29 Prunier, *Africa's World War*, pp. 267–269.
30 Reyntjens, *The Great African War*, p. 259.
31 Prunier, *Africa's World War*, pp. 344–345.
32 D.M. Tull, "Peacekeeping in the Democratic Republic of Congo: Waging Peace and Fighting War", *International Peacekeeping* 16, 2009, pp. 215–230, 217.

33 *Ibid.*, p. 216.
34 Prunier, *Africa's World War*, p. 296.
35 E. Rogier, "MONUC and the Challenges of Peace Implementation in the DRC: A Participant's Perspective", in Malan and Gomes Porto (eds), *Challenges of Peace Implementation: The UN Mission in the Democratic Republic of Congo*, Pretoria: ISS, 2004, pp. 255–268, 265; Prunier, *Africa's World War*, pp. 292–293.
36 Reyntjens, *The Great African War*, pp. 218–220.
37 Prunier, *Africa's World War*, p. 297.
38 T. Turner, *The Congo Wars: Conflict, Myth and Reality*, London and New York: Zed Books, 2007, pp. 101 and 160; Prunier, *Africa's World War*, p. 298.
39 Reyntjens, *The Great African War*, pp. 211–213.
40 *Ibid.*, p. 209; Prunier, *Africa's World War*, p. 309.
41 UN Security Council Resolution 1493, 28 July 2003.
42 Tull, "Peacekeeping", p. 218.
43 Reyntjens, *The Great African War*, p. 221.
44 *Ibid.*, p. 211.
45 *Ibid.*, p. 214.
46 Prunier, *Africa's World War*, p. 308.
47 D. Johnson, "Interessenlagen der Akteure im Kongo bei der Stationierung von EUFOR", in H.-G. Justenhoven and H.-G. Ehrhart (eds), *Intervention im Kongo: Eine kritische Analyse der Befriedungspolitik von UN und EU*, Stuttgart: Kohlhammer, 2008, pp. 14–29, 24.
48 M. Bøås, "'Just Another Day' – The North Kivu Security Predicament After the 2006 Congolese Elections", *African Security* 1, 2008, pp. 53–68, 55.
49 T. Dagne, *The Democratic Republic of Congo: Background and Current Developments*, Congressional Research Service, Washington DC, 1 September 2011, p. 5.
50 D. Fahey, "Guns and Butter: Uganda's Involvement in Northeastern Congo 2003–2009", paper presented at the African Studies Association 2009 Annual Meeting, New Orleans, 20 November 2009, p. 18; International Crisis Group (ICG), *No Stability in Kivu despite a Rapprochement with Rwanda*, Africa Report 165, 16 November 2010, p. 16.
51 ICG, *No Stability*, pp. i, 10; ICG, *Congo: A Comprehensive Strategy to Disarm the FDLR*, Africa Report 151, 9 July 2009, p. i.
52 ICG, *Congo*, p. ii; ICG, *No Stability*, p. 11.
53 UN Security Council Resolution 2098, 28 March 2013.
54 "Peace, Security and Cooperation Framework for DRC and the region", AU, 24 February 2013, available at www.peaceau.org/uploads/scanned-on-24022013-125543.pdf, accessed 3 June 2013.
55 UN Security Council Resolution 1744, 20 February 2007, p. 1.
56 Bah, "Broader Horn of Africa", p. 501.
57 Dagne, *Somalia*, , pp. 9–10; *Have All the Options Run Out*, ISS Situation Report, 13 November 2007, p. 6.
58 J. Fisher, "Managing Donor Perception: Contextualizing Uganda's 2007 Intervention in Somalia", *African Affairs* 111, 2012, pp. 404–423, 421; later on these forces were joined by troops from Burundi and Djibouti.
59 A. Ramsbotham, "An African Solution to Somalia? A Conversation with Nicolas Bwakira", in Bradbury and Healy (eds), *Whose Peace Is It Anyway? Connecting Somali and International Peacemaking*, Accord 21, London: Conciliation Resources, 2010, pp. 30–31, 30.
60 M. Preston McGhie, "Mediating Djibouti", in Bradbury and Healy (eds), *Whose Peace Is It Anyway? Connecting Somali and International Peacemaking*, Accord 21, London: Conciliation Resources, 2010, pp. 20–23, 20; Bradbury and Healy, "Brief History", p. 14.
61 D. Dehéz, "Die Vereinten Nationen und Somalia", *Zeitschrift Vereinte Nationen*

57, 2009, pp. 117–122, 121; Bah, "Broader Horn of Africa", pp. 504–505; ICG, *Somalia: To move Beyond the Failed State*, Africa Report 147, 23 December 2008, p. 20.

62 Bah, "Broader Horn of Africa", pp. 504–505.

63 D.H. Shinn, *Assessing the Consequences of the Failed State of Somalia*, Joint Hearing, House Subcommittee on Africa, Global Health, and Human Rights, Washington DC, 7 July 2011, p. 3.

64 K.P. Apuuli, "Somalia after the United Nations-led Djibouti Peace Process", *African Security Review* 20, 2011, pp. 45–53, 51.

65 Human Rights Watch, *Harsh War*, p. 57.

66 "Report of the Chairperson of the Commission on the Situation in Somalia, Peace and Security Council, 293th meeting", AU, PSC/PR/2(CCXCIII), 13 September 2011, p. 8.

67 Bradbury, *State-building*, p. 6; Ramsbotham, "African Solution", p. 30.

68 J. Cilliers, H. Boshoff and F.B. Aboagye, "Somalia: The Intervention Dilemma", *ISS Policy Brief* 20, 20 August 2010, p. 8.

69 "Ethiopia, Kenya and Somalia: More but not Merrier", *The Economist*, 28 November 2011; B.E. Bruton, *Somalia: A New Approach*, New York: Council of Foreign Relations, Council Special Report 52, March 2010, p. 32.

70 K. Menkhaus, *After the Kenyan Intervention in Somalia*, The Enough Project, January 2012, p. 2.

71 Human Rights Watch, *"You Don't Know Who to Blame": War Crimes in Somalia*, New York, August 2011, p. 13.

72 Menkhaus, op. cit., p. 4.

73 ICG, *The Kenyan Military Intervention in Somalia*, Africa Report 184, 15 February 2012, p. i.

74 Menkhaus, *After the Kenyan Intervention*, p. 5.

75 ICG, *Kenyan Military Intervention*, p. i.

76 "Communique of the 19th Extra-ordinary Session of the IGAD Assembly of Heads of State and Government on the Situation in Somalia and a Briefing on the Outstanding Issues of the Sudan Comprehensive Peace Agreement", IGAD, 25 November 2012, p. 3.

77 UN Security Council Resolution 2036, 22 February 2012, p. 4.

78 Dersso, *Somalia Dilemmas*, p. 16; ICG, *Kenyan Military Intervention*, pp. 3–5 and 12–13.

79 "February 2013 Monthly Forecast, Somalia", Security Council Report, 31 January 2013, available at www.securitycouncilreport.org/monthly-forecast/2013–02/somalia4.php, accessed 1 April 2013.

80 M. Yusuf, "AMISOM to Replace Ethiopian Troops in Central Somalia", *Voice of America*, 14 March 2012, available at www.voanews.com/content/amisom-to-replace-ethiopian-troops-in-central-somalia-142807215/179831.html, accessed 13 October 2012.

81 ICG, *Kenyan Military Intervention*, p. 11.

82 D.W. Throup, "Kenya's Intervention in Somalia", Center for Strategic and International Studies, 16 February 2012, available at http://csis.org/print/35302, accessed 20 October 2012.

83 Reuters, "Ethiopia says Preparing to Pull Troops Out of Somalia", 23 April 2013, available at http://uk.reuters.com/article/2013/04/23/uk-somalia-ethiopia-troops-idUKBRE93M19A20130423, accessed 3 June 2013.

84 UN Security Council Resolution 2102, 2 May 2013.

85 W.C. Saalax and A.A. Ibrahim "Xildhiban", "Somali Peace Agreements", in Bradbury and Healy (eds), *Whose Peace Is It Anyway? Connecting Somali and International Peacemaking*, Accord 21, London: Conciliation Resources, 2010, pp. 32–33, 36.

9 The long path to MINUSMA

Assessing the international response to the crisis in Mali

Lori-Anne Théroux-Bénoni

Introduction

The complex and multidimensional crisis in Mali has put regional, continental and international security arrangements through a tough test. Multilateral responses to the outbreak of the armed Tuareg secessionist rebellion of January 2012, the coup d'état of March 2012 and the subsequent occupation of northern Mali by a mixture of terrorist, extremist and criminal groups clearly lacked direction, coherence and coordination. The broad support received by the French Operation "Serval", launched in January 2013 to counter the offensive of the Northern armed groups, was illustrative of the absence of credible and timely alternatives to respond to the threat. This situation, in turn, revealed the shortcomings of the existing security architecture at the level of the Economic Community of West African States (ECOWAS), the African Union (AU) and the UN, as well as weaknesses in their interactions. In tracing the evolving international response to the situation in Mali, from the March 2012 coup to the April 2013 authorization of the UN Multidimensional Integrated Stabilization Mission in Mali (MINUSMA), this chapter explores the shortcomings of current multilateral security frameworks and draws lessons, in order to address more effectively the changing nature of threats to peace and security in Africa.[1]

The chapter is in two sections. The first section analyses the security and military responses articulated in Mali by international organizations. Broadly, these responses can be classified into four phases, which are overlapping to some extent. Phase one is centred on the regional response made through the ECOWAS Mission in Mali (MICEMA) following the putsch. Phase two relates to the progressive Africanization and internationalization of the response, which led to the African-led International Support Mission in Mali (AFISMA). Phase three saw the launch of the French military Operation Serval, followed by the hasty deployment of AFISMA and the United Nations Office in Mali (UNOM), as well as the establishment of the European Union Training Mission to Mali (EUTM Mali). Phase four revolves around the establishment of MINUSMA, through the integration of UNOM and the re-hatting of AFISMA. This section analyses the parameters that have contributed to framing each of the military responses identified above, as well as the challenges that made it necessary to move to the next step.

These challenges are further discussed in the second section, which analyses the shortcomings of the current multilateral security architecture. The management of the Malian crisis highlighted major weaknesses in the functioning of the various components of the emerging African Peace and Security Architecture (APSA). It made evident the need if not for a doctrinal evolution on the part of the UN, at least for a closer cooperation, more creative partnership and enhanced synergy between the world body and regional arrangements based on their respective comparative advantages.

Multilateral attempts to address the Malian crisis

Phase 1: MICEMA – an attempt to regionalize the response

The initial response to the crisis in Mali, which spans the period from the March 2012 coup to the consultations between the African organizations and the UN in New York in June 2012, was regional in character. Articulated by ECOWAS, it was centred on the decision to deploy a stabilization mission in Mali. This decision, however, never went beyond the planning stages, having faced three main obstacles: first, the junta's hostility to any armed presence in Bamako, and ECOWAS's then primary focus on restoring constitutional order, before tackling the situation in the northern part of the country; second, the absence of consensus on the way forward within ECOWAS and between ECOWAS and other countries considered central in the search of a solution, namely Algeria and Mauritania; third, logistical and financial constraints, which made it impossible to effectively deploy the planned mission in the absence of international support.

Understanding the first hurdle – disagreements between the junta, which took the name of the *Comité National de Redressement de la Démocratie et de Restauration de l'État*, and ECOWAS – calls for a brief analysis of the background of the "accidental" coup of 22 March 2012.[2] The anger that led to the putsch first manifested itself in the form of a mutiny in protest against the appalling conditions in which soldiers were fighting in the north, following the rebellion led by the National Movement for the Liberation of Azawad (*Mouvement National de Libération de l'Azawad*, MNLA) in January 2012. Many practices within the Malian army persistently undermined the country's security apparatus: recruitment based on nepotism and cronyism; promotion not always founded on merit and competence; integration into the army of former rebel fighters without sufficient training or monitoring; involvement of senior military officers in various sorts of trafficking; lack of equipment; and the reliance of the central government on tribal militia rather than the regular army in the management of security in northern Mali.[3] This situation reflected the military facet of a decadent governance that had prevailed for many years.

The March coup created a constitutional vacuum, precipitated the disintegration of what remained of the army's chain of command, and facilitated the advance of the rebellion and other armed extremist and terrorist groups, such as Al-Qaeda in the Islamic Maghreb (AQIM), Ansar Dine, and the Movement for Unity and Jihad in West Africa (MUJWA), which gained control of the main northern population centres from which they progressively chased MNLA fighters. Against this backdrop, ECOWAS focused on the return to constitutional order and the restoration of territorial integrity, as stated in the communiqué of the extraordinary session of its Assembly of Heads of State and Government held in Abidjan on 27 March 2012. This meeting authorized the activation of the ECOWAS Standby Force "to deal with any eventuality", which appears in the section dealing with the return to constitutional order.[4] It seems that, for ECOWAS, the threat was emanating as much from the junta as from the northern armed groups.

Following the coup, mediation efforts undertaken by ECOWAS under the auspices of the President of Burkina Faso, Blaise Compaoré,[5] led to the Framework Agreement of 6 April 2012. This agreement put in place fragile institutional arrangements within the framework of the Malian Constitution of 1992. It entrusted the post of Interim President to the Speaker of the National Assembly, Dioncounda Traoré, following the resignation of ousted Head of State Amadou Toumani Touré. Since the Framework Agreement was signed between the mediation and the junta, the latter became somewhat legitimized as an actor in the transition.[6]

Following the signing of the Framework Agreement, the ECOWAS Mediation and Security Council adopted the recommendations of the Military Staff Committee to mandate the ECOWAS standby force to restore territorial integrity and constitutional order in Mali.[7] In mid-April, the envisaged deployment of the Standby Force took the name MICEMA (ECOWAS Mission in Mali).[8] Notably, mission planning envisaged the deployment of troops in Bamako in order to secure the transitional institutions as well as the ECOWAS civilian, police and military personnel.

During the early stages of this response, a growing gap developed between, on the one hand, the normative approach of ECOWAS and that of the larger international community, predicated on the restoration of the institutional arrangements that had existed before the putsch, and, on the other, the perception of some Malian actors for whom the restoration of constitutional order was tantamount to "bringing back a corrupt regime and a dubious governance system".[9] Taking advantage of this gap, the junta adopted a populist posture with nationalistic undertones and mobilized local support to resist the demands of an international community perceived as trying to bring back to power a discredited political class held responsible for the defeat of the Malian army by the armed groups in the north.

The disagreement between the junta and ECOWAS had especially to do with the priority lent to the various stages of the mission proposed in MICEMA's concept of operations and the role of the Malian army in its implementation. The lengthy discussions that ensued revealed the depth of the mistrust between Bamako and the West African organization, and complicated efforts towards reaching a consensus beyond the region.

The second constraint that hindered the regional approach pertains to the absence of agreement on the way forward: first, within ECOWAS, and second, between ECOWAS and Algeria as well as, to a lesser extent, Mauritania. Within ECOWAS, the Commission, the mediation led by Burkina Faso, with Nigeria later appointed as associate mediator,[10] the Chair (Côte d'Ivoire), and individual countries did not always agree on the position to adopt, and neither did they act in a coordinated fashion. Although most ECOWAS countries strongly supported military action, opinions diverged on the modalities of the negotiation process with northern armed groups. Outside of ECOWAS, Algeria was far more cautious regarding military action, favouring dialogue with some of the armed groups such as the MNLA and Ansar Dine. Since AQIM was largely built on the former Algerian *Groupe Salafiste pour la Prédication et le Combat*, Algiers was perceived as a key actor in the search for a solution.[11] Mauritania's changing position appears to have largely been framed by its support for military action without its direct participation and by the presence, in Nouakchott, of the political wing of the MNLA, which it may have perceived as an ally in the fight against terrorism.[12]

In spite of the ECOWAS efforts to include non-ECOWAS countries in the resolution of the crisis, not much progress was made in reaching a regional consensus, notably with Algeria. More generally, while what was needed was a truly regional solution, what was provided was an ECOWAS solution with a limited geographical and political outreach. The absence of a strong and structured North African organization that could have been ECOWAS's counterpart in a horizontal cooperation also hampered the prospects of coming up with an inclusive cross-regional solution.

Third, although ECOWAS envisaged the deployment of its Standby Force less than a week after the coup and discussed its funding in the document that created MICEMA,[13] the organization did not have the means to deploy and maintain such an operation over time. With an estimated yearly budget of US$227 million, the deployment of MICEMA therefore depended on support from other stakeholders, particularly the UN.

From a theoretical perspective, this episode may cast doubts on discourses that advocate regional crisis management, as well as on the role and legitimacy of ECOWAS as a sub-regional organization. The management of the Malian crisis by ECOWAS does not support the claim that regional actors are necessarily better positioned to understand crises in their backyards, to respond swiftly, to enlist the cooperation of conflicting parties or to facilitate consensus among member states. Concluding that ECOWAS failed in the management of the Malian crisis, however, would not do justice to regional efforts, which led to the return to constitutional order, as well as to the initiatives taken to advance mediation. In spite of the limitations of the regional response, it laid the ground for subsequent initiatives. Lessons should nonetheless be drawn regarding the functioning of APSA at the regional level and coordination between the regional, continental, and international levels of crisis management.

Phase 2: AFISMA – Africanization as the way forward?

The AU, which initially limited its efforts to supporting ECOWAS, started playing a more active role in June 2012. The continental organization's involvement was framed by the limitations which became apparent in ECOWAS's response. First, in a context where neither ECOWAS nor the AU had the necessary funding to support the envisaged mission, the AU attempted to secure financial support from the UN. Then, by transforming MICEMA into AFISMA, the AU simultaneously attempted, at the national level, to create conditions that would facilitate the deployment of an international force and, at the regional level, to overcome the reluctance of Algeria through the "continentalization" of the initiative.

Following its meeting held in New York on 12 June 2012, the AU Peace and Security Council (PSC) issued a communiqué that comes across as an attempt to reframe, within APSA, the ECOWAS decision to activate its Standby Force. The communiqué "authorize[d]" ECOWAS, "in collaboration as appropriate with the core countries, namely Algeria, Mauritania and Niger, to put in place the required military and security arrangements" in order to perform the following tasks: ensuring the security of the transitional institutions; restructuring and reorganizing the Malian security and defence forces; and restoring State authority over the northern part of the country and combating terrorism and criminal networks. The communiqué also sought "authorization for the provision of a support package funded by UN-assessed contributions".[14]

During a joint meeting of the UN Security Council (UNSC) and the AU PSC held on 13 June, the Security Council requested a clearer description of the political strategy underpinning the military approach. It stressed the need for the military strategy to be part of a wider approach to solve the crisis.[15] The request for a more comprehensive strategy was further reiterated in UNSC Resolution 2056 adopted on 5 July 2012. The Security Council also requested ECOWAS to collaborate more closely with the AU, among others, and to provide further details about "the objectives, means and modalities of the envisaged deployment and other possible measures".[16]

In parallel, steps were taken to find a compromise with the Malian actors on the primary objectives of the foreign intervention and on the role to be given to the Malian army in the northern campaign. A series of joint planning conferences were held in that regard between concerned international stakeholders and Malian representatives. Other key moments include, on 26 September 2012, the holding of a high-level meeting on the Sahel, on the margins of the UN General Assembly session, and the unanimous adoption by the UN Security Council, on 12 October, of Resolution 2071 on Mali. This resolution paved the way for the deployment of an "international military force" and requested the UN Secretary-General to provide military and security planners to assist joint ECOWAS and AU planning efforts.[17] The resolution also asked for a report which would include the "means and modalities of the envisaged deployment, in particular the concept of operations, force generation capabilities strength and financial costs".[18]

Against this backdrop, a continental approach was progressively promoted. In the run-up to the 19 October 2012 meeting of the Support and Follow-up Group on the situation in Mali, the AU, ECOWAS and their partners developed the "Strategic Concept for the Resolution of the Crises in Mali".[19] The PSC adopted the document on 24 October and welcomed the "on-going efforts for the rapid finalization of the joint planning for the deployment of an African-led international force in Mali".[20] The Strategic Concept informed the subsequent planning conference, which concluded its work in Bamako in November 2012, and during which an agreement was reached on the "harmonized" concept of operation for what became AFISMA.[21]

The Strategic Concept marked a shift with the previous ECOWAS approach by placing Malian national actors at the centre of the decision-making process in an operation in which the Malian army was supposed to have a lead role and was no longer a potential target for the military operation. It also moved the leadership to the continental level and enlarged the framework of the response to garner support from outside the continent.

On his part, the UN Secretary-General stated, in the report on the situation in Mali submitted in pursuance of Resolution 2071, that the UN was unfit for the task at hand in Mali. More specifically, he underlined that

> it would be more appropriate for the UN's partners in Mali, the region and the international community to do what may be required in other areas, such as counter-terrorism and a potential offensive military operation in the north, where the UN is not best suited to play a direct role.[22]

The Secretary-General, however, noted that "consideration could be given … to the possible deployment of a United Nations peacekeeping operation after the end of major combat operations".[23]

In terms of limitations, the transition from MICEMA to AFISMA was marked by a lack of coordination and, at times, tension between ECOWAS and the AU, which hampered the efforts to rapidly reach a consensus. In addition, the crucial issue of resource mobilization to sustain AFISMA could not be resolved. Although Security Council Resolution 2085 of 20 December 2012 authorized the mission, it did so under very stringent conditions[24] and did not provide the requested financial and logistical support package funded through assessed contributions. In effect, this resolution dashed any hope of a speedy deployment of AFISMA and highlighted, once more, the need for African organizations to find ways to fund their operations. The last limitation of this response, which appeared clearly during the offensive by the armed groups against the city of Konna, in early January 2013, was the limited capacity of the Malian army, expected to spearhead the campaign to regain control of the North.

Phase 3: French Operation Serval – revealing the shortcomings of multilateral responses

To some extent, extra-continental actors acted as if the situation on the ground would remain frozen until they managed to articulate a coherent response. The statement of the UN Special Envoy for the Sahel, Romano Prodi, who declared in December 2012 that a military operation could not take place before September 2013, is telling in this regard.[25] With hindsight, this assumption was based on a wrong assessment of the nature of the groups in northern Mali, the balance of forces among them and their ultimate objectives.

On 10 January 2013, about 20 days after the adoption by the Security Council of the resolution authorizing the deployment of AFISMA, Ansar Dine, MUJWA and AQIM launched what could be analysed as a preemptive offensive on the city of Kona, in the region of Mopti, swiftly overrunning the Malian army's positions. Military analysts believed that the attack against Konna was meant to be the first step towards taking Sévaré, where both an international airport and the Malian army's operational headquarters for the campaign in the north were located. Control of this town would have cut off the Malian army from the theater of operation, hampered the deployment of AFISMA, and facilitated the takeover of the south of the country.[26] On the one hand, this attack clarified the targets of the military response and showed them to include Ansar Dine, which had been, until then, perceived by some regional and international actors as a group to negotiate with. On the other hand, it called for an urgent response that the Malian army, whose reorganization and training by the EU had not yet commenced, and AFISMA – then still struggling to finalize its planning documents, generate forces and mobilize sufficient resources for its deployment – could not deliver.

At the request of the Malian transitional authorities, France launched Operation Serval on 11 January. This marked the beginning of the third phase of the international response. Although France had, until then, announced it would only support an African-led operation through technical advice, logistics and funding, what became Operation Serval had in fact long existed as a contingency plan.[27] The French ended up undertaking a major military intervention that blocked the southbound advance of the armed groups and subsequently regained control of the major cities in the north.

Operation Serval brought about a number of consequences. First, it induced a change in the way both the Malian authorities and their partners sequenced their military response. Originally, the plan was first to build the capacity of the Malian army with the help of the EU to enable it to play the lead role in regaining control of the North; then to progressively deploy AFISMA in support of the Malian army; and finally to launch a joint offensive military operation, with the Malian army ultimately taking over from foreign forces. In the wake of Operation Serval, the Malian army was expected to rebuild while engaged in operations on the ground. Second, AFISMA was expected to speed up its deployment and eventually take over from the French troops before the issues of its legal framework, financing, management, and command and control, including with its Chadian component, had been resolved. Finally, what was required was no longer to liberate the northern regions, but rather to secure and stabilize them.

While French and, later, Chadian troops were attempting to uproot the fighters of Ansar Dine, AQIM and MUJWA from the main northern population centres, AFISMA's concept of operations was revised to adjust to the new situation[28] and troops were progressively deployed on the ground. As of March 2013, about 6,200 of the uniformed personnel out of the 7,727 pledged were on the ground and securing liberated cities.[29] In parallel, EUTM was officially launched in February 2013.

In a few weeks, Serval broke the offensive of the armed groups, regained control of the major northern cities and tracked the terrorist and extremist armed groups in an attempt to chase them from their northern hideouts. Aimed at addressing the urgency of the crisis, the operation was not to be a long-term solution. For political and financial reasons, France wished to promptly reduce the volume of its forces and to "multilateralize" its commitment. Hence the emergence, at France's initiative, of the idea of a UN mission with more secure funding to take over from AFISMA. The principle of such a re-hatting was agreed upon by ECOWAS and the AU under certain conditions, such as ensuring a robust mandate for the UN mission, adequate consultation with African actors throughout the proposed transformation process, mobilization of support for AFISMA to facilitate the transformation, support for a political role for ECOWAS and the AU, and support for regional cooperation in the field of security.[30]

Phase 4: Entering unchartered territory? The United Nations in Mali

Initially, the UN Secretariat was averse to any idea of deployment on the ground, since the prevailing conditions did not lend themselves to the type of operation that the organization has the ability and will to conduct.[31] Under pressure from some members of the Security Council, the Secretariat softened its position. Two options were provided in the Secretary-General's March 2013 report with regards to the role of the UN in Mali. Option 1 put forward an integrated and multidimensional presence alongside a military force under African leadership. Option 2 proposed an integrated and multidimensional stabilization mission authorized under Chapter VII and supported by a parallel force. In the weeks prior to the adoption of Security Council Resolution 2100 establishing MINUSMA, it was already public knowledge that the second formula was garnering the support of the majority of the Council's members.[32]

The report acknowledged that "the UN is operating in a new geopolitical context and faces threats that have not been encountered before in a peacekeeping context". Therefore, it stated that

> it is critical that a clear distinction be maintained between the core peacekeeping tasks of an envisaged UN stabilization mission and the peace enforcement and counter-terrorist activities of the parallel force that will necessarily need to be established to preserve the hard-won security gains achieved so far.[33]

Resolution 2100 decided the transfer of authority from AFISMA to MINUSMA as of 1 July 2013 if major combat operations led by the international community in the immediate vicinity of the envisaged mission area of responsibility had ceased, and if the capacity of terrorist forces to pose a major threat were significantly reduced.[34] MINUSMA would comprise up to 11,200 military personnel, including reserve battalions capable of deploying rapidly within the country as and when required, and 1,440 police personnel. In addition, French troops were authorized to intervene on the Secretary-General's request in support of elements of MINUSMA when "under imminent and serious threat".[35]

The volatile nature of the security situation and the asymmetric warfare carried out by the extremist groups in the North calls for the kind of coercive action that the UN has been reluctant to undertake, hence the provision for a rapid deployment capability and for the continued presence of French troops. The UN has so far preferred the conventional concept of peacekeeping based on the principles of consent of the parties, impartiality and non-use of force except in self-defence and in defence of the mandate, as reiterated in Resolution 2100.[36] The type of mandate required[37] by the Malian situation, however, is more akin to a peace support operation, such as the one being conducted by the AU in Somalia, than to a traditional UN peacekeeping operation.[38] Two major elements appear to be framing the UN response, which aims at consolidating the military gains achieved. The first one is France's expressed desire to scale down its presence or, at least to "multilateralize" its commitment. The second is the difficulty for AFISMA of fully discharging its mandate given the lack of financial and logistical means.

Reacting to UN Resolution 2100, the AU PSC held a meeting on 25 April 2013 to express its disenchantment with the content of the resolution. In a communiqué, the PSC noted "with concern" that "Africa [had] not [been] appropriately consulted in the drafting and the consultation process that led to the adoption of the resolution authorizing MINUSMA"; that the resolution did not "adequately take into account the foundation laid by the African stakeholders"; and that it did not "take into account the concerns formally expressed by the AU and ECOWAS".[39] The PSC further stressed that "this situation [was] not in consonance with the spirit of partnership that the AU and the UN have been striving to promote for many years, on the basis of the provision of Chapter VIII of the UN Charter".[40] The AU supported the transformation of the mission into a UN operation but with certain caveats which, according to the African organization, were not taken into consideration.[41]

Among the shortcomings of the UN action in the run-up to Resolution 2100, one should note the refusal by the Security Council to authorize, based on the Somalia model, a support package funded by assessed contributions. Even the middle-of-the-road solution of the establishment of a Trust Fund has proven to be ineffective. At the doctrinal level, the stabilization of northern Mali, which requires an offensive mandate, goes far beyond the scope of peacekeeping operations as understood and conducted by the UN. Finally, there were some problems in the UN management of its relationship with African actors during the decision-making process, which did not facilitate the smooth transition from AFISMA to MINUSMA or the subsequent cooperation between African organizations and the UN. The adoption of the resolution authorizing MINUSMA opened up a new phase which promises to be challenging. It also marked the conclusion of the long process of trial and error by which the international community has sought to manage the security dimension of the Malian crisis.

Limitations of the global peace and security architecture

From MICEMA, which never went beyond the planning stage, to the hasty deployment of AFISMA, following the launch of French Operation Serval, and the re-hatting of AFISMA into MINUSMA, the crisis in Mali has underlined the shortcomings of multilateral organizations that inhibit their ability to collectively prevent and respond to the threat posed by the Malian crisis. This situation has unveiled the limitations of the regional, continental and international security architecture, as well as gaps in the relationships between ECOWAS, the AU and the UN. Identifying those gaps provides avenues for enhancing the existing mechanisms.[42]

The need to fully operationalize APSA

At the continental level, the shortcomings of ECOWAS and the AU are emblematic of the long road that lies ahead before the full operationalization of the African Peace and Security Architecture (APSA). APSA is a set of interrelated structures and policies provided for in the AU Peace and Security Council Protocol with the objective of facilitating an integrated, coherent and effective African response to the challenges of conflict prevention, conflict management, conflict resolution and post-conflict reconstruction.[43] It comprises the Peace and Security Council, the African Standby Force (ASF), the Panel of the Wise, the Peace Fund, the Continental Early Warning System, and the relationship with the Regional Mechanisms for Conflict Prevention, Management and Resolution.[44] The practical definition of APSA has been widened to include policies on a variety of security-related issues.

The Malian crisis revealed five important dimensions of the emerging APSA that would require major improvement: preventive action; cross-regional institutional development; funding; operationalization of the ASF, especially its rapid deployment capability; and coordination between the regional and continental levels.

First, the crisis in Mali has highlighted the gap between the rhetoric of prevention, which lies at the heart of the objectives of the AU and ECOWAS, and its actual practice. While the AU warned against the consequences of the Libyan crisis,[45] particularly on Mali, it did not take the full measure of the fragility of the Malian state. Neither of the two organizations pointed to the increasingly glaring governance shortcomings in Mali, nor did they take the necessary initiatives to address them. This situation can be explained by the fact that, for decades, the international community has tried to set Mali up as a democratic model. It has seen the country solely through the lens of electoral democracy, which, in itself, was not free from defects, as evidenced by the low voter turnout in elections and the emptiness of the democratic debate in the past few years. It is therefore hardly surprising that some Malian actors have seen evidence of hypocrisy in the international rhetoric about great democratic principles and constitutional legality after the coup.

Second, the management of the crisis was complicated by the absence of an ECOWAS counterpart in the northern region. A block of countries including Mauritania, Algeria, Tunisia, Libya and Egypt, speaking under the umbrella of the North African Regional Community (NARC), might have allowed for a regional management of the situation instead of the dialogue that happened between ECOWAS, as an institution, and Algeria and Mauritania, as individual non-members states. Ideally, if there was a similar level of institutional development among the regional mechanisms, two regional economic communities could collaborate horizontally to respond to a conflict affecting both groupings. Given the existing capacity disparities between the regions, when the situation ran into a deadlock at the regional level, coordination became vertical, between ECOWAS and the AU.

With regard to regional cooperation, the structures put in place by the core countries (Algeria, Mali, Mauritania and Niger) to address their common security challenges, namely the Liaison and Fusion Unit located in Algiers and the Tamanrasset-based Joint Operational Command, have not proven their efficacy. Nevertheless, efforts should aim at strengthening the existing structures in order to address the various interrelated threats confronting the region.[46] The process of consultations initiated in Nouakchott, in March 2013, on "the modalities for the operationalization of the APSA in the Sahelo-Saharan region, particularly considering the fact that the geographic coverage of the existing APSA structures do not exactly correspond to the configuration of the region", implies that the African peace and security architecture has been conceptualized as if conflicts were to occur only in the confined limits of a given regional economic community or region. Discussions about the operationalization of the security architecture for the Sahel region might be a productive starting point.[47] However, the Malian crisis has showed the limits of the currently geographically bound security ensemble, and might call for an architecture that is less reliant on limited geographical areas. Lessons should be learned on the inappropriateness of the geographical coverage of the different existing structures, the need for greater synergy among the regions, and the necessity to build the required operational capability within regional groupings to address the challenges faced on the ground.

Third, the Malian crisis has once more pointed out the inability of African institutions to fund and, therefore, to retain political leadership and ownership over their own initiatives. The inadequacy of the AU Peace Fund, which is not sufficiently supplied by African resources to allow the AU and the Regional Mechanisms to finance their operations, became glaring. Much time has been spent by African actors on creating the conditions for international support, and in particular UN funding, for the regional and the envisaged continental operation. It is in part the absence of funding that underlined the insistent request for authorization by the UN. Between the activation of the ECOWAS Standby Force in March 2012 and the authorization of AFISMA by the Security Council in December 2012, with only voluntary-based funding, ten months went by during which the armed groups consolidated their grasp on Northern Mali. When the Security Council rejected the establishment of the requested AMISOM-like support package, the deployment of AFISMA became hypothetical. Even the middle-of-the-road solution of establishing a trust fund had, until the re-hatting into a UN operation, been ineffective. The budget of

MICEMA, for 3,300 personnel, was estimated at US$227 million. AFISMA's budget included US$458.5 million for 5,500 personnel and US$930 million for 8,000 troops. The pledges recorded during the donor conference held in Addis Ababa at the end of January 2013, amounting to US$455 million, did not cover the financial needs of the mission. In addition, they were not always honored in practice. Five years after the Prodi Report on the funding of African operations,[48] African peace and security actors must find viable sources of funding, including through their institutional assessed contributions as provided for by the PSC Protocol.[49]

Fourth, the Malian situation underlined the limited military capability of ECOWAS and the AU to react promptly to emergency situations and, hence, the urgency of making the ASF operational, including its rapid deployment capability (RDC).[50] The ASF is composed of standby multidisciplinary contingents stationed in their respective countries of origin and ready for deployment as required. Its key doctrinal documents have been developed, planning elements have been established at continental and regional levels, and its initial operational capability was achieved in 2011. The ASF is supposed to reach its full continental operational capability by 2015 and was, therefore, not expected to provide a response during the Malian crisis.[51]

The rapid deployment capability, a key component of the ASF conceived as an entry point to be deployed as a precursor to a larger mission, aims to enable the AU to respond to situations corresponding to scenario 6 of the ASF (intervention in a member state in case of grave circumstances – war crimes, crimes against humanity and genocide – or intervention at the request of a state to restore peace and security). The RDC should have been operational in 2012. As a transitional arrangement to fill the gaps revealed by the shortcomings of an African-led response to the crisis in Mali and at the request of the January 2013 AU Summit, the AU Commission proposed, in April 2013, the establishment of the African Capability for the Immediate Response to Crisis (ACIRC) as an interim measure before the full operationalization of the ASF and the RDC.

According to the report of the chairperson of the Commission,[52] the ACIRC would provide a robust force that can be deployed quickly to conduct certain types of operations limited in both their goals and their duration. It would consist of military capabilities, force multipliers and resources from the continent. The document states that "the use of force will conform to the prevailing modes of decisions within the AU". After intense discussions, the 21st Ordinary Session of the Assembly of Heads of State and Government of the AU, held in Addis Ababa on 26 and 27 May 2013, endorsed the creation of this mechanism. This attempt to promote "Africa's collective self-reliance" through the implementation of the ACIRC raises hopes of a greater responsiveness on the part of the AU.[53]

Finally, the management of the crisis also brought to the fore the limitations of the coordination between the continental body and sub-regional structures. Genuine cooperation between the sub-regional and continental levels, based on the comparative advantages of the different organizations and compliance with the processes of the APSA, was largely absent in the pre-Serval phase of the management of the crisis. The launch of Operation Serval appears to have, to some extent, brought African actors together. The rivalry that seemed to characterize the relations between ECOWAS and the AU was based more on institutions' competition than on any substantive disagreements on the way forward. Some lessons should be learned from the Malian crisis in terms of sub-regional and continental coordination.[54] While the PSC Protocol and the Memorandum of Understanding between the AU and the Regional Mechanisms asserts the primacy of the first and details rules for cooperation in the management of conflicts, in practice the relationships between the AU and ECOWAS were marked, at best, by a lack of coordination. Article 16 of the PSC Protocol deals with the relationships with regional mechanisms for conflict prevention, management and resolution.[55] It does not actually use the word subsidiarity, but rather states that the modalities of the partnership "shall be determined by the comparative advantage of each and the prevailing circumstances". This article provides for flexibility, but in light of the Malian situation, it appears that all stakeholders did not understand the hierarchy between the continental and sub-regional levels in the same way. Hence the need for a shared understanding of the principles underlying the architecture, their effective implementation, and sustained dialogue between the different parties concerned.[56]

Rethinking the AU-UN partnership

The Malian conundrum highlighted the need if not for a doctrinal evolution on the part of the world body, then at least for a closer and more creative partnership between the UN and regional arrangements, based on their respective comparative advantages and with an enhanced synergy. Although the UN recognized the changing nature of the threat and the fact that peacekeeping principles were not in tune with the reality of the Malian crisis, it nonetheless agreed to deploy, and counted on a parallel force to do the peace enforcement work.

While the UN Secretariat generally insists on deploying operations only when there is a peace to keep and to limit its activities to peacekeeping, the continental and regional organizations believe that a deployment can contribute to the advent of peace that will then be kept. Reflective of these different understandings is a difference in terminology between the UN and the AU, in what they respectively call peacekeeping and peace support operation.[57]

These diverging approaches should not be seen as an obstacle to cooperation. On the contrary, they create opportunities for complementarity between the two organizations. This implies a division of labour, where the

AU carries the burden of peace enforcement before transitioning to the UN, which undertakes the long-term stabilization and post-conflict reconstruction process.[58]

Such a division of labour poses in specific terms the contentious issue of funding, which was extensively addressed in the 2008 Prodi report.[59] The AU's understanding of Chapter VIII of the UN Charter on cooperation with regional arrangements is that the UN has the responsibility for international peace and security, but that if it cannot and does not want to deploy an operation, it should give the means to regional organizations to do so, in order to enable the world body to intervene later on when there is a peace to keep.

Conclusion

The deteriorating political and security situation in Mali and in the Sahel and the gradual evolution of the international response from MICEMA to AFISMA, to Serval and, finally, to MINUSMA, have stretched existing arrangements at the levels of ECOWAS, the AU and the UN. The Malian crisis revealed the shortcomings of the multilateral security architecture and called for a double action. At the continental level, full effect must be given to all the components of the African Peace and Security Architecture, which should be conceived as a flexible structure able to adapt to the ever-changing peace and security challenges facing Africa. At the UN level, it is more necessary than ever to overcome the reluctance that characterizes its relationship with regional arrangements, in order to build a partnership adapted to the complex challenges to peace and security in Africa.

Domestic political, economic and political governance failures, compounded by regional transnational terrorism, criminality and religious extremism, have led to the collapse of the Malian state. Such a combination of ingredients is by no means exceptional to Mali and can be found in many African countries. Indeed, the "crisis in Mali" might be better described as an "African crisis in Mali". Hence there is a need to learn lessons in order to improve mechanisms at the sub-regional, continental and international levels for the prevention, management and resolution of conflict.

Notes

1 This chapter is based on field research conducted in Bamako, Abidjan, Ouagadougou and Addis Ababa between August 2012 and June 2013. An earlier version of this chapter was presented at the International Peacekeeping in Africa conference organized by the CSS in Zurich in November 2012.

2 F. Donki Diarra with A.K. Coulibaly and M. Traoré, *Les insurgés de Kati*, Bamako: La Sahelienne and L'Harmattan, 2013.

3 See L.-A. Théroux-Bénoni and D. Zounmenou, with P.M. Toupane and A. Faye

Daou, *Mali: Making Peace while Preparing for War*, ECOWAS Peace and Security Report 1, Institute for Security Studies (ISS), October 2012, available at www.issafrica.org/pgcontent.php?UID=31876, accessed 1 November 2012.

4 "Final Communiqué of the ECOWAS Extraordinary Summit", ECOWAS, 27 March 2012.

5 *Ibid.*

6 "Framework Agreement on the Solemn Declaration on the Return to Constitutional Order of 1st of April", signed on the 6 April 2012.

7 "Extraordinary Session of the ECOWAS Mediation and Security Council, Recommendation MSC/RES.1/04/12 Relating to the Mandate of the ECOWAS Standby Force to Restore Territorial Integrity and Constitutional Order in the Republic of Mali", ECOWAS, 12 April 2012.

8 "Decision MSC/AHSG/DEC.2/04/12 Mandating the ECOWAS Standby Force to Restore Territorial Integrity and Constitutional Order in the Republic of Mali, Signed by ECOWAS Chair, Ivorian President Alassane Ouattara, on 16 April 2012", ECOWAS.

9 L.-A. Théroux-Bénoni, "Mali in the Aftermath of the French Military Intervention: New Opportunities or Back to Square One?", *Situation Report*, ISS, 25 February 2012, available at www.issafrica.org/uploads/SitRep2013_18_03Mali.pdf, accessed on 27 February 2012.

10 "Final Communiqué of the ECOWAS Extraordinary Summit", ECOWAS, 26 April 2012.

11 Y. Zoubir, "Algeria and the Sahelian Embroglio: Preventing War and Fighting Terrorism", Report of the Al Jazeera Center for Studies, 25 November 2012, available at http://studies.aljazeera.net/ResourceGallery/media/Documents/2012/11/25/201211259572872058OAlgeria%20and%20the%20Sahelian%20Imbroglio.pdf, accessed 27 March 2012. See also S. Chena, "Portée et limites de l'hégémonie algérienne dans l'aire sahélo-maghrébine", *Hérodote* 142, 2011, pp. 108–124.

12 For more details on Mauritania's role, see A. Tisseron et J. Pigné, "La Mauritanie face à la crise malienne: Changement de stratégie?", Institut Thomas More, 24 October 2012, available at www.institut-thomas-more.org/actualite/la-mauritanie-face-a-la-crise-au-nord-mali-changement-de-strategie–2.html, accessed 4 April 2013.

13 Article 6 of Decision MSC/AHSG/DEC.2/04/12 mandating the ECOWAS Standby Force to restore territorial integrity and constitutional order in the Republic of Mali states that "the funding of MICEMA will come from the resources of ECOWAS. Funding can also come from the United Nations, the African Union, the European Union, voluntary contributions, subsidies, as well as bilateral and multilateral cooperation" (author's translation).

14 "Communiqué of the 323rd MEETING of the Peace and Security Council", AU, PSC/PR/COMM.(CCCXXIII), 12 June 2012.

15 "UN Security Council Press Statement on Mali", UN, SC/10676AFR/2407, 18 June 2012.

16 UN Security Council Resolution 2056, 5 July 2012.

17 UN Security Council Resolution 2071, 12 October 2012.

18 *Ibid.*

19 The idea of the strategic concept emerged in June following the consultations between the AU PSC and UNSC, with the objective of responding to the UNSC request that any military operation in Northern Mali be part of a larger political process. The first PSC decision to make a specific reference to this concept was adopted on 14 July 2012.

20 "Communiqué of the 339th Meeting of the Peace and Security Council", AU, PSC/MIN/COMM.2(CCCXXXIX), 24 October 2012.

21 See "Communiqué of the Extraordinary Session of the ECOWAS Assembly of Heads of State and Government", ECOWAS, 11 November 2012, and "Communiqué of the 341st Meeting of the Peace and Security Council", AU, PSC/PR/COMM.2(CCCXLI), 13 November 2012.
22 "Report of the UN Secretary-General on the Situation in Mali", UN, S/2012/894, 28 November 2012, para. 100.
23 *Ibid.*, para. 97.
24 E.g., the AU and ECOWAS were supposed to report on "the operational readiness of AFISMA, including the level of staffing leadership and equipment of the units, their operational adaptation to the climate and terrain conditions and ability to conduct joint armed operations with logistical, air and ground fire support" (Operative para. 10).
25 "Mali: Pas d'intervention militaire avant septembre 2013, selon Romano Prodi", Radio France Internationale, 21 November 2012, available at www.rfi.fr/afrique/20121121-mali-intervention-militaire-prodi-sahel-onu-cedeao-aqmi-mnla-mujao, accessed 27 March 2012.
26 For more details, see Théroux-Bénoni, "Mali in the Aftermath".
27 R. Marchal, "Military (Mis-)Adventure in Mali", *African Affairs* 112, 2013, pp. 486–497.
28 "Communiqué of the 358th Meeting of the Peace and Security Council and Progress Report of the Chairperson of the Commission of the African-led International Support Mission in Mali", AU, PSC/PR/2(CCCLVIII), 7 March 2013, p. 3.
29 *Ibid.*
30 At its 5 February 2012 meeting in Brussels, the Support and Follow-up Group supported the transformation of AFISMA into a UN operation under certain conditions (para. 8). This support was reiterated by ECOWAS at its 42nd Ordinary Session of the Authority of Heads of State and Government held in Yamoussoukro, from 27–28 February 2013, as well as by the AU PSC in its communiqué PSC/PR/COMM(CCCLVIII) of its 358th meeting held in Addis Ababa on 7 March 2012.
31 "Report of the Secretary-General on the Situation in Mali", UN, S/2012/894, 28 November 2012.
32 "Mali Briefing and Consultations: What's in Blue", Security Council Report, 2 April 2013, available at www.whatsinblue.org/2013/04/mali-briefing-and-consultations-2.php, accessed 3 April 2013.
33 "Report of the UN Secretary-General on the Situation in Mali", UN, S/2013/189, 26 March 2012, para. 99 and 100.
34 UN Security Council Resolution 2100, 25 April 2013, para 8.
35 *Ibid.*, para. 18.
36 *Ibid.*, third preambular reference.
37 Conclusions of the meeting of the Support and Follow-up Group held in Brussels on 5 February 2013, while expressing the hope that the UN Security Council "will positively consider the change, at the appropriate time, of AFISMA into a United Nations operation", underscored that such an operation should be provided "with an appropriate mandate, determined in consultation with Mali and contributing towards strengthening the Malian State's authority over its entire territory and the safeguard of the country's unity and territorial integrity".
38 See L.-A. Théroux-Bénoni, "Stabilising Northern Mali: Different Approaches to Peace Operations", *ISS Today*, ISS, 12 March 2013, available at www.issafrica.org/iss_today.php?ID=1607, accessed 13 March 2013.
39 "Communiqué of the 371st Meeting of the Peace and Security Council", AU, PSC/PR/COMM.(CCCLXXI), 25 April 2013, para. 10.

40 *Ibid.*

41 "Communiqué of the 358th Meeting of the Peace and Security Council", AU, PSC/PR/COMM.(CCCLVIII), 7 April 2013, para. 13.

42 An earlier version of this section was published in L.-A. Théroux-Bénoni, "Lessons from the Malian Crisis for the International Security Architecture", *ISS Today*, ISS, 15 April 2013, available at www.issafrica.org/iss-today/lessons-from-the-malian-crisis-for-the-international-security-architecture, accessed 16 April 2013.

43 "Protocol Relating to the Establishment of the Peace and Security Council of the African Union (PSC Protocol), Adopted by the First Ordinary Session of the Assembly of the African Union in Durban South Africa, on 9 July 2002", AU, available at www.africa-union.org/root/AU/organs/psc/Protocol_peace%20and%20security.pdf, accessed 13 April 2013.

44 See, e.g., U. Engel and J. Gomes Porto (eds), *Africa's New Peace and Security Architecture: Promoting Norms and Institutionalizing Solutions,* Farnham: Ashgate, 2010.

45 "Statement of the Chairperson of the AU Commission, Jean Ping, at the Meeting of the International Contact Group on Libya, Rome, Italy", AU, 5 May 2011, pp. 1–2.

46 At its meeting in Brussels on 5 February 2013, the Support and Follow-up Group reiterated the "importance of cooperation among the neighbouring countries of Mali on intelligence and border-control, in order to enhance the effectiveness of efforts to counter terrorist and criminal networks and facilitate the implementation of the mandate of AFISMA".

47 "Nouakchott Conclusion, Ministerial Meeting on the Enhancement of Security Cooperation and the Operationalisation of the African Peace and Security Architecture in the Sahelo-Saharan Region, Nouakchott, Mauritania", AU Peace and Security Council, 17 March 2013.

48 "Report of the African Union-United Nations Panel on Modalities for Support to African Union Peacekeeping Operations", UN, A/63/666 and S/2008/813, 31 December 2008.

49 Although the PSC held at the level of heads of state and government decided "to recommend to the Assembly of the Union to instruct that part of AFISMA budget be covered by assessed contributions from AU members States" (PSC/AHG/COMM/2.(CCCLIII)), this option provided for by Article 21 of the Protocol was, in practice, not implemented.

50 The need for the early operationalization of the ASF's rapid deployment capability, within the framework of APSA, was stressed during the 353th meeting at the level of heads of state and government held in Addis Ababa on 25 January 2013 (PSC/AHG/COMM/2.(CCCLIII). In his statement to the sixth meeting of the specialized technical committee on Defense, Safety and Security, AU Commissioner for Peace and Security Ramtane Lamamra stated:

> The January decisions were made against the background of the then evolving situation in Mali and our inability, as Africans, to swiftly respond to the request for assistance made by the Malian Government following the offensive launched by armed terrorist and criminal groups against the positions of the Malian army in the area of Konna.

51 "Roadmap III on the Operationalization of the African Standby Force Adopted by the Ministers of Defense in October 2011, and Endorsed by the Executive Council in January 2012", AU Commission.

52 "Report of the Chairperson of the Commission on the Operationalisation of the Rapid Deployment Capability of the African Standby Force and the Establishment of an 'African Capacity for Immediate Response to Crises', RPT/Exp/

VI/STCDSS/(i-a)2013, 6th Ordinary Meeting of the Specialised Technical Committee on Defence, Safety and Security, Preparatory Meeting of Chiefs of Staff, Addis Ababa, Ethiopia", AU Commission, 29–30 April 2013.

53 L.-A. Théroux-Bénoni 2013, "Enhancing Africa's Responsiveness to Crisis Situation", *ISS Today*, ISS, 3 June 2013, available at www.issafrica.org/iss-today/enhancing-africas-responsiveness-to-crisis-situations, accessed 3 June 2013.

54 "Communiqué of the 371st Meeting of the Peace and Security Council", AU, PSC/PR/COMM.(CCCLXXI), 25 April 2013, para. 16.

55 "Article 16 of the Protocol Relating to the Establishment of the Peace and Security Council of the African Union (PSC Protocol), Adopted by the First Ordinary Session of the Assembly of the African Union in Durban South Africa, on 9 July 2002, and Entered into Force on 26 December 2009", AU, available at www.africa-union.org/root/AU/organs/psc/Protocol_peace%20and%20security.pdf, accessed 13 April 2013.

56 "Communiqué of the 370th Meeting of the Peace and Security Council", AU, PSC/PR/COMM.(CCCLXX), 24 April 2013.

57 See L.-A. Théroux-Bénoni, "Stabilizing Northern Mali".

58 Such transitions happened in Burundi, when the UN took over the AU Mission in Burundi (AMIB) through the creation of the UN Operation in Burundi (ONUB), and in Darfur following the establishment of the UN-AU Hybrid Operation in Darfur (UNAMID), an experiment based on the "re-hatting" of the AU Mission in Sudan (AMIS). The AU also hopes that, at some point, AMISOM will evolve into a UN operation (see E. Wane, "L'Union africaine à l'épreuve des operations de paix: entre innovations institutionnelles et contraintes opérationnelles", in D. Morin and L.-A. Théroux-Bénoni, *Guide du maintien de la paix: L'Afrique et les opérations de paix*, Montréal: Athéna, 2011).

59 "Report of the African Union–United Nations Panel on Modalities for Support to African Union Peacekeeping Operations", UN, A/63/666 and S/2008/813, 31 December 2008.

10 The Democratic Republic of Congo

A laboratory for international peace operations

Meike Froitzheim

Introduction

The conflict that unfolded in the Democratic Republic of Congo (DRC) – the former Zaire – in the mid-1990s has often been referred to as "Africa's world war".[1] During the first and second Congo wars, lasting from 1996 to 1997 and 1998 to 2002 respectively, more than five million people lost their lives, untold numbers became refugees and millions were injured, raped, and orphaned.[2] Following the official ending of the second Congo war in 2002, a national power-sharing agreement was implemented; one year later a transitional period began, leading to the first round of national elections in 2006. However, conflict in the DRC, and especially in the country's eastern provinces, continued even after the war had officially ended. The devastating situation of the population provoked not only massive interventions in terms of humanitarian assistance but also, increasingly, peace- and statebuilding interventions and stabilisation efforts on the part of the international community.

This chapter specifically focuses on the implementation process of the international stabilisation efforts under the framework of the International Security and Stabilization Support Strategy (ISSSS). The latter was developed by UN agencies, international organisations and foreign donors in 2008/2009 to consolidate and strengthen the political progress made in the aftermath of the 2006 elections. The motivation was to lay the foundations for sustainable peacebuilding by combining security, political, statebuilding and return and recovery interventions. Simultaneously, the ISSSS became the main vehicle of external actors in supporting the Congolese government in its own national stabilisation approaches defined in the Stabilization and Reconstruction Plan for War-Affected Areas (STAREC).[3]

The ISSSS is of particular interest as it manifests a case in which stabilisation as an objective, alongside the protection of civilians, has not only become legitimised by the international community but has also become the primary strategy interlinking the broader peacebuilding, statebuilding, development and humanitarian efforts in the DRC. The objective of stabilisation has furthermore become the guiding principle of the ongoing UN peacekeeping mission in the DRC, which was renamed in 2010 from the UN Organization Mission in the DRC (MONUC) to the UN Organization Stabilization Mission in the DRC (MONUSCO).

Despite the large budget expended by the international community, however, stability and sustainable peace seem distant, especially in eastern Congo. The latest rebellion started in mid-2012 in the province of North Kivu, when the "March 23" movement (M23) defected from the Congolese army. As a consequence, nearly two million internally displaced persons were counted in the DRC in May 2012, of which 70 per cent were displaced in the eastern provinces of North and South Kivu alone.[4]

Against this background, the purpose of the chapter is to focus on how the international stabilisation strategy has been put into practice in eastern DRC. By doing so, the key aim is to outline challenges and obstacles in relation to the stabilisation objective and its implementation. The analysis is built upon interviews conducted with a wide range of actors in Goma, the provincial capital of North Kivu, in October 2012. It is further informed by the findings of two previous field trips to the Great Lakes Region in 2010, and by primary and secondary sources, such as academic articles and books, as well as policy papers and progress and evaluation reports.[5]

The chapter elaborates on the significance of focusing on the outcomes of putting stabilisation into practice. In combination with the evidence derived from the field, this provides the framework for the analytical sections of the chapter. This is followed by a descriptive overview of the conflict context in the DRC and the stabilisation efforts of the international community in relation to the national stabilisation approach. The stabilisation laboratory of eastern DRC is then examined by scrutinising both the formulation of the ISSSS and the priorities determined in the strategy. Furthermore, the relationship between the international community and the Congolese government is investigated: the performance of the ISSSS is scrutinised by looking at one of the five key objectives, namely the rebuilding of state authority. Finally, some general conclusions regarding the stabilisation efforts are drawn, highlighting the challenges faced by the various actors.

Framework of analysis: highlighting outcomes

Since the end of the Cold War, the UN as well as a number of state and non-state actors have consistently increased their commitment to various forms of peace operations in conflict areas. This trend is certainly reflected in the extensive engagement of external actors in the DRC. Simultaneously, the amount of research analysing peace operations has substantially increased. The predominant understanding that has developed considers most of these interventions as failures and locates the reasons mainly in material constraints and lack of political will, coordination problems between and among the actors, and the imposition of liberal values.[6] Furthermore, the relationship and the prevalent power disparity between the external interveners and the local counterparts, the "intervened upon", is increasingly being identified as an obstacle.[7]

A recurring approach in studies questioning the success or failure of peace operations is the focus on whether the mission's mandate has been implemented adequately. The result is that peace operations have mainly been analysed through their *outputs*, which can be defined as the "measures decided by and implemented within a political system".[8] In practice, this questions whether the number of trained local officials conforms to the previously agreed number. This is comprehensible since peace operations are primarily accountable to external entities, be it peacebuilding missions accounting to the UN Security Council or NGOs accounting to donors.[9] This approach has furthermore informed the understanding that peacebuilding missions will be successful once the technical and operational obstacles have been solved.[10] However, any analysis should not only centre on the outputs but should concentrate further on the implementation processes of these activities, which are understood as generating any potential *outcome* of peace operations. Outcomes can be defined as "the things that are actually achieved", whether intended or unintended.[11] This implies that a distinction has to be drawn between the efforts made by the international community and the actual outcome of these efforts or, in other words, the impact achieved on the ground.[12] It is therefore of specific interest not only to scrutinise the formulation of the policy but also to understand what happens after a policy is formulated and to point out those factors that either facilitate or hamper the realisation of policy objectives.[13] This approach becomes significant because irrespective of the policy (or programme) in focus, one important aspect remains the same, namely that knowing the objectives of the programme usually gives only an indication of how those responsible for the programme will carry it out.[14] Of interest therefore are all events and activities that occur after a policy directive has been issued, which implies both "the behaviour of the administrative body which has responsibility for the program and the compliance of the target groups" and "the web of direct and indirect political, economic, and social forces that bear on the behaviour of all those involved, and ultimately on the impacts – both intended and unintended – of the program".[15]

The significance of focusing on the implementation and the outcomes of peace operations is rooted in the fact that in contrast to traditional or "first generation" peacekeeping missions, which aimed at maintaining the status quo in a conflict situation, contemporary peace operations have become far more complex in their transformational role. Hence, instead of being neutral, they evoke an increasing number of side-effects. In this regard, the involvement of external actors in the DRC serves as a primary example, with the ISSSS providing a framework for the various activities of the international community ranging from classical peacekeeping tasks to peace- and statebuilding, as well as humanitarian and development efforts. Thus, focusing on the outcomes of the ISSSS reminds us that "policy delivery and impact are rarely a matter of a straight-line relationship between a single policy instrument or organization interacting with its environment to produce a clear-cut impact".[16] Determining the outcomes of peace operations is essential; otherwise, their legitimacy becomes contestable and opportunities for learning lessons are missed.[17]

The international community's stabilisation efforts in the DRC

The history of the DRC can be best described as a history of plunder, predation and pillaging, starting under Belgian colonial rule and continuing under the decades-long misrule of President Mobutu Sese Seko (1965–1997). Over the past 15 years, the situation has not improved tangibly and can be pictured as one of "intractable armed conflict, poor governance, pervasive poverty, and massive humanitarian suffering, including widespread human rights violations and large-scale population displacement".[18] Congolese political space "continues to be defined by those who bear arms and money". Four inseparably linked factors provide for continuing instability, namely the absence of a functioning state, the fragility of state power, continued tensions over land connected to citizenship, and the externalisation of neighbouring instability, particularly in relation to Rwanda.[19]

The initial reaction of the UN was to establish MONUC in November 1999, four months after the Lusaka Ceasefire Agreement had been signed.[20] However, Ugandan and Rwandan troops remained in the DRC for another three years until they were eventually withdrawn. In April 2002, the Sun City peace deal[21] was signed by all Congolese belligerents and political parties. This marked the beginning of the transition phase and led, with extensive support from a wide range of external actors, to a first round of parliamentary and presidential elections in 2006. However, during this transition phase, the conflict in eastern DRC continued. Rebel groups, including foreign militias such as the Hutu group *Forces Démocratiques de Libération du Rwanda*, as well as local Mai Mai groups continued fighting for land and resources. In 2003, massive violence in the province of Ituri could be halted only with the deployment of the EU military mission "Artemis", after the UN had failed to contain the clashes. In the following years and in addition to the UN-led peacekeeping mission, the EU deployed another four civil and military missions in the DRC, of which two are still ongoing, namely the EU Police Mission for the DRC (EUPOL RD Congo) and the EU Security Sector Reform Mission in the DRC (EUSEC RD Congo).[22]

Despite international efforts, the magnitude of ongoing violence, deaths and displacement led the UN to depict eastern DRC in May 2005 as the "world's worst humanitarian crisis".[23] It is in this environment that the UN and other actors tried to become active in the stabilisation of the DRC from 2006 onwards. At the end of the transition phase and following the elections, MONUC formulated a first stabilisation strategy, the so-called UN Security and Stabilization Support Strategy, aiming at facilitating "the transition of the UN's role from peacekeeping to supporting peacebuilding and development, laying the groundwork for the mission's eventual 'hand over' of security tasks to the government and withdrawal from the country".[24] However, this strategy was put on hold due to the re-emergence of rebellion in the Kivu provinces in 2007. At the end of 2008, following the historical rapprochement between Kigali and Kinshasa, regional relations were realigned; as a consequence, a new peace deal, the 23 March 2009 Agreement, was signed by the Congolese Government and the Tutsi-led *Congrès National pour la Défense du Peuple*. The signing of this peace agreement was understood as finally constituting a security shift in the Kivu provinces and it paved the way for the launch of the ISSSS in 2008–2009. The ISSSS was intended to become the primary strategy tying international support to the national stabilisation framework, STAREC.[25] In line with this development, MONUC was renamed MONUSCO with an "S", meaning that stabilisation efforts had become part of the mandate alongside the protection of civilians.[26] In addition, several donors, such as the United States Agency for International Development (USAID) or the British Department for International Development (DFID), have continued to support peacebuilding and stabilisation initiatives bilaterally; these initiatives are implemented by NGOs and focus, among other things, on establishing community-driven conflict resolution mechanisms and governance activities.[27]

Although stabilisation has become an increasingly prominent approach in addressing the needs of so-called fragile, failing or failed states, the concept remains vague and its meaning depends on the context in which it is applied. According to Bailey, stabilisation is "[g]rounded in the security imperative of removing or reducing threats such as armed groups [and] encompasses both 'hard' (military) and 'soft' (civilian) interventions".[28] Thus stabilisation approaches can range from direct security action countering threats to aspiring social transformation through interlinking peacebuilding, statebuilding and development initiatives.[29] Following this understanding and the application of stabilisation in diverse contexts such as Afghanistan, Timor-Leste and Haiti, one can conclude that "stabilization has therefore emerged as a key component of a broader liberal, transformative peacebuilding project".[30] In this regard, improving stability becomes reliant on a number of objectives, such as the creation of a safe and secure environment, the achievement of stable governance and a feasible market economy, and the facilitation of the social and psychological well-being of the population.[31] In the DRC context, the overall aim of the ISSSS is "to address specific root causes and consequences of conflict, support the implementation of peace initiatives at local level, and help stabilise areas where conflict has recently ceased".[32] In support of this aim, five objectives are outlined: improving security; supporting political processes; strengthening state authority; facilitating return, reintegration and recovery; and combating sexual violence.[33] To implement these objectives, each component involves different actors, including MONUSCO, as well as various UN agencies such as the UN Development Programme, the UN Children's Fund, the UN Human Settlements Programme and the UN High Commissioner for Refugees. In addition, international NGOs, such as the International Organization for Migration, Oxfam and International Alert, as well as national partners, namely NGOs and private contractors, are involved.

The funding of the ISSSS consists predominantly of bilateral donor support and mission resources. While the total budget requested is roughly US$835 million, as of April 2012 the ISSSS had US$338.41 million in resources, of which US$203.88 million had been spent in the first three years.[34] In contrast, the annual budget of MONUSCO is US$1.4 billion, while as of 2012 the Congolese government has provided as little as US$20.32 million to STAREC.[35]

Because it integrates the stabilisation objective into an ongoing peacekeeping mandate and because it interlinks this external approach with STAREC, the Congolese-owned national stabilisation plan, the ISSSS can be seen as an innovative attempt to respond to the demanding and ever changing conflict context in the DRC. However, and not least against the background of the latest outbreak of violence following the M23 rebellion in 2012, it is of the utmost significance to question the actual implications of this stabilisation attempt.

The stabilisation laboratory of Eastern DRC: "a mess at the moment, no doubt about it"[36]

The extensive stabilisation efforts in the DRC suffer from various challenges and obstacles, to the extent that the actors involved broadly confess that the activities undertaken "did not really bring stability".[37] In line with the literature highlighting the importance of focusing not only on policy outputs but also on policy outcomes, the following section analyses the process of putting the stabilisation strategy into practice. This implies pointing out challenges and obstacles in relation to (1) the formulation of the ISSSS, (2) the priorities determined in the stabilisation strategy, (3) the relationship between the international community and the Congolese government, and (4) performance in relation to the objective of rebuilding state authority.

The equivocality of the stabilisation strategy

As highlighted before, the concept of stabilisation in this context is fairly new, and therefore rather limited experience and knowledge have been gained up to now regarding its implementation, especially when stabilisation is introduced into the mandate of an ongoing peacekeeping mission. Relating to the DRC, this even implies that a common definition of what stabilisation means, as applied in the ISSSS, has not yet been established. It was not until 2012 that the international community started to work on a common definition, yet without integrating its Congolese partners. According to a UN official, one reason for this is that it is considered "impossible to get everyone around one table".[38] Consequently, what has remained unclear, even two years after the integration of stabilisation into the peacekeeping mandate, is whether this change constitutes a genuine shift in strategy or rather simply re-labels the existing political and security objectives.[39] A further consequence of this is, as pointed out by one interviewee, that the ISSSS still "has a slightly ambiguous mandate with MONUSCO". What is much needed is a clear definition of the "S" to provide more clarity regarding the roles and activities of the various bodies and actors involved.[40] While the priority of MONUSCO, as defined in its mandate, is the protection of civilians, one respondent confessed that the headline of the mission's approach is indeed "to stabilise this place" according to the counterinsurgency logic of "clear – hold – build".[41] However, the prevailing understanding of interviewees working in the development sector was that stabilisation as applied in the DRC implies a softer, peacebuilding-oriented approach including, for example, projects to increase the capacity of local conflict prevention and resolution mechanisms.[42]

A further ambiguity is rooted in the fact that the Stabilization Support Unit, which is the secretarial unit for the ISSSS, is semi-autonomous but placed within MONUSCO and staffed by UN agencies, donors and MONUSCO. This leads to a situation in which the unit "belongs to everybody and nobody ... it is everybody's and nobody's baby at the same time".[43] At the conceptual level this is considered positive because it does not exclude actors. However, in practical terms it renders the work more difficult as it takes away responsibility in cases of failure. In other words, no one feels responsible if something does not work out.[44] One suggestion to make it more acceptable and accountable is therefore to place the responsibility for stabilisation on one body, which is then also in charge of the outcome.[45]

Due to the definitional gap and the lack of accountability and clarity regarding the structural setup (in particular regarding the interaction with MONUSCO), any efforts to put the ISSSS into action were significantly hampered from the onset. While the underlying idea – of integrating the stabilisation efforts into the established structures of the peacekeeping mission – seemed promising, the implementation has been insufficient. This internal ambiguity has in turn negatively affected the relationship with the stabilisation plan of the Congolese Government, STAREC. Since the envisioned "twin stabilization plans" are "similar but not the same",[46] confusion prevails among the various actors involved, and there is no coherent vision of stabilisation – either within or between the two plans. The ISSSS and STAREC differ first of all in their geographical scope: projects under the ISSSS are concentrated along several strategic axes, in contrast to STAREC projects which are spread out over a much larger geographical area. Also, while the political objective of supporting the realisation of existing peace agreements is included only in the ISSSS, humanitarian aid delivery is solely part of STAREC. The two plans have furthermore two different orientations: donor-oriented for the ISSSS versus national for STAREC.[47] Consequently, and besides the persistent nebulosity regarding the actual content of "stabilisation", there seems to be no shared vision or strategy on how to achieve the ambitious goal of "stabilising" eastern DRC.

The priorities of stabilisation: a local perspective and political processes

The gap between the international community on the one side and the Congolese on the other side becomes further visible when looking at conflict analysis and the general picture of the challenges the DRC faces and upon which the ISSSS has been developed. According to one interviewee, there is a lot of "propaganda, wrong information and a biased way of looking at things" leading to a situation in which "the international community is not aware of the fact that they promote ideas that are not based on facts, but on prejudices and biased information".[48] This understanding is supported by other interviewees distinguishing between the perspective of those directly involved in the implementation of the ISSSS on the ground versus those involved in the ISSSS from a Kinshasa and donor perspective. The former claim to better understand the prevailing complexity of the conflict situation and the requirements for any successful implementation of the stabilisation approach, and they accuse the latter of not accepting this reality and its consequences. This becomes evident when focusing on the initiation of the ISSSS in 2008–2009. By that time, widespread optimism prevailed that the conflict in eastern DRC had come to an end. However, as it was frankly put by one interviewee: "Our initial hypothesis was faulty. We [the architects of the ISSSS] didn't know enough about the situation".[49] Another respondent accuses the external actors in the DRC as not even being willing to see the complexity of the conflict, which inevitably led to a failure of the international stabilisation approach. The current outbreak of violence is therefore considered "useful" by a number of interviewees, because it is perceived as demonstrating both that the conflict had never ended and that a closer engagement is required.

Since 2012, as a response to the first three years of the ISSSS, the strategy has been under revision; the revised version that is supposed to be implemented in 2013 will presumably have a stronger focus on local peacebuilding initiatives. The aim with this shift is to identify and support local initiatives that can make a difference, for example by working jointly on solutions for land disputes, which are understood as root causes of the conflict. The intention is to increase the commitment of local communities with regard to stabilisation.[50]

In line with these changes, a modification of the geographical focus of the stabilisation efforts is under consideration with the aim of achieving more successful stabilisation outcomes. From 2009 to 2012, during the first phase of the ISSSS, stabilisation activities have been targeted predominantly at so-called high-risk areas. This approach, however, has been analysed as being faulty since no sustainable achievements were in fact realised in any of the highly insecure areas in the eastern provinces. Drawing lessons from these experiences, the hope is that "if we focus our work on areas where there is a minimum of stabilization, we can make a difference".[51] This could be achieved, for example, through supporting local initiatives in the more stable areas. At the same time, MONUSCO should continue to target the high-risk spots. The intention behind reversing the approach for the second phase of the ISSSS is to eventually materialise trickle-down effects from the more stable to the less stable areas. This modification is based on the experience that it has not been successful the other way round.[52]

In addition, based on the lessons learned from the first three years of the ISSSS, a broad consensus among the international actors has emerged that political processes instead of security aspects must constitute the principal component of any stabilisation approach. While labelling security as a top priority is understandable due to the high levels of ongoing violence, any success in stabilisation is increasingly understood as being primarily dependent on political exercises including security sector reform (SSR) initiatives and disarmament, demobilisation and reintegration (DDR) efforts. This argument of putting political processes first is understood to be "supported" by the ongoing grievance of M23, which may be seen as politically motivated since it accuses the Congolese government of not complying with the peace agreement of 2009.

The relationship between the international community and the Congolese government

Connected with the argument of putting political processes first is the responsibility of the Congolese government to actively drive this process, since stabilisation efforts, such as the rebuilding of state authority, lies at the heart of its sovereignty. In practice, however, being confronted with a government that seems to lack both the political capacity and the will to lead the stabilisation process, it is the international community that has taken the driver's seat, thus challenging the principle of ownership.

Both in the field of development policies and in relation to post-conflict interventions the concept of ownership has increasingly become a buzzword, while at the same time its operational implications have remained unclear. In terms of post-conflict reconstruction and statebuilding, Chesterman argues that the notion of "ownership" in a more positive understanding "reflects a desire on the part of external actors to avoid undermining pre-existing local processes that may be the most effective response to local political questions".[53] However, the term "ownership" can also be used more defensively "to avoid the appearance of paternalism or neo-colonialism".[54]

Questioning the principle of ownership in relation to the stabilisation approach in the DRC, it is worth looking at the behaviour of those responsible for implementing the stabilisation endeavours, be they international actors or the Congolese government. In this regard, the recurring theme in every single interview is the profound lack of political capacity and will on behalf of the Congolese government on the one hand, and a strongly donor-led stabilisation approach, undermining the principle of ownership, on the other hand.

Focusing first on the Congolese government, the prevailing view throughout the interviews was that the political will to implement those processes required to stabilise the country was insufficient or even completely lacking. Instead, the Congolese government was characterised as "not working as a real government but strongly divided along group and personal interests".[55] Since the ISSSS is supposed to support the government's stabilisation endeavours as defined in STAREC, the national stabilisation plan, any lack of political will negatively affects the outcomes of the ISSSS.

The interdependency of international and national efforts becomes obvious with regard to the reform of the Congolese security sector, where the lack of a political framework led to a situation in which SSR initiatives were not sufficiently contextualised. Although SSR is understood as being essential to stability, it is not part of STAREC; as a consequence, the SSR process, which has been heavily supported by the international community, has remained "up in the air", which means that it is "not part of a comprehensive project with a long-term plan".[56] Any capacity gap is seen by international actors as a starting point for external support, as it can be filled through training, for example; in contrast, the lack of political will is understood as a severe obstacle because "we cannot do anything against their will".[57] This implies that "if we don't have the support at the national level, we will fail".[58] This failure becomes apparent in the international support to the reform of the Congolese National Police. Extensive capacity-building and training programmes were carried out, yet due to a weak political back-up of the process, the Congolese police are still far from being professional, well-paid and cohesive.[59]

At the same time, critique is raised regarding the virtually "imposed" character of the ISSSS and more specifically the understanding that "we're the donors, we have the money and we know what to do".[60] According to an interviewee, this has provoked a situation in which "the ISSSS has not been able to sell the soul of stabilization. What the Congolese see is the money, not the outcomes or bigger results". The need to include some aspects of conditionality was highlighted as a necessary response on the part of the donor.[61]

While the call for conditionality is rooted in the apparent deficiencies of the Congolese government, missing coordination is identified as an obstacle on the side of the international community. The donor community is described as "much divided", to the point where even a shared conflict analysis does not necessarily mean that donors push in the same direction: "they all have their own interests",[62] stated one interviewee. These interests can be economically motivated – for example by the wealth of natural resources and raw materials in eastern DRC – or politically driven, defined in terms of former colonial interests and the intention to sustain influence in the region or, put more simply, to ensure visibility.[63] As a consequence, programmes on the ground are not sufficiently coordinated and police and military training, for example, is carried out by different actors. This leads to confusion on the Congolese side, but also to frustration for those implementing the training. One interviewee accuses the external actors of behaving like market actors, competing against each other to attract as many participants as possible instead of coordinating the various training programmes carried out in eastern DRC.[64] This understanding is shared by another respondent, who cynically remarked that "a positive result of the war is that it shows that the training schemes didn't work whether they were carried out by the US, the EU or the UN. So what is needed is a common, joint approach".[65]

Performance of the ISSSS: rebuilding state authority

Based on the preceding sections, which scrutinised both the formulation of the ISSSS and the stabilisation priorities determined, as well as the relation between the international and the Congolese actors involved in the stabilisation process, this section focuses on the outcomes in relation to the aim of restoring and strengthening state authority. This objective of the ISSSS, the extension of state presence in sensitive territories, has to be understood against the current situation of non-existent state authority in many parts of eastern Congo. This has led to situations of insecurity and to a lack of confidence in the state on the part of the population, which sees it as "abusive rather than as a provider of services".[66]

It is in this environment that a number of projects targeted at the rebuilding of state authority have been implemented under the ISSSS. In this regard, many interviewees questioned the actual outcomes of the

ISSSS's activity; what is being challenged is the impact of the projects on the ground instead of merely the activities that have been carried out. The general conclusion drawn regarding changes achieved was, then, predominantly negative, highlighting that "there is hardly any positive impact" visible in eastern DRC.[67] More specifically, stabilisation efforts have not improved the security situation in high-risk areas, nor has the Congolese state deployed functional civil servants to these territories.[68]

In this regard, two interviewees talking about the attempt to rebuild state authority compared specific projects under the ISSSS to a stone that is tossed into water creating ever widening and vanishing patterns of concentric ripples. However, both of them remarked that projects implemented under the ISSSS have not caused the concentric ripples, or in other words the broader impact, that they had hoped for. Instead, a recurring example of an output with hardly any impact was the focus of infrastructure projects.[69]

The largest share of the funds of the ISSSS has been allocated to the rebuilding of state authority, which is also a priority of STAREC. With regard to the police, the justice sector, the civil administration and the improvement of road infrastructure, internationally assisted stabilisation efforts have primarily focused on what were repeatedly referred to as "hardware aspects": the construction of police stations, prisons and courts. On the "software side", training for police and other state officials were conducted. According to Dixon, more than 600 km of roads have been rehabilitated, 81 police buildings were built, and more than 900 police officers and more than 200 administrative officials received training by the UN only.[70] At first glance, this seems to be a noticeable result. However, it has been heavily criticised for being ineffective due to the fact that the international community was

> building buildings where there was no legitimacy of the actors. No work on legitimacy was done before the construction of the buildings. In the end, armed groups have taken over the buildings and there are court houses where there has never been a judge. So in a country where the state is as dysfunctional and corrupt as in the DRC, the understanding to build buildings to restore state authority does not and cannot work.[71]

One could counter-argue that there have been extensive efforts regarding training and capacity-building of police officers and civil administrators, at least when focusing on the number of officials that received training. However, an analysis of whether these capacity-building initiatives have been successful gives a rather bleak picture. One UN official highlighted that what is needed is a change in attitudes, but "people [Congolese officials] don't identify with it, they don't think it's important".[72] More specifically, one NGO representative asserted of the Congolese police that no substantial improvement has been achieved, although they should have increased their capacity after three to four years of training. Hence, a generally positive development is not observable, not least because one of the main incentives for participation appears to be the receipt of a *per diem* and a new diploma at the end of the training session. Nevertheless, the same respondent pointed out that "15 per cent are very engaged and interested and apply what they have been taught" – which still marks a substantial increase, because "at the beginning, no one was engaged".[73]

Also problematic are the deployment policies of the Congolese government. In accordance with international practices, police officers who have received training to become trainers are supposed to be employed in designated training centres. In many cases, however, they are deployed as "regular" police officers somewhere else in the country. Something similar can be observed with regard to both the Congolese army and the judicial system: while 85 facilities for the permanent garrisoning of soldiers were constructed, less than half of the personnel trained for deployment were actually stationed there in mid-2011. In addition, not a single judicial and corrections officer, out of a group of 305 people, had actually been deployed to eastern DRC.[74] This problem, which has left a "vacuum of personnel", is understood as being of a political nature, demonstrating that "the anticipated national ownership of the stabilisation process has still not taken place".[75]

Conclusion

In examining how the ISSSS has been put into practice in eastern DRC with a specific focus on potential outcomes, it is hard to avoid the conclusion that the stabilisation strategy has not been very successful. From the onset, the international community had built its stabilisation efforts on the optimistic but faulty understanding that the conflict in eastern DRC had come to an end. In addition, after three years of doing stabilisation under the ISSSS framework, no common understanding has emerged about what stabilisation actually means in the specific conflict context of the DRC and from the perspective of the various actors involved. Furthermore, the relationship between the ISSSS and MONUSCO remains ambiguous as to their roles and activities and the distribution of competences and responsibilities. This further impinges upon any intended collaboration with STAREC, the government-led stabilisation plan. In addition to these obstacles, which were built into the stabilisation strategy from the onset, international actors seem to be somehow surprised by, and unable to respond to, the lack of political capacity and ownership of the Congolese government. In the meantime they pursue a strong donor-led approach, leading one interviewee to conclude that it is only the international community and not the Congolese government that is concerned with stabilisation.[76]

Against this background and focusing on the performance of the ISSSS in rebuilding state authority, the necessity to distinguish between outputs and outcomes becomes obvious. While the international actors have indeed been able to produce outputs, such as the construction of police and court houses in the eastern provinces, as well as the delivery of training programmes for administrative and police officials, the outcomes of these activities remain unimpressive. Furthermore, the absence of tangible outcomes has led the population to lose trust, as pointed out by one UN official:

> We built these beautiful buildings ... which are now looted, destroyed or taken over by the rebels. We lost the credibility and the reputation with the local population – and that is much more serious than losing buildings.... They tell us: "you promised us – but look where we are now!"

The activities carried out so far have been not only ineffective but even harmful when judging from the perspective of the local population, who had initially put trust in the international community's stabilisation efforts: "It is not only a setback to zero but we're beyond where we started".[77]

Insofar as the way forward is concerned, two main and interlinked aspects have repeatedly been discussed as being absolutely essential: (1) the implementation of a revised strategy on behalf of the international community, which takes a local approach to responding to the actual situation in eastern DRC, and (2) a changed understanding on the part of the Congolese government of its role in the stabilisation process, effected, if necessary, through the imposition of conditionalities.

The first aspect of having a more locally-based approach responds to the necessity to better adapt to the security situation by being more flexible, and to be able to directly tackle the root causes of conflict. This, however, does not imply that the national level becomes less significant. On the contrary, the shared understanding is that a local focus has to be supported both by MONUSCO and by the government, since the local and the national levels are closely interlinked; as highlighted by one interviewee, "there is a strong link between what we do [on the ground] and central reform, for example in terms of decentralization".[78] This aspect directly connects to the second aspect, the role of the Congolese government, which has consistently been criticised as not being interested or caring for its own people. The role of the international community is understood as being to "push" the government because "it won't work if they [the international community] don't put demands on the government.... Without the international engagement, you're stuck".[79] At the same time, the actors of the international community are divided; they do not necessarily push in the same direction, but rather follow their own strategic and often economic or political interests.

In light of these findings, it becomes obvious that the efforts of the international community to foster stabilisation as well as peace- and state-building in eastern DRC can hardly be deemed a success story. However, one has to keep in mind that due to the novelty of the stabilisation approach in general and particularly in relation to an ongoing peacekeeping mission, there are hardly any cases, or lessons learned, that the different actors involved can turn to. The ongoing debate on the strategic review of the ISSSS therefore raises the hope that the experiences of the last three years might be turned into more promising approaches in the future. And as much as the new outbreak of violence in 2012 implied a severe setback in the few developments that had actually been achieved, one can hope that it finally serves as an eye-opener, and shows the myriad of underlying problems and complexities that have to be tackled in order to achieve a minimum level of stabilisation. This is a precondition for any sustainable progress in the DRC.

Notes

1 G. Prunier, *Africa's World War: Congo, the Rwandan Genocide, and the Making of a Continental Catastrophe*, Oxford and New York: Oxford University Press, 2009.

2 T. Turner, *The Congo Wars: Conflict, Myth and Reality*, London and New York: Zed Books, 2007, pp. 1–3.

3 MONUSCO, *The ISSSS*, 2010, available at http://monusco.unmissions.org/Default.aspx?tabid=10831&language=en-US, accessed 26 March 2013.

4 UN Office for the Coordination of Humanitarian Affairs (UNOCHA), *DR Congo: Stepping up Support for Two Million Displaced*, available at www.unocha.org/top-stories/all-stories/dr-congo-stepping-support-two-million-displaced, accessed 23 November 2012.

5 In October 2012, the author conducted 19 interviews with UN, EU and non-governmental organisation (NGO) representatives involved in the formulation, administration or implementation of the ISSSS in eastern DRC. In addition, member states representatives and associates of a research institute were targeted.

6 Regarding the lack of political will, see for example R. Thakur, *The United Nations, Peace and Security: From Collective Security to the Responsibility to Protect*, Cambridge: Cambridge University Press, 2005, and M.W. Doyle and N. Sambanis, *United Nations Peace Operations: Making War & Building Peace*, Princeton: Princeton University Press, 2006. On the coordination problems see C. de Coning, *Coherence and Coordination in United Nations Peacebuilding and Integrated Missions – A Norwegian Perspective*, Oslo: Norwegian Institute of International Affairs, 2007; as well as M. Lurweg, "Coherent Actor or Institution Wrangler? The European Union as a Development and Security Actor in Eastern Democratic Republic of the Congo", *African Security* 4, 2011, pp. 100–126; and on the imposition of liberal values see R. Paris, *At War's End: Building Peace after Civil Conflict*, Cambridge: Cambridge University Press, 2004; as well as O.P. Richmond, *The Transformation of Peace*, Basingstoke: Palgrave Macmillan, 2005.

7 See for example B. Pouligny, *Peace Operations Seen from Below: UN Missions and Local People*, London: Hurst & Company, 2006; S. Autesserre, *The Trouble with the Congo: Local Violence and the Failure of International Peacebuilding*, Cambridge: Cambridge University Press, 2010; and L. Gelot and F. Söderbaum, "Interveners and

Intervened Upon: The Missing Link in Building Peace and Avoiding Conflict", in H. Fjelde and K. Höglund (eds), *Building Peace, Creating Conflict? Conflictual Dimensions of Local and International Peace-building*, Lund: Nordic Academic Press, 2011, pp. 73–88.

8 J.-E. Lane and S. Ersson, *The New Institutional Politics: Performance and Outcomes*, New York: Routledge, 2000, p. 61.

9 S. Autesserre, *Peacebuilders: An Ethnography of International Intervention*, Cambridge: Cambridge University Press (forthcoming 2014).

10 Gelot and Söderbaum, "Interveners"; and R. MacGinty, "Routine Peace: Technocracy and Peacebuilding", *Cooperation and Conflict* 47, 2012, pp. 287–308.

11 Lane and Ersson, *New Institutional Politics*, p. 63.

12 G.A. Almond, G. Bingham Powell and R.J. Mundt, *Comparative Politics: A Theoretical Framework*, New York: HarperCollins College Publishers, 1993, p. 20.

13 D.S. Van Meter and C.E. Van Horn, "The Policy Implementation Process", *Administration & Society* 6, 1975, p. 448.

14 D.A. Mazmanian and P.A. Sabatier, *Implementation and Public Policy*, Lanham MD: University Press of America, 1989, p. 4.

15 *Ibid.*

16 B.W. Hogwood and L.A. Gunn, *Policy Analysis for the Real World*, Oxford: Oxford University Press, 1984, p. 17.

17 K. Menkhaus, *Impact Assessment in Post-Conflict Peacebuilding: Challenges and Future Directions*, Interpeace: International Peacebuilding Alliance, 2004, p. 4.

18 E. Paddon and G. Lacaille, *Stabilising the Congo*, Forced Migration Policy Briefing, Oxford: Refugee Studies Centre, 2011, p. 5.

19 *Ibid.*

20 The Lusaka Ceasefire Agreement, signed on 10 July 1999, was an attempt to end the second Congo war through a ceasefire, a declaration of attempt to address the security concerns in the DRC and its neighbouring countries and through the deployment of an international UN-led peacekeeping force. The agreement is available at http://reliefweb.int/report/democratic-republic-congo/dr-congo-lusaka-ceasefire-agreement, accessed 20 October 2012.

21 The Sun City peace deal was reached on 19 April 2002 between the *Mouvement pour la libération du Congo* (MLC) led by Jean-Pierre Bemba and the government of Joseph Kabila; see International Crisis Group (ICG), *Storm Clouds over Sun City: The Urgent Need to Recast the Congolese Peace Process*, Africa Report 44, 14 May 2002, available at www.crisisgroup.org/en/regions/africa/central-africa/dr-congo/044-storm-clouds-over-sun-city-the-urgent-need-to-recast-the-congolese-peace-process.aspx, accessed 20 October 2012.

22 Besides Artemis, EUPOL and EUSEC RD Congo missions, the EU had further deployed the civilian EUPOL Kinshasa mission from 2005 to 2007 to support the Integrated Police Unit of the National Police in Kinshasa (this was the predecessor of EUPOL RD Congo) and the military EUFOR RD Congo mission in 2006 to support MONUC during the election process (for more information on the EU missions in the DRC, see M. Froitzheim, F. Söderbaum and I. Taylor, *The Limits of the EU as a Peace and Security Actor in the Democratic Republic of the Congo, Africa Spectrum* 46, 2011, pp. 45–70).

23 ICG, *DR Congo Conflict History*, Brussels, 2010, available at www.crisisgroup.org/fr/publication-type/key-issues/Research%20Resources/Conflict%20Histories/DR%20Congo%20Conflict%20History.aspx, accessed 4 October 2012.

24 ISSSS, *Generating a Joint Political Approach to Stabilization*, DRC, 2012, p. 4.

25 Gouvernement de la République Démocratique du Congo, *Programme de Stabilisation et de Reconstruction des Zones sortant des conflits armés (STAREC)*, Kinshasa, 2009.

26 ISSSS, *Generating*, p. 5.

27 See for example the USAID approach under the "Democracy, Human Rights and Governance" theme: USAID, "Democracy, Human Rights and Governance", last updated 25 February 2013, available at www.usaid.gov/democratic-republic-congo/democracy-human-rights-and-governance, accessed 26 March 2013; and the DFID project "TUUNGANE (Let's unite) – Community Driven Reconstruction Programme in DRC", available at http://projects.dfid.gov.uk/project.aspx?Project=105862, accessed 26 March 2013.
28 S. Bailey, *Humanitarian Action, Early Recovery and Stabilisation in the Democratic Republic of Congo*, London: Overseas Development Institute, 2011, p. 5.
29 Paddon and Lacaille, *Stabilising the Congo*, p. 2.
30 S. Collison, S. Elhawary and R. Muggah, *States of Fragility: Stabilisation and its Implications for Humanitarian Action*, HPG Working Paper, London: Overseas Development Institute, 2010, p. 5.
31 *Ibid.*
32 UN, *Integrated Programme Framework (IPF), 2009–2012. Democratic Republic of Congo*, 2009, p. 7.
33 *Ibid.*, p. 2.
34 The largest bilateral donors are the US (US$95.1 million), followed by the Netherlands (US$72.44) and the UK (US$57.24 million).
35 Stabilization Support Unit (SSU), "International Security and Stabilization Support Strategy for the Democratic Republic of the Congo", *Quarterly Report April to June 2012*, Kinshasa and Goma, 2012, p. 3.
36 Interview with a UN representative in Goma, 15 October 2012.
37 Interview with a UN representative in Goma, 6 October 2012.
38 Interview with a UN representative in Goma, 15 October 2012.
39 Bailey, *Humanitarian Action*, p. 5.
40 Interview with a UN representative in Goma, 15 October 2012.
41 Interview with a UN representative in Goma, 10 October 2012.
42 Interview with a NGO representative in Goma, 15 October 2012.
43 Interview with a UN representative in Goma, 15 October 2012.
44 *Ibid.*
45 *Ibid.*
46 S. Dixon, *"For Me, but Without Me, is Against Me". Why Efforts to Stabilise the Democratic Republic of Congo are Not Working*, Oxfam International, 2012, p. 14.
47 Interview with a UN representative in Goma, 15 October 2012.
48 Interview with a UN representative in Goma, 6 October 2012.
49 Interview with a UN representative in Goma, 15 October 2012.
50 Interview with a UN representative in Goma, 6 October 2012; see also SSU, "International Security".
51 Interview with a UN representative in Goma, 16 October 2012.
52 *Ibid.*
53 S. Chesterman, "Ownership in Theory and in Practice: Transfer of Authority in UN Statebuilding Operations", *Journal of Intervention and Statebuilding* 1, 2007, p. 9.
54 *Ibid.*
55 Interview with a UN representative in Goma, 6 October 2012.
56 Interview with an NGO representative in Goma, 15 October 2012.
57 Interview with a UN representative in Goma, 11 October 2012.
58 Interview with a UN representative in Goma, 6 October 2012.
59 Dixon, *"For Me, but Without Me"*, p. 30.
60 Interview with a UN representative in Goma, 15 October 2012.
61 While the ICG also argues for the need to increase the political will on the part of the Congolese government, they deny that the stabilization strategy as such has to be revised. See ICG, "Eastern Congo: Why Stabilisation Failed", *Africa*

Briefing 91, 4 October 2012. This understanding, however, was not shared during the interviews carried out in Goma in October 2012.
62 Interview with a UN representative in Goma, 6 October 2012.
63 Lurweg, "Coherent Actor", p. 117 and Froitzheim *et al.*, *Limits of the EU*, p. 45.
64 Interview with an EU representative in Goma, 8 October 2012.
65 Interview with a UN representative in Goma, 6 October 2012.
66 Dixon, *"For Me, but Without Me"*, p. 20.
67 Interview with a UN representative in Goma, 6 October 2012. See also Paddon and Lacaille, *Stabilising the Congo*, p. 13.
68 Paddon and Lacaille, *Stabilising the Congo*, p. 20.
69 See also Dixon, *"For Me, but Without Me"*, pp. 20–21.
70 *Ibid.* In addition to the UN, the EU, through the EUPOL RD Congo mission, as well as the Chinese have further been active in training police officers.
71 Interview with a UN representative in Goma, 6 October 2012.
72 Interview with a UN representative in Goma, 15 October 2012.
73 Interview with a NGO representative in Goma, 10 October 2012.
74 Paddon and Lacaille, *Stabilising the Congo*, p. 16.
75 *Ibid.*
76 Interview with a NGO representative in Goma, 15 October 2012.
77 Interview with a UN representative in Goma, 15 October 2012.
78 Interview with a UN representative in Goma, 9 October 2012.
79 *Ibid.*

11 The perils of peacekeeping as a tool of RtoP

The case of Darfur

David Lanz[1]

Introduction

This chapter is concerned with the role of peacekeeping in wider normative processes and structures of world politics. At its inception, peacekeeping derived from a Westphalian conception of world order based on state sovereignty and non-intervention. This was exemplified by the first UN peacekeeping force, which was deployed in 1956 in the Sinai: peacekeepers were interposed between two conflicting states, and they abided by strict neutrality and non-use of force (except in self-defence). The blueprint changed after the end of the Cold War, when traditional peacekeeping gave way to missions that incorporated elements of a post-Westphalian conception of "liberal peace" based on democracy, human rights, and the rule of law.[2] Peacekeepers thus received broad mandates, which often included statebuilding tasks, and they were expected to protect civilians in a proactive way, using all necessary means at their disposal. The new functions did not replace traditional peacekeeping principles, but they were juxtaposed with them. Indeed, peacekeeping as defined by the UN Department of Peacekeeping Operations (UNDPKO) still rests on the three basic principles of consent of the parties, impartiality, and non-use of force except in self-defence and in defence of the mandate.[3]

The evolution of peacekeeping shows that its doctrine and practice reflect the normative context of world politics. This raises the question of how peacekeeping interacts with the emerging norm of the "Responsibility to Protect" (RtoP), which seeks to prevent mass atrocities worldwide. The primary responsibility lies with the state, but if a state proves unable or unwilling to provide protection, the onus falls on the international community.[4] Contrary to the earlier "right of interference" (*droit d'ingérence* in French), RtoP casts human rights and sovereignty as being compatible, amending the notion of sovereignty to include a state's decent treatment of its citizens. This framing notwithstanding, RtoP represents a liberal internationalist project that clearly breaks with traditional, Westphalian conceptions of state sovereignty, which consider a state's behavior towards its citizens an exclusively domestic affair. There is much discussion about the status and impact of the RtoP norm.[5] However, it seems clear that it has recently gained momentum. States endorsed RtoP in the 2005 World Summit Outcome Document, albeit in a somewhat watered-down version.[6] Also, there is increasing reference to RtoP in international crisis management, most recently in Libya and Côte d'Ivoire.[7]

The talk of RtoP has elevated protection as an activity in which international interveners should engage. One consequence is that "protection of civilians" is increasingly included in the mandates of peacekeeping operations. Beyond the mandate, the convergence of RtoP and peacekeeping raises a number of questions. Is peacekeeping a tool of RtoP? How does it affect the politics surrounding the establishment of new peacekeeping missions? How does it influence expectations vis-à-vis peacekeepers? This chapter addresses these questions by examining the case of Darfur.[8] Indeed, the crisis in Darfur, which erupted in 2003, reached its climax in 2004, and since then has featured a less intense but unresolved conflict, triggered a far-reaching response in terms of peacekeeping. The AU deployed its largest ever peacekeeping mission to Darfur, the AU Mission to Darfur (AMIS), which was replaced in 2008 by the AU-UN Hybrid operation in Darfur (UNAMID) – likewise one of the largest and most expensive peacekeeping missions the UN has ever commanded.

The idea of sending peacekeepers to Darfur, and the creation of UNAMID in particular, was intrinsically linked to RtoP. It emerged from a context that framed Darfur as a test case of RtoP and demanded that policymakers "do something" to address the crisis. Since non-consensual intervention was not feasible, activists and policymakers focused on robust peacekeeping. This chapter argues that the energies thus unleashed made possible the creation of a mission of the magnitude of UNAMID. At the same time, however, the framing of peacekeeping as a tool of RtoP also posed problems. It politicized UNAMID and complicated relations with the Sudanese government, which feared that peacekeepers were at the vanguard of Western-instigated regime change. The RtoP language also raised unrealistic expectations among the local population about what a peacekeeping mission can achieve in a context like Darfur. As their hopes were disappointed, UNAMID, and with it the international community as a whole, has been discredited.

The chapter is structured as follows: the first section provides a brief background of the conflict and traces how Darfur became a test case of RtoP. The second section looks at the manifestations of RtoP in Darfur, with a focus on AMIS and UNAMID. The third section considers the implications of infusing peacekeeping with RtoP language in terms of perceptions of UNAMID in the Sudanese government and among the local population in Darfur. The conclusion makes a number of general observations, as peacekeeping and RtoP increasingly converge.

Darfur in the context of the Responsibility to Protect

This section explains the context in which the international response to the Darfur conflict took shape. It offers some background on the conflict and then traces its transformation from a forgotten conflict to a global *cause célèbre* since 2004. A crucial factor in this process was the framing of Darfur as a test case of RtoP, which set the stage for robust peacekeeping later on.

From a forgotten conflict ...

Darfur is the size of Spain and is situated in the western periphery of the Sudanese state, bordering South Sudan, the Central African Republic (CAR), Chad, and Libya. Around 2000, a series of local insurgencies formed in Darfur in response to inter-tribal violence and owing to the government's long-standing policy of neglect and marginalization.[9] The conflict escalated in early 2003 when different rebel groups joined together and were supplied with arms from South Sudan and from governments of neighboring countries. A concerted attack in April on the army garrison in the capital of North Darfur made the Sudanese government realize that the rebels were a force to be reckoned with.[10] The government, at the time engaged in delicate peace negotiations with rebels from the South, reacted severely. It mounted local militia forces, the "Janjaweed", comprised primarily of Arab groups from North Darfur, and unleashed them with the aim of destroying the civilian support base of the rebels.[11] The conflict was at its most intense in the period between the last months of 2003 and mid-2004, during which hundreds of villages were destroyed, 130,000 died, and over one million Darfuris were displaced.[12]

At the outset, states and international organizations largely ignored Darfur. Humanitarian organizations from Darfur had repeatedly warned that mass violence was imminent, but their calls did not lead to any response. The same was true in 2003 when Amnesty International and the International Crisis Group (ICG) spoke about the escalating violence in Darfur.[13] Moreover, at the height of the brutal counter-insurgency campaign in late 2003, humanitarian organizations, whose staff witnessed the atrocities, sounded the alarm bell. The resonance was again negligible. Some governments agreed to fund humanitarian aid, but none was willing to act on the political dimension of the crisis. The media also ignored Darfur: no major international newspaper reported the conflict before 2004.[14]

... to an RtoP test case

Darfur stopped being ignored in March 2004 when several UN officials began to speak out. Most importantly, Mukesh Kapila, the UN's humanitarian coordinator in Sudan, said that "the only difference between Rwanda and Darfur now is the numbers involved".[15] This statement had a strong impact. Subsequently, media reports multiplied, making Darfur one of the world's most publicized conflicts within a few months.[16] The media reports presented Darfur as an unambiguous case of mass atrocities, perpetuated by Arabs with the intention of cleansing Darfur of its black African tribes. Insofar as the world had learned from Rwanda, it needed to mount a forceful intervention to stop the crimes.[17]

Even if at the outset there were few explicit references, the core idea of RtoP – if a state is unable or unwilling, the onus of protection falls on the international community – became the primary lens through which the world viewed Darfur. This is exemplified by various statements by world leaders. On 7 April 2004, UN Secretary-General Kofi Annan talked about Darfur at the UN Commission on Human Rights:

> It is vital that international humanitarian workers and human rights experts be given full access to the region, and to the victims, without further delay. If that is denied, the international community must be prepared to take swift and appropriate action. By "action" in such situations I mean a continuum of steps, which may include military action.[18]

Two weeks later the US representative, Richard Williamson, stated:

> [T]en years from now, the 60th Commission on Human Rights will be remembered for one thing and one thing alone: Did we have the courage and strength to take strong action against the "ethnic cleansing" in Darfur. We will be asked, "Where were you at the time of the ethnic cleansing?" "What did you do?" ... [T]he horrific events in Darfur demand strong action.[19]

Another example is the UK Prime Minister Tony Blair. In July 2004, he raised the possibility of sending troops to Darfur, as he stated that "we have a moral responsibility to deal with this and deal with it by any means we can".[20]

RtoP also framed civil society engagement on Darfur, as NGOs promoting RtoP took up Darfur. In this context, Gareth Evans, president of ICG and co-chair of the international commission that proposed the notion of RtoP at its inception in 2001, described Darfur as a "test case" of the RtoP principles.[21] In the summer of 2004, a broad-based civil society platform emerged in North America to spearhead the advocacy effort on Darfur. Tellingly, the platform was named the "Save Darfur Coalition", the idea of "saving" the victims of mass atrocities being strongly linked to the core idea of RtoP.[22] After 2005, RtoP was regularly invoked. The long-time Sudan activist Eric Reeves, for example, stated:

> The UN World Summit of September 2005 produced an "outcome document" ... that commits the international community to a "responsibility to protect" civilians who are victims of genocide, ethnic cleansing or crimes against humanity. This "responsibility" was explicitly framed as superseding claims of national sovereignty such as Khartoum continues to assert. If the world fails to intervene in Darfur ... the fleeting ideal of an international "responsibility to protect" civilians at the most acute risk will have collapsed.[23]

In a nutshell, Darfur was framed in the media, by civil society activists, and in statements by world leaders as a case of mass atrocities perpetuated by a criminal regime against innocent civilians in need of rescue. This made Darfur a test case for the emerging RtoP norm, which thus formed the context against which policymakers contemplated responses to the crisis.

Peacekeepers as RtoP implementers

Given the framing of Darfur as a test case of RtoP, it is not surprising that policymakers put a strong emphasis on protection. One approach consisted of putting pressure on the Sudanese government – the main culprit of the atrocities – in order to change its cost-benefit analysis of using mass atrocities. Western countries made strong statements condemning Khartoum's actions; the US, Canada, and the EU imposed sanctions against members of the Sudanese government; and the UN Security Council referred the situation in Darfur to the International Criminal Court (ICC). However, the limits of this approach rapidly became apparent. Given Khartoum's intransigence, public opinion demanded other forms of intervention to directly protect Darfuris, and this is how policymakers turned to peacekeeping. Against this, this section first traces the emergence of peacekeeping as the primary protection response to the crisis in Darfur, before looking at the manifestations of this response: the deployment of two successive peacekeeping operations, AMIS and UNAMID.

Settling for second best

Calls for non-consensual military intervention in Darfur, similar to NATO's actions in Kosovo in 1999, were rare even among Darfur advocates, which included people in the media, civil society, and a few committed policymakers that were the driving forces behind the international response to the Darfur conflict.[24] A few people, such as Eric Reeves, continuously advocated for non-consensual intervention,[25] but this never represented the mainstream position of the movement. The reluctance may appear strange considering that the media and activists were painting a picture of Darfur as the site of genocide on a par with Rwanda, where thousands of innocent civilians were being brutally slaughtered every month. If this were the case, then Darfur would surely meet the threshold for military intervention as set forth in the RtoP doctrine. So why did so few people call for this course of action?

The answer is that Darfur advocates knew that in the post-Afghanistan, post-Iraq world, another US-led military intervention in a predominantly Muslim country was not on the cards. The commentary of *New York Times* columnist Nicholas Kristof is a case in point. In his editorials, he often gave graphic details of the atrocities. However, as far as remedies were concerned, he was pragmatic: "The US is not going to invade Sudan. That's not a plausible option. But we can pass a tough UN Security Council resolution authorizing troops, as well as more support for African peacekeepers".[26] Another example is ICG. In 2005, the organization conducted a survey to gauge US citizens' opinions regarding Darfur. The survey showed that 76 percent of respondents were in favour of "offer[ing] NATO logistical and troop support for an expanded African peacekeeping force", but only 38 percent wanted to "insert US soldiers on the ground".[27] Not surprisingly, this was taken up in a report published one month after the survey was released: ICG recommended that the existing AU peacekeeping force should be strengthened and extended, possibly with help from NATO.[28]

Given that other, more forceful options were not realistic, those advocating for Darfur settled for the second best option for the implementation of RtoP: sending peacekeepers. The problem, however, was that while the advocates were flexible on the means of intervention, they were rigid on the end: peacekeepers had to speak truth to power to Khartoum, and they should offer full-fledged protection to Darfuris. As Romeo Dallaire wrote in an opinion editorial, AU peacekeepers could, with some help from NATO, "protect Darfur's displaced people in their camps and remaining villages, and eliminate or incarcerate the Janjaweed".[29] Complicating factors were excluded from consideration: that peacekeepers rely on the consent of the host country and that the sheer size of the Darfur territory posed serious limitations for what they could achieve.

AMIS: in and out of favour

At first, activists and policymakers settled for outsourcing peacekeeping to the AU, without however appreciating the operational limitations of AU peacekeeping as well as the political realities of the African context. The story of AMIS is telling in this regard. AMIS observers were first deployed in June 2004. A few months later, the mission strength was boosted to 2,200 armed personnel and its mandate extended "in a way that responded to humanitarian appeals but at the same time satisfied the Sudanese host state, the AU membership and the foreign donors".[30] Specifically, the AU Peace and Security Council (AUPSC) tasked AMIS with "protecting civilians whom it encounters under imminent threat and in the immediate vicinity, within resources and capability, it being understood that the protection of the civilian population is the responsibility of the government of Sudan".[31] In 2005, the AUPSC decided on a phased increase of the mission, and by September 2006, AMIS had over 7,000 armed personnel operating all over Darfur.[32]

Initially, AMIS received a lot of international support. Its budget was entirely covered by international donors. The EU contributed €300 million altogether. The US government gave nearly US$300 million to build AMIS's bases.[33] Canada paid for helicopters, which were rented from private contractors. NATO airlifted AU troops in and out of Darfur. These contributions were strongly supported by Darfur advocates on the grounds that the AU peacekeepers were "the only people who will stand between civilians and their killers on the ground in Darfur".[34]

What impact did AMIS's presence have in Darfur? It is not surprising that different evaluations concluded that the impact of AMIS in terms of protecting civilians was limited.[35] Various factors contributed to this: AMIS operated in an ongoing civil war and it had to cover a territory the size of Spain with just a few thousand peacekeepers. It did not have significant force projection capability and given the AU's limited peacekeeping experience, it faced logistical and capacity constraints. Despite these constraints, AMIS improved the security of Darfuris in some respects. AU peacekeepers made preventative deployments in areas where it anticipated fighting or where fighting had taken place and there was a danger that it would reignite. They also patrolled the main travel routes in order to prevent attacks on humanitarian convoys. In many internally displaced person (IDP) camps, AMIS established a police presence, which generally increased security for camp residents.[36]

Despite these achievements, a new policy priority crystallized in early 2006: replacement of AMIS with a UN-led peacekeeping force featuring a robust Chapter VII mandate to protect civilians in Darfur. This may appear surprising since Darfur activists, policymakers, and pundits had previously argued that the protection of civilians in Darfur required beefing up AMIS, strengthening its mandate, increasing its troop size, and giving it financial and logistical support. However, towards the end of 2005, the mood shifted. Negative reports about AMIS and its inability to prevent abuses against civilians multiplied in the media. The Western countries that were bankrolling AMIS also had a change of heart, calling into question the system of voluntary funding that paid for the mission. Congress reduced funding, as did the EU on the grounds that AMIS's accounting procedures were improper. Within a year, AMIS turned from a straw man for saving strangers in Darfur into an institution that embodied the world's inaction in the face of genocide.[37]

UN peacekeepers in Darfur: a long time coming

With AMIS increasingly discredited, the deployment of a robust UN peacekeeping force became a rallying cry for Darfur advocates. Thus, the Save Darfur Coalition ran expensive newspaper advertisements and organized several rallies in New York to call for a UN force in Darfur.[38] Many policymakers heeded the call, as it allowed them to show that they were "doing something" on Darfur. Moreover, within the US government, the UN force emerged as a compromise between those calling for more forceful measures – such as establishing a no-fly zone or sending NATO troops to Darfur – and others who did not think Darfur was relevant to US interests.[39] European governments, in particular the UK and France, picked up the idea too. An additional incentive for AMIS donors was that a UN mission would be funded through the regular peacekeeping budget, to which all UN member states contributed.

In May 2006, the Sudanese government and a break-away rebel group signed the Darfur Peace Agreement in Abuja.[40] The agreement was never implemented, but it paved the way for the UN Security Council in its Resolution 1706 to authorize the expansion to Darfur of the existing UN Mission in Sudan (UNMIS) – created in 2005 to support the implementation of the North-South peace agreement. RtoP was a central reference point, as the resolution mentioned the World Summit Outcome Document and several ambassadors referred to RtoP when explaining their vote.[41] However, to nip Khartoum's hostility in the bud, and to assuage the concerns of China, which insisted on respect for host state sovereignty,[42] the drafters of Resolution 1706 had inserted a clause "inviting" Khartoum's consent to the deployment of the mission.[43] Khartoum seized on this. According to MacKinnon, "Khartoum's sustained opposition to the resolution won the day and the resolution was effectively shelved in November 2006".[44] As a way out of the impasse, Kofi Annan proposed a new plan: a hybrid mission that would be jointly authorized and operated by the UN and the AU. Thus, in July 2007, the UN Security Council created UNAMID, authorizing the deployment of up to 19,555 troops and 3,772 police officers and giving the mission an explicit mandate to protect civilians under Chapter VII of the UN Charter.[45]

UNAMID took over from AMIS in January 2008 and became the largest and – with running costs between US$1.3 and 1.7 billion – the most expensive UN peacekeeping mission to date.[46] Given the nature of politics surrounding UN peacekeeping, which is characterized by the existence of multiple veto players, the creation of UNAMID was a significant development. Had it not been for advocacy groups campaigning for forceful intervention in Darfur, and more generally, had Darfur not been framed as an RtoP test case, it is unlikely that UNAMID would ever have seen the light of the day. These factors were crucial in convincing the US, France, and the UK to invest significant political capital in the creation of UNAMID.

The activist pressure, in particular the "Genocide Olympics" campaign, also helped to overcome China's resistance against a Chapter VII mission in Darfur.

UNAMID on the ground[47]

How does the performance of UNAMID compare to the intentions of its creators? After nearly five years of deployment, UNAMID's record does not appear to be very different from that of AMIS. UNAMID has made some difference in Darfur. Where it is physically present, the mission seems to have some deterrent effect. This may have contributed to lowering the level of violence in Darfur – indeed, in 2008, a study reported 2,112 battle-related deaths in Darfur, 585 of whom were civilians.[48] This represents a striking contrast to the most violent phase of the conflict in 2003–2004. UNAMID peacekeepers have also improved security in IDP camps, and there have been instances where they directly protected civilians from the effects of violence.

However, the mission's overall ability to offer protection of civilians, in the sense of taking proactive measures to ensure that civilians are safe from attacks and that the belligerents do not deliberately target them, is limited. This is especially the case in areas where peacekeepers are not physically present. Overall, the impact of peacekeepers in Darfur has been a far cry from the ideals of RtoP. There are multiple reasons for this. One is undoubtedly UNAMID's inadequacy in the number of troops, which is insufficient to protect civilians in a territory that is as big, as populated, and as unstable as Darfur.[49] The force's equipment is also inadequate; for example, UNAMID has a limited number of tactical helicopters, which reduces its force projection capability. Also, UNAMID has not received the kind of political support necessary to confront the Sudanese government. This has allowed Khartoum, under the pretext of the consent requirement, to put all kinds of obstacles in the way of the work of the UN-AU peacekeepers.

To sum up, RtoP helped muster the political support that was necessary first to boost AMIS and later to establish a mission of the magnitude of UNAMID. However, despite a few improvements, the impact of peacekeepers has been limited. The conflict remains unresolved; a third of Darfur's population lives in displaced camps; and many Darfuris continue to be as vulnerable as they were at the outset of the conflict. This shows that peacekeepers are inherently limited in an ongoing civil war like Darfur – whether or not they have a Chapter VII mandate to protect civilians.

Local implications of peacekeeping as a tool of RtoP

The effectiveness of peacekeepers depends to a large degree on cooperation with local actors. Therefore, a relevant question pertains to the impact of the RtoP language on the work of the mission on the ground. How did the utilization of RtoP language influence perceptions and expectations of local political actors in Sudan? This section first considers the role of the Sudanese government before turning to the local population in Darfur.

Defying the West

The ruling party of Sudan, the National Congress Party (NCP), is headed by Omar al-Bashir, whose regime has ruled Sudan since a coup brought its predecessor, the National Islamic Front, to power in 1989. The NCP has long claimed it is the victim of a Western-led conspiracy to bring about regime change in Sudan. This is partly strategic, as it helps to conjure up support in the Arab world, thereby lessening the pressure that Khartoum has faced due to its catastrophic human rights record. At the same time, it reflects a deeply held belief among the NCP ruling elites, which goes back to the 1990s when Sudan embraced Islamic extremism and hosted Osama bin Laden for several years.[50] Unsurprisingly, Khartoum got a very hostile reception in Washington at the time, even after it moderated its stance following the involvement of members of Khartoum's security cabal in an unsuccessful assassination attempt on Egyptian president Mubarak in 1995. Some members of the Clinton Administration, especially Secretary of State Madeleine Albright, sympathized with the Southern Sudanese rebels and openly contemplated regime change in Khartoum.[51] Many NCP members see the Darfur campaigns as a continuation of this policy. This translates into a deep suspicion about any form of Western intervention, including the activities of humanitarian organizations.[52]

Against this, it is not surprising that the idea of deploying peacekeepers endowed with a Chapter VII mandate to protect civilians sounded alarm bells in Khartoum. This was compounded by the ICC investigations against the Sudanese government, which culminated in the indictment of Omar al-Bashir in 2009, and by the deployment of an EU protection force across the border from Darfur in eastern Chad and north-eastern CAR. Khartoum feared that peacekeepers would eventually spearhead a more forceful, NATO-led intervention. In this context, the portrayal of UN peacekeeping as an instrument of RtoP seems to have enhanced such fears. It has heightened the perception that peacekeeping is a strategic tool of the West, and it has thus been one factor fuelling Khartoum's defiance and its systematic obstruction of UNAMID operations. Certainly, there are other reasons why Sudan opposes a strong peacekeeping force in Darfur: it does not want evidence of past and current crimes, for which the government is responsible, to be brought to light. However, UNAMID has never attempted to collect such evidence, and the very cautious approach it adopted during the first years of deployment should have made it clear that the mission was far from a vanguard for regime change.

Another consideration is that while Khartoum fiercely resisted peacekeepers in Darfur, it gave the green light for the deployment of another mission, UNMIS, which also had a Chapter VII mandate to protect civilians.

In order to fully understand the NCP regime's resistance against UNAMID it is necessary to look at the level of norms and symbols. This chapter advances the argument that the RtoP-infused discourse has elevated UNAMID to being a poster child for Western interventionism. This meant that obstructing the mission became a way for the government to assert its independence and to defy the West. The government also sought to create resonance with voices in the Global South, which have portrayed RtoP as a "Trojan horse" legitimizing Western intrusion under a humanitarian pretext.[53] Reports published in government-controlled news sources confirm this dynamic. For example, in November 2006, Sudan TV broadcast a speech by Omar al-Bashir in which he strongly stated his objection to the deployment of international peacekeepers in Darfur: "[Sudan] does not want to become a field in which international political scores are settled. It does not also want to become an inlet for the forces of international hegemony".[54] Likewise, an NCP member said in an interview with the author:

> The government did not trust the international forces.... The fear was that these forces were subject to manipulation by the Americans, like in Iraq, where international troops forced their agenda.... There was a sense that international forces foster regime change.[55]

Khartoum was eventually forced to accept UNAMID because its primary ally, China, who wanted to diffuse the bad publicity that the "Genocide Olympics" campaign generated, insisted on it.[56] However, this has not prevented the government from hindering the deployment and operation of the mission. This has manifested itself in numerous obstructions, which were small-scale but which in the aggregate represent a significant constraint. For example, the Sudanese government has withheld visas for UNAMID staff; prevented the importation of necessary material; hindered the acquisition of real estate in Darfur; imposed curfews; and prohibited night patrols. Another common practice is for the Sudanese government to declare expats whom they consider too proactive as *persona non grata* and expel them from the country.[57] As a UN official stated in an interview with the author, "the government never gave authentic consent. The objective was to limit the mission to something primitive. The government's consent was barely acceptable to the functioning of the mission".[58]

Why has the government been so obstructionist? One aspect is that Khartoum is getting away with it. For all the rhetoric about Darfur, and all the political capital that was invested in the establishment of UNAMID, the mission has not had sufficient political backing to confront the government. This chapter focuses on another aspect, namely that UNAMID, along with the ICC, came to be viewed as a symbol of a Western-led agenda to undermine the independence of Sudan. In this context, obstructing UNAMID makes sense, as it is a way for the government to defy the West and thereby assert its legitimacy and independence.

The saviour that never came

The local reality of Darfur seems far away from the centres of global policy in New York, Washington, or Geneva. However, Darfuris at the grassroots, who considered the Sudanese government responsible for their suffering, were acutely aware of international discussions about their fate. RtoP was important in this regard. It is not difficult to understand how Darfuris' expectations were raised, as time and again they heard international personalities denounce the crimes in Darfur, compare the situation to Rwanda, and treat Omar al-Bashir as a war criminal. It meant that Darfuris expected the arrival of an external saviour, who would bring justice and make sure they could go home and reclaim their land. The account of journalist Rob Crilly of what he experienced on one of his visits to a displaced camp in Darfur is telling:

> Children began streaming into the camp from all directions, laughing and shouting. Each carried a home-made banner, often little more than a piece of white paper covered in childish writing. "Go on International Criminal Court" read one. "Welcome UN", said another.... The message could be summed up in one simple phrase: "Come and Save Us."[59]

The researchers of "24 Hours for Darfur", a video advocacy campaign, collected statements from Darfuri refugees that illustrate this attitude as well:

> Let the international forces come to Darfur and prosecute the criminals, disarm the Janjaweed, and then after that, God willing, we can return. We realize it will take a lot of work. On behalf of the widows and orphans, we are calling on the UN to do more than they have done.[60]

This demonstrates that local Darfuris projected their hopes and expectations onto the promised UN peacekeeping force, especially since they had to wait for over two years until the mission was finally deployed. In this context, it is not difficult to understand that the portrayal of UN peacekeeping as an instrument of RtoP left a strong impression at the local level. Darfur expected a mission that would protect them from harm. They were hoping the mission would stand up to the government, bring their killers to justice, and allow them to return to their homes. In short, they expected a saviour. However, the saviour never came. As mentioned above, while UNAMID may have improved security in some areas, its ability to provide protection has been limited. Obviously, the mission fell far short of what Darfuris were expecting. One consequence is that Darfuris became cynical about the international community and about the notion of RtoP in particular. As a Darfuri lawyer stated in an interview with the author, "RtoP means nothing! Even in the presence of UNAMID atrocities continue to happen. Nobody protects the people of Darfur. In the context of the international community, RtoP produces no acts".[61]

The credibility of UNAMID forces on the ground suffered immensely as well. A Sudanese journalist working in Darfur tellingly stated in an interview with the author:

> People in the camps think that UNAMID is not capable of solving their problems. And so they say to UNAMID that if you are not capable of solving our problem you should get out of Darfur, you rather let us die. In the beginning people expected problems to be solved by UNAMID, they expected to be able to return to their lands, to have peace, to be paid compensation, to have their basic services in health and education met.[62]

The loss in credibility has impeded UNAMID's ability to effectively operate in Darfur, as the local population has sometimes been reluctant to cooperate with the peacekeepers. For example, peacekeepers have been unable to secure access to certain areas controlled by the rebels, which accused UNAMID of colluding with the government.[63] In one instance, a rebel group captured 49 UNAMID soldiers and held them for a few days on the grounds that they entered their territory without permission.[64]

Another consequence is that people's disappointed hopes have fostered the perception of UNAMID as being weak. The notion that UNAMID peacekeepers are incapable of protecting themselves has thus become a slogan among Darfuris. This seriously undermined the deterrence effect, which is crucial for any peacekeeping mission, and for UNAMID in particular since the mission operates in an ongoing civil war and covers a territory the size of Spain with a mere 20,000 soldiers. It seems plausible that the perception of weakness has been one factor explaining the frequent attacks against UNAMID peacekeepers, even if the highly volatile overall security situation is the main cause. By February 2013, UNAMID has suffered 145 fatalities.[65] In addition, armed groups have repeatedly abducted UNAMID staff, demanding large sums of money in ransom.[66]

To sum up, the portrayal of peacekeeping as an instrument of RtoP has been problematic for UNAMID, as it has inflated the local population's expectations of what the mission can achieve. A Darfuri NGO worker said in this regard:

> Actually people have expectation that these forces will keep the peace. But from their experience they say that UNAMID is weak. Even their cars were attacked, their soldiers were kidnapped. There was a lot of hope when UNAMID was deployed.... But people are not aware of what the mandate of UNAMID is. The mission and the mandate were not clear. What are peacekeepers? Why are they so weak, why are they attacked? People did not understand this. People hope that UNAMID can help in their return.[67]

This gets to the heart of the problem of infusing a peacekeeping mission with RtoP language. It creates expectations that peacekeeping missions, regardless of how determined their staff or how well they are equipped, will have difficulties fulfilling.

Conclusion

This chapter has discussed the convergence of peacekeeping and RtoP. It has examined the conflict in Darfur, where the RtoP norm has been the primary prism through which international actors contemplated their responses. Given that non-consensual intervention was not deemed realistic, the activists and policymakers that were pushing for a more forceful response settled on the deployment of a robust peacekeeping force endowed with a Chapter VII mandate to protect civilians. The reference to RtoP was useful in galvanizing political support for the creation of such a force; indeed, without it, it is unlikely that UNAMID would have been established. However, a strong mandate based on RtoP does not do away with the political and operational difficulties that peacekeepers, which have limited means and depend on the consent of the host state, inevitably encounter in the context of an ongoing civil war like Darfur. It is not surprising, therefore, that UNAMID's record in terms of protecting civilians is ambiguous. In some respects, the reference to RtoP has even been problematic, as it politicized the mission vis-à-vis the host government and raised unrealistic expectations among the local population that quickly turned into cynicism.

One lesson is that implementing RtoP requires a pragmatic attitude based on considerations of efficiency. In the case of Darfur, one can argue that the enormous resources in terms of political capital, money and time that were invested in the creation of UNAMID could have been spent more efficiently otherwise. One option would have been to beef up the existing AU force instead of creating a new mission. Also, more attention should have been paid to peace negotiations leading to a sustainable agreement signed by all relevant actors. A peacekeeping force benefitting from the full consent of all parties could subsequently have been created to help implement the agreement. Another lesson from Darfur, in line with Thierry Tardy's recent argument,[68] holds that if the goal is to effectively protect civilians on the ground, it is wise to be cautious about conflating peacekeeping and RtoP, as this could politicize a mission and create unrealistic expectations of what it can achieve.

In terms of future research, it would be useful to analyse other cases of peacekeeping missions that were framed in terms of RtoP. Two questions are particularly interesting in this respect. One pertains to the effect of framing peacekeeping as a tool of RtoP on the consent of the host government and on the perceptions of the local population. In Darfur, RtoP seems to have been problematic on both accounts, and it would be relevant to evaluate whether this was the case for other missions as well. Second, it would be interesting to examine how the nature and structure of the host state affects peacekeepers' ability to implement a protection mandate. Sudan features an authoritarian government, which in spite of its fragility has the ability to obstruct the conduct of a peacekeeping mission. It would appear that in other contexts, where the central government does not possess effective control over a mission's area of deployment, it is easier to implement the RtoP agenda.

Notes

1 The opinions expressed in this chapter are the author's own and in no way represent the views of his employer. The chapter includes excerpts of David Lanz's PhD thesis (viva expected in 2014).

2 A.J. Bellamy, P.D. Williams and S. Griffin, *Understanding Peacekeeping*, Cambridge: Polity, 2004, Chapter 4.

3 UNDPKO, *What is Peacekeeping?*, available at www.un.org/en/peacekeeping/operations/peacekeeping.shtml, accessed 27 October 2012.

4 G. Evans, *The Responsibility to Protect: Ending Mass Atrocity Crimes Once and for All*, Washington DC: Brookings Institution Press, 2008, chapter 2.

5 For generally sympathetic accounts of RtoP, see, e.g., R. Thakur and T.G. Weiss, "R2P: From Idea to Norm – and Action?", *Global Responsibility to Protect* 1, 2009, pp. 22–53; A.J. Bellamy, "Realizing the Responsibility to Protect", *International Studies Perspectives* 10, 2009, pp. 111–128; C.G. Badescu, *Humanitarian Intervention and the Responsibility to Protect: Security and Human Rights*, Milton Park: Routledge, 2011. For critical assessments, see, e.g., D. Chandler, "Unravelling the Paradox of 'The Responsibility to Protect'", *Irish Studies in International Affairs* 20, 2009, pp. 27–39; A. Hehir, "The Responsibility to Protect: 'Sound and Fury Signifying Nothing'?", *International Relations* 24, 2010, pp. 218–239. On the legal debates around RtoP, see, e.g., C. Stahn, "Responsibility to Protect: Political Rhetoric or Emerging Legal Norm?", *American Journal of International Law* 101, 2007, pp. 99–120.

6 For assessments of RtoP in the context of the 2005 World Summit, see A.J. Bellamy, "Whither the Responsibility to Protect? Humanitarian Intervention and the 2005 World Summit", *Ethics & International Affairs* 20, 2006, pp. 143–169; N.J. Wheeler, "A Victory for Common Humanity? The Responsibility to Protect after the 2005 World Summit", *Journal of International Law and International Relations* 2, 2005, pp. 95–106.

7 See A.J. Bellamy and P.D. Williams, "The New Politics of Protection? Côte d'Ivoire, Libya and the Responsibility to Protect", *International Affairs* 87, 2011, pp. 825–850.

8 Darfur is not treated here as a full-fledged case study in the sense of building a theory that is applicable to a larger set of cases. The chapter aims primarily to make sense of Darfur, although it does aim also to generate a set of general observations that future studies can elaborate on.
9 On Darfur's status as a marginalized periphery within the Sudanese state, see M.W. Daly, *Darfur's Sorrow: The Forgotten History of a Humanitarian Disaster*, 2nd edn, Cambridge: Cambridge University Press, 2010.
10 G. Prunier, *Darfur: The Ambiguous Genocide*, Ithaca NY: Cornell University Press, 2007, pp. 95–99.
11 J. Flint and A. de Waal, *Darfur: A New History of a Long War*, rev. ed., London: Zed Books, 2008, Chapter 3.
12 The Belgium-based Centre for Research on the Epidemiology of Disasters (CRED) estimated that 158,000 people had died in Darfur between September 2003 and June 2004, of which 131,000 were excess deaths. (See US Government Accountability Office, *Darfur Crisis: Death Estimates Demonstrate Severity of Crisis, but Their Accuracy and Credibility Could Be Enhanced*, Washington DC, November 2006).
13 E.g., Amnesty International, "Sudan: Urgent Call for Commission of Inquiry in Darfur as Situation Deteriorates", Press Release, 21 February 2003; International Crisis Group (ICG), *Sudan's Other Wars*, Brussels: ICG, 25 June 2003.
14 The first significant reports about the Darfur conflict in major Western newspapers were published in January 2004: S. Sengupta, "War in Western Darfur Overshadows Peace in the South", *New York Times*, 17 January 2004; J.-P. Rémy, "Khartoum écrase la rébellion au Darfour par le feu et le sang", *Le Monde*, 20 January 2004.
15 Quoted in IRIN News, "Sudan: Darfur is World's Greatest Humanitarian Disaster, Says UN Official", 22 March 2004, available at http://allafrica.com/stories/200403220078.html, accessed 24 June 2012.
16 From March to December 2005, the *New York Times* and the *Washington Post* alone published 63 opinion editorials about the conflict in Darfur.
17 On the role of meaning-making narratives in internationalizing Darfur, see D. Lanz, "The Globalisation of Darfur: Making Sense of a Trajectory from Forgotten Conflict to Cause Célèbre", paper presented at the Annual Convention of the International Studies Association, Montreal, 16–19 March 2011.
18 K. Annan, "Action Plan to Prevent Genocide", Prevent Genocide International, 7 April 2004, available at www.preventgenocide.org/prevent/UNdocs/KofiAnnansActionPlantoPreventGenocide7Apr2004.htm, accessed 26 June 2012.
19 R. Williamson, "Speech Delivered to the UN Commission on Human Rights", 23 April 2004, available at www.usembassy.it/viewer/article.asp?article=/file2004_04/alia/a4042309.htm, accessed 30 July 2012.
20 Quoted in "UK Must 'Deal' with Sudan Crisis", BBC World News, 22 July 2004, available at http://news.bbc.co.uk/2/hi/uk_news/politics/3917041.stm, accessed 26 July 2012.
21 G. Evans, "Darfur and the Responsibility to Protect", *The Diplomat*, 1 August 2004.
22 D. Lanz, "Save Darfur: A Movement and its Discontents", *African Affairs* 108, 2009, pp. 669–677.
23 E. Reeves, "Accommodating Genocide", *Washington Post*, 3 September 2006.
24 D. Lanz, "Why Darfur? The Responsibility to Protect as a Rallying Cry for Transnational Advocacy Groups", *Global Responsibility to Protect* 3, 2011, pp. 239–41.
25 See, e.g., Reeves, "Accommodating Genocide".
26 N. Kristof, "Dithering as Others Die", *New York Times*, 26 June 2004.
27 ICG, *Do Americans Care about Darfur? An International Crisis Group/Zogby International Opinion Survey*, Brussels: ICG, 1 June 2005, p. 4.

28 ICG, *The AU's Mission in Darfur: Bridging the Gaps*, Brussels: ICG, 6 July 2005, pp. 1–2.
29 R. Dallaire, "Looking at Darfur, Seeing Rwanda", *Toronto Star*, 5 October 2004.
30 C.G. Badescu and L. Bergholm, "The Responsibility To Protect and the Conflict in Darfur: The Big Let-Down", *Security Dialogue* 40, 2009, pp. 287–309, 297.
31 Quoted in Human Rights Watch, *Imperatives for Immediate Change: The African Union Mission in Sudan*, New York, January 2006, p. 16.
32 A. Ekengard, "The African Union Mission in Sudan (AMIS): Experiences and Lessons Learned", Stockholm: FOI, Swedish Defence Research Agency, 2008, p. 20.
33 C.G. Badescu and L. Bergholm, "The African Union", in D.R. Black and P.D. Williams (eds) *The International Politics of Mass Atrocities: The Case of Darfur*, London: Routledge, 2010, p. 106.
34 R. Hamilton, "Building a Permanent Anti-Genocide Constituency", speech delivered on 4 November 2005, video available at www.facinghistory.org/video/rebecca-hamilton-building-permanent-anti-gen, accessed 23 July 2012.
35 See S. Chin and J. Morgenstein, *No Power to Protect: The African Union Mission in Sudan*, Washington DC: Refugees International, November 2005; W.G. O'Neill and V. Cassis, *Protecting Two Million Internally Displaced: The Successes and Shortcomings of the African Union in Darfur*, Washington DC and Bern: The Brookings Institution–University of Bern Project on Internal Displacement, November 2005; ICG, *The AU's Mission in Darfur*; Human Rights Watch, *Imperatives*; P.D. Williams, "Military Responses to Mass Killing: The African Union Mission in Sudan", *International Peacekeeping* 13, 2006, pp. 168–183; P. Kagwanja and P. Mutahi, *Protection of Civilians in African Peace Missions: The Case of the African Union Mission in Sudan, Darfur*, Pretoria: Institute for Security Studies, May 2007; A. Ekengard, 'African Union Mission'; Badescu and Bergholm, "The African Union".
36 For an overview and assessment of AMIS's protection activities, see O'Neill and Cassis, *Protecting Two Million*, pp. 35–49.
37 See M. Mamdani, "Blue-Hatting Darfur", *London Review of Books* 29, 2007, pp. 18–20.
38 See "Rally in New York's Central Park to Call for UN Peacekeepers", Save Darfur Coalition, September 2006, available at http://ww20.savedarfur.org/index.php/pages/press/save_darfur_coalition_rally_in_new_yorks_central_park_to_call_for_un_peacek, accessed 28 March 2013.
39 Hamilton, *Fighting for Darfur: Public Action and the Struggle to Stop Genocide*, Basingstoke: Palgrave Macmillan, 2011, Chapter 6.
40 See L. Nathan, *No Ownership, No Peace: the Darfur Peace Agreement*, Working Paper 5, London: LSE Crisis States Research Centre, September 2006.
41 "Security Council Expands Mandate of UN Mission in Sudan to Include Darfur", UN Department of Public Information, 31 August 2006, available at www.un.org/News/Press/docs/2006/sc8821.doc.htm, accessed 28 March 2013.
42 See N.P. Contessi, "Multilateralism, Intervention and Norm Contestation: China's Stance on Darfur in the UN Security Council", *Security Dialogue* 41, 2010, pp. 323–344.
43 UN Security Council Resolution 1706, 31 August 2006.
44 M.G. MacKinnon, "The United Nations Security Council", in D.R. Black and P.D. Williams (eds), *The International Politics of Mass Atrocities: The Case of Darfur*, New York: Routledge, 2010, pp. 71–99, at p. 80.
45 UN Security Council Resolution 1769, 31 July 2007.
46 In fact, UNAMID has been the most expensive UN peacekeeping mission for five consecutive years, even as the resources approved for UNAMID fluctuated between US$1.276 (for the 2007–2008 cycle), US$1.5 (2009–2009), US$1.599 (2009–2010), US$1.808 (2010–2011), and US$1.689 (2011–2012) billion. Data

available on the UNDPKO website, available at www.un.org/en/peacekeeping/operations/financing.shtml, accessed 9 August 2012.

47 This section draws on an earlier work, which provides a more detailed assessment of UNAMID's impact on the ground: D. Lanz, "African-Union United Nations Hybrid Operation in Darfur (UNAMID)", in J.A. Koops, N. MacQueen, T. Tardy and P.D. Williams (eds), *Oxford Handbook of United Nations Peacekeeping Operations*, New York: Oxford University Press, forthcoming 2014, Chapter 67.

48 See A. de Waal, C. Hazlett, C. Davenport and J. Kennedy, *Evidence-Based Peacekeeping: Exploring the Epidemiology of Lethal Violence in Darfur*, Cambridge MA: Harvard Humanitarian Initiative, March 2010, p. 6.

49 For a discussion of the necessary troop numbers in a civilian protection force in relation to the size of the territory on which it is operating and the number of people it has to protect, see Williams, "Military Responses", pp. 176–177.

50 R.O. Collins, *A History of Modern Sudan*, New York: Cambridge University Press, 2008, Chapter 7.

51 A. de Waal and A.H. Abdel Salam, "Islamism, State Power, and *Jihad* in Sudan", in A. de Waal (ed.), *Islamism and its Enemies in the Horn of Africa*, Bloomington IN: Indiana University Press, 2004, pp. 71–113.

52 This conclusion emerges from the author's interviews with members of the Sudanese regime.

53 This argument has appeared in international debates about Darfur since the beginning of the crisis. See A.J. Bellamy, "Responsibility to Protect or Trojan Horse? The Crisis in Darfur and Humanitarian Intervention after Iraq", *Ethics & International Affairs* 19, 2005, pp. 31–53.

54 "Sudanese Leader Reiterates Objection to International Peacekeepers", Sudan TV, 26 November 2006 (retrieved from and translated by BBC Monitoring).

55 Interview with NCP member, Khartoum, 26 October 2012.

56 A.C. Budabin, "Genocide Olympics: How Activists Linked China, Darfur & Beijing 2008", in D. Large and L.A. Patey (eds), *Sudan Looks East: China, India and the Politics of Asian Alternatives*, Woodbridge: James Currey, 2011, pp. 139–156.

57 These examples are derived from the author's own experience working for UNMIS and from several interviews with UN officials.

58 Interview with UN official, New York, 24 March 2011.

59 R. Crilly, *Saving Darfur: Everyone's Favourite African War*, London: Reportage Press, 2010, p. 38.

60 "Messages from Darfurians, Please Do More", Darfurian Voices, video transcript translated from Arabic, uploaded on 1 May 2009, available at www.darfurian-voices.org/video.php?videoID=uPUw6yjpOoI&videoTitle=Please%20Do%20More, accessed 1 November 2012.

61 Interview with Darfuri lawyer, Khartoum, 30 November 2010.

62 Interview with Sudanese journalist, Khartoum, 22 November 2010.

63 Interview with UN official, Khartoum, 27 October 2010.

64 "Sudan Jem Darfur Rebels 'Release UNAMID Peacekeepers'", BBC World News, 21 February 2012, available at www.bbc.co.uk/news/world-africa-17103522, accessed 2 November 2012.

65 UNDPKO, *Fatalities by Mission and Appointment Type*, available at www.un.org/en/peacekeeping/fatalities/documents/stats_3.pdf, accessed 28 March 2013.

66 E.g., "Militia Asking Ransom for Kidnapped UNAMID Peacekeeper in Darfur", online article, Radio Dabanga, 12 April 2010, available at www.radiodabanga.org/node/544, accessed 2 November 2012.

67 Interview with Darfuri NGO staff, Khartoum, 25 November 2010.

68 T. Tardy, "The Dangerous Liaisons of the Responsibility to Protect and the Protection of Civilians in Peacekeeping Operations", *Global Responsibility to Protect* 4, 2012, pp. 424–448.

12 The dilemmas of state consent in United Nations peace operations

The case of the United Nations operation in Côte d'Ivoire

Giulia Piccolino

Introduction

The year 2010 was a difficult one for UN peacekeeping. On 31 December, the UN Mission in the Central African Republic and Chad officially completed its withdrawal at the request of the Chadian government, after less than three years on the ground. The President of Chad, Idriss Déby, insisted that the mission was useless and unable to fulfil its civilian protection mandate. In the same period, the President of the Democratic Republic of Congo (DRC), Joseph Kabila, asked for the progressive withdrawal of the UN Organization Mission in the DRC (MONUC), one of the most substantial recent UN operations in terms of duration, personnel and financial burden. Kabila's request for the completion of the withdrawal after the 2011 presidential elections was unrealistic, but the mission was downsized and renamed the UN Organization Stabilization Mission in the DRC (MONUSCO). In Côte d'Ivoire, after certifying the victory at the polls of opponent Alassane Dramane Ouattara in December, the UN Operation in Côte d'Ivoire (UNOCI) was ordered to leave the country by incumbent president Laurent Gbagbo. The mission refused to comply, but Gbagbo's hostility to its presence meant its inability to fulfil its mandate, and the situation developed into open conflict between President Gbagbo and UNOCI in 2011.

The difficulties that the UN experienced in Chad, the DRC and Côte d'Ivoire did not stem from organizational or technical shortcomings but from a more fundamental challenge: the deterioration of the peacekeepers' relationship with the authorities of the African states where they were deployed, which culminated in the withdrawal of the state's consent to UN operations.[1]

UN difficulties with African host authorities raise a series of questions, concerning both the significance of the principle of consent for the UN and the ambiguities of the ostensibly consent-based relationships of the UN with its African counterparts. First, what is consent in UN peacekeeping? Is the principle of consent just "organized hypocrisy", or does it still matter and, if so, in which way for UN operations? Second, why is consent so fragile and uncertain? What does the volatility of consent reveal about the relationships of the UN with African authorities? Third, which options are offered to the UN when consent is uncertain and ambiguous or appears to deteriorate?

The first section of this chapter looks at the meaning and relevance of consent in today's peace operations. The second section places consent within the context of Africa's external relations and conceptualizes state consent as a bargaining relation between UN peacekeepers and African rulers. The rest of the chapter illustrates the debate on how the UN can respond to a situation of uncertain consent using UNOCI in Côte d'Ivoire as a case study. From its deployment in 2004 until the fall of President Laurent Gbagbo in 2011, UNOCI had to struggle with the Ivorian authorities' uncertain consent. In the end, after the 2010 presidential elections, the mission broke with the rule of consent, generating considerable controversy at the international level.

This chapter argues that, although its meaning has been partially altered by recent normative development in UN peacekeeping, state consent still matters very much for UN peacekeepers, in both operational and normative terms. However, the particular nature of the UN's relations with host African states renders consent particularly fragile and problematic, with major implications for the work of UN peacekeepers.

The meaning of consent in UN peacekeeping today

Consent occupies a central place in the normative structure of UN peacekeeping, but at the same time it remains "a contested and not very well specified concept".[2] UN post-Cold War policy documents, including the Report of the Panel on UN Peace Operations (Brahimi Report)[3] and the UN Principles and Guidelines on Peacekeeping (Capstone doctrine),[4] have insisted that the principle of consent remains a bedrock of UN peacekeeping. Yet defining consent in today's multidimensional peacekeeping is substantially more difficult than in first-generation operations.

The official UN Secretariat position on consent is given by the 2008 Capstone doctrine. This sees consent as implying "a commitment by the parties to a political process and their acceptance of a peacekeeping operation mandated to support that process".[5] It also establishes a distinction between consent at the "strategic" and at the "tactical" level. Consent from "the main parties to the conflict"[6] is considered an indispensable precondition for UN peacekeeping. On the other hand, the Capstone doctrine accepts that UN missions can use force against local "spoilers". Thus examples of "robust peacekeeping", such as MONUC's military operations in the Ituri region of the DRC in 2005, targeting locally-based militias that were not part of the national peace process, are not seen as violating the principle of consent. On the other hand, the line between peacekeeping and peace enforcement would be crossed in cases of UN peacekeepers confronting one of the main warring parties, including notably the host state authorities.

Several authors have noticed that in contemporary peace operations the line between consent and no consent is blurred in practice. Ian Johnstone observes that consent is often qualified in three ways: it may be unreliable (when the main warring parties do not fully control their followers or proxies), under pressure (brought about by aggressive international diplomatic efforts or even economic and military sanctions) or open-ended (the political process supported by the UN is so broad and complex that unforeseen problems can emerge at a later stage). Going further, Michael Lipson has argued that consent in today's peace operations would amount to "organized hypocrisy" – "inconsistent rhetoric and action resulting from conflicting material and normative pressures".[7] He argues that the principle of consent, while retaining normative force, is in contrast with the requirements for effectiveness in the complex environments where contemporary peace operations take place, and is thus regularly violated on the ground.[8]

However, although the hypocrisy argument is suggestive, some of the examples of "robust peacekeeping" given in support of the notion that consent would be obsolete, such as the DRC and Haiti, are cases of the use of force at the "tactical level" that are consistent with the current UN doctrine. To understand inconsistencies in UN peacekeeping in terms of "hypocrisy" means, moreover, to neglect the fact that peacekeeping is an evolving, rather than static, field and an essentially contested concept. The evolution of UN peacekeeping in recent years has had a particularly ambiguous impact on host states' consent. While certain post-Cold War normative developments have weakened the rule of host state consent, others have strengthened the centrality of state actors and the importance for UN peacekeepers of gaining and retaining their consent.

A case in point is the current paradigm of state weakness and state fragility. Many contemporary peacekeeping and peacebuilding operations are requested to support state institutions and/or contribute to the re-establishment of state authority across the national territory.[9] In Africa, the weak capacities of most African states and their historical emergence from decolonization as juridical "quasi-states"[10] have been invoked for interpreting many of Africa's current conflicts, such as in Somalia, the DRC, Liberia and Sierra Leone, as crises of the state.[11] Statebuilding tasks are notably included in the mandates of MONUSCO, UNOCI, the UN Mission in the Republic of South Sudan, and the UN Mission in Liberia. The focus on the restoration of state authority reinforces the qualitative difference between state consent and consent from non-state armed actors and the importance, for UN officers, of maintaining and nurturing state consent. Expecting the UN to help them in reasserting their control over the national territory, state authorities have an incentive to welcome UN missions and facilitate their work. However, as the post-conflict reconstruction process advances and the state becomes stronger, national authorities' dependency on the UN gradually withers and state officials become more assertive vis-à-vis the UN.[12]

Current peace operations are, however, also viewed as instruments for protecting the civilian population. Notably, all peace operations currently deployed in Africa – with the exception of the UN Mission for the Referendum in Western Sahara – include the protection of civilians in their mandate.[13] Protection mandates place the missions in a difficult and potentially antagonistic position with the host state. In Africa, there are many examples of conflicts where state authorities have been accused of being responsible for egregious human rights violations or of having done nothing to stop them. The cases of Darfur (Sudan) and Côte d'Ivoire, where current or former state rulers are under indictment by the International Criminal Court (ICC), are the most visible examples.[14]

Furthermore, peacebuilding mandates focusing on the promotion of democracy and the rule of law, which are also part of most current UN operations, have an ambiguous effect on state consent. On the one hand they may put peacebuilders in conflict with state rulers, who are preoccupied above all with their political survival and who have little interest in democratization and human rights. On the other hand, however, liberal peacebuilding is predicated on the developmental principle of "ownership". Although the effective scope and content of ownership is debated,[15] the notion surely encompasses the need of negotiating and obtaining the adhesion of national actors – both state and non-state – to the liberal peace agenda.

To sum up, while the significance of consent may have evolved, consent from host state authorities still matters, and not only in a rhetorical sense, for UN peacekeepers. Without state consent, most of the tasks currently assigned to UN peacekeepers are impossible to execute. The problem is, however, that consent from host state authorities is inherently fragile and volatile. While host states may not raise official objections to the deployment of peacekeepers, they may have very different priorities to those of UN operations.

Peace operations in the African arena

The relationships between peacekeepers and African "peacekept" – the term employed by Christopher Clapham[16] for the local warring parties of peace operations' recipient countries – are inherently complex and tense. Looking at peacekeeping in the African landscape, it is important to stress that peace operations do not fall into a historical and political void.[17] The view of African elites on UN peacekeeping and peacebuilding is shaped by their previous experience of a long series of intrusive external interventions of different kinds, from colonialism to Cold War sponsorship, development aid and structural adjustment programs. Peacekeeping will be seen in a context characterized by long-term dynamics of neo-patrimonial politics[18] and political and economic extraversion.[19] Conflict-affected African countries have been compared to a "political marketplace", which functions according to a neo-patrimonial logic.[20] Moreover, because of their weakness and their dependent position within the international system, African states have, since their independence, developed a whole battery of strategies for capturing external resources for the internal aims of "state survival", while avoiding the strings of conditionality that often come attached to them.[21] Hence, paradoxically, although African states are considered to be weak, their leaders may be quite successful at resisting external imperatives.[22]

As Johnston suggests,[23] consent is often granted by the "peacekept" under international pressure to stop military action, engage in negotiations and accept peacekeepers' deployment. Yet state authorities may have little commitment to engage in the negotiation process and may continue to nurture the hope that a military solution is at hand. Liberal reforms promoted by peacekeepers constitute another possible source of tension. In Africa, externally-sponsored post-conflict democratization has been most successful in cases such as Namibia and Mozambique, where state elites issued from liberation movements could expect post-conflict elections to reinforce their position.[24] In most cases, however, the democratic reforms peacekeepers are pushing for are at odds with the preferences of state elites. Nevertheless, international peacekeepers also bring opportunities, in the form of security from insurgents, international legitimacy and material resources, such as development aid and technical cooperation. These opportunities are particularly welcome when the threat posed by insurgents is significant and access to alternative resources is limited.[25]

Peacekeepers and state authorities typically engage in a bargaining process[26] where consent to the deployment of UN peacekeepers is traded by state authorities in exchange for security and external aid. In some cases, however, acceptance of the deployment of peacekeepers may just be a tactical move that can be easily reversed when state authorities perceive the UN presence to be no longer useful, or even harmful, to their interests. Internal rulers often have a strengthened hand on outsiders, because of their better grasp of their own societies and the option to threaten them with violence or non-cooperation, up to the explicit withdrawal of consent.[27]

The "peacebuilder bargain" creates a dilemma for international peacekeepers and peacebuilders, as they cannot implement their mandate, especially when it involves the extension of state authority and the organization of elections, without the cooperation of national authorities. The options that they have when they perceive that national authorities are not genuinely cooperative are, however, limited. First, they may choose to confront state authorities by denouncing non-compliance, exercising pressures and threatening sanctions. This avenue is risky: it can generate even more resistance and can result in an explicit withdrawal of consent, and confrontation may escalate to violence. Alternatively, peacekeepers can try to accommodate host authorities' interests. Here, one faces a very tight line between managing consent – creating space for the UN to operate through instruments such as dialogue, negotiation and persuasion – and "abdicating responsibility"[28] – bending to the will of national authorities at the cost of renouncing the other principles that are supposed to guide the work of a peace operation. The UN Security Council can also choose not to deploy an operation at all, or to withdraw, if it perceives that the environment is unfavourable and national authorities are trying to manipulate the UN. Although this option would be equivalent to an admission of defeat, it would have the merit of making the bad faith of state authorities apparent and avoiding a waste of material resources and political efforts.

UNOCI provides an example of an operation that had to strive, from its launch in 2003 up to the fall of the incumbent Ivorian regime in 2011, with limited consent from host state authorities. UNOCI tried several options to "manage consent", which were unsuccessful in the end, as the conflict with Ivorian president Laurent Gbagbo became open after the contested 2010 elections. The mandate of certification of the elections attributed to the head of the mission in the end provided an escape from the constraints of consent. In the next section, UNOCI's experience with state consent will be discussed, as well as the different strategies through which UNOCI tried to respond to the challenges that it was experiencing.

Managing consent in practice – The UNOCI experience

The launch of UNOCI and its initial mandate

UNOCI was officially established on 27 February 2004 by UNSC Resolution 1528.[29] The operation's mandate outlined two main tasks: to monitor the ceasefire by deploying along the buffer zone – *zone de confiance* – established between the government-controlled south and the rebel-controlled north; and to assist the Government of National Reconciliation in the implementation of the January 2003 Linas–Marcoussis peace agreement.

Although the Ivorian authorities had ostensibly given their consent to the deployment of UNOCI, the operation's relations with President Laurent Gbagbo and his Front Populaire Ivoirien (FPI) party were from the start characterized by tensions and mistrust. The Special Representative of the Secretary-General (SRSG) Albert Tévoédjrè was depicted as an enemy of Côte d'Ivoire by the pro-Gbagbo press[30] and UN officers remember that a general atmosphere of hostility surrounded the UN as soon as they started to deploy.[31]

The events that had preceded the launch of UNOCI contribute to explaining these difficulties. Before 2004, the Ivorian peace process had been dominated by two main features: the military and diplomatic involvement of France and the strong antagonism between French peacemakers and president Gbagbo.[32] France was Côte d'Ivoire's former colonial master and had historically maintained very strong ties with the country, including a permanent military base in the de facto capital Abidjan.[33] Just after the beginning of the civil war in September 2002, the French mission Licorne had stopped the fighting and interposed between the Ivorian loyalist forces and the rebels of the *Forces Nouvelles* (FN).[34] Operation Licorne was at the centre of a debate, as Gbagbo contended that, under the 1961 defence accords between France and Côte d'Ivoire,[35] France should help the *Forces Armées Nationales de Côte d'Ivoire*, the loyalist army, in crushing the rebellion. Gbagbo and his supporters argued that France refused to honour its commitments out of mistrust for a president who had criticized France's neo-colonial role in Côte d'Ivoire. Gbagbo was playing on the ambivalent feelings that France's post-colonial presence in Côte d'Ivoire generated among the Ivorian public.[36] The situation got worse with the French-sponsored Linas–Marcoussis negotiations in January 2003,[37] which were denounced – not without any reason – as partial and "neo-colonialist" by Gbagbo's supporters. Nationalist youth groups close to the presidency, the *jeunes patriotes* (young patriots), sparked anti-French riots and demonstrations, and the agreement soon proved inapplicable in its integral form.

Aware of its delicate position, the French government had hoped from the start that Operation Licorne could be replaced by an operation either managed by the ECOWAS or by the UN.[38] However, this proved impossible for several reasons. ECOWAS set up its own military mission, ECOMICI, at the end of 2002, but technical and financial problems as well as political difficulties delayed its deployment. The insistence by France that the UN should get involved in Côte d'Ivoire was frustrated by the attitude of the United States, which blocked any Security Council Resolution on Côte d'Ivoire in the first months of the crisis.[39]

The involvement of the UN in Côte d'Ivoire was thus slow and gradual. In February 2003, UNSC Resolution 1464[40] eventually endorsed the Linas–Marcoussis agreement, gave Operation Licorne and ECOMICI a Security Council mandate and nominated a UN SRSG for Côte d'Ivoire. In May, the UN reinforced its political presence by establishing the UN Mission in Côte d'Ivoire (MINUCI). Almost one year passed before the UN turned MINUCI into UNOCI, a full-scale peace operation that also integrated the troops of ECOMICI. For financial and security reasons, however, the Security Council decided to maintain Operation Licorne, with its separate chain of command, as a rapid reaction force alongside UNOCI.[41]

The fragility of the political process that UNOCI was in charge of supporting, and the presence of Operation Licorne, had important implications for UNOCI and for host state consent. If, in line with the UN Capstone doctrine, consent depends on the commitment of the warring parties to a "political process", Côte d'Ivoire was a case of "consent under pressure".[42] Gbagbo felt that he had been forced to engage in the peace process by the French, who had stopped the fighting and pressured him into going to the negotiation table. However, even on the eve of the Linas–Marcoussis talks, he remained openly critical of peace talks that would have put both belligerents on the same level.[43] Yet, while avoiding admitting it publicly, Gbagbo and his associates were conscious of the weakness of the national army and knew that without France's intervention in 2002 the rebels would have advanced towards Abidjan. As long as a FN attack remained a possibility, they presumably saw UNOCI, and even more so Operation Licorne, as "buffers" that at least guaranteed the preservation of the military status quo. In fact, in spite of the frequently-expressed criticism of France's policy, during the first two years of the crisis the Ivorian regime never mentioned the possibility of a withdrawal of Licorne. Its relationship with France was very ambivalent, and phases of reconciliation regularly followed moments of tension.[44]

The presence of Operation Licorne was a mixed blessing for UNOCI. From the military point of view, the operation was a great asset. However, looking at the principle of consent, the coexistence between UNOCI and Operation Licorne was problematic. It can be said that, at the time of its deployment, Operation Licorne had also received the "consent" of the Ivorian government, but this consent stemmed from a different rationale. Operation Licorne had found its initial legal justification not in the UN doctrine but on different grounds, the protection of the French community in Côte d'Ivoire and the Franco-Ivorian defence agreements.[45] Although the interpretation of the agreements was controversial, there is little doubt that they had originally been designed as a means to protect the incumbent government, rather than to foster a process of dialogue between conflicting parties. France's subsequent effort to present Operation Licorne as a peace operation aiming at promoting a political solution, apparently placing it in line with the UN approach to peacekeeping, went against the preferences of Gbagbo, who had hoped that the French could support him against the insurgents.[46]

Although the Linas–Marcoussis agreement required extensive international support for its implementation, the fact that Gbagbo and his supporters militated for reducing the political space of external actors meant that UNOCI was given a mandate that was "broad in terms of areas to be covered" but "limited in the sense that the mission was to 'assist' the Ivorian government in almost all areas".[47] Paradoxically, UNOCI's position was complicated by the fact that Côte d'Ivoire was not a "failed state" to the same degree as other post-conflict African countries where the UN had carried out peace operations, such as neighboring Liberia and Sierra Leone.[48] This meant that UNOCI had to work all the time alongside state institutions, and its position in the "peacebuilder bargain" was thus considerably weaker.

UNOCI was facing a difficult dilemma. Consent was indispensable for carrying out a mandate that implied the cooperation of the Ivorian parties. However, if the mission interpreted too strictly its consent-based mandate, it risked being reduced to insignificance and impotence. If, on the other hand, UNOCI chose to put pressure on the Ivorian regime, it could definitively compromise its relations with Gbagbo and host state consent.

2003–2007: managing consent through dialogue or pressure

Fostering consent in Côte d'Ivoire meant revitalizing the political process on which consent depended. Thus the initial response to the hostility of the Ivorian president consisted of efforts to renegotiate some aspects of the Linas–Marcoussis agreement and make it more acceptable to the Ivorian participants, especially Gbagbo. UN Secretary-General Kofi Annan was personally involved in one of the new rounds of peace talks, held in Ghana at the end of July 2004. In November 2004, however, a violation of the ceasefire by the Ivorian loyalist forces struck a new blow to the peace process and marked the peak of the Franco-Ivorian antagonism. Airstrikes on the rebel-controlled north, called *Opération Dignité* by the Ivorian regime, degenerated into a quasi-war between Côte d'Ivoire and France after the still mysterious bombing of a French military camp by the loyalist troops.[49] UNOCI was not directly involved in the clashes, which however highlighted the problems that the UN were facing in Côte d'Ivoire: the risk of an overall collapse of a peace process that rested on fragile ground, the ambiguities of the consent-based mandate with respect to ceasefire violations, and the tendency of France to act independently from the UN, rather than as a support force.

In the wake of these events, the Security Council adopted Resolution 1572,[50] by which it established an arms embargo and nominated a Sanction Committee in charge of adopting sanctions against those responsible for egregious human rights violations and obstructions to the peace process. Resolution 1572 could have led UNOCI to go beyond its consent-based mandate. Its impact, however, was counterbalanced by the fact that South African president Thabo Mbeki, just appointed mediator by the African Union (AU), thought that more meaningful progress could be made by restoring trust among the conflict parties. In the end, the adoption of targeted sanctions was postponed and UNOCI was given a limited mandate that allowed the mission only to monitor compliance with the arms embargo.[51]

A subtler source of tension on the principle of consent emerged through the outcome of the Pretoria talks sponsored by Mbeki, in which the role that the UN was supposed to play in the post-conflict electoral process was discussed. Elections would have been organized by a revised Ivorian Independent Electoral Commission (IEC), but a "competent authority acting in the name of the international community" was to be mandated "to guarantee transparency and the strict respect of the rules governing the election".[52] The role of the "competent authority" was not "consensual" in the sense that its decisions were supposed to be independent of the will of the parties and motivated only by concern about the fairness of the electoral process. In fact, the unprecedented decision of the UN Secretary-General to nominate a High Representative for Elections (HRE) independent from UNOCI and from the UN SRSG suggested that the UN was aware of the difficulty of conciliating the consent-based mandate of UNOCI with the new task.[53]

A new paralysis in the peace process was, however, leading to an indefinite postponement of the elections. In order to avoid an institutional deadlock, the Peace and Security Council of the AU met on 6 October 2005, taking a series of decisions that were subsequently endorsed by UN Security Council Resolution 1633.[54] The Prime Minister of the national unity government, Seydou Diarra, was replaced by the former governor of the Central Bank of West African States, Charles Konan Banny. At the same time, a ministerial-level International Working Group (IWG) was mandated "to evaluate, monitor and follow-up the peace process",[55] establishing what was seen at the time to be a sort of "international trusteeship" on Côte d'Ivoire. Resolution 1633 also used, for the first time, the term "certification" for describing the mandate of the HRE.[56]

UNOCI was actively involved in the IWG, as Tévoédjrè's successor Pierre Schori was given the co-presidency of the new organ. Such involvement contributed to the deterioration of the relations with President Gbagbo and his supporters and to the further fragilization of host state consent. In January 2006, the *jeunes patriotes* took to the streets, claiming that a statement of the IWG, which acknowledged the expiration of the Ivorian National Assembly and pleaded for a non-extension, constituted an attack against Ivorian institutions. They paralysed Abidjan for three days and encircled the headquarters of UNOCI. In the volatile town of Guiglo, the situation degenerated as UN peacekeepers opened fire on the demonstrators, killing five.[57] It was the first time that UNOCI openly clashed with the followers of the Ivorian president. In the wake of these events, targeted sanctions were adopted for the first time against two pro-Gbagbo youth leaders and one FN commander.

In the meantime, rumours circulated that Gbagbo was engaging in diplomatic steps for obtaining the replacement of Operation Licorne with a South African-led peacekeeping mission under the aegis of the AU. Although these rumours only concerned the possible expulsion of Licorne, the president apparently also insisted that the UN had to be excluded from the management of the Ivorian peace process.[58] Thus by mid-2006 consent from the Ivorian authorities looked more fragile than ever.

Moreover, international pressure did not seem to produce the outcome that was hoped for. UNSC Resolution 1721 of November 2006[59] responded to the lack of advances in the peace process by reaffirming and detailing the special powers of the prime minister and the international support for him. Given the lack of enforcement mechanisms, the resolution was judged unrealistic by many UN officers.[60] Indeed, if the "trusteeship" option was to be pushed to its ultimate consequences, it would have meant that the principle of consent had to be overcome. Yet, even if UNOCI were given a different mandate and different resources, leading the country to post-conflict elections without the cooperation of the Ivorian warring parties would still have hardly been possible. While the deadlock seemed unsolvable, this time the initiative came unexpectedly from Gbagbo himself.

The Ouagadougou Political Agreement: successful management of consent?

In October 2006, after the vote of UNSC Resolution 1721, Gbagbo declared that he would seek a new roadmap for peace through "direct dialogue" with the FN. On 4 March 2007, the Ouagadougou Political Agreement (OPA) was signed and FN leader Guillaume Soro was designated to be the new transitional prime minister. On substantial matters the agreement differed little from the Linas–Marcoussis accord, but the implementation formula was changed. Responsibility for the conduct of the transition was transferred to Gbagbo and to Soro, thus eliminating the impartial prime minister equidistant from the parties to the conflict that had been a cornerstone of the transitional arrangement set for by Linas–Marcoussis.[61]

For the first time since 2002 the Ivorian parties had taken the initiative to go to the negotiating table. In this sense, the OPA seemed to lay down new grounds for consent-based peacekeeping in Côte d'Ivoire: unlike Linas–Marcoussis, which had been perceived as an agreement to some extent imposed, it represented a political process initiated and freely accepted by the conflict participants.

For Gbagbo and his supporters, the OPA was also a way to curtail international influence over the peace process, while responding to international criticism by showing that the warring parties were committed to peace implementation. Ivorian actors insisted that the peace process was now "nationally owned". Diplomats close to the Gbagbo regime were candid in admitting that one of the objectives of the direct dialogue was "to keep the UN out";[62] it seems that a total marginalization of UNOCI was what the Ivorian authorities initially had in mind, and was what the UN feared.[63] UN officers were, however, able to persuade the Ivorian parties that excluding UNOCI was not realistic, as the support of an impartial actor was still needed in order to implement many practical aspects of the new agreement. Eventually, the Ivorian presidency seemed to be satisfied with a solution that implied curtailing UNOCI's political influence.

In UNSC Resolution 1765,[64] which endorsed the OPA, the role of UNOCI was redefined as one of providing financial, and to some extent technical, support to an internally defined process: a mission that in French was described as *accompagnement*. The ability of UNOCI to provide security was reduced, as the buffer zone was dismantled and a new internal body put in charge of election security. The post of HRE was also eliminated, although, by demand of the FN and the Ivorian opposition, the "certification" mandate was transferred to the UN SRSG and to a newly created "certification cell" within UNOCI.[65]

If one accepts that the OPA proved a viable framework and that the commitment of the warring parties to its implementation was genuine,[66] the fact that UNOCI had less influence over the peace process was not a worrying development but rather represented the return of UNOCI to its original mandate. In this sense, Côte d'Ivoire could have looked at mid-2007 as a successful case of consent management. In spite of the hostility manifested by the Ivorian regime, UNOCI had been able to stay in Côte d'Ivoire, and open clashes with the Ivorian authorities had been limited to the 2006 episode. International pressures, although in themselves unable to re-launch the peace process, had eventually convinced the Ivorian parties that they had to abandon their unconstructive attitude and find a viable agreement.

An alternative interpretation was that the Ivorian parties had not abandoned their antagonism or their "winner takes all" approach to politics. They had realized that the situation of no war, no peace was internally and internationally untenable. However, the OPA was a short-term and opportunistic arrangement, rather than a fundamental step in the resolution of the crisis. The marginalization of the UN helped the Ivorian parties – which profited, in political and economic terms, from the division of the country – to pursue their game of postponement and mutual deception. In fact, presidential elections, scheduled for 2005 according to the electoral calendar, were postponed many times between 2007 and 2010. The disarmament, demobilization and reintegration (DDR) process, another centrepiece of the OPA, stalled in spite of the conclusion of a series of complementary agreements dealing with it.[67] Thus, the mission of *accompagnement* of UNOCI proved more ambiguous than was initially suggested by the term.

As time passed and the roadmap envisaged by the OPA was not followed, the prevailing feeling at UNOCI's headquarters was disillusionment. It seemed that, to avoid endangering consent and falling back to the 2006 scenario, the UN had chosen a position of passivity and acquiescence. Attempts to block the peace process were rarely denounced in public by UN senior officers and the Sanction Committee avoided adopting any further targeted sanctions. Particularly significant was the UN SRSG's acquiescence in February 2010, when the Gbagbo camp accused the chairman of the IEC of fraud, and the president dismissed both the IEC and the government.[68]

In spite of the apparently passive attitude of UNOCI towards the Ivorian parties, certain aspects of the UN mandate that went beyond the logic of *accompagnement* still bore the seeds of a potential conflict with the principle of consent, particularly the mandate of certification now conferred on the UN SRSG. The problematic aspect of the certification mandate was all the more notable as South Korean Young Jin Choi, who had taken the lead of UNOCI after the conclusion of the OPA, interpreted the mandate in a particularly strong manner – not just as being about assessing the fairness of elections, but also safeguarding the respect of the results, even by employing force if necessary.[69]

A second aspect of UNOCI's mandate that could still clash with the principle of consent was the task of protecting civilians, although the scope of this task was limited to the mission's area of operations. Between 2007 and 2010, the human rights situation throughout the country had improved, but a rapid deterioration was always a possibility. Its protection mandate could lead UNOCI to clash with the Ivorian regime in case of violations of human rights and humanitarian law.

The 2010 elections and the collapse of consent

As time passed, the continual postponement of the presidential election appeared unsustainable. In October 2010, the time eventually appeared to be right. Pressure on Gbagbo was mounting and he had been convinced by opinion polls that he was now in a position to win. Those expectations turned out to be wrong: Gbagbo ended up ahead of the other candidates in the first round, but in the second round the alliance concluded between the main opposition parties proved to be successful and former Prime Minister Alassane Ouattara obtained most of the votes. The follow-up demonstrated that Gbagbo was not prepared to relinquish power even in such circumstances. The FPI-controlled Ivorian Constitutional Council tried to reverse the results by invalidating the vote in northern districts, which had been favourable to the rival, and proclaimed the incumbent president the effective winner of the elections.[70]

In his certification of the elections, the UN SRSG argued that the alleged frauds were either minor or non-existent.[71] While the certification mandate led to an irreparable break between UNOCI and Gbagbo, it provided a partial way out from the principle of state consent. By officially designating a winner in the elections, the certification changed Gbagbo's status from head of the Ivorian state to an illegitimate authority. The international recognition of Ouattara as the elected president – which deprived Gbagbo of the cover of sovereignty – was arguably the factor that allowed UN peacekeepers to ignore the order to leave the country, which had been given by the "illegal" government nominated by Gbagbo. The latter, however, without any doubt, remained one of the main warring parties to the conflict, and his withdrawal of consent had major consequences, both in normative and operational terms. UNOCI was prevented from operating normally and, in the months following the elections, harassment and even physical aggression against UN peacekeepers became a frequent occurrence. The mission concentrated on protecting the elected president and his government, trapped in their headquarters at the Hotel du Golf, but seemed unable to stop the wave of political repression unfolding in Abidjan. The situation escalated in February, when a guerrilla movement started to conduct attacks on the loyalist forces in an Abidjan neighbourhood reputed to be favourable to Ouattara. In response, the incumbent regime took a series of indiscriminate actions, such as the shelling of a marketplace in the popular Abobo neighbourhood.

In a reaction to this, under France's and Nigeria's initiative, the Security Council met and adopted Resolution 1975. The resolution, adopted on 30 March 2011, was framed as "civilian protection" and authorized UNOCI "to prevent the use of heavy weapons against the civilian population"[72] by all necessary means. The implementation of Resolution 1975 was all the more delicate because by the time of its adoption the former FN, now renamed *Forces Républicaines de Côte d'Ivoire* (FRCI) and allied with Ouattara, were starting a major military offensive, encountering minimal resistance until their entry into Abidjan. Resolution 1975 could thus easily be read as a covert authorization for UNOCI to support the FRCI against Gbagbo.[73]

While the battle for Abidjan intensified, UN peacekeepers were attacked and the mission's headquarters were repeatedly shelled by the pro-Gbagbo forces. Eventually, exasperation and the prospect of a disastrous extension of the conflict persuaded UNOCI to intervene. On 4 April, UNOCI started a first helicopter attack over Gbagbo's last strongholds, also targeting the presidential residence in further raids. Operation Licorne stepped in and its military strength played a determinant role in the eventual success of the raids. After a failed effort to obtain Gbagbo's negotiated surrender, the attacks resumed on 10 April. The day after, Gbagbo's troops were finally conquered and the former president was taken into custody.

UNOCI's action notably raised criticism from two Security Council members, Russia and South Africa, who accused the mission of having gone beyond Resolution 1975.[74] UN SRSG Choi, however, strongly defended the actions undertaken by UNOCI, arguing that the UN had played a crucial role both in defending democracy and in protecting the civilian population.[75] Choi was supported by UN Secretary-General Ban Ki Moon, who stated that UNOCI had acted in self-defence and to protect civilians in conformity with its mandate.[76]

Conclusions

The emergence of robust peacekeeping and of the Responsibility to Protect in the last decade have led some authors to prematurely proclaim the "death of consent", which would have turned into "organized hypocrisy". However, looking more closely, the norm of consent, particularly when it comes to consent from the host state authorities, still has a fundamental impact on the work of UN peacekeepers, although the necessity to maintain consent may clash with other UN-supported norms and principles. This is why, in contemporary multidimensional operations, managing consent requires a delicate balance between firmness and flexibility.

The case of UNOCI proves the continuous importance of consent in UN peacekeeping. Discussions about UNOCI have focused almost exclusively on the actions undertaken by the mission after 2010, and UNOCI has been called an example of "the new politics of protection".[77] However, a deeper analysis shows that, until the 2010 elections, maintaining and nurturing consent constituted one of the major preoccupations of the mission. This preoccupation was partially in contrast to the other main imperative that drove the work of UNOCI, namely to ensure that the peace process progressed, in spite of the game of duplicity and manipulation played by the Ivorian parties. Originating as a fully consent-based mission, UNOCI gradually took on a series of tasks that posed potential challenges to the principle of consent. After the tensions of 2005–2006, UNOCI's senior officers became very cautious in avoiding any open clash with the Ivorian state authorities. However, the excessively complaisant attitude demonstrated by UNOCI between 2007 and 2010 may have contributed to the outbreak of the post-election crisis, encouraging Gbagbo's expectation that his electoral holdup was not going to meet significant resistance.

With the events of 2010–2011, UNOCI had to radically reconsider its position. Clearly, UNOCI's actions violated the principle of consent as delineated by the Capstone doctrine. Two main warring parties were engaged in violent conflict, and the use of force was pursued at the strategic level. Somewhat paradoxically, a UN mission that was at its outset constrained by a narrow mandate of "assistance" to national authorities ended up breaking with the principle of consent. An innovative mandate – the certification – led to an irreducible conflict between the safeguard of election results, and thus of democracy, and the principle of consent.

It is difficult to tell whether UNOCI will constitute a precedent. In particular, the impact of the certification mandate on the principle of consent may lead the Security Council to exercise more caution in future in assigning this task to a peacekeeping mission again, and may lead the warring parties to avoid asking the UN to play this role. Moreover, although much of the responsibility for the course of action taken by UNOCI goes to SRSG Choi, who was convinced that the UN had the right and the duty to break with the principle of consent in order to defend the election results, UNOCI would probably have been unable to intervene militarily without Operation Licorne and without the diplomatic support of a large section of the "international community".[78] Also, given the current difficulty for peacekeeping missions in securing well-trained troops, it is arguable that UNOCI's break with the norm of consent will remain an exceptional case.

Notes

1 For a general discussion, see D. Tull, "When they Overstay their Welcome: UN Peacekeepers in Africa", German Institute for International and Security Affairs, *Comment Paper* 15, 2011; G. Piccolino and J. Karlsrud, "Withering Consent but Mutual Dependency? UN Peace Operations and African Assertiveness", *Conflict, Security & Development* 11, 2011, pp. 447–471.

2 I. Johnstone, "Managing Consent in Contemporary Peacekeeping Operations", *International Peacekeeping* 18, 2011, p. 178.

3 "Report of the Panel on United Nations Peace Operations [Brahimi Report]", UN, A/55/305-S/2000/809, 21 August 2000.

4 UN, *United Nations Peacekeeping Operations: Principles and Guidelines [Capstone Doctrine]*, New York: United Nations Department of Peacekeeping Operations/Department of Field Support, 2008.

5 UN, *Principles and Guidelines*, p. 31.

6 *Ibid.*

7 M. Lipson, "Peacekeeping: Organized Hypocrisy?", *European Journal of International Relations* 13, 2007, p. 6.

8 *Ibid.*, pp. 20–21.

9 R. Gowan and I. Johnstone, "New Challenges for Peacekeeping: Protection, Peacebuilding and the 'War on Terror'", *Coping with CRISIS working Papers Series*, International Peace Academy, 2007, p. 7.

10 R.H. Jackson, *Quasi-states: Sovereignty, International Relations and the Third World*, Cambridge: Cambridge University Press, 1990.

11 African countries typically receive the worst scores compared to other regions of the world in the various indexes of "failure" and "fragility" that have mushroomed in recent years. Among the most well-known ones, see the Failed States Index issued by the Fund for Peace, available at www.fundforpeace.org/global/?q=fsi, accessed 2 February 2013; and the State Fragility Index and Matrix 2008 (Center for the Systemic Peace and Center for Global Policy), available at www.systemicpeace.org/SFImatrix08c.pdf, accessed 2 February 2013.

12 Piccolino and Karlsrud, "Withering Consent"; D. Edelstein, "Foreign Militaries, Sustainable Institutions, and Postwar Statebuilding", in R. Paris and T.D. Sisk (eds), *The Dilemmas of Statebuilding: Confronting the Contradictions of Postwar Peace Operations*, London: Routledge, 2009, pp. 81–103.

13 See UNDPKO official website: available at www.un.org/en/peacekeeping/operations/current.shtml, accessed 2 February 2013. See also P.D. Williams, "Enhancing Civilian Protection in Peace Operations: Insights from Africa", Research Paper, Africa Center for Strategic Studies, September 2010.

14 Information about the charges raised against Bashir and Gbagbo is available on the website of the ICC: www.icc-cpi.int/EN_Menus/ICC/Situations%20and%20Cases/Situations/Situation%20ICC%200205/Pages/situation%20icc-0205.aspx, accessed 23 March 2013; and www.icc-cpi.int/EN_Menus/ICC/Situations%20and%20Cases/Situations/ICC0211/Pages/situation%20index.aspx, accessed 23 March 2013.

15 For discussions of ownership, see T. Donais, "Empowerment or Imposition? Dilemmas of Local Ownership in Post-Conflict Peacebuilding Processes", *Peace & Change* 34, 2009, pp. 3–26.

16 C. Clapham, "Being Peacekept", in O. Furley and R. May (eds), *Peacekeeping in Africa*, Aldershot: Ashgate, 1998, pp. 303–319.
17 For a discussion of the impact of historical legacies – in particular post-colonial legacies – on peace operations see M. Berdal, *Building Peace after War*, Adelphi Paper 49, Abingdon: Routledge, 2009; and B. Pouligny, *Peace Operations Seen from Below: UN Missions and Local People*, London: Hurst & Co., 2006.
18 For discussions of African neo-patrimonial politics and its relation to civil wars, see P.D. Williams, *War and Conflict in Africa*, New York: Wiley, 2011; and A. De Waal, "Mission Without End? Peacekeeping in the African Political Marketplace", *International Affairs* 85, 2009, pp. 99–113.
19 J.-F. Bayart, "Africa in the World: A History of Extraversion", *African Affairs* 99, 2000, pp. 217–267; C. Clapham, *Africa and the International System: The Politics of State Survival*, Cambridge and New York: Cambridge University Press, 1996.
20 De Waal, "Mission Without End?".
21 Clapham, *Africa and the International System.*
22 D.M. Tull, "Weak States and Successful Elites: Extraversion Strategies in Africa", *Research Paper* 9, German Institute of International Affairs, August 2011.
23 Johnstone, "Managing Consent".
24 C. Zürcher, "Building Democracy While Building Peace", *Journal of Democracy* 22, 2011, pp. 81–95.
25 Piccolino and Karlsrud, "Withering Consent".
26 I. Johnstone, "Managing Consent"; M. Barnett and C. Zürcher, "The Peacebuilder's Contract: How External Statebuilding Reinforces Weak Statehood", in R. Paris and T. Sisk (eds), *The Dilemmas of Statebuilding: Confronting the Contradictions of Postwar Peace Operations*, London: Routledge, 2009, pp. 25–52.
27 See Barnett and Zürcher's typology of "confrontational peacebuilding", "Peacebuilder's Contract", p. 33.
28 Johnstone, "Managing Consent", p. 180.
29 UN Security Council Resolution 1528, 27 February 2004.
30 See for instance the commentaries of the FPI newspaper *Notre Voie* at the departure of Tévoédjré from Côte d'Ivoire: A.V. Sanogo, "Pourquoi Tévoédjré a été limogé", *Notre Voie*, 7 December 2004.
31 Interview with senior UN officer, Abidjan, 24 August 2011.
32 For a general discussion of the role of France, see Marco Wyss's contribution in this volume. About the first phase of the Ivorian crisis, see also S.W. Smith, "La politique d'engagement de la France à l'épreuve de la Cote d'Ivoire", *Politique Africaine* 89, 2003, pp. 112–126; R. Marshall, "La France en Côte d'Ivoire: l'interventionnisme à l'épreuve des faits", *Politique Africaine* 98, 2005, pp. 21–41.
33 On post-colonial relations between France and Côte d'Ivoire see for instance J.-P. Dozon, *Frères et sujets: la France et l'Afrique en perspective*, Paris: Flammarion, 2003.
34 This denomination of the insurgents is being used for the sake of clarity (the insurgents took the name *Forces Nouvelles* (New Forces) only in January 2003).
35 "Accord de défense entre les Gouvernements de la République de Côte d'Ivoire, de la République du Dahomey, de la République française et de la République du Niger", Presidency of Côte d'Ivoire, 24 April 1961, available at www.cotedivoirepr.ci/files/pdf/Accords_de_defense_entre_la_Cote_d_Ivoire_et_la_France.pdf, accessed 16 December 2010. However, the additional protocols to the agreement remain confidential.
36 On the political exploitation of the rhetoric of "second independence", see G. Piccolino, "David against Goliath in Côte d'Ivoire? Laurent Gbagbo's war against Global Governance", *African Affairs* 111, 2012, pp. 1–23. On Ivorian nationalism under Gbagbo and the movement of the *jeunes patriotes*, see also R.

Banégas, "Côte d'Ivoire: Patriotism, Ethnonationalism and other African Modes of Self-writing", *African Affairs* 105, 2006, pp. 535–552; R. Marshall, "The War of 'Who Is Who': Autochthony, Nationalism, and Citizenship in the Ivorian Crisis", *African Studies Review* 49, 2006, pp. 9–43.

37 For the official English version of the Linas–Marcoussis agreement see Republic of Côte d'Ivoire, *Linas Marcoussis Agreement*, Annex I to the letter dated 27 January 2003 from the Permanent Representative of France to the United Nations addressed to the President of the Security Council, New York: United Nations.

38 Smith, "La politique d'engagement", pp. 121–122.

39 H. Serequeberhan, "Le réengagement français dans les conflits africains et le défi ivoirien", *Annuaire Français de Relations Internationales 2005* vi, pp. 323–339.

40 UN Security Council Resolution 1464, 4 February 2003.

41 The UN Secretariat had notably proposed, as an alternative, the creation of a larger UN mission: see "Report of the Secretary General on the UN Mission in Côte d'Ivoire Submitted Pursuant to SC Resolution 1514 (2003) of 13 November 2003", UN, 6 January 2004.

42 Johnstone, "Managing Consent", p. 170.

43 S. Smith, "Laurent Gbagbo: 'Il n'y a pas de transition à organiser, il y a un ordre légal à rétablir!' ", *Le Monde*, 16 January 2003.

44 Smith, "La politique d'engagement"; L. D'Ersu, "La crise ivoirienne, une intrigue franco-française", *Politique africaine* 105, 2007, pp. 85–104.

45 For an international law perspective on Operation Licorne, see L. Balmond, "Sur quelques enseignements de 'l'Opération Licorne' ", *Arès* XXI, 2004, pp. 83–96.

46 D'Ersu, "La crise ivoirienne".

47 G. Yabi, "Côte d'Ivoire", in M. Edgren-Schori, D. García-Orrico, P. Schori, S. Tadjbakhsh and G. Yabi, *Security Council Resolutions Under Chapter VII*, Madrid: Fundación par las Relaciones Internacionales y el Diálogo Exterior (FRIDE), 2009, p. 155. For a discussion of UNOCI's mandate and its limitations, see also A.J. Bellamy and P.D. Williams, "Local Politics and International Partnerships: The UN Operation in Côte d'Ivoire (UNOCI)", *Journal of International Peacekeeping*, 2012, 16(3–4), pp. 252–281.

48 Interviews with UNOCI political officer, Abidjan, 16 July 2010, and with senior UNOCI officer, Abidjan, 28 July 2010.

49 About the November 2004 events, see Y. Konaté, "Côte d'Ivoire: le canari d'eau de Jacques Chirac", *Politique Africaine* 97, 2005, pp. 117–132.

50 UN Security Council Resolution 1572, 15 November 2004.

51 UN Security Council Resolution 1584, 1 February 2005.

52 "Letter dated 23 May 2005 from the Permanent Representative of South Africa to the United Nations addressed to the President of the Security Council", UN, 24 May 2005.

53 UN Security Council Resolution 1603, 3 June 2005. On the role of the UN in overseeing the Ivorian electoral process, see L.-A. Théroux-Bénoni, "Lessons for UN Electoral Certification from the 2010 Disputed Presidential Poll in Côte d'Ivoire", *Africa Initiative Policy Brief*, Waterloo ON: Centre for International Governance Innovation (CIGI), 2012.

54 "Communiqué of the 40th meeting of the Peace and Security Council", AU, 6 October 2005; UN Security Council Resolution 1633, 21 October 2005.

55 "Communiqué of the 40th meeting of the Peace and Security Council", AU, 6 October 2005, para. 10-V.

56 Théroux-Benoni, "Lessons for UN Electoral Certification".

57 See ICG, *Côte d'Ivoire: La Paix comme Option*, Africa Report 109, 2006.

58 "Nouveau processus de sortie de crise: Voici les propositions de Gbagbo à Mbeki et Compaoré", *Le Temps*, 28 September 2006.

59 UN Security Council Resolution 1721, 1 November 2006.
60 Interview with UN officer from the Department of Political Affairs (DPA), Abidjan, 5 August 2010.
61 République de Côte d'Ivoire, "Accord Politique de Ouagadougou (APO)", edition including complementary agreements and implementing decisions, Abidjan: Centre d'Information et de la Communication Gouvernementale, 2010. For an analysis of the agreement see T. Charles and S.P.A. Handy, "L'Accord politique de Ouagadougou. Vers une sortie de crise pérenne en Côte d'Ivoire?", *Annuaire Français de Relations Internationales 2008* ix, 2008, pp. 653–667.
62 Interview with senior Ivorian diplomat, Abidjan, 18 August 2010.
63 Interview with UN officer from DPA, Abidjan, 5 August 2010. Interview with senior UNOCI officer, Abidjan, 28 July 2010.
64 UN Security Council Resolution 1765, 16 July 2007.
65 Théroux-Bénoni, "Lessons for UN Electoral Certification".
66 This is notably the view hold by A.B. Bah, "Democracy and Civil War: Citizenship and Peacemaking in Côte d'Ivoire", *African Affairs* 109, 2010, pp. 597–615.
67 République de Côte d'Ivoire, "Accord Politique".
68 Bah, "Democracy and Civil War".
69 Interview with senior UN officer, Abidjan, 24 August 2011. According to the interviewee, Choi insisted personally on the inclusion in a leaflet on the certification released by UNOCI of a few lines stating that the UN SRSG would have safeguarded the results "by all means at his disposal" (UNOCI, "Certification des Elections en Côte d'Ivoire/The Certification of Elections in Côte d'Ivoire", para. 9, available online. English version available at www.onuci.org/pdf/faqcertificationen.pdf, accessed 3 March 2013.
70 For an analysis of the electoral process and its results, see T. Basset, "Winning Coalition, Sore Loser: Côte d'Ivoire's 2010 Presidential Elections", *African Affairs* 110, 2011, pp. 469–479; European Union Election Observation Mission, "Côte d'Ivoire: Election Présidentielle 31 octobre – 28 novembre 2010. Rapport Final", Brussels: 2011. On the post-election crisis and the following international intervention, see also Marco Wyss's contribution in this volume.
71 Y.J. Choi, "Statement on the Certification of the Result of the Second Round of the Presidential Election Held on 28 November 2010", UNOCI, Abidjan, 3 December 2010.
72 UN Security Council Resolution 1975, 30 March 2011, para. 6.
73 On the adoption of Resolution 1975 and the conflicting interpretations of the resolution by different members of the Security Council, see also A.J. Bellamy and P.D. Williams, "The New Politics of Protection? Côte d'Ivoire, Libya and the Responsibility to Protect", *International Affairs*, 2011, 87(4), pp. 834–835; and Bellamy and Williams, "Local Politics", p. 65.
74 Bellamy and Williams, "Local Politics", p. 66. Interview with South African diplomat, Abidjan, August 2011.
75 P. Cherruau and A. Khady Sé, "Après l'élection, Gbagbo a perdu contact avec la réalité", interview with Young-jin Choi, *SlateAfrique*, 25 April 2011, available at www.slateafrique.com/1641/election-laurent-gbagbo-perdu-contact-avec-realite, accessed 30 April 2011.
76 Bellamy and Williams, "Local Politics", p. 66.
77 Bellamy and Williams, "New Politics of Protection".
78 See Marco Wyss's contribution in this volume.

Conclusion

"New wine in old bottles" – the struggle for a new African security architecture

Karen A. Mingst

Peace operations have entered a new era. The goals of traditional peacekeeping have expanded. No longer are missions concerned only with abating, containing, or settling conflict. Expanded goals include disarmament, demobilization, and reintegration; election supervision; democratization; humanitarian assistance; and human rights protection. To achieve these multiple goals, as contested as they may be, both the types of actors and their numbers have proliferated. They include international governmental organizations (IGOs) and regional IGOs, but also civilian police, non-governmental organizations (NGOs), and private security firms. Nowhere in the world has this proliferation of goals, actors, and activities been seen as much as it has in Africa. The contributions in this volume explore this evolution in terms of institutions, actors, complex cases, and controversial ideas. In this concluding chapter, we elucidate some of the trends and dilemmas which are challenging both academics and policymakers.

The UN system increasingly works alongside regional IGOs in what are labelled as partnerships. It was conceived as a way that the "United Nations efforts could not only lighten the burden of the Council but also contribute to a deeper sense of participation, consensus and democratization in international affairs".[1] The need for resources (money and specialized skills) and the desire to add new expertise to the organization at a reduced cost propel organizations into these relationships. Theoretically each institution brings to the relationship a strength which the other lacks, including enhanced legitimacy and greater ownership of the issue closer to the source of the problem. However, as this volume confirms, that relationship is complex and is not always as presented on paper.

In this "multi-actor game of peacekeeping in Africa" over the last decade,[2] there is an evolving new security approach, the AU's African Peace and Security Architecture. After 2002, the member states of the newly constituted AU agreed to accept a greater legal capacity to participate in peacekeeping operations, which Okeke (Chapter 2) examines. In a radical departure from the Organization of African Unity, the AU under Article 4(h) of the Constitutive Act may intervene in the affairs of other states in "grave circumstances, namely war crimes, genocide and crimes against humanity". Also, the AU Peace and Security Council has explicitly acknowledged a "Responsibility to Protect" (RtoP), which has evolved slowly ("internalized unevenly") from non-intervention "to what is now commonly referred to as the doctrine of non-indifference".[3] In addition, Article 13 of the AU Protocol calls for the African Standby Force, composed of "standby multidisciplinary contingents with civilian and military components in their countries of origin and ready for rapid deployment at appropriate notice". But that change has been slow to evolve.

Changes in the EU have also occurred that affect the African security architecture, as Mattelaer and Marijnen (Chapter 3) delineate. The EU's Lisbon Treaty (2009) gave the Union an enhanced capacity to develop a foreign and security policy. While the EU has a responsibility to act when UN rules are broken, as stated in the 2003 European Security Strategy under the concept of "effective multilateralism", the primacy of the UN in security affairs has remained and the EU military component is constrained by political will as much as by diverging security priorities.

This new security architecture is developing as the international security environment is changing. As Gleason-Roberts and Kugel (Chapter 1) make clear, these institutions recognize that military solutions cannot always be the best approach when states face a wide range of threats: political, socioeconomic, and transnational threats such as crime, corruption, and drugs. Faced with these problems, the institutions are resource-constrained. Given this background, what are the challenges and dilemmas facing them?

Institutional challenges and dilemmas

First, the UN is developing new and broader tools for crisis management and has been employing more political missions, as Gleason-Roberts and Kugel (Chapter 1) note. These missions include not only prominent individuals, but also missions with police, local civilian staff, and UN volunteers. Field-based political missions provide a lower-cost alternative and are designed to meet the various kinds of broad-based threats. These missions depend, however, on partnerships both at the headquarters of regional partners and in the field. In reality, though, these partnerships are often developed in an ad hoc fashion, and are driven by emergency conditions. Partnerships are the rhetoric, but not yet the reality.

Second, as much as the UN and the AU strive toward partnerships, the fact is that the two organizations have increasingly operated according to different conceptions of appropriate peace operations.[4] The UN, stung by past failures, prefers peace operations to begin once there is some kind of ceasefire, where there is consent of the host country, impartiality in operation, and use of force only in self-defence. In contrast, the AU supports operations to establish peace, as in Somalia. Partnerships can never be effectively implemented when the basic ideas of what is to be accomplished are at variance.

Third, although the relationship between the UN and the AU, as well as the sub-regionals, may be one of partnership or integration in theory, the reality is characterized by competition and rivalry. Each organization competes for scarce resources from member states and in the case of the AU from external donors. Each seeks to develop a reputation for effectiveness and legitimacy, and this may lead to rivalry at the operational level. This was illustrated in the case of Mali, where the ability of the UN, the AU, and ECOWAS to work together was hampered by profound differences in their respective operational and financial capacities.

Fourth, despite the AU's goal to broaden the security architecture, the AU itself remains weak in terms of both political will and institutional capacities. Ambrosetti and Esmenjaud (Chapter 4) illustrate the lack of political will by referring to the fact that the AU is still guided by state consent rather than sovereignty as a responsibility. The AU's experience in Burundi, Darfur, and Somalia shows its weaknesses in a military logistical capacity. Furthermore, the minimal staffing in the Peace and Security Operation Division in the AU itself[5] and the inordinate delays in operationalizing the African Standby Force confirm this lack of political will.

Nowhere is that weakness more evident than in financing operations. The chapters by Okeke and by Ambrosetti and Esmenjaud show the AU's dependence on external donors. Only once has the AU funded an African-led operation from its own budget: the 2013 International Support Mission to Mali. Yet that mission is also funded in part by the EU through its African Peace Facility. As Ambrosetti and Esmenjaud show, funding is a negotiated process conducted with regional organizations (NATO, the EU), the UN, and concerned states. Given the AU's institutional weaknesses, both political and financial, Okeke's conclusion is not only accurate but revealing: "its [the AU's] institutionalization based on Africa's ownership remains a distant reality".

Fifth, the member states of the EU may have the hypothetical military capacity that the African states lack, but the EU's actions have shown a lack of political willingness to use that military capacity in any sustained effort. Instead, as Mattelaer and Marijnen (Chapter 3) describe, the EU undertakes limited niche tasks, such as supporting local security sector reform (SSR), capacity-building and financing (through the EU African Peace Facility) in order to maintain its "affordable influence". Occasionally, the EU may provide a bridging operation until a wider UN operation is mobilized. And it is financially committed to Africans building their own security architecture. However, the EU remains a selective and somewhat distant actor in Africa.

Sixth, the fact is neither the UN, the AU, nor the EU has institutionalized or even prioritized the development of civilian capacities in peace operations, even though the numbers of civilians have significantly increased – by 27 percent over the past five years.

Police deployments have also substantially increased – by 80 percent in the past five years versus 13 percent for military deployments.[6] The introduction of police to address the various threats leads to a number of challenges. Police forces need key pieces of equipment (transport, communication instruments, and weapons). Just as international military peacekeepers have been under-resourced and under-equipped, so, too, have the police contingents. In addition, police units are seldom schooled in foreign cultures or trained in the language of the hosting country. And their assignments are generally much shorter than those of the military, making it less likely they would become conversant in the language or acculturated. Yet the success of policing depends on being able to "read" the local environment. While such knowledge may be helpful to the military in peace operations, they are there to keep warring factions at bay and to use coercive force in enforcement actions when necessary. With two different missions, the key is getting both the military and police to understand the different functional roles played by each and to not see each other as being in competition.

Seventh, both the UN and regional organizations have the potential to be captured by hegemonic states' interests or to reflect one member state's priorities more than those of its multilateral partners, as the chapters by Okeke and by Ambrosetti and Esmenjaud acknowledge. That carries dangers of politicizing the mission in ways that, also, may jeopardize its overall legitimacy. France's role in pushing the EU to act in sub-Saharan Africa had led many to assert that France was acting through the EU (and the UN) to multilateralize its African interests, reinforcing its economic interests (Chad and Mali) and securing its cultural/linguistic ties with the DRC.

Eighth, the precise nature of the relationship between the organizations is, in most cases, negotiated on a case-by-case basis. Underlying those negotiations are perceptions of legitimacy and political considerations, regardless of capacity or commitment. African participation either through the UN or, even better, through the AU supports the legitimacy of an African response to African problems. Legitimacy and commitment are important considerations; however, if political willingness is absent and institutional capacity so weak as to jeopardize the effectiveness and outcome of the operation, does that not undermine legitimacy?

Dilemmas emerging from state actors

In this context, a series of current dilemmas stem from state actors' capacities and policies. First, none of the international institutions has independent operational capacity. They depend on member states to contribute soldiers, civilians, and materials. At one level, the units are responsible for instituting the mandate from the principal institution, but the troops remain under the national command of individual member states. What follows is divided and often confusing authority.

India, one of the most active states contributing to international peacekeeping, encountered this difficulty in the DRC. As Mampilly (Chapter 6) asserts, India's unit was subject to multiple, often confusing mandates and the leaders on the ground were hamstrung by a lack of local authority close to the action. Valid as that criticism is, an alternative explanation for India's poor performance in terms of corruption and sexual misconduct is that India's leaders seek to achieve broader national objectives by supporting Indian participation, even if their performance is not evaluated positively. National militaries retain jurisdiction over personnel, and generally few punitive actions have been taken for misbehavior. As we have seen with respect to the DRC, poor performance by key troop contributors undermines not only perceptions of state competence, but also the competence of the UN and the legitimacy of its engagement.

Second, France's colonial and neo-colonial history puts it in a unique position. Having pulled back from Africa during the 1990s, France has taken actions in Côte d'Ivoire as of 2002 and in Mali in 2013 that illustrate a reassertion of French interests and use of the military, albeit in both cases at the request of the sitting government and when African states themselves were at an impasse. Can France's actions be seen as another phase of post-colonial intrusive involvement? Or does the fact that France's actions were swift and limited and that their activities were subsequently turned over to multilateral bodies undermine the post-colonial rhetoric? Wyss (Chapter 7) concludes that while France provided essential support, France's involvement also "undermined the credibility and impartiality of the international community". That conclusion may well be valid for the ongoing Mali intervention, where the UN's MINUSMA has accepted the proviso that French troops are authorized to intervene when a threat is posed (Théroux-Bénoni, Chapter 9).

Third, of the state actors, China remains the "wild card". While its extraordinary investment and foreign aid to African states make it a significant economic player in the continent, its actions on security issues have been relatively weak. Taylor (Chapter 5) traces the subtle change in China's support for multilateral peace operations when there is host government agreement. China has provided personnel for a number of African operations in Liberia, the DRC, Côte d'Ivoire, and Sudan, namely support personnel, engineers, and medics, rather than combat forces. Whether that "wild card" will step up to support combat boots on the ground and whether it will keep its commitment to requiring host government approval is unknown.

Dilemmas emerging from contemporary peace operations: the DRC, Mali, Somalia, and Sudan

Finally, dilemmas of conflict management in Africa also come from the operations per se. First, partnerships are the rhetorical norm, but, the reality is that in these complicated cases partnerships are ad hoc, and often take the form of a sequencing among organizations and actors. Some operations have begun as a regional endeavour and transitioned to the UN. Some have been authorized by the UN Security Council, but have been carried out independently; some were even established by a regional organization and then given retroactive authorization by the UN Security Council. In only rare cases has there been a real hybrid mission such as UNAMID, emerging as a political compromise which gave the operation the necessary equipment, funding, and logistical capacities, while retaining its "predominantly African character".

Nowhere is this sequencing more complicated than in Mali, where, as Théroux-Bénoni (Chapter 9) describes, missions have evolved through at least four sequences from the failure of ECOWAS to achieve consensus, to an African-led approach, to French military action in Operation Serval, and then to the UN's MINUSMA. In such a complicated case, where the nature of the threat is so different and the terrain so forbidding, one size does not fit all. This may be a unique case where a major external power seized the initiative, and then turned the case over to the international community. This is unlikely to be a model for the future. As a matter of fact, no such external actor has stepped up in the DRC, Sudan, or Somalia.

Second, these contemporary cases are complicated by the fact that they are local, regional, and international at the same time and the relative salience of each level has varied over time. When the International Security and Stabilization Support Strategy began, not only was fighting continuing, but there was little understanding of what stabilization entailed. As Froitzheim (Chapter 10) details, there was a lack of both Congolese government and local ownership in the process.

Vorrath (Chapter 8) focuses on the failure to realize that these cases are also regional in scope. Often regional actors may be part of the problem and may also need to be part of the solution: "neighbors keep a foot in the door". The chapter traces the regional dynamics in the case of Somalia (Ethiopia/Kenya tensions) and the DRC (Rwanda/Uganda rivalries). No effective resolution will be reached until accommodation is made at each level, yet as each of the cases illustrates, not only do the parties to the conflict change, but their respective interests also evolve over time.

Third, these cases bring up the dilemma of who should give consent. The UN has prioritized the necessity to have consent. But in rapidly changing cases, who gives consent? Is the consent of a military government such as that in Mali acceptable? How is it given? If consent has been given, can it also be taken away? What does that mean for the peace operation? These are critical issues raised by Piccolino (Chapter 12). Seeing consent as a negotiated process, rather than as an absolute, helps to explain the dynamics in these complex cases.

Fourth, each of these cases includes humanitarian crises – which explain the multiplicity of actors. By the time that Darfur had appeared on the international agenda, the Responsibility to Protect (RtoP) was being discussed and affirmed in principle. So, as Lanz (Chapter 11) shows, Darfur became the test case for RtoP, where civil society groups (e.g., the Save Darfur movement and others) pushed for an international response, and where the mandate became one of protecting individuals who were being abused by their own government. However, the limited ability of both the AU Mission in Sudan and UNAMID to provide that protection disappointed locals who expected more. Does the infusion of RtoP language only inflate the expectations of both locals and supporters, or does it provide a galvanizing effect such that civil society supporters and even celebrity diplomats have continued to keep this complex case on the international agenda? Almost ten years after its formal adoption by the UN General Assembly, the possibilities and limitations of RtoP are still to be clarified, in particular in relation to peacekeeping.

Under the nascent African Peace and Security Architecture, the trend is towards more partnerships and regionalization. Since 2003 alone, the AU has supported seven missions, and the EU eight limited engagements. This trend is not surprising; no single institution – certainly not the UN, nor any particular state – has the will or the capacity to shoulder the responsibility for all peace operations. Yet as much as the AU has enhanced legitimacy and has developed innovative approaches, is closer to the action, and has accepted enforcement actions where UN members have not dared to tread, it still continues to struggle with forging a political consensus, using its newly-acquired powers, and backing up that power with funding. The glacially slow process of operationalizing the African Standby Force is indicative of this situation. As the studies in this volume show, the AU's reliance on external funding undermines its claim of African solutions for African problems. French involvement in Côte d'Ivoire and Mali does not bode well for a new strong African architecture. Rather, complex peace operations continue to illustrate the core dilemmas of ad hoc partnerships, consent continuously negotiated, and changing local, regional, and international interests. These dilemmas are embedded in this "multi-actor game" of peace operations in twenty-first century Africa.

Notes

1 B. Boutros-Ghali, *An Agenda for Peace: Preventive Diplomacy, Peacemaking and Peacekeeping*, New York: United Nations, 1992, p. 64.
2 M. Brosig, "The Multi-actor Game of Peacekeeping in Africa", *International Peacekeeping* 17, 2010, pp. 327–342.
3 P.D. Williams, "From Non-Intervention to Non-Indifference: The Origins and Development of the African Union's Security Culture", *African Affairs* 106, 2007, pp. 253–279.
4 A. Boutellis and P.D. Williams, *Peace Operations, the African Union, and the United Nations: Toward More Effective Partnerships*, New York: International Peace Institute, April 2013, pp. 7–9.
5 Brosig, "Multi-actor Game".
6 Center on International Cooperation, "*Annual Review of Global Peace Operations* 2012 Briefing Paper", New York, March 2012.

Index

Made in United States
North Haven, CT
19 October 2024

59172997R00154